ORELA
MULTIPLE SUBJECTS
001, 002, 003

XAMonline, INC.
Boston

To obtain permission(s) to use the material from this work for any purpose including workshops or seminars, please submit a written request to:

XAMonline, Inc.
25 First Street, Suite 106
Cambridge, MA 02141
Toll Free 1-800-509-4128
Email: info@xamonline.com
Web: www.xamonline.com
Fax: 1-617-583-5552

Library of Congress Cataloging-in-Publication Data

Wynne, Sharon A.
    ORELA Multiple Subjects 001, 002, 003 / Sharon A. Wynne. 3rd ed
    ISBN 978-1-60787-015-9
    1. Multiple Subjects 001, 002, 003
    2. Study Guides
    3. ORELA
    4. Teachers' Certification & Licensure
    5. Careers

Disclaimer:

The opinions expressed in this publication are the sole works of XAMonline and were created independently from the National Education Association, Educational Testing Service, or any State Department of Education, National Evaluation Systems or other testing affiliates.

Between the time of publication and printing, state specific standards as well as testing formats and Web site information may change and therefore would not be included in part or in whole within this product. Sample test questions are developed by XAMonline and reflect content similar to that on real tests; however, they are not former test questions. XAMonline assembles content that aligns with state standards but makes no claims nor guarantees teacher candidates a passing score. Numerical scores are determined by testing companies such as NES or ETS and then are compared with individual state standards. A passing score varies from state to state.

Printed in the United States of America   œ-1

ORELA Multiple Subjects 001, 002, 003
ISBN: 978-1-60787-015-9

Table of Contents

COMPETENCY 7

UNDERSTAND IMPORTANT THEORIES, CONCEPTS, AND TERMINOLOGY RELATED TO GEOGRAPHY 66

COMPETENCY 8

UNDERSTAND IMPORTANT EVENTS, CONCEPTS, AND TERMINOLOGY RELATED TO WORLD HISTORY 72

COMPETENCY 9

UNDERSTAND IMPORTANT EVENTS, CONCEPTS, AND TERMINOLOGY RELATED TO THE HISTORY OF THE UNITED STATES AND THE STATE OF OREGON 90

COMPETENCY 10
UNDERSTAND METHODS OF SOCIAL SCIENCE RESEARCH AND ANALYSIS 122

DOMAIN III
THE ARTS 127

COMPETENCY 11
UNDERSTAND TECHNIQUES AND MATERIALS ASSOCIATED WITH THE VISUAL ARTS AND THE CULTURAL, POLITICAL, AND HISTORICAL SIGNIFICANCE OF THE VISUAL ARTS.......................... 129

COMPETENCY 12
UNDERSTAND TECHNIQUES AND MATERIALS ASSOCIATED WITH THEATER AND DANCE AND THE CULTURAL, POLITICAL, AND HISTORICAL SIGNIFICANCE OF THEATER AND DANCE 133

COMPETENCY 13
UNDERSTAND TECHNIQUES AND MATERIALS ASSOCIATED WITH MUSIC AND THE CULTURAL, POLITICAL, AND HISTORICAL SIGNIFICANCE OF MUSICAL GENRES AND STYLES.............. 139

COMPETENCY 17
UNDERSTAND READING COMPREHENSION AND FLUENCY 180

COMPETENCY 18
UNDERSTAND READING COMPREHENSION STRATEGIES FOR LITERARY AND INFORMATIONAL TEXT 210

DOMAIN V
MATHEMATICS 217

COMPETENCY 19
UNDERSTAND MATHEMATICAL COMMUNICATION 221

COMPETENCY 36

COMPETENCY 37

SAMPLE TEST

ORELA

ORELA

MULTIPLE SUBJECTS
001, 002, 003

SECTION 1
ABOUT XAMONLINE

XAMonline—A Specialty Teacher Certification Company

Created in 1996, XAMonline was the first company to publish study guides for state-specific teacher certification examinations. Founder Sharon Wynne found it frustrating that materials were not available for teacher certification preparation and decided to create the first single, state-specific guide. XAMonline has grown into a company of over 1,800 contributors and writers and offers over 300 titles for the entire PRAXIS series and every state examination. No matter what state you plan on teaching in, XAMonline has a unique teacher certification study guide just for you.

XAMonline—Value and Innovation

We are committed to providing value and innovation. Our print-on-demand technology allows us to be the first in the market to reflect changes in test standards and user feedback as they occur. Our guides are written by experienced teachers who are experts in their fields. And our content reflects the highest standards of quality. Comprehensive practice tests with varied levels of rigor means that your study experience will closely match the actual in-test experience.

To date, XAMonline has helped nearly 600,000 teachers pass their certification or licensing exams. Our commitment to preparation exceeds simply providing the proper material for study—it extends to helping teachers **gain mastery** of the subject matter, giving them the **tools** to become the most effective classroom leaders possible, and ushering today's students toward a **successful future**.

SECTION 2
ABOUT THIS STUDY GUIDE

Purpose of This Guide

Is there a little voice inside of you saying, "Am I ready?" Our goal is to replace that little voice and remove all doubt with a new voice that says, "I AM READY. **Bring it on!**" by offering the highest quality of teacher certification study guides.

Organization of Content

You will see that while every test may start with overlapping general topics, each is very unique in the skills they wish to test. Only XAMonline presents custom content that analyzes deeper than a title, a subarea, or an objective. Only XAMonline presents content and sample test assessments along with **focus statements**, the deepest-level rationale and interpretation of the skills that are unique to the exam.

Title and field number of test

→Each exam has its own name and number. XAMonline's guides are written to give you the content you need to know for the specific exam you are taking. You can be confident when you buy our guide that it contains the information you need to study for the specific test you are taking.

Subareas

→These are the major content categories found on the exam. XAMonline's guides are written to cover all of the subareas found in the test frameworks developed for the exam.

Objectives

→These are standards that are unique to the exam and represent the main subcategories of the subareas/content categories. XAMonline's guides are written to address every specific objective required to pass the exam.

Focus statements

→These are examples and interpretations of the objectives. You find them in parenthesis directly following the objective. They provide detailed examples of the range, type, and level of content that appear on the test questions. **Only XAMonline's guides drill down to this level.**

How Do We Compare with Our Competitors?

XAMonline—drills down to the focus statement level.
CliffsNotes and REA—organized at the objective level
Kaplan—provides only links to content
MoMedia—content not specific to the state test

Each subarea is divided into manageable sections that cover the specific skill areas. Explanations are easy to understand and thorough. You'll find that every test answer contains a rejoinder so if you need a refresher or further review after taking the test, you'll know exactly to which section you must return.

How to Use This Book

Our informal polls show that most people begin studying up to eight weeks prior to the test date, so start early. Then ask yourself some questions: How much do you really know? Are you coming to the test straight from your teacher-education program or are you having to review subjects you haven't considered in ten years? Either way, take a **diagnostic or assessment test** first. Also, spend time on sample tests so that you become accustomed to the way the actual test will appear.

This guide comes with an online diagnostic test of 30 questions found online at *www.XAMonline.com*. It is a little boot camp to get you up for the task and reveal things about your compendium of knowledge in general. Although this guide is structured to follow the order of the test, you are not required to study in that order. By finding a time-management and study plan that fits your life you will be more effective. The results of your diagnostic or self-assessment test can be a guide for how to manage your time and point you toward an area that needs more attention.

After taking the diagnostic exam, fill out the **Personalized Study Plan** page at the beginning of each chapter. Review the competencies and skills covered in that chapter and check the boxes that apply to your study needs. If there are sections you already know you can skip, check the "skip it" box. Taking this step will give you a study plan for each chapter.

Week	Activity
8 weeks prior to test	Take a diagnostic test found at www.XAMonline.com
7 weeks prior to test	Build your Personalized Study Plan for each chapter. Check the "skip it" box for sections you feel you are already strong in. ✗ SKIP IT ☐
6-3 weeks prior to test	For each of these four weeks, choose a content area to study. You don't have to go in the order of the book. It may be that you start with the content that needs the most review. Alternately, you may want to ease yourself into plan by starting with the most familiar material.
2 weeks prior to test	Take the sample test, score it, and create a review plan for the final week before the test.
1 week prior to test	Following your plan (which will likely be aligned with the areas that need the most review) go back and study the sections that align with the questions you may have gotten wrong. Then go back and study the sections related to the questions you answered correctly. If need be, create flashcards and drill yourself on any area that you makes you anxious.

SECTION 3
ABOUT THE ORELA MULTIPLE SUBJECTS EXAM

What is the ORELA Multiple Subjects Exam?

The ORELA Multiple Subjects exam assesses candidate's qualification for Oregon initial licensure with authorization to teach at the early childhood, elementary, and middle school levels. It is administered by Pearson Education on behalf of the Oregon Department of Education.

Often **your own state's requirements** determine whether or not you should take any particular test. The most reliable source of information regarding this is your state's Department of Education. This resource should have a complete list of testing centers and dates. Test dates vary by subject area and not all test dates necessarily include your particular test, so be sure to check carefully.

If you are in a teacher-education program, check with the Education Department or the Certification Officer for specific information for testing and testing time-lines. The Certification Office should have most of the information you need.

If you choose an alternative route to certification you can either rely on our website at *www.XAMonline.com* or on the resources provided by an alternative certification program. Many states now have specific agencies devoted to alternative certification and there are some national organizations as well, for example:

National Association for Alternative Certification
http://www.alt-teachercert.org/index.asp

Interpreting Test Results

Contrary to what you may have heard, the results of the ORELA Multiple Subjects test are not based on time. More accurately, you will be scored on the raw number of points you earn in relation to the raw number of points available. Each question is worth one raw point. It is likely to your benefit to complete as many questions in the time allotted, but it will not necessarily work to your advantage if you hurry through the test.

Follow the guidelines provided by Pearson for interpreting your score. The web site offers a sample test score sheet and clearly explains how/whether the scores are scaled and what to expect if you have an essay portion on your test.

Scores are available by mail four weeks after the test date and scores will be sent to you and your chosen institution(s).

What's on the Test?

The ORELA Multiple Subjects exam consists of three subtests. For candidates in any Oregon pre-service program who have never held a permanent teaching certificate, it is necessary to pass subtest I and II. All other candidates are required to pass subtests II and III. The test lasts 4 hours and consists of both multiple-choice questions and constructed-response essays. The breakdown of the questions is as follows:

Category	Approximate Number of Multiple Choice Questions	Constructed Response Essays
SUBTEST I:		
Language Arts	18-20	1
Social Science	27-29	1
Arts	12-14	
SUBTEST II:		
Mathematics	30-32	1
Science	18-20	1
Health and Physical Education	9-11	
SUBTEST III:		
Language Arts	18-20	1
Social Science	27-29	1
Arts	12-14	
Reading Instruction	19-21	

Question Types

You're probably thinking, enough already, I want to study! Indulge us a little longer while we explain that there is actually more than one type of multiple-choice question. You can thank us later after you realize how well prepared you are for your exam.

1. **Complete the Statement.** The name says it all. In this question type you'll be asked to choose the correct completion of a given statement. For example:

> **The Dolch Basic Sight Words consist of a relatively short list of words that children should be able to:**
>
> A. Sound out
>
> B. Know the meaning of
>
> C. Recognize on sight
>
> D. Use in a sentence

The correct answer is A. In order to check your answer, test out the statement by adding the choices to the end of it.

2. **Which of the Following.** One way to test your answer choice for this type of question is to replace the phrase "which of the following" with your selection. Use this example:

> **Which of the following words is one of the twelve most frequently used in children's reading texts:**
>
> A. There
>
> B. This
>
> C. The
>
> D. An

Don't look! Test your answer. _____ is one of the twelve most frequently used in children's reading texts. Did you guess C? Then you guessed correctly.

3. **Roman Numeral Choices.** This question type is used when there is more than one possible correct answer. For example:

Which of the following two arguments accurately supports the use of cooperative learning as an effective method of instruction?

I.   Cooperative learning groups facilitate healthy competition between individuals in the group.

II.   Cooperative learning groups allow academic achievers to carry or cover for academic underachievers.

III.   Cooperative learning groups make each student in the group accountable for the success of the group.

IV.   Cooperative learning groups make it possible for students to reward other group members for achieving.

A. I and II

B. II and III

C. I and III

D. III and IV

Notice that the question states there are **two** possible answers. It's best to read all the possibilities first before looking at the answer choices. In this case, the correct answer is D.

4. Negative Questions. This type of question contains words such as "not," "least," and "except." Each correct answer will be the statement that does **not** fit the situation described in the question. Such as:

Multicultural education is not

A. An idea or concept

B. A "tack-on" to the school curriculum

C. An educational reform movement

D. A process

Think to yourself that the statement could be anything but the correct answer. This question form is more open to interpretation than other types, so read carefully and don't forget that you're answering a negative statement.

5. Questions that Include Graphs, Tables, or Reading Passages. As always, read the question carefully. It likely asks for a very

specific answer and not a broad interpretation of the visual. Here is a simple (though not statistically accurate) example of a graph question:

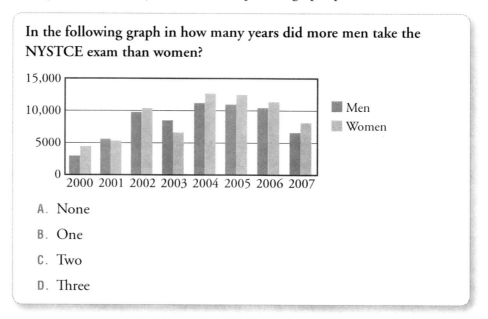

In the following graph in how many years did more men take the NYSTCE exam than women?

A. None

B. One

C. Two

D. Three

It may help you to simply circle the two years that answer the question. Make sure you've read the question thoroughly and once you've made your determination, double check your work. The correct answer is C.

SECTION 4
HELPFUL HINTS

Study Tips

1. You are what you eat. Certain foods aid the learning process by releasing natural memory enhancers called CCKs (cholecystokinin) composed of tryptophan, choline, and phenylalanine. All of these chemicals enhance the neurotransmitters associated with memory and certain foods release memory enhancing chemicals. A light meal or snacks of one of the following foods fall into this category:

• Milk	• Rice	• Eggs	• Fish
• Nuts and seeds	• Oats	• Turkey	

The better the connections, the more you comprehend!

2. **The pen is mightier than the sword.** Learn to take great notes. A by-product of our modern culture is that we have grown accustomed to getting our information in short doses. We've subconsciously trained ourselves to assimilate information into neat little packages. Messy notes fragment the flow of information. Your notes can be much clearer with proper formatting. **The Cornell Method** is one such format. This method was popularized in *How to Study in College*, Ninth Edition, by Walter Pauk. You can benefit from the method without purchasing an additional book by simply looking up the method online. Below is a sample of how *The Cornell Method* can be adapted for use with this guide.

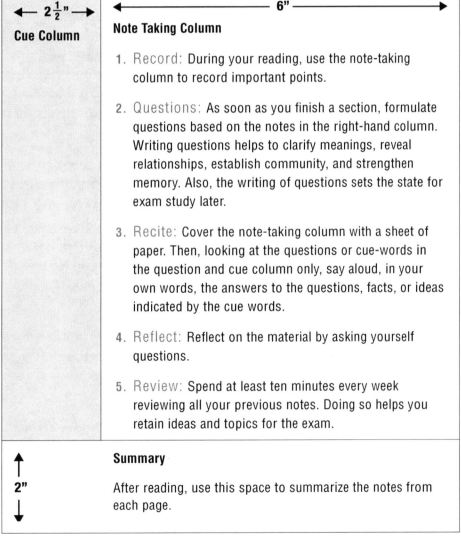

← 2½" →

Cue Column

← 6" →

Note Taking Column

1. Record: During your reading, use the note-taking column to record important points.

2. Questions: As soon as you finish a section, formulate questions based on the notes in the right-hand column. Writing questions helps to clarify meanings, reveal relationships, establish community, and strengthen memory. Also, the writing of questions sets the state for exam study later.

3. Recite: Cover the note-taking column with a sheet of paper. Then, looking at the questions or cue-words in the question and cue column only, say aloud, in your own words, the answers to the questions, facts, or ideas indicated by the cue words.

4. Reflect: Reflect on the material by asking yourself questions.

5. Review: Spend at least ten minutes every week reviewing all your previous notes. Doing so helps you retain ideas and topics for the exam.

2"

Summary

After reading, use this space to summarize the notes from each page.

Adapted from How to Study in College, Ninth Edition, by Walter Pauk, ©2008 Wadsworth

3. See the forest for the trees. In other words, get the concept before you look at the details. One way to do this is to take notes as you read, paraphrasing or summarizing in your own words. Putting the concept in terms that are comfortable and familiar may increase retention.

4. Question authority. Ask why, why, why? Pull apart written material paragraph by paragraph and don't forget the captions under the illustrations. For example, if a heading reads *Stream Erosion* put it in the form of a question (Why do streams erode? What is stream erosion?) then find the answer within the material. If you train your mind to think in this manner you will learn more and prepare yourself for answering test questions.

5. Play mind games. Using your brain for reading or puzzles keeps it flexible. Even with a limited amount of time your brain can take in data (much like a computer) and store it for later use. In ten minutes you can: read two paragraphs (at least), quiz yourself with flash cards, or review notes. Even if you don't fully understand something on the first pass, your mind stores it for recall, which is why frequent reading or review increases chances of retention and comprehension.

6. Place yourself in exile and set the mood. Set aside a particular place and time to study that best suits your personal needs and biorhythms. If you're a night person, burn the midnight oil. If you're a morning person set yourself up with some coffee and get to it. Make your study time and place as free from distraction as possible and surround yourself with what you need, be it silence or music. Studies have shown that music can aid in concentration, absorption, and retrieval of information. Not all music, though. Classical music is said to work best

7. Get pointed in the right direction. Use arrows to point to important passages or pieces of information. It's easier to read than a page full of yellow highlights. Highlighting can be used sparingly, but add an arrow to the margin to call attention to it.

8. Check your budget. You should at least review all the content material before your test, but allocate the most amount of time to the areas that need the most refreshing. It sounds obvious, but it's easy to forget. You can use the study rubric above to balance your study budget.

> The proctor will write the start time where it can be seen and then, later, provide the time remaining, typically fifteen minutes before the end of the test.

Testing Tips

1. Get smart, play dumb. Sometimes a question is just a question. No one is out to trick you, so don't assume that the test writer is looking for something other than what was asked. Stick to the question as written and don't overanalyze.

2. Do a double take. Read test questions and answer choices at least twice because it's easy to miss something, to transpose a word or some letters. If you have no idea what the correct answer is, skip it and come back later if there's time. If you're still clueless, it's okay to guess. Remember, you're scored on the number of questions you answer correctly and you're not penalized for wrong answers. The worst case scenario is that you miss a point from a good guess.

3. Turn it on its ear. The syntax of a question can often provide a clue, so make things interesting and turn the question into a statement to see if it changes the meaning or relates better (or worse) to the answer choices.

4. Get out your magnifying glass. Look for hidden clues in the questions because it's difficult to write a multiple-choice question without giving away part of the answer in the options presented. In most questions you can readily eliminate one or two potential answers, increasing your chances of answering correctly to 50/50, which will help out if you've skipped a question and gone back to it (see tip #2).

5. Call it intuition. Often your first instinct is correct. If you've been studying the content you've likely absorbed something and have subconsciously retained the knowledge. On questions you're not sure about trust your instincts because a first impression is usually correct.

6. Graffiti. Sometimes it's a good idea to mark your answers directly on the test booklet and go back to fill in the optical scan sheet later. You don't get extra points for perfectly blackened ovals. If you choose to manage your test this way, be sure not to mismark your answers when you transcribe to the scan sheet.

7. Become a clock-watcher. You have a set amount of time to answer the questions. Don't get bogged down laboring over a question you're not sure about when there are ten others you could answer more readily. If you choose to follow the advice of tip #6, be sure you leave time near the end to go back and fill in the scan sheet.

Do the Drill

No matter how prepared you feel it's sometimes a good idea to apply Murphy's Law. So the following tips might seem silly, mundane, or obvious, but we're including them anyway.

1. Remember, you are what you eat, so bring a snack. Choose from the list of energizing foods that appear earlier in the introduction.

2. You're not too sexy for your test. Wear comfortable clothes. You'll be distracted if your belt is too tight or if you're too cold or too hot.

3. **Lie to yourself.** Even if you think you're a prompt person, pretend you're not and leave plenty of time to get to the testing center. Map it out ahead of time and do a dry run if you have to. There's no need to add road rage to your list of anxieties.

4. **Bring sharp number 2 pencils.** It may seem impossible to forget this need from your school days, but you might. And make sure the erasers are intact, too.

5. **No ticket, no test.** Bring your admission ticket as well as **two** forms of identification, including one with a picture and signature. You will not be admitted to the test without these things.

6. **You can't take it with you.** Leave any study aids, dictionaries, notebooks, computers, and the like at home. Certain tests **do** allow a scientific or four-function calculator, so check ahead of time to see if your test does.

7. **Prepare for the desert.** Any time spent on a bathroom break **cannot** be made up later, so use your judgment on the amount you eat or drink.

8. **Quiet, Please!** Keeping your own time is a good idea, but not with a timepiece that has a loud ticker. If you use a watch, take it off and place it nearby but not so that it distracts you. And **silence your cell phone**.

To the best of our ability, we have compiled the content you need to know in this book and in the accompanying online resources. The rest is up to you. You can use the study and testing tips or you can follow your own methods. Either way, you can be confident that there aren't any missing pieces of information and there shouldn't be any surprises in the content on the test.

If you have questions about test fees, registration, electronic testing, or other content verification issues please visit *www.orela.nesinc.com*.

Good luck!

Sharon Wynne
Founder, XAMonline

D O M A I N   I
LANGUAGE ARTS

Available for purchase at www.XAMonline.com:

eFlashcards: a digital representation of a card represented with words, numbers or symbols or any combination of each and briefly displayed as part of a learning drill. eFlashcards takes away the burden of carrying around traditional cards that could easily be disarranged, dropped, or soiled. Available at www.XAMonline.com/flashcards

More Sample Tests: more ways to assess how much you know and how much further you need to study. Ultimately, makes you more prepared and attain mastery in the skills and techniques of passing the test the FIRST TIME! Available at www.XAMonline.com/sampletests

PERSONALIZED STUDY PLAN

KNOWN MATERIAL/ SKIP IT

PAGE	COMPETENCY AND SKILL	
3	**1: Understand the effective expression of information and ideas through oral and visual communication**	☐
	1.1: Identify methods of organizing and presenting ideas, information, and feelings	☐
	1.2: Recognize elements of nonverbal communication	☐
	1.3: Recognize elements of visual language	☐
	1.4: Demonstrate knowledge of principles of active listening and of barriers to effective listening	☐
	1.5: Demonstrate knowledge of structures of oral, visual, and multimedia presentations	☐
	1.6: Recognize the principles of using spoken and visual language	☐
8	**2: Understand the effective expression of information and ideas through writing and the appropriate elements and conventions of standard written English**	☐
	2.1: Demonstrate knowledge of elements of the writing process	☐
	2.2: Describe characteristics of and purposes for different writing forms and modes	☐
	2.3: Recognize elements of sentence and paragraph structure and formatting	☐
	2.4: Demonstrate knowledge of the use of introductions, main ideas, transitions, conclusions, and other forms of organization in writing	☐
	2.5: Apply elements of appropriate grammar and usage	☐
	2.6: Apply elements of appropriate punctuation and capitalization	☐
27	**3: Understand features and forms of literature**	☐
	3.1: Identify characteristics of literary forms and genres	☐
	3.2: Identify characteristics of genres of nonfiction	☐
	3.3: Identify characteristics and functions of literary elements and devices	☐
	3.4: Recognize influences of cultural, social, biographical, and historical factors on the creation and development of literature	☐
	3.5: Demonstrate knowledge of genres, themes, authors, and works of literature written for children and adolescents	☐
	3.6: Recognize influence of nontraditional literary forms	☐
38	**4: Understand research methods**	☐
	4.1: Demonstrate knowledge of strategies for developing topics, questions, and purposes for inquiry	☐
	4.2: Demonstrate knowledge of strategies for gathering, analyzing, synthesizing, and evaluating data	☐
	4.3: Analyze ethical issues related to the use of resources, human subjects, materials, and the Internet	☐

COMPETENCY 1
UNDERSTAND THE EFFECTIVE EXPRESSION OF INFORMATION AND IDEAS THROUGH ORAL AND VISUAL COMMUNICATION

SKILL 1.1 Identify methods of organizing and presenting ideas, information, and feelings when speaking to diverse audiences and for various purposes

One way to organize information when speaking or writing is to make an outline. Outlines help you organize important information and ideas and help you see how these ideas are related to each other. Outlines give a quick visual summary of ideas that will be presented. Below is an example of what an outline might look like.

Outlines give a quick visual summary of ideas that will be presented.

I. First main idea

    A. Detail supporting the first main idea

        1. Detail supporting point A

        2. Another detail supporting point A

            a. Detail supporting point 2

            b. Another detail supporting point 2

        3. Another detail supporting point A

II. Second main idea

Another way to organize information is in the reverse order of its importance. This organizational method ensures that listeners remember the most important part of your presentation because it is the last thing they hear. Placing the most important information at the conclusion of a presentation leaves the audience with a clear impression of the speaker's main ideas

The attitude in which information is presented is the TONE. Tone is passed on to an audience through the speaker's choice of words, body language, and mannerisms. For example, tone can be humorous, serious, sad, friendly, hostile or angry. The writer or speaker's purpose determines the tone.

TONE: the attitude in which information is presented

SKILL 1.2 Recognize elements of nonverbal communication including their uses in different cultural contexts for specific audiences and/or purposes

In public speaking, not all speeches require the same type of speaking style. For example, when making a humorous speech, it is important to utilize body language in order to accent humorous moments. However, when giving instructions, it is extremely important to speak clearly and slowly, carefully noting the mood of the audience, so that if the audience seems confused or lost, the speaker can go back and clarify as necessary.

In group discussions, it is important for speakers to ensure that they are listening to the other speakers carefully and tailoring their messages so that they fit into the general mood and topic of the discussion at hand. When giving an oral presentation, the mood should be both serious and friendly. The speaker should focus on ensuring that the content is covered, while also relating to audience members as much as possible.

As students practice these skills, they can receive guidance and modeling from recordings of various types of speeches appropriate to the types they are giving themselves. Also, the various attributes of each type of oral speaking strategy should be covered with students so that they clearly hear the differences.

There is more to communication than just good and bad or effective and ineffective. We must take into consideration that we must adjust our communication styles for various audiences. While we should not stereotype audiences, we can still recognize that certain methods of communication are more appropriate with certain people than with others. Age is an easy factor to consider: Adults know that when they talk to children, they should come across as pleasant and nonthreatening and that they should use vocabulary that is simple for children to understand. On the other hand, teenagers realize that they should not speak to their grandmothers the way they speak with their peers. When dealing with communication between cultures and genders, people must be sensitive, considerate, and appropriate.

Teachers must also consider these aspects as they deal with colleagues, parents, community members, and students. They must realize that all communication should be tailored so that it conveys appropriate messages and tones to listeners.

The steps of persuasive speaking should be explicitly taught to students. They are:

1. *Expressing an opinion*
2. *Staying focused on topic of discussion*
3. *Supporting opinions with detail*
4. *Using good speaking etiquette in discussions*

Teachers must model unspoken rules of communication and have high expectations for students inside and outside of the classroom.

SKILL 1.3   Recognize elements of visual language *(e.g., symbols, shapes, colors)*

Learning to spell, like learning to speak, is a constructive developmental process. This writing process begins with the child's early efforts to form letters. Children pass through various stages of writing, from drawing symbols and creating shapes that indicate thoughts and words to random letters that stand for complete sentences.

Young children's writing is often made up of muddled strings of letters and numbers to represent words or a complete message. Children learn to analyze each letter into sections such as horizontal, vertical, and diagonal line segments.

One of the best methods to initiate letter learning is by using the letters in a child's name.

Word Shapes

- Write a word on the board
- Have the students identify the "short," "tall," and "tail" letters
- Have the students write the "short," "tall," and "tail" letters

Explain to students that each word has a shape and that remembering the shape of the word can help them spell the word correctly.

SKILL 1.4   Demonstrate knowledge of principles of active listening and of barriers to effective listening

Oral speech can be very difficult to follow, because listeners typically have no written record in which to "reread" things they didn't hear or understand. In addition, oral speech can be much less structured than written language. At the same time, many of the skills and strategies that help students in reading comprehension can help them in listening comprehension. For example, as soon as students start listening to something new, they should tap into their prior knowledge in order to attach new information to what they already know. This will not only help in understanding, but it will also assist in remembering the material.

We can also look for transitions between ideas. Sometimes, in oral speech, these are fairly simple to find (such as when voice tone or body language change).

Although we don't have the luxury of looking at paragraphs in oral language, we do have the animation that comes along with live speech. Human beings have to try very hard to be completely nonexpressive in their speech. Listeners should take advantage of this and notice how the speaker changes character and voice to signal a transition of ideas.

Listeners can better comprehend the underlying intent of a speaker by paying attention to nonverbal cues.

Listeners can also better comprehend the underlying intent of a speaker when they notice nonverbal cues. For example, looking to see an expression on the face of a speaker that signals irony is often simpler than trying to extract irony from written words. Another good way to follow oral speech is to take notes, outlining the major points. Because oral speech can be more circular (as opposed to linear) than written text, it can be of great assistance to keep track of an author's message. Students can practice this strategy in many ways in the classroom, including taking notes during the teacher's oral messages as well as during other students' presentations and speeches.

Additional classroom methods can help students to learn good listening skills. For example, teachers can have students practice following complex directions. They can also have students orally retell stories or retell (in writing or in oral speech) oral presentations of stories or other materials. These activities give students direct practice in the very important skills of listening. They provide students with out-lets in which they can slowly improve their abilities to comprehend oral language; they also allow students to take decisive action based on oral speech.

SKILL 1.5 Demonstrate knowledge of structures of oral, visual, and multimedia presentations *(e.g., sequence, connections, transitions)*

Multimedia Teaching Model

Step 1. Diagnose

- Figure out what students need to know
- Assess what students already know

Step 2. Design

- Design tests of learning achievement
- Identify effective instructional strategies
- Select suitable media
- Sequence learning activities within program

- Plan introductory activities

- Plan follow-up activities

Step 3. Procure

- Secure materials at hand

- Obtain new materials

Step 4. Produce

- Modify existing materials

- Create new materials

Step 5. Refine

- Conduct small-scale test of program

- Evaluate procedures and achievements

- Revise program accordingly

- Conduct classroom test of program

- Evaluate procedures and achievements

- Revise in anticipation of next school term

Tips for using print media and visual aids

- Use pictures rather than words whenever possible

- Present one key point per visual

- Use no more than 3 to 4 colors per visual to avoid clutter and confusion

- Use contrasting colors such as dark blue and bright yellow

- Use a maximum of 25 to 35 numbers per visual aid

- Use bullets instead of paragraphs when possible

- Make sure it is student-centered, not media-centered; delivery is just as important as the media presented

Tips for using film and television

- Study programs in advance

- Obtain supplementary materials such as printed transcripts of the narrative or study guides

- Provide your students with background information, explain unfamiliar concepts, and anticipate outcomes

- Assign outside readings based on the material

- Ask cuing questions

- Watch along with students

- Observe students' reactions

- Follow up viewing with discussions and related activities

SKILL 1.6 **Recognize the principles of using spoken and visual language for a variety of purposes** *(e.g., learning, enjoyment, persuasion, exchanging ideas)*

See Skill 2.2

COMPETENCY 2

UNDERSTAND THE EFFECTIVE EXPRESSION OF INFORMATION AND IDEAS THROUGH WRITING AND THE APPROPRIATE ELEMENTS AND CONVENTIONS OF STANDARD WRITTEN ENGLISH

SKILL 2.1 **Demonstrate knowledge of elements of the writing process** *(e.g., brainstorming, drafting, revising, publishing)* **and techniques for taking notes and developing drafts**

Writing is a recursive process. As students engage in the various stages of writing, they develop and improve not only their writing skills, but also their thinking skills. The stages of the writing process are as follows:

- Prewriting: Students gather ideas before writing. Prewriting may include clustering, listing, brainstorming, mapping, free writing, and charting. Providing many ways for students to develop ideas on a topic will increase their chances of success.

- Writing: Students compose the first draft.

- Revising: Students examine their work and make changes in sentences, wording, details, and ideas. Revise comes from the Latin word revidere, meaning "to see again."

- Editing: Students proofread the draft for punctuation and mechanical errors.

- Publishing: Students may have their work displayed on a bulletin board, read aloud in class, or printed in a literary magazine or school anthology. It is important to realize that these steps are recursive; as students engage in each aspect of the writing process, they may begin with prewriting and then writing, revising, writing, revising, editing, and publishing. Students do not engage in this process in a lockstep manner; it is more circular.

Teaching Composition

Prewriting activities

1. Class discussion of the topic

2. Map out ideas, questions, and graphic organizers on the chalkboard

3. Break into small groups to discuss different ways of approaching the topic, develop an organizational plan, and create a thesis statement

4. Research the topic if necessary

Drafting and revising

1. Students write a first draft in class or at home

2. Students engage in peer response and class discussion

3. Using checklists or a rubric, students critique each other's writing and make suggestions for revising the writing

4. Students revise the writing

Editing and proofreading

1. Students, working in pairs, analyze sentences for variety

2. Students work in groups to review papers for punctuation and mechanics

3. Students perform final edit

SKILL 2.2 Describe characteristics of and purposes for different writing forms *(e.g., essays, stories, reports)* **and modes** *(e.g., narrative, imaginative, expository, persuasive)*

Different Types of Writing

Most nonfiction writing falls into one of four different forms:

1. Narrative

2. Descriptive

3. Expository

4. Persuasive

Persuasive writing

PERSUASION is a piece of writing, the purpose of which is to change the minds of the readers or listeners or to get them to do something. This is achieved in a variety of ways:

> **PERSUASION:** a piece of writing, the purpose of which is to change the minds of the audience members or to get them to do something

1. The credibility of the writer/speaker might lead the listeners/readers to a change of mind or a recommended action.

2. Reasoning is important in persuasive discourse. Reasoning that is persuasive uses logic to convince an audience.

3. The third and most powerful force that leads to acceptance or action is emotional appeal. Even if audience members have been logically persuaded that they should believe the writer or speaker, they are unlikely to act unless moved emotionally. A person with resources might be convinced that people suffered in New Orleans after Katrina, but he or she will not be likely to do anything about it until he or she feels a deeper emotional connection to the disaster.

Expository writing

> **EXPOSITORY WRITING:** a form of writing where the purpose is to inform

In contrast to persuasion, the purpose of exposition is to inform. EXPOSITORY WRITING is not interested in changing anyone's mind or getting anyone to take a certain action. It exists to give information. Some examples include directions to a particular place or the directions for putting together a toy that arrives unassembled. In these instances, the writer only wants to be sure you have the information in case you do decide to use it.

Narrative writing

> **NARRATION:** discourse that is arranged chronologically

NARRATION is discourse that is arranged chronologically—something happened, and then something else happened, and then something else happened. A story is an example of narration. News reports are often narrative in nature, as are records of trips or experiences.

Descriptive writing

DESCRIPTIVE WRITING makes an experience available through one of the five senses—seeing, smelling, hearing, feeling (as with the fingers), and tasting. Descriptive words are used to make it possible for readers to "see" with their mind's eye, "hear" through their mind's ear, "smell" through their mind's nose, "taste" with their mind's tongue, and "feel" with their mind's fingers. This is how language moves people. Only by experiencing an event can the emotions become involved. Poets are experts in descriptive language. Descriptive writing is typically used to make sure the point is established emotionally.

Persuasive writing often uses all forms of discourse. The introduction may be a history or background of the idea being presented—exposition. Details supporting some of the points may be stories—narrations. Descriptive writing will be used to make sure the point is established emotionally.

PARAPHRASE is a rewording of a piece of writing. The result will not necessarily be shorter than the original. It will use different vocabulary and possibly a different arrangement of details. Paraphrases are sometimes written to clarify a complex piece of writing. Sometimes, material is paraphrased because it cannot be borrowed verbatim due to copyright restraints.

SUMMARY is a distillation of the elements of a piece of writing or speech. It will be much shorter than the original. To write a good summary, the writer must determine what the "bones" of the original piece are. What is its structure? What is the thesis and what are the subpoints? A summary does not make judgments about the original; it simply reports the original in condensed form.

LETTERS are often expository in nature; their purpose is to give information. However, letters are also often persuasive—the writer wants to persuade or get the recipient to do something. They are also sometimes descriptive or narrative—the writer will share an experience or tell about an event.

RESEARCH REPORTS are a special kind of expository writing. A topic is researched—explored by some appropriate means such as searching literature, interviewing experts, or even conducting experiments—and the findings written up in such a way that a particular audience may know what was discovered. They can be very simple, such as delving into the history of an event, or very complex, such as a report on a scientific phenomenon that requires complicated testing and reasoning to explain. A research report often reports possible conclusions but puts forth one as the best answer to the question that inspired the research in the first place this is the thesis of the report.

DESCRIPTIVE WRITING: an experience available through one of the five senses—seeing, smelling, hearing, feeling (as with the fingers), and tasting

PARAPHRASE: a rewording of a piece of writing

SUMMARY: a distilling of the elements of a piece of writing or speech

LETTERS: expository in nature, intended to give information or to persuade

RESEARCH REPORTS: the written product of a literature search, interview or an experiment

SKILL 2.3 **Recognize elements of sentence and paragraph structure and formatting**

Sentence Completeness

Avoid fragments and run-on sentences. Recognition of sentence elements necessary to make a complete thought, proper use of independent and dependent clauses, and proper punctuation will correct such errors.

Sentence Structure

Recognize simple, compound, complex, and compound-complex sentences. Use dependent (subordinate) and independent clauses correctly to create these sentence structures.

Simple	Joyce wrote a letter.
Compound	Joyce wrote a letter, and Dot drew a picture.
Complex	While Joyce wrote a letter, Dot drew a picture.
Compound/Complex	When Mother asked the girls to demonstrate their new-found skills, Joyce wrote a letter, and Dot drew a picture.

Note: Do not confuse compound sentence elements with compound sentences.

Simple sentence with compound subject	Joyce and Dot wrote letters. The girl in row three and the boy next to her were passing notes across the aisle.
Simple sentence with compound predicate	Joyce wrote letters and drew pictures. The captain of the high school debate team graduated with honors and studied broadcast journalism in college.
Simple sentence with compound object of preposition	Colleen graded the students' essays for style and mechanical accuracy.

Parallelism

Recognize parallel structures using phrases (prepositional, gerund, participial, and infinitive) and omissions from sentences that create the lack of parallelism.

Prepositional Phrase/Single Modifier

Incorrect: *Colleen ate the ice cream with enthusiasm and hurriedly.*

Correct: *Colleen ate the ice cream with enthusiasm and in a hurry.*

Correct: *Colleen ate the ice cream enthusiastically and hurriedly.*

Participial Phrase/Infinitive Phrase

Incorrect: *After hiking for hours and to sweat profusely, Joe sat down to rest and drinking water.*

Correct: *After hiking for hours and sweating profusely, Joe sat down to rest and drink water.*

Recognition of Dangling Modifiers

Dangling phrases are attached to sentence parts in such a way they create ambiguity and potentionally incorrect meanings.

Participial phrase

Incorrect: *Hanging from her skirt, Dot tugged at a loose thread.*

Correct: *Dot tugged at a loose thread hanging from her skirt.*

Incorrect: *Relaxing in the bathtub, the telephone rang.*

Correct: *While I was relaxing in the bathtub, the telephone rang.*

Infinitive phrase

Incorrect: *To improve his behavior, the dean warned Fred.*

Correct: *The dean warned Fred to improve his behavior.*

Prepositional phrase

Incorrect: *On the floor, Father saw the dog eating table scraps.*

Correct: *Father saw the dog eating table scraps on the floor.*

Recognition of Syntactical Redundancy or Omission

These errors occur when superfluous words are added to a sentence or key words are omitted from a sentence.

Redundancy

Incorrect: *Joyce made sure that when her plane arrived that she retrieved all of her luggage.*

Correct: *Joyce made sure that when her plane arrived she retrieved all of her luggage.*

Incorrect: *He was a mere skeleton of his former self.*

Correct: *He was a skeleton of his former self*

Omission

Incorrect: *Sue opened her book, recited her textbook, and answered the teacher's subsequent question.*

Correct: *Sue opened her book, recited from the textbook, and answered the teacher's subsequent question.*

Avoidance of Double Negatives

This error occurs from positioning two negatives that, in fact, cancel each other in meaning.

Incorrect: *Harold couldn't care less whether he passes this class.*

Correct: *Harold could care less whether he passes this class.*

Incorrect: *Dot didn't have no double negatives in her paper.*

Correct: *Dot didn't have any double negatives in her paper.*

Correct Use of Coordination and Subordination

Connect independent clauses with the coordinating conjunctions—*and, but, or, for,* or *nor*—when their content is of equal importance. Use subordinating conjunctions—*although, because, before, if, since, though, until, when, whenever, where*—and relative pronouns—*that, who, whom, which*—to introduce clauses that express ideas that are subordinate to main ideas expressed in independent clauses. Be sure to place the conjunctions so that they express the proper relationship between ideas (cause/effect, condition, time, space).

Incorrect: *Because mother scolded me, I was late.*

Correct: *Mother scolded me because I was late.*

Incorrect: *The sun rose after the fog lifted.*

Correct: *The fog lifted after the sun rose.*

Notice that placement of the conjunction can completely change the meaning of the sentence. Main emphasis is shifted by the change.

> *Although Jenny was pleased, the teacher was disappointed. Although the teacher was disappointed, Jenny was pleased.*
>
> *The boys who wrote the essay won the contest. The boys who won the contest wrote the essay.*

Note: While not syntactically incorrect, the second sentence makes it appear that the boys won the contest for something else before they wrote the essay.

SKILL 2.4 Demonstrate knowledge of the use of introductions, main ideas, transitions, conclusions, and other forms of text organization in writing

If the concepts are not too complex, reading an essay should not require extensive re-reading. The ideas should be clear and straightforward. Anyone who has tried to write an essay knows that this sounds much easier than it really is! How do teachers help students to become proficient at writing multi-paragraph essays in ways that allow them to clearly communicate their ideas? The trick is to help them understand that various conventions of writing make comprehension easier for their readers. Those conventions include good paragraphing; transitions between paragraphs, ideas, and sentences; topic sentences; concluding sentences; appropriate vocabulary; and sufficient context.

If the concepts are not too complex, reading an essay should not require extensive re-reading.

Good paragraphing entails dividing up ideas into easily processed chunks. A good paragraph typically includes a topic sentence that explains the content of the paragraph. A good paragraph also includes sufficient explanation of that topic sentence. For example, if a topic sentence suggests that the paragraph will be about the causes of the Civil War, the rest of the paragraph should explain specific causes of the Civil War.

As writers transition from one paragraph to another—or from one sentence to another—they will usually provide transitional phrases that give signposts to readers about what is coming next. Words like "however," "furthermore," "although," and "likewise" are good ways of communicating intention to readers. When ideas are thrown together on a page, it is hard to tell what the writer is actually doing with those ideas. Therefore, students need to become familiar with using transitional phrases.

Concluding sentences often are unnecessary, but when done right, they provide a nice closing to a piece of writing. Students do not always need to use concluding sentences in paragraphs; however, they should be alerted to their potential benefits.

When writers use appropriate vocabulary, they are sensitive to the audience for and purpose of what they are writing. For example, if a professor writes an essay on a scientific concept for a group of nonscientists, he will not use specialized vocabulary to explain concepts. However, if he were writing for a group of scientists, specialized vocabulary would be appropriate, and even expected. Therefore, students need to learn early on that all writing has a purpose, and that because of that purpose, good writers will make conscious decisions about how to arrange their texts, which words to use, and which examples and metaphors to include.

Finally, when writers provide sufficient context, they ensure that readers do not have to extensively question the text to figure out what is going on. Again, this is related to the audience. Using the scientific concept example from above, the professor would need to provide more context if the audience were a group of nonscientists than he would if the audience were scientists. In other words, he would have to provide more background so that the nonscientists could understand the concepts.

SKILL 2.5	**Apply elements of appropriate grammar and usage** (e.g., noun-pronoun agreement, subject-verb agreement, consistent verb tense)

Subject-Verb Agreement

A verb should always agree in number with its subject. Making them agree relies on the ability to properly identify the subject of a sentence.

> *One of the boys was playing too rough.*
>
> *No one in the class, not the teacher nor the students, was listening to the message from the intercom.*
>
> *The candidates, including a grandmother and a teenager, are debating some controversial issues.*

If two singular subjects are connected by *and*, the verb must be plural.

> *A man* and *his dog were jogging on the beach.*

If two singular subjects are connected by *or* or *nor*, a singular verb is required.

> *Neither Dot* nor *Joyce has missed a day of school this year.*
> *Either Fran* or *Paul is missing.*

If one singular subject and one plural subject are connected by *or* or *nor*, the verb agrees with the subject nearest to the verb.

> *Neither the coach* nor *the players were able to sleep on the bus.*

If the subject is a collective noun, its sense of number in the sentence determines the verb: it is singular if the noun represents a group or unit, and plural if the noun represents individuals.

> *The House of Representatives has adjourned for the holidays.*
> *The House of Representatives have failed to reach agreement on the subject of adjournment.*

Verbs (Tense)

Present tense is used to express that which is currently happening or is always true.

> *Randy is playing the piano.*
> *Randy plays the piano like a pro.*

Past tense is used to express action that occurred in a past time.

> *Randy learned to play the piano when he was six years old.*

Future tense is used to express action or a condition of future time.

> *Randy will probably earn a music scholarship.*

Present perfect tense is used to express action or a condition that started in the past and is continued to or completed in the present.

> *Randy has practiced piano every day for the last ten years.*
> *Randy has never been bored with practice.*

Past perfect tense expresses action or a condition that occurred as a precedent to some other action or condition.

> *Randy had considered playing clarinet before he discovered the piano.*

Future perfect tense expresses action that started in the past or the present and will conclude at some time in the future.

> *By the time he goes to college, Randy will have been an accomplished pianist for more than half of his life.*

Verbs (Mood)

Indicative mood is used to make unconditional statements; subjunctive mood is used for conditional clauses or wish statements that pose untrue conditions. Verbs in subjunctive mood are plural with both singular and plural subjects.

> *If I were a bird, I would fly.*
>
> *I wish I were as rich as Donald Trump.*

Conjugation of verbs

The conjugation of verbs follows the patterns used in the discussion of tense above. However, the most frequent problems in verb use stem from the improper formation of past and past participial forms.

The most frequent problems in verb use stem from the improper formation of past and past participial forms.

> Regular verb: *believe, believed, (have) believed*
>
> Irregular verbs: *run, ran, run; sit, sat, sat; teach, taught, taught*

Other problems stem from the use of verbs that are the same in some tenses but have different forms and different meanings in other tenses.

> *I lie on the ground. I lay on the ground yesterday. I have lain down.*
>
> *I lay the blanket on the bed. I laid the blanket there yesterday. I have laid the blanket on the bed every night.*
>
> *The sun rises. The sun rose. The sun has risen. He raises the flag. He raised the flag. He had raised the flag.*
>
> *I sit on the porch. I sat on the porch. I have sat in the porch swing.*
>
> *I set the plate on the table. I set the plate there yesterday. I had set the table before dinner.*

Two other common verb problems stem from misusing the preposition *of* for the verb auxiliary *have* and misusing the verb *ought* (now rare).

Incorrect:	*I should of gone to bed.*
Correct:	*I should have gone to bed.*
Incorrect:	*He hadn't ought to get so angry.*
Correct:	*He ought not to get so angry.*

Pronouns

A pronoun used as a subject of predicate nominative is in nominative case.

She was the drum majorette. The lead trombonists were Joe and he. The band director accepted whoever could march in step.

A pronoun used as a direct object, indirect object, or object of a preposition is in objective case.

The teacher praised him. She gave him an A on the test. Her praise of him was appreciated. The students whom she did not praise will work harder next time.

Some common pronoun errors occur from the misuse of reflexive pronouns:

Singular:	*myself, yourself, herself, himself, itself*
Plural:	*ourselves, yourselves, themselves*
Incorrect:	*Jack cut hisself shaving.*
Correct:	*Jack cut himself shaving.*
Incorrect:	*They backed theirselves into a corner.*
Correct:	*They backed themselves into a corner.*

Adjectives

An adjective should agree with its antecedent in number.

Those apples are rotten. This one is ripe. These peaches are hard.

Comparative adjectives end in *-er* and superlatives in *-est*, with some exceptions like *worse* and *worst*. Some adjectives that cannot easily make comparative inflections are preceded by *more* and *most*.

Mrs. Carmichael is the better of the two basketball coaches.
That is the hastiest excuse you have ever contrived.

Avoid double comparisons.

Incorrect:	*This is the worstest headache I ever had.*
Correct:	*This is the worst headache I ever had.*

When comparing one thing to others in a group, exclude the thing under comparison from the rest of the group.

Incorrect:	*Joey is larger than any baby I have ever seen. (Since you have seen him, he cannot be larger than himself.)*
Correct:	*Joey is larger than <u>any other</u> baby I have ever seen.*

Include all the words necessary to make a comparison clear in meaning.

I am as tall as my mother. I am as tall as she (is).
My cats are better behaved than those of my neighbor.

Plurals

This section will focus on spelling plurals and possessives. The multiplicity and complexity of spelling rules based on phonics, letter doubling, and exceptions to rules that are not mastered by adulthood should be replaced by a good dictionary. As spelling mastery is also difficult for adolescents, the recommendation is the same: Learning the use of a dictionary and thesaurus will be a more rewarding use of time.

Most plurals of nouns that end in hard consonant sounds followed by a silent *e* are made by adding *s*. Some words ending in vowels also only add an *s*.

fingers, numerals, banks, bugs, riots, homes, gates, radios, bananas

For nouns that end in the soft consonant sounds *s, j, x, z, ch*, and *sh*, add *es* to make them plural. Some nouns ending in *o* also add *es*.

dresses, waxes, churches, brushes, tomatoes, potatoes

Nouns ending in y preceded by a vowel are pluralized by adding *s*.

boys, alleys

For nouns ending in *y* preceded by a consonant, change the *y* to *i* and add *es* to make them plural.

> *babies, corollaries, frugalities, poppies*

Some noun plurals are formed irregularly or remain the same.

> *sheep, deer, children, leaves, oxen*

Some nouns derived from foreign words, especially Latin, may make their plurals in two different ways. Sometimes, the meanings are the same; other times, the two plurals are used in slightly different contexts. It is always wise to consult the dictionary.

> *appendices, appendixes*   *criterion, criteria*
> *indexes, indices*   *crisis, crises*

Make the plurals of closed (solid) compound words in the usual way except for words ending in *ful*, which make their plurals on the root word.

> *timelines, hairpins, cupsful*

Make the plurals of open or hyphenated compounds by adding the change in inflection to the word that changes in number.

> *fathers-in-law, courts-martial, masters of art, doctors of medicine*

Make the plurals of letters, numbers, and abbreviations by adding *s*.

> *fives and tens, IBMs, 1990s, ps and qs*

Possessives

Make the possessives of singular nouns by adding an apostrophe followed by the letter *s* ('s).

> *baby's bottle, father's job, elephant's eye, teacher's desk, sympathizer's protests, week's postponement*

Make the possessive of singular nouns ending in *s* by adding either an apostrophe or an *'s* depending upon common usage or sound. When making the possessive causes difficulty, use a prepositional phrase instead. Even with the sibilant ending, with a few exceptions, it is advisable to use the *'s* construction.

> *dress's color, species's characteristics or characteristics of the species, James' hat or James's hat, Delores's shirt.*

Make the possessive of plural nouns ending in *s* by adding the apostrophe after the *s*.

> *horses' coats, jockeys' times, four days' time*

Make possessives of plural nouns that do not end in *s* the same as singular nouns by adding *'s*.

> *children's shoes, deer's antlers, cattle's horns*

Make possessives of compound nouns by adding the inflection at the end of the word or phrase.

> *the mayor of Los Angeles' campaign, the mailman's new truck, the mailmen's new trucks, my father-in-law's first wife, the keepsakes' values, several daughters-in-law's husbands*

Note: Because a gerund functions as a noun, any noun preceding it and operating as a possessive adjective must reflect the necessary inflection. However, if the gerundive following the noun is a participle, no inflection is added.

SKILL 2.6 Apply elements of appropriate punctuation and capitalization (e.g., commas, apostrophes, quotation marks)

The candidate should be cognizant of proper rules and conventions of punctuation, capitalization, and spelling. Competency exams will generally test the ability to apply the more advanced skills; thus, a limited number of more frustrating rules are presented here. Rules should be applied according to the American style of English, i.e., spelling *theater* instead of *theatre* and placing terminal marks of punctuation almost exclusively within other marks of punctuation.

Using Terminal Punctuation in Relation to Quotation Marks

In a quoted statement that is either declarative or imperative, place the period inside the closing quotation marks.

> *"The airplane crashed on the runway during takeoff."*

If the quotation is followed by other words in the sentence, place a comma inside the closing quotations marks and a period at the end of the sentence.

> *"The airplane crashed on the runway during takeoff," said the announcer.*

In most instances in which a quoted title or expression occurs at the end of a sentence, the period is placed before either the single or double quotation marks.

> *The educator worried, "The middle school readers were unprepared to understand Bryant's poem 'Thanatopsis.'"*
>
> *Early book-length adventure stories like* Don Quixote *and* The Three Musketeers *are known as "picaresque novels."*

There is an instance in which the final quotation mark precedes the period: if the content of the sentence is about a speech or quote, and the understanding of the meaning might be confused by the placement of the period.

> *The first thing out of his mouth was "Hi, I'm home."*
>
> *–BUT–*
>
> *The first line of his speech began "I arrived home to an empty house".*

In sentences that are interrogatory or exclamatory, the question mark or exclamation point should be positioned outside the closing quotation marks if the quote itself is a statement or command or a cited title.

> *Who decided to lead us in the recitation of the "Pledge of Allegiance"?*
>
> *Why was Tillie shaking as she began her recitation, "Once upon a midnight dreary..."?*
>
> *I was embarrassed when Mrs. White said, "Your slip is showing"!*

In sentences that are declarative but in which the quotation is a question or an exclamation, place the question mark or exclamation point inside the quotation marks.

> *The hall monitor yelled, "Fire! Fire!"*
>
> *"Fire! Fire!" yelled the hall monitor.*
>
> *Cory shrieked, "Is there a mouse in the room?" (In this instance, the question supersedes the exclamation.)*

Using Periods with Parentheses or Brackets

Place the period inside the parentheses or brackets if they enclose a complete sentence, independent of the other sentences around it.

> *Stephen Crane was a confirmed alcohol and drug addict. (He admitted as much to other journalists in Cuba.)*

If the parenthetical expression is a statement inserted within another statement, the period in the enclosure is omitted.

> *Mark Twain used the character Indian Joe (He also appeared in* The Adventures of Tom Sawyer*) as a foil for Jim in* The Adventures of Huckleberry Finn.

When enclosed matter comes at the end of a sentence requiring quotation marks, place the period outside the parentheses or brackets.

> *"The secretary of state consulted with the ambassador [Powell]."*

Using commas

Use commas to separate two or more coordinate adjectives modifying the same word and three or more nouns, phrases, or clauses in a list.

> *Maggie's hair was dull, dirty, and lice-ridden.*
>
> *Dickens portrayed the Artful Dodger as skillful pickpocket, loyal follower of Fagin, and defendant of Oliver Twist.*
>
> *Ellen daydreamed about getting out of the rain, taking a shower, and eating a hot dinner.*
>
> *In Elizabethan England, Ben Jonson wrote comedy, Christopher Marlowe wrote tragedies, and William Shakespeare composed both.*

Use commas to separate antithetical or complimentary expressions from the rest of the sentence.

> *The veterinarian, not his assistant, would perform the delicate surgery.*
>
> *The more he knew about her, the less he wished he had known.*
>
> *Randy hopes to, and probably will, get an appointment to the Naval Academy.*

Using double quotation marks with other punctuation

Quotations—whether words, phrases, or clauses—should be punctuated according to the rules of the grammatical function they serve in the sentence.

> The works of Shakespeare, "the Bard of Avon," have been contested as originating with other authors.
>
> "You'll get my money," the old man warned, "when Hell freezes over."
>
> Sheila cited the passage that began "Four score and seven years ago...." (Note the ellipsis followed by an enclosed period.)
>
> "Old Ironsides" inspired the preservation of the U.S.S. Constitution.

Use quotation marks to enclose the titles of shorter works: songs, short poems, short stories, essays, and chapters of books. (See "Using Italics" for rules on punctuating longer titles.)

> "The Tell-Tale Heart" (short story)
>
> "Casey at the Bat" (poem)
>
> "America the Beautiful" (song)

Using semicolons

Use semicolons to separate independent clauses when the second clause is introduced by a transitional adverb. (These clauses may also be written as separate sentences, preferably by placing the adverb within the second sentence.)

> The Elizabethans modified the rhyme scheme of the sonnet; thus, it was called the English sonnet.
>
> –OR–
>
> The Elizabethans modified the rhyme scheme of the sonnet. It thus was called the English sonnet.

Use semicolons to separate items in a series that are long and complex or have internal punctuation.

> The Italian Renaissance produced masters in the fine arts: Dante Alighieri, author of the Divine Comedy; Leonardo da Vinci, painter of The Last Supper; and Donatello, sculptor of the Quattro Coronati, the Four Saints.
>
> The leading scorers in the WNBA were Haizhaw Zheng, averaging 23.9 points per game; Lisa Leslie, 22; and Cynthia Cooper, 19.5.

Using colons

Place a colon at the beginning of a list of items. (Note its use in the sentence about Renaissance Italians previously.)

> The teacher directed us to compare Faulkner's three symbolic novels: Absalom, Absalom; As I Lay Dying; and Light in August.

Do *not* use a comma if the list is preceded by a verb.

> *Three of Faulkner's symbolic novels are* Absalom, Absalom; As I Lay Dying; *and* Light in August.

Using dashes

Place dashes (called "em" dashes) to denote sudden breaks in thought.

> *Some periods in literature—the Romantic Age, for example—spanned different time periods in different countries.*

Use dashes instead of commas if commas are already used elsewhere in the sentence for amplification or explanation.

> *The Fireside Poets included three Brahmans—James Russell Lowell, Henry David Wadsworth, and Oliver Wendell Holmes—and John Greenleaf Whittier.*

Capitalization

Capitalize all proper names of persons (including specific organizations or agencies of government); places (countries, states, cities, parks, and specific geographical areas); things (political parties, structures, historical and cultural terms, and calendar and time designations); and religious terms (any deity, revered person or group, sacred writings).

> *Percy Bysshe Shelley, Argentina, Mount Rainier National Park, Grand Canyon, League of Nations, the Sears Tower, Birmingham, Lyric Theater, Americans, Midwesterners, Democrats, Renaissance, Boy Scouts of America, Easter, God, Bible, Dead Sea Scrolls, Koran*

Capitalize proper adjectives and titles used with proper names.

> *California gold rush, President John Adams, French fries, Homeric epic, Romanesque architecture, Senator John Glenn*

COMPETENCY 3
UNDERSTAND FEATURES AND FORMS OF LITERATURE

SKILL 3.1 **Identify characteristics of literary forms** *(e.g., poetry, plays, novels, short stories)* **and genres** *(e.g., science fiction, mystery, historical fiction*

The major literary genres in literature include allegory, ballad, drama, epic, epistle, essay, fable, novel, poem, romance, and the short story. At times, even books written for adults are appropriate for children. These major genres are detailed below.

Allegory: A story in verse or prose with characters that represent virtues and vices. There are two meanings: symbolic and literal. John Bunyan's *The Pilgrim's Progress* is the most renowned of this genre.

Ballad: An *in medias res* story that is told or sung—usually in verse—and accompanied by music. Literary devices found in ballads include the refrain (repeated section) and incremental repetition (anaphora) for effect. Earliest forms were anonymous folk ballads. Later forms include Coleridge's Romantic masterpiece, "The Rime of the Ancient Mariner."

Drama: Plays (comedy, modern, or tragedy) that are typically performed in five acts. Traditionalists and neoclassicists adhere to Aristotle's unities of time, place, and action. Plot development is advanced through dialogue. Literary devices include asides, soliloquies, and the chorus, which represents public opinion. Considered by many to be the greatest of all dramatists/playwrights is William Shakespeare. Other playwrights include Ibsen, Williams, Miller, Shaw, Stoppard, Racine, Moliére, Sophocles, Aeschylus, Euripides, and Aristophanes.

Epic: A long poem, usually of book length, that reflects values inherent in the generative society. Epic devices include an invocation to a Muse for inspiration, an overall purpose for writing, universal setting, a protagonist and antagonist who possess supernatural strength and acumen, and interventions of a God or the gods. Comparatively, there are few epics in literature: Homer's *Iliad* and *Odyssey*, Virgil's *Aeneid*, Milton's *Paradise Lost*, Spenser's *The Fairie Queene*, Barrett Browning's *Aurora Leigh*, and Pope's mock-epic, *The Rape of the Lock*.

Epistle: A letter that is not always originally intended for public distribution, but due to the fame of the sender and/or recipient, one that becomes public domain. For example, Paul wrote epistles that were later placed in the Bible.

Essay: Typically, a limited length prose work focusing on a topic and propounding a definite point of view and authoritative tone. Great essayists include Carlyle, Lamb, DeQuincy, Emerson, and Montaigne (who is credited with defining this genre).

Fable: A terse tale offering a moral or exemplum. Chaucer's "The Nun's Priest's Tale" is a fine example of a *bete fabliau* (or beast fable) in which animals speak and act characteristically human, illustrating human foibles.

Legend: A traditional narrative or collection of related narratives, popularly regarded as historically factual but actually a mixture of fact and fiction.

Myth: Stories that are more or less universally shared within a culture to explain its history and traditions.

Novel: The longest form of fictional prose, containing a variety of characterizations, settings, local color, and regionalism. Most have complex plots, expanded description, and attention to detail. Some of the great novelists include Austen, the Brontës, Twain, Tolstoy, Hugo, Hardy, Dickens, Hawthorne, Forster, and Flaubert.

Poem: The only requirement of this genre is rhythm. Subgenres include fixed types of literature such as the sonnet, elegy, ode, pastoral, and villanelle. Unfixed types of literature include blank verse and dramatic monologue.

Romance: A highly imaginative tale set in a fantastical realm that deals with the conflicts between heroes, villains, and/or monsters. "The Knight's Tale" from Chaucer's *Canterbury Tales, Sir Gawain and the Green Knight*, and Keats' "The Eve of St. Agnes" are well-known examples.

Short Story: A concise narrative that has less background than a novel, but that typically includes many of the same plot developments and techniques. As mentioned before, some of the most notable short story writers include Hemingway, Faulkner, Twain, Joyce, Jackson, O'Connor, de Maupassant, Saki, Poe, and Pushkin.

SKILL 3.2 Identify characteristics of genres of nonfiction (e.g., essays, biographies, autobiographies, informational text)

Biography/Autobiography: Narrative of a person's life; a true story about a real person.

Essay: A short literary composition that reflects the author's outlook or point of view.

Narrative Nonfiction: Factual information presented in a format that tells a story.

Nonfiction: Informational text dealing with an actual, real-life subject.

Speech: Public address or discourse.

SKILL 3.3 Identify characteristics and functions of literary elements and devices (e.g., setting, plot, dialect, point of view, symbolism)

Students need to be able to distinguish between fiction and nonfiction in order to determine the author's or narrator's perspective. Generally fiction is divided into three main areas:

- Story
- Novel
- Novella

These usually have a main character, setting, plot, climax, and resolution. Non-fiction, on the other hand, is usually intended to inform the reader. Common types of nonfiction include:

- Essays
- Documentaries
- Biographies
- Autobiographies
- Informational books

The meaning of the message conveyed by each author or narrator comes through in the words of the text. Abstract themes of love, hatred, friendship, honor, good, justice, and power become real through the words and actions of the characters

Abstract themes of love, hatred, friendship, honor, good, justice, and power become real through the words and actions of the characters in works of fiction.

in works of fiction. In order to teach students to find the perspective used by the author or narrator, the teacher has to help them analyze the work. This means that, through discussion and direct teaching, the students can look at the characters, actions, problems, and dialogue in order to discern how they relate to or help develop the theme.

Some of the ways to determine themes in fiction are:

- Main ideas expressed through the text and speech of the characters

- The actual statements that the characters make

- Narrators tell readers how they feel about a topic by inserting their own ideas into the text

- The actions and words of characters who may be in conflict with each other

- The use of figurative language

Figurative language is present in both fiction and nonfiction. This is one element of reading that often poses difficulties for students. Therefore, the teacher has to help them find the symbolism in the text. In literature, a symbol can be an idea, an object, or a person that the writer is using to make a point, develop a theme, or create a mood. Symbols can be underlying tenets of a culture, or even biblical or mythological in nature. Once students decide on the symbolism used in a text, they need to judge its importance in the work.

There are also fiction texts that teach a lesson, such as fables and parables. These are short stories that the teacher can read to the class and have the students discuss what lesson the story is teaching. Modeling and practice is the key here. Students should not be expected to read a fable and guess its meaning if they have not been previously exposed to this type of writing. The classroom should also contain multiple texts that the students can read on their own.

The author's or narrator's perspective is easier to discern in nonfiction. This is because the meaning comes from the writer's thesis, which is often found in the very first paragraph. However, it is not always directly stated, and may be implied. Students have to read between the lines of the text to find out exactly what the author's feelings toward the topic are.

There are four main types of nonfiction writing:

1. Expository: Explains a topic or how to do something

2. Persuasive: Tries to persuade the reader to adopt the author's or narrator's point of view

3. Descriptive: Transmits descriptions and images through words. In other words, descriptive writing excites the senses.

4. Narrative: Informs by telling a story. This form of nonfiction usually presents a series of actions to let the reader know what has happened at some point in time.

Teachers should model questioning for the students when identifying the author's or narrator's perspective in both fiction and nonfiction. This includes such questions as:

- Is the text fiction or nonfiction? How do you know?

- Why do you think the author wrote this work?

- What feelings does the text evoke in you?

- What is the author's main idea?

- How do the setting, characters, actions, and central problem help bring out the meaning or the author's point of view in the text?

Students should be encouraged to make personal responses to the texts they read (e.g., how it made them feel, if it reminded them of anything in their own lives, which part they liked best, or what they learned from the reading). Depending on the grade level, students can use a variety of ways of responding, such as drawings, retellings, talking, and painting.

> *Students should be encouraged to make personal responses to the texts they read (e.g., how it made them feel, if it reminded them of anything in their own lives, which part they liked best, or what they learned from the reading).*

SKILL 3.4 Recognize influences of cultural, social, biographical, and historical factors on the creation and development of literature

One way of interpreting literature is to examine the various contexts in which it was written.

Historical and Cultural Context

Local color

LOCAL COLOR is defined as the presentation of the peculiarities of a particular locality and its inhabitants. Local color was introduced primarily after the Civil War, although there were certainly precursors, such as Washington Irving and his depiction of life in the Catskill Mountains of New York. However, the local colorist movement is generally considered to have begun in 1865, when humor began to permeate the writing of those who were focusing on a particular region of the country.

> **LOCAL COLOR:** the presentation of the peculiarities of a particular locality and its inhabitants

Read more about regional realism:

http://www.learner.org/amerpass/unit08/usingvideo.html

Samuel L. Clemens (Mark Twain) is best known for his humorous works about the Southwest, such as "The Notorious Jumping Frog of Calaveras County." The country had just emerged from its "long night of the soul," a time when death, despair, and disaster had preoccupied the nation for almost five years. It's no wonder that artists sought to relieve the grief and pain and lift spirits, nor is it surprising that their efforts brought such a strong response. Mark Twain is generally considered to be not only one of America's funniest writers but also one who wrote great and enduring fiction.

Other examples of local colorists inlcude:

- George Washington Cable
- Joel Chandler Harris
- Bret Hart
- Sarah Orne Jewett
- Harriet Beecher Stowe

Slavery

The most well-known of the early writers who used fiction to make a political statement about slavery is Harriet Beecher Stowe, author of *Uncle Tom's Cabin*. *Uncle Tom's Cabin* was Stowe's first novel. It was published first as a serial in 1851, and then as a book in 1852. This antislavery book infuriated many Southerners. However, Stowe herself had been angered by the 1850 Fugitive Slave Law that made it legal to indict those who assisted runaway slaves. The law took away the rights not only of the runaways but also of free slaves. Stowe intended to generate a protest of the law and of slavery in general. *Uncle Tom's Cabin* was the first effort to depict the lives of slaves from their standpoint.

The novel is about three Kentucky slaves, Tom, Eliza, and George. Eliza and George are married to each other but have different masters. They successfully escape with their little boy, but Tom does not escape. Although he has a wife and children, he is sold, ending up the property of the monstrous Simon Legree, on whose property he eventually dies.

Stowe cleverly used depictions of motherhood and Christianity to stir her readers. When President Lincoln met her, he told her it was her book that started the Civil War.

Many writers used the printed word to protest slavery:

- Frederick Douglass
- William Lloyd Garrison
- Benjamin Lay, a Quaker

- Jonathan Edwards, a Connecticut theologian

- Susan B. Anthony

Immigration

Immigration has been a popular topic in literature since the time of the Louisiana Purchase in 1804. The recent work *Undaunted Courage* by Stephen E. Ambrose is ostensibly the autobiography of Meriwether Lewis but is actually a recounting of the Lewis and Clark expedition. Presented as a scientific expedition by President Jefferson, the expedition was actually intended to provide maps and information for the expansion of the American West. A well-known novel depicting the settling of the West by immigrants from other countries is *Giants in the Earth* by Ole Edvart Rolvaag, himself a descendant of immigrants.

During the twentieth century, immigration increased rapidly and the population of the United States swelled. Literature documented the resultant changes in the American culture. For example, John Steinbeck's *Cannery Row* and *Tortilla Flats* glorify the lives of Mexican migrants in California. Amy Tan's *The Joy Luck Club* deals with the problems faced by Chinese immigrants.

Leon Uris's *Exodus* explores the social history that led to the founding of the modern state of Israel. It was published in 1958, only a short time after the Holocaust. It deals with the attempts of concentration camp survivors to get to the land that had become the new Israel. In many ways, it is the quintessential work on immigration causes and effects.

Civil rights

Many of the abolitionists were also early crusaders for civil rights. However, the 1960s Civil Rights movement focused attention on the plight of the people who had been "freed" by the Civil War. The movement brought about long-overdue changes in the opportunities for and rights of African Americans.

David Halberstam, who was a reporter in Nashville at the time of the sit-ins by eight young black college students that initiated the Civil Rights movement, wrote *The Children*, published in 1998 by Random House, to remind Americans of these students' courage, suffering, and achievements. Congressman John Lewis, Fifth District, Georgia, was one of those eight young men. Lewis has gone on to a life of public service. Halberstam records that when older black ministers tried to persuade these young people not to pursue their protest, John Lewis responded: "If not us, then who? If not now, then when?"

Some examples of protest literature include:

- James Baldwin, *Blues for Mister Charlie*

- Martin Luther King, *Where Do We Go from Here?*

- Langston Hughes, *Fight for Freedom: The Story of the NAACP*

- Eldridge Cleaver, *Soul on Ice*

- Malcolm X, *The Autobiography of Malcolm X*

- Stokely Carmichael and Charles V. Hamilton, *Black Power*

- Leroi Jones, *Home*

Vietnam

An America that was already divided over the Civil Rights movement faced even greater divisions over the war in Vietnam. Those who were in favor of the war and who opposed withdrawal saw it as the major front in the war against communism. Those who opposed the war and who favored withdrawal of the troops believed that it would not serve to defeat communism and was a quagmire.

Though set in the last years of World War II, *Catch-22* by Joseph Heller was a popular antiwar novel that became a successful movie of the time.

Authors Take Sides on Vietnam, edited by Cecil Woolf and John Bagguley, is a collection of essays by 168 well-known authors throughout the world. *Where is Vietnam?*, edited by Walter Lowenfels, consists of ninety-two poems about the war.

SKILL 3.5 **Demonstrate knowledge of genres, themes, authors, and works of literature written for children and adolescents**

The social changes of post-World War II significantly affected adolescent literature. Issues such as the Civil Rights movement, feminism, the protest of the Vietnam conflict, issues surrounding homelessness, neglect, teen pregnancy, drugs, and violence have all created a new vein of contemporary fiction that helps adolescents understand and cope with the world they live in.

Popular books for preadolescents often deal with establishing relationships with members of the opposite sex (*Sweet Valley High* series) and learning to cope with their changing bodies, personalities, or life situations, as in Judy Blume's *Are You There, God? It's Me, Margaret*. Adolescents are still interested in the fantasy and science fiction genres as well as popular juvenile fiction. Middle school students still read the *Little House on the Prairie* series and the mysteries of the Hardy boys and Nancy Drew. Teens value the works of Emily and Charlotte Bronte, Willa Cather, Jack London, William Shakespeare, and Mark Twain as much as those of Piers Anthony, S.E. Hinton, Madeleine L'Engle, Stephen King, and J.R.R. Tolkien, because they're fun to read, whatever their underlying worth may be.

FAVORITE AUTHORS BY GENRE	
Fantasy	Piers Anthony, Ursula LeGuin, Ann McCaffrey
Horror	V.C. Andrews, Stephen King
Juvenile Fiction	Judy Blume, Robert Cormier, Rosa Guy, Virginia Hamilton, S.E. Hinton, M.E. Kerr, Harry Mazer, Norma Fox Mazer, Richard Newton Peck, Cynthia Voight, Paul Zindel
Science Fiction	Isaac Asimov, Ray Bradbury, Arthur C. Clarke, Frank Herbert, Larry Niven, H.G. Wells.

For Sixth Grade

These classic and contemporary works combine the characteristics of multiple theories. Functioning at the concrete operations stage (Piaget), being of the "good person" orientation (Kohlberg), still highly dependent on external rewards (Bandura), and exhibiting all five needs discussed from Maslow's hierarchy, these eleven- to twelve-year-olds should appreciate the following titles, grouped by reading level. These titles are also cited for interest at that grade level and do not reflect high-interest titles for older readers who do not read at grade level. Some high-interest titles will be cited later.

READING LEVEL 6.0 TO 6.9	
Barrett, William	*Lilies of the Field*
Cormier, Robert	*Other Bells for Us to Ring*
Dahl, Roald	*Danny, Champion of the World; Charlie and the Chocolate Factory*
Lindgren, Astrid	*Pippi Longstocking*
Lindbergh, Anne	*Three Lives to Live*
Lowry, Lois	*Rabble Starkey*
Naylor, Phyllis	*The Year of the Gopher, Reluctantly Alice*
Peck, Robert Newton	*Arly*
Speare, Elizabeth	*The Witch of Blackbird Pond*
Sleator, William	*The Boy Who Reversed Himself*

For Seventh and Eighth Grades

Most seventh- and eighth-grade students, according to learning theory, are still functioning cognitively, psychologically, and morally as sixth graders. However, because these are not inflexible standards, there are some twelve- and thirteen-year-olds who are much more mature socially, intellectually, and physically than the younger children who share the same school.

These students are becoming concerned with establishing individual and peer group identities that often present conflicts with breaking from authority and the rigidity of rules. Some students at this age are still tied firmly to the family and its expectations, while others identify more with those their own age or older. Enrichment reading for this group must help them cope with life's rapid changes or provide escape, and thus must be either realistic or fantastic depending on the child's needs. Adventures and mysteries (the Hardy Boys and Nancy Drew series) are still popular today. These preteens also become more interested in biographies of contemporary figures rather than legendary figures of the past.

READING LEVEL 7.0 TO 7.9	
Armstrong, William	*Sounder*
Bagnold, Enid	*National Velvet*
Barrie, James	*Peter Pan*
London, Jack	*White Fang, Call of the Wild*
Lowry, Lois	*Taking Care of Terrific*
McCaffrey, Anne	*The Dragonsinger* series
Montgomery, L. M.	*Anne of Green Gables* and sequels
Steinbeck, John	*The Pearl*
Tolkien, J. R. R.	*The Hobbit*
Zindel, Paul	*The Pigman*

READING LEVEL 8.0 TO 8.9	
Cormier, Robert	*I Am the Cheese*
McCullers, Carson	*The Member of the Wedding*

Continued on next page

North, Sterling	*Rascal*
Twain, Mark	*The Adventures of Tom Sawyer*
Zindel, Paul	*My Darling, My Hamburger*

> **SKILL** **Recognize influence of nontraditional literary forms** *(e.g., editorial*
> **3.6** *cartoons, media, advertising)*

Editorial Cartoons

An editorial cartoon is a symbolic drawing that comically represents the author's ideas. These types of cartoons are usually humorous with a satirical attitude.

The origins of the modern editorial cartoon can be traced back to the 16th century. Political and religious leaders used editorial cartoons as a propaganda tool during the ongoing religious debates of the Reformation Era. The use of the caricature style of cartoon was invented in the 1800s in the country of Britain.

The origins of the modern editorial cartoon can be traced back to the 16th century.

Editorial cartoons are often viewed as an important part of American politics throughout much of the history of the United States. Over the past years, children have become more interested in editorial cartoons and, consequently, these types of cartoons have become an important source of political and social information in their lives.

Editorial cartoons can play a significant role in the discussion of many social topics. Use of editorial cartoons is an excellent way for students to identify the author's point of view.

Prominent editorial cartoonist

Dr. Seuss (Theodor Seuss Geisel, 1904-1991) was a life-long cartoonist. Because of the fame of his children's books, his political cartoons have remained largely unread by the general public. However, for two years, 1941-1943, he was the principal editorial cartoonist for the New York newspaper *PM*, drawing over 400 editorial cartoons.

Dr. Seuss Goes to War by historian Richard H. Minear (The New Press, 1999) reproduced some two hundred of the *PM* cartoons. Dr. Seuss also drew a set of war "cartoons" which were published in numerous newspapers.

For more information about Richard H. Minear see:

http://orpheus.ucsd.edu

Students can also create their own cartoons on the topics of the editorial cartoons using an easy-to-read storybook format for their own personal commentaries.

Media and Advertising

Advertising aimed towards children usually includes paid advertisements or commercials that appear in TV programs that are specifically created for children: cartoons, children's game shows, etc. Children are highly susceptible to advertising because they are often unable to make a distinction of the validity of advertising. Many advertisers use visual effects that can mislead children about the performance or the value of the product. Advertisers can use visual effects to capture the viewers' attention and to convince them to identify with the advertiser's point of view.

Discussion

- Explain to students that visual effects are ways of changing an image to add a message or to create a certain impression in a viewer's mind.

- Discuss with students how TV fiction and nonfiction programs can affect their perception of the world around them.

- In order for students to understand the influence of advertising on them as consumers, ask them to compare their experience, for example, eating a Happy Meal sandwich from McDonald's to the paid actor on TV who also eats a Happy Meal sandwich from McDonald's.

COMPETENCY 4
UNDERSTAND RESEARCH METHODS

SKILL 4.1 Demonstrate knowledge of strategies for developing topics, questions, and purposes for inquiry prior to planning for and conducting research

---

Prewriting

PREWRITING: may include clustering, listing, brainstorming, mapping, free writing, and charting

Students gather ideas before writing. PREWRITING may include clustering, listing, brainstorming, mapping, free writing, and charting. Providing many ways for a student to develop ideas on a topic will increase his or her chances for success.

Remind students that as they prewrite they need to consider their audience. Prewriting strategies assist students in a variety of ways. Listed below are the most common prewriting strategies students can use to explore, plan, and write on a topic. It is important to remember when teaching these strategies that not all prewriting must eventually produce a finished piece of writing. In fact, in the initial lesson about prewriting strategies, it might be more effective to have students practice prewriting strategies without the pressure of having to write a finished product.

- Keep an idea book so that they can jot down ideas that come to mind.

- Write in a daily journal.

- Write down whatever comes to mind; this is called free writing. Students do not stop to make corrections or interrupt the flow of ideas.

A variation of this technique is focused FREE WRITING—writing on a specific topic—to prepare for an essay.

- Make a list of all ideas connected with their topic; this is called BRAINSTORMING.

- Make sure students know that this technique works best when they let their mind work freely. After completing the list, students should analyze the list to see if there is a pattern or way to group the ideas.

- Ask the questions Who? What? When? Where? When? and How? Help the writer approach a topic from several perspectives.

- Create a visual map on paper to gather ideas. Cluster circles and lines to show connections between ideas. Students should try to identify the relationship that exists between their ideas. If they cannot see the relationships, have them pair up, and exchange papers and have their partners look for some related ideas.

- Observe details of sight, hearing, taste, touch, and smell.

- Visualize by making mental images of something and write down the details in a list.

FREE WRITING: writing on a specific topic

BRAINSTORMING: making a list of all ideas connected with their topic

Creating a Working Outline

A good thesis gives structure to your essay and helps focus your thoughts. When forming your thesis, look at your prewriting strategy—clustering, questioning, or brainstorming. Then decide quickly which two or three major areas you'll discuss. Remember, you must limit the scope of the paper because of the time factor.

The OUTLINE lists those main areas or points as topics for each paragraph.

OUTLINE: lists those main areas or points as topics for each paragraph

Looking at the prewriting cluster on computers, you might choose several areas in which computers help us—for example, in science and medicine, business, and education. You might also consider people's reliance on this "wonder" and include at least one paragraph about this reliance. A formal outline for this essay might look like this:

> I. Introduction and thesis
> II. Computers used in science and medicine
> III. Computers used in business
> IV. Computers used in education
> V. People's reliance on computers
> VI. Conclusion

Under time pressure, however, you may use a shorter organizational plan, such as abbreviated key words in a list. For example:

> 1. intro: wonders of the computer OR
> 2. science
> 3. med
> 4. schools
> 5. business
> 6. conclusion
>
> A. intro: wonders of computers—science
> B. in the space industry
> C. in medical technology
> D. conclusion

After they have practiced with each of these prewriting strategies, ask them to pick out the ones they prefer and ask them to discuss how they might use the techniques to help them with future writing assignments. It is important to remember that they can use more than one prewriting strategy at a time. They may find that different writing situations suggest certain techniques.

| SKILL 4.2 | Demonstrate knowledge of strategies for gathering, analyzing, synthesizing, and evaluating data from a variety of sources (e.g., print and nonprint texts, artifacts, people, libraries, databases, computer networks, videos) |

Research and Documentation

Whether researching for your own purposes or teaching students to research, the best place to start research is usually at a library. The library has numerous books, videos, and periodicals you can use as references, and the librarian is always a valuable resource who can help you retrieve relevant information. In spite of the abundance of online resources, researchers still need librarians.

Those who declared librarians obsolete when the Internet rage first appeared are now red-faced. We need them more than ever. The Internet is full of "stuff" but its value and readability is often questionable. "Stuff" doesn't give you a competitive edge; high-quality related information does.

—Patricia Schroeder, President of the Association of American Publishers

Gathering data

Keep content and context in mind when researching. Remember that there are multiple ways to get the information you need. Read an encyclopedia article about your topic to get a general overview, and then focus from there. Note names of important people associated with your subject, time periods, and geographic areas. Make a list of key words and their synonyms to use while searching for information. And finally, don't forget about articles in magazines and newspapers, or even personal interviews with experts related to your field of interest. As you gather information, be sure to do the following:

- Keep a record of any sources consulted during the research process

- As you take notes, avoid unintentional plagiarism

- Summarize and paraphrase in your own words without the source in front of you

To be lifelong learners, students should learn to conduct their own research. Thus, they need to know what resources are available to them and how to use them.

Dictionaries are useful for spelling, writing, and reading. Looking up a word in the dictionary should be an expected behavior, not a punishment or busy work.

Model the correct way to use the dictionary, as some students have never been taught proper dictionary skills. As the teacher, you need to demonstrate that as an adult reader and writer, you routinely and happily use the dictionary.

Encyclopedias in print or online are the beginning point for many research projects. While these entries may sometimes lack timeliness, they do provide students with general background.

Databases hold billions of records. Students should be taught effective search techniques, such as using key words and Boolean operators.

Learning that "and" and "or" will increase the number of hits while "not" or "and not" will decrease the number of hits can save researchers time and effort.

The Internet is a multi-faceted goldmine of information, but you must be careful to discriminate between reliable and unreliable sources. Use sites that are associated with an academic institution, such as a university or a scholarly organization. Typical domain names will end in "edu" or "org."

Students should evaluate any piece of information gleaned from the Internet. For example, if you google "etymology," you will find a multitude of sources. Don't trust just one. The information should be validated by at least three sources. Wikipedia is very useful, but it can be changed by anyone who chooses, so any information on it should be backed up by other sources.

Primary and secondary sources

The resources used to support a piece of writing can be divided into two major groups: primary sources and secondary sources.

> **PRIMARY SOURCES:**
> works, records, and the like that were created during the period being studied or immediately after

> **SECONDARY SOURCES:**
> works written significantly after the period being studied and are based on primary sources

> *Primary sources are the basic materials that provide raw data and information. Secondary sources are works that contain the explications of, and judgments on, this primary material.*

PRIMARY SOURCES are works, records, and the like that were created during the period being studied or immediately after. SECONDARY SOURCES are works written significantly after the period being studied and are based on primary sources. Primary sources are the basic materials that provide raw data and information. Secondary sources are works that contain the explications of, and judgments on, this primary material.

Primary sources include the following kinds of materials:

- Documents that reflect the immediate, everyday concerns of people: memoranda, bills, deeds, charters, newspaper reports, pamphlets, graffiti, popular writings, journals or diaries, records of decision-making bodies, letters, receipts, snapshots, and so on.

- Theoretical writings that reflect care and consideration in composition and that attempt to convince or persuade. The topic will generally be deeper and more pervasive than is the case with "immediate" documents. Theoretical writings may include newspaper or magazine editorials, sermons, political speeches, or philosophical writings.

- Narrative accounts of events, ideas, and trends written with intentionality by someone contemporary with the events described.

- Statistical data, although statistics may be misleading.

- Literature and nonverbal materials, novels, stories, poetry, and essays from the period, as well as coins, archaeological artifacts, and art produced during the period.

Secondary sources include the following kinds of materials:

- Books written on the basis of primary materials about the period of time.

- Books written on the basis of primary materials about persons who played a major role in the events under consideration.

- Books and articles written on the basis of primary materials about the culture, the social norms, the language, and the values of the period.

- Quotations from primary sources.

- Statistical data on the period.

- The conclusions and inferences of other historians.

- Multiple interpretations of the ethos of the time.

Questions for analyzing sources

To determine the authenticity or credibility of your sources, consider these questions:

1. Who created the source, and why? Was it created through a spur-of-the-moment act, a routine transaction, or a thoughtful, deliberate process?

2. Did the recorder have firsthand knowledge of the event? Or, did the recorder report what others saw and heard?

3. Was the recorder a neutral party, or did the recorder have opinions or interests that might have influenced what was recorded?

4. Did the recorder produce the source for personal use, for one or more individuals, or for a large audience?

5. Was the source meant to be public or private?

6. Did the recorder wish to inform or persuade others? Did the recorder have reasons to be honest or dishonest?

7. Was the information recorded during the event, immediately after the event, or after some lapse of time? How large a lapse of time?

> *Learn more about assessing the credibility of online sources:*
>
> *http://www. webcredible.co.uk/ user-friendly-resources/ web-credibility/assessing-credibility-online-sources. shtml*

SKILL 4.3 **Analyze ethical issues related to the use of resources, human subjects, materials, and the Internet** *(e.g., copyright, citations)*

Documentation

Documentation is an important skill when incorporating outside information into a piece of writing. Students must learn that research involves more than cutting and pasting from the Internet and that plagiarism is a serious academic offense.

Students must recognize that stealing intellectual property is an academic and, in some cases, a legal crime; thus, students need to learn how to give credit where credit is due.

Students should be aware of the rules that apply to borrowing ideas from various sources. The consequences for violating these rules are becoming more severe. Pleading ignorance is less and less of a defense. Such consequences include failing an assignment, losing credit for an entire course, expulsion from a learning environment, and civil penalties. Software exists that enables teachers and other interested individuals to determine quickly whether a given paper includes plagiarized material. As members of society in the information age, students are expected to recognize the basic justice of intellectual honesty and to conform to the systems meant to ensure it.

There are several style guides for documenting sources. Each guide has its own particular ways of signaling that information has been directly borrowed or paraphrased, and familiarity with the relevant details of the major style guides is essential for students. Many libraries publish overviews of the major style guides, and most bookstores will carry full guides for the major systems. Relevant information is readily available on the web as well.

Documentation of sources takes two main forms. The first form applies when citing sources in the text of the document or as footnotes or endnotes. In-text documentation is sometimes called parenthetical documentation and requires specific information within parentheses placed immediately after borrowed material. Footnotes or endnotes are placed either at the bottom of relevant pages or at the end of the document.

In addition to citing sources within the text, style guides also require a bibliography, a references section, or a works cited section at the end of the document. Sources for any borrowed material are to be listed according to the rules of the particular guide. In some cases, a "works consulted" listing may be required even though no material is directly cited or paraphrased to the extent that an in-text citation is required.

The major style guides include the *Modern Language Association Handbook (MLA)*, the *Manual of the American Psychological Association (APA)*, the *Chicago Manuel of Style, Turabian,* and *Scientific Style and Format: the CBE Manual.*

Documentation of sources from the Internet is particularly involved and continues to evolve at a rapid pace. It is important to consult the most recent online update for a particular style guide.

Learn more about MLA works cited documentation:

http://www.studyguide.org/ MLAdocumentation.htm

Tips for documentation

- Keep a record of all sources consulted during the research process.

- As you take notes, avoid unintentional plagiarism. Summarize and paraphrase in your own words without the source in front of you. If you use a direct quote, copy it exactly as written and enclose it in quotation marks.

- Cite anything that is not common knowledge. This includes direct quotes as well as ideas or statistics.

- Within the body of your document, follow this blueprint for standard attribution following MLA style:

    1. Begin the sentence with, "According to _____..."

    2. Proceed with the material being cited, followed by the page number in parentheses.

In-text citation example

According to Steve Mandel, "our average conversational rate of speech is about 125 words per minute" (78).

Once students have mastered this basic approach, they can learn more sophisticated methods, such as embedding information.

Each source used within the document should have a complete citation in a bibliography or works cited page.

Works cited entry

Mandel, Steve. Effective Presentation Skills. Menlo Park, California: Crisp Publications, 1993.

DOMAIN II
SOCIAL SCIENCE

Available for purchase at www.XAMonline.com:

eFlashcards: a digital representation of a card represented with words, numbers or symbols or any combination of each and briefly displayed as part of a learning drill. eFlashcards takes away the burden of carrying around traditional cards that could easily be disarranged, dropped, or soiled. Available at www. XAMonline.com/flashcards

More Sample Tests: more ways to assess how much you know and how much further you need to study. Ultimately, makes you more prepared and attain mastery in the skills and techniques of passing the test the FIRST TIME! Available at www. XAMonline.com/sampletests

PERSONALIZED STUDY PLAN

KNOWN MATERIAL/ SKIP IT

PAGE	COMPETENCY AND SKILL	
53	**5:** **Understand important theories, concepts, and terminology related to civics and government**	☐
	5.1: Recognize the purposes of government and the basic constitutional principles of the U.S. government	☐
	5.2: Identify the responsibilities and interrelationships among national, state, and local governments	☐
	5.3: Identify roles and powers of the executive, legislative, and judicial branches	☐
	5.4: Identify the roles, rights, responsibilities, and participatory obligations of U.S. citizens, resident aliens, immigrants, and refugees	☐
	5.5: Recognize different ways that governments are organized and hold power	☐
	5.6: Recognize ways in which the U.S. government relates to and interacts with other nations	☐
61	**6:** **Understand important theories, concepts, and terminology related to economics**	☐
	6.1: Recognize the economic concepts of scarcity and supply and demand, and the purposes and functions of currency	☐
	6.2: Recognize that trade-offs and opportunity costs can be measured in terms of costs and benefits	☐
	6.3: Identify the philosophies and characteristics of various economic systems	☐
	6.4: Identify the role of government and institutions in an economy	☐
	6.5: Identify the knowledge and skills necessary to make reasoned and responsible financial decisions	☐
68	**7:** **Understand important theories, concepts, and terminology related to geography**	☐
	7.1: Apply knowledge of spatial concepts of geography	☐
	7.2: Apply knowledge of the purpose of maps, globes, and geographic tools	☐
	7.3: Apply knowledge of physical and population characteristics of places and regions	☐
	7.4: Describe the distribution and movement of people, ideas, and products	☐
	7.5: Identify how humans affect physical environments, and how physical characteristics and changes in the environment affect human activities	☐

PERSONALIZED STUDY PLAN

KNOWN MATERIAL/ SKIP IT

PAGE	COMPETENCY AND SKILL	
74	**8: Understand important events, concepts, and terminology related to world history**	☐
	8.1: Recognize chronological relationships and patterns of change and continuity over time in world history	☐
	8.2: Demonstrate knowledge of early civilizations, including the development of empires and kingdoms	☐
	8.3: Recognize the importance and lasting influence of events, issues, and developments in world history	☐
	8.4: Recognize the importance and lasting influence of major world conflicts	☐
	8.5: Analyze cause-and-effect relationships in world history	☐
	8.6: Analyze various perspectives and interpretations of events, issues, and developments in world history	☐
92	**9: Understand important events, concepts, and terminology related to the history of the United States and the state of Oregon**	☐
	9.1: Recognize chronological relationships and patterns of change and continuity over time in U.S. and Oregon history	☐
	9.2: Recognize the importance and lasting influence of people, events, issues, and developments in Oregon history	☐
	9.3: Recognize the importance and lasting influence of events, issues, and developments in U.S. history	☐
	9.4: Analyze cause-and-effect relationships in the history of the United States and Oregon	☐
	9.5: Analyze various perspectives and interpretations of issues and events in U.S. and Oregon history	☐
	9.6: Demonstrate knowledge of strategies for interpreting events, issues, and developments in local history	☐
124	**10: Understand methods of social science research and analysis**	☐
	10.1: Recognize methods for analyzing an event, issue, problem, or phenomenon and its significance to society	☐
	10.2: Identify strategies for gathering, using, and evaluating information to support analysis and conclusions	☐
	10.3: Identify approaches for analyzing an event, issue, problem, or phenomenon from multiple perspectives	☐
	10.4: Recognize methods for analyzing characteristics, causes, and consequences of an event, issue, problem, or phenomenon	☐
	10.5: Recognize ways of comparing and evaluating outcomes, responses, or solutions	☐

COMPETENCY 5

UNDERSTAND IMPORTANT THEORIES, CONCEPTS, AND TERMINOLOGY RELATED TO CIVICS AND GOVERNMENT

SKILL 5.1 Recognize the purposes of government and the basic constitutional principles of the U.S. government as a republic

Government ultimately began as a form of protection. A strong person, usually one of the best warriors or someone who had the support of many strong men, assumed command of a people or a city or a land. The power to rule those people rested in this person's hands. Laws existed as the pronouncements and decision of the ruler and were not often written down, leading to inconsistency. Religious leaders had a strong hand in governing the lives of people, and in many instances the political leader was also the primary religious figure.

In Greece, Rome, and then in other places throughout the world, the idea of government by more than one person or a handful of people developed. Even though more people were involved, the purpose of government hadn't changed. These governments still existed to keep the peace and protect their people from encroachments by both inside and outside forces.

From the Middle Ages to the twentieth century, many countries have had monarchs as their heads of state. These monarchs make and uphold laws, but the laws are designed to protect the welfare of the people and the state.

Today, people are subject to laws made by many levels of government.

SKILL 5.2 Identify the responsibilities and interrelationships among national, state, and local governments in the United States

Powers Delegated to the Federal Government

1. To tax

2. To borrow and coin money

3. To establish a postal service

4. To grant patents and copyrights

5. To regulate interstate and foreign commerce

6. To establish courts

7. To declare war

8. To raise and support the armed forces

9. To govern territories

10. To define and punish felonies and piracy on the high seas

11. To fix standards of weights and measures

12. To conduct foreign affairs

Powers Reserved to the States

1. To regulate intrastate trade

2. To establish local governments

3. To protect general welfare

4. To protect life and property

5. To ratify amendments

6. To conduct elections

7. To make state and local laws

Concurrent Powers of the Federal Government and States

1. Both federal and state governments may tax

2. Both may borrow money

3. Both may charter banks and corporations

4. Both may establish courts

5. Both may make and enforce laws

6. Both may take property for public purposes

7. Both may spend money to provide for the public welfare

Implied Powers of the Federal Government

1. To establish banks or other corporations implied from delegated powers to tax, borrow, and to regulate commerce.

2. To spend money for roads, schools, health, insurance, etc. implied from powers, to establish post roads, to tax to provide for general welfare and defense, and to regulate commerce.

3. To create military academies, implied from powers to raise and support an armed force.

4. To locate and generate sources of power and sell surplus implied from powers to dispose of government property, commerce, and war powers.

5. To assist and regulate agriculture implied from power to tax and spend for general welfare and regulate commerce.

SKILL 5.3 **Identify roles and powers of the executive, legislative, and judicial branches**

Legislative

Article I of the Constitution established the legislative, or law-making, branch of the government called the Congress. It is made up of two houses, the House of Representatives and the Senate. Voters in all states elect the members who serve in each respective House of Congress. The Legislative branch is responsible for making laws, raising and printing money, regulating trade, establishing the postal service and federal courts, approving the President's appointments, declaring war, and supporting the armed forces. The Congress also has the power to change the Constitution itself, and to impeach (bring charges against) the President. Charges for impeachment are brought by the House of Representatives, and are then tried in the Senate.

Article I of the Constitution established the legislative, or law-making, branch of the government called the Congress

Executive

Article II of the Constitution created the Executive branch of the government, headed by the President, who leads the country, recommends new laws, and can veto bills passed by the Legislative branch. As the chief of state, the President is responsible for carrying out the laws of the country and the treaties and declarations of war passed by the Legislative branch. The President also appoints federal judges and is commander-in-chief of the military when it is called into service. Other members of the Executive branch include the Vice-President, also elected,

Article II of the Constitution created the Executive branch of the government, headed by the President, who leads the country, recommends new laws, and can veto bills passed by the Legislative branch

and various cabinet members the president appoints, such as ambassadors, presidential advisors, members of the armed forces, and other appointed and civil servants of government agencies, departments and bureaus. Though the President appoints them, they must be approved by the Legislative branch.

Judicial

Article III of the Constitution established the Judicial branch of government headed by the Supreme Court. The Supreme Court has the power to rule that a law passed by the legislature, or an act of the Executive branch, is illegal and unconstitutional. Citizens, businesses, and government officials can ask the Supreme Court to review a decision made in a lower court if they believe that the ruling by a judge is unconstitutional. The Judicial branch also includes lower federal courts, known as federal district courts, that have been established by the Congress. These courts try lawbreakers and review cases referred from other courts.

> Article III of the Constitution established the Judicial branch of government headed by the Supreme Court

---

SKILL 5.4 Identify the roles, rights, responsibilities, and participatory obligations of U.S. citizens, resident aliens, immigrants, and refugees

---

Citizenship in a democracy bestows on an individual certain rights, foremost being the right to participate in one's own government. Along with these rights come responsibilities, including the responsibility of a citizen to participate. The most basic form of participation is the vote. Those who have reached the age of 18 in the United States are eligible to vote in public elections. With this right comes the responsibility to be informed before voting, and not to sell or otherwise give away one's vote. Citizens are also eligible to run for public office. Along with the right to run for office comes the responsibility to represent the electors as fairly as possible and to perform the duties expected of a government representative.

In the United States, citizens are guaranteed the right to free speech; that is, the right to express an opinion on public issues. In turn, citizens have the responsibility to allow others to speak freely. At the community level, this might mean speaking at a city council hearing while allowing others with different or opposing viewpoints to have their say without interruption or comment.

The U.S. Constitution also guarantees freedom of religion. This means that the government may not impose an official religion on its citizens, and that people are free to practice their religion. Citizens are also responsible for allowing those of other religions to practice freely without obstruction. Occasionally, religious issues will be put before the public at the state level in the form of ballot measures or initiatives.

The U.S. Constitution also guarantees that all citizens be treated equally by the law. In addition, federal and state laws make it a crime to discriminate against citizens based on their sex, race, religion, and other factors. To ensure that all people are treated equally, citizens have the responsibility to follow these laws.

Resident aliens are people from foreign countries who have been granted permission to live and sometimes to work in the United States. Their roles and responsibilities are much the same as U.S. citizens, and they enjoy some of the same rights. Resident aliens do not automatically have the right to vote. Some states and cities have extended voting rights on certain matters to resident aliens, giving them the same obligations to participate in and be informed of local government as citizens have.

IMMIGRANTS AND REFUGEES are people who have come to the United States to live permanently for various reasons. In the case of refugees, they may have been persecuted or threatened in their home country. Refugees from certain countries are granted some protection by the U.S., but must apply for and be granted status as a refugee to remain in the U.S. Other immigrants are obligated to receive permission from the U.S. government to live permanently and to work in the U.S. Refugees and other immigrants may be eligible to become citizens of the U.S. through various procedures, including a test. Once they are citizens, they are entitled to nearly all the rights of a native citizen. Some rights are reserved for native citizens only, however, such as eligibility to serve as President of the United States.

> **IMMIGRANTS AND REFUGEES:** people who have come to the United States to live permanently for various reasons

---

> **SKILL 5.5** Recognize different ways that governments are organized and hold power, and ways in which individuals, groups, and international organizations influence government

- Anarchism: A political movement believing in the elimination of all government and its replacement by a cooperative community of individuals. Sometimes it has involved political violence such as assassinations of important political or governmental figures. The historical banner of the movement is a black flag.

- Communism: A belief as well as a political system, characterized by the ideology of class conflict and revolution, a one-party state, government control of the media, and government ownership of the means of production and distribution of goods and services. Communism is a revolutionary ideology preaching the eventual overthrow of all other political orders and the establishment of one world Communist government. The historical banner of the movement is a red flag and variation of stars and hammer and sickles, representing the various types of workers.

- Dictatorship: The rule by an individual or small group of individuals (oligarchy) that centralizes all political control in itself and enforces its will through the military or a police force.

- Fascism: A belief as well as a political system, opposed ideologically to Communism though similar in basic structure, with a one party state, centralized political control and a repressive police system. However, it tolerates private ownership of the means of production, though it maintains tight overall control. Central to its belief is the idolization of the Leader, a "Cult of Personality," and most often an expansionist ideology. Examples are German Nazism and Italian Fascism.

- Monarchy: The rule of a nation by a monarch, a non-elected leader usually determined by heredity, most often a king or queen. It may or may not be accompanied by some measure of democratic open institutions and elections at various levels. A modern example is Great Britain, which is called a Constitutional Monarchy.

- Parliamentary System: A system of government with a legislature, usually involving a multiplicity of political parties and often coalition politics. There is division between the head of state and the head of government. The head of government is usually known as a Prime Minister, who is also usually the head of the largest party. The head of government and cabinet usually both sit and vote in the parliament. The head of state is most often an elected president (though in the case of a constitutional monarchy, like Great Britain, the sovereign may take the place of a president as head of state). A government may fall when a majority in parliament votes "no confidence" in the government.

- Presidential System: A system of government with a legislature, it can involve few or many political parties, and has no division between head of state and head of government. The President serves in both capacities. The President is elected either by direct or indirect election. A President and cabinet usually do not sit or vote in the legislature, and the President may or may not be the head of the largest political party. A President can thus rule even without a majority in the legislature. He can only be removed from office before an election for major infractions of the law.

- Socialism: A political belief and system in which the state takes a guiding role in the national economy and provides extensive social services to its population. It may or may not own the means of production, but even where it does not, it exercises tight control. It usually promotes democracy, (Democratic-Socialism), though with heavy state involvement. Taken to an extreme, it may lead to Communism if government control increases and democratic practice decreases.

SKILL 5.6	Recognize ways in which the U.S. government relates to and interacts with other nations

The national or federal government of the United States derives its power from the U.S. Constitution and has three branches: the legislative, executive and judicial. The federal government exists to make national policy and to legislate matters that affect the residents of all states, and to settle matters between states. National income tax is the primary source of federal funding.

The U.S. Constitution also provides the federal government with the authority to make treaties and enter agreements with foreign countries, creating a body of international law. While there is no authoritative international government, organizations such as the United Nations, the European Union, and other smaller groups exist to promote economic and political cooperation between nations.

The elements of the U.S. Government that pursue and conduct foreign policy are large and varied. Some are in the Legislative Branch; others are in the Executive Branch.

The most well-known foreign policy advocate is the SECRETARY OF STATE, who is part of the Executive Branch and is appointed by the President and confirmed by Congress. The Secretary of State is the country's primary ambassador to other countries, having prime responsibilities in this regard for attending international meetings, brokering peace deals, and negotiating treaties. The Secretary of State often acts as the "voice of the country," speaking for the interests of the United States to the rest of the world. Since the Secretary of State is appointed by the President, he or she is expected to follow the policy directives of the President. It is usually the case that the two people are of the same political party and share political views on important issues. The result of this is that, in some cases, the views and actions of the Secretary of State are in line with many, but not all, U.S. citizens. Such is the nature of politics.

SECRETARY OF STATE: The most well-known foreign policy advocate; the Secretary is part of the Executive Branch and is appointed by the President and confirmed by congress

The Executive Branch also has a NATIONAL SECURITY COUNCIL, which advises the President on matters of foreign policy. Members of this group are not nearly as visible or well-traveled as the Secretary of State, but they do provide the President and other members of the government with valuable information about activity elsewhere in the world.

NATIONAL SECURITY COUNCIL: advises the President on matters of foreign policy

The most numerous of the Executive Branch members involved in foreign policy are the AMBASSADORS. Most countries throughout the world have ambassadors, people who reside in other countries in order to be lobbyists for their home countries' interests. The United States has ambassadors to most countries in the world; by the same token, most countries in the world have embassies, buildings

AMBASSADORS: people who reside in other countries in order to be lobbyists for their home countries' interests and organizations that contain offices for these ambassadors. These ambassadors attend official functions in their "adopted" countries and speak for their countries in international meetings.

The Legislative Branch plays an important role in U.S. foreign policy as well. The Senate in particular is responsible for approving treaties and ambassadorial appointments. Both houses of Congress have committees of lawmakers who specialize in foreign policy. These lawmakers keep abreast of happenings elsewhere in the world and advise their fellow lawmakers on foreign businesses, issues, and conflicts. These foreign policy-focused lawmakers often tour other countries and attend state functions, but they don't have the voice or responsibility of ambassadors.

Increasingly, state and local governments practice foreign policy as well.

Increasingly, state and local governments practice foreign policy as well. Governors and lawmakers of many states have trade agreements with other countries; these agreements are not on the order of national agreements, but they do deal with foreign relations, mainly with economics. Local governments, too, get involved with things overseas. A good example of this is the growing practice of implementing a "sister city," whereby a city in the U.S. "adopts" a city in another country and exchanges ideas, goods, services, and technology and other resources with its new "companion."

Since the United States is based on the principles of freedoms, it is active in trying to compel other nations to respect the rights of their own citizens. This concern for democratic principles and human rights has involved the United States in World War II and other international conflicts. Troops were sent to Serbia to halt the genocide that was taking place and to restore a democratic government. The U.S. and other nations were instrumental in bringing Serbian leaders to trial for war crimes. The United States has also been involved in conflicts in Vietnam, Korea, and, most recently, Iraq and Afghanistan.

Some of this is accomplished through the United Nations; some of this is accomplished outside of the United Nations.

Many different ethnic cultures are thriving in the U.S.

The United States is said to be a melting pot. Its population consists of immigrants and descendants of immigrants. The U.S. respects the different ethnicities and cultures of other people and those that choose to settle in the U.S. America is affected by the politics of other nations, just as every nation is. Our politics reflect our beliefs in freedom.

COMPETENCY 6

UNDERSTAND IMPORTANT THEORIES, CONCEPTS, AND TERMINOLOGY RELATED TO ECONOMICS

SKILL 6.1 Recognize the economic concepts of scarcity and supply and demand, and the purposes and functions of currency in the economy

Consumer economics refers to how consumers make their decisions and the role that consumer decision-making plays in a capitalist economy. Consumers buy the goods and services that give them satisfaction, or utility. They want to obtain the most utility they can for their dollar. The quantity of goods and services that consumers are willing and able to purchase at different prices during a given period of time is referred to as DEMAND. Aggregating all of the individual demands yields the market demand for a good or service.

> **DEMAND:** the quantity of goods and services that consumers are willing and able to purchase at different prices during a given period of time

Since consumers buy the goods and services that give them satisfaction, this means that, for the most part, they don't buy the goods and services that don't give them satisfaction. Consumers are, in effect, voting for the goods and services that they want with their dollars. This is called dollar voting. Consumers are basically signaling to firms how they want society's scarce resources used with their dollar votes. A good that society wants acquires enough dollar votes for the producer to experience profits—a situation where the firm's revenues exceed the firm's costs. The existence of profits indicates to the firm that it is producing the goods and services that consumers want and that society's scarce resources are being used in accordance with consumer preferences. When a firm does not have a profitable product, it is because that product is not tabulating enough dollar votes from consumers.

This process where consumers vote with their dollars is called consumer sovereignty. Consumers are basically directing the allocation of scarce resources in the economy with their dollar spending. Firms, who are in business to earn profit, then hire resources, or inputs, in accordance with consumer preferences. This is the way in which resources are allocated in a market economy. This is the manner in which society achieves the output mix that it desires.

Price plays an important role in a market economy. Supply is based on production costs. The supply of a good or service is defined as the quantities of a good or service that a producer is willing and able to sell at different prices during a given period of time. Market equilibrium occurs where the buying decisions of buyers are equal to the selling decision of seller, or where the demand and supply curves intersect. At this point, the quantity that sellers want to sell at a price is equal to the quantity the buyers want to buy at that same price. This is the market equilibrium price.

Money functions as a medium of exchange, a unit of account, and a store of value. Unit of account means it is a way of measuring the value of a good or service. A medium of exchange means it is used in exchange for goods and services. And store of value means it is a way of holding or storing wealth.

> Market equilibrium occurs where the buying decisions of buyers are equal to the selling decisions of sellers, or where the demand and supply curves intersect.

Money facilitates exchange. Instead of bartering, exchanging one good or service for another, money makes it easier for trade and commerce to take place. Money functions as a medium of exchange and is accepted in exchange for all goods or services on an international basis.

SKILL 6.2 Recognize that trade-offs and opportunity costs are decisions that can be measured in terms of costs and benefits

> ECONOMICS: a study of how scarce resources are allocated to satisfy unlimited wants

The scarcity of resources is the basis for the existence of economics. ECONOMICS is defined as a study of how scarce resources are allocated to satisfy unlimited wants. Resources refer to the four factors of production: labor, capital, land and entrepreneurs. Labor refers to anyone who sells the ability to produce goods and services. Capital is anything that is manufactured to be used in the production process. Land refers to the land itself and everything occurring naturally on it, like oil, minerals lumber, etc. Entrepreneurship is the ability of an individual to combine the three inputs with his own talents to produce a viable good or service. The entrepreneur takes the risk and experiences the losses or profits.

The fact that the supply of these resources is finite means that society cannot have as much of everything that it wants. There is a constraint on production and consumption and on the kinds of goods and services that can be produced and consumed. Scarcity means that choices have to be made. If society decides to produce more of one good, this means that there are fewer resources available for the production of other goods. Assume a society can produce two goods, good X and good Y. The society uses resources in the production of each good. If producing one unit of good X results in an amount of resources used to produce three units of good Y, then producing one more unit of good X results in a decrease in 3 units of good Y. In effect, one unit of good X "costs" three units of good Y. This cost is referred to as opportunity cost. Opportunity cost, or tradeoffs, is the value of the sacrificed alternative, the value of what had to be given up in order to have the output of good X. Opportunity cost does not just refer to production. Your opportunity cost of studying with this guide is the value of what you are not doing because you are studying, whether it is watching TV, spending time with family, or working. Every choice has an opportunity cost.

If wants were limited and/or if resources were unlimited, then the concepts of choice and opportunity cost would not exist, and neither would the field of economics. There would be enough resources to satisfy the wants of consumers, businesses and governments. The allocation of resources wouldn't be a problem. Society could have more of both good X and good Y without having to give up anything. There would be no opportunity cost. But this isn't the situation that societies are faced with.

Because resources are scarce, society doesn't want to waste them. Society wants to obtain the most satisfaction it can from the consumption of the goods and services produced with its scarce resources. The members of the society don't want their scarce resources wasted through inefficiency. This means that producers must choose an efficient production process, which is the lowest cost means of production. High costs mean wasted resources. Consumers also don't want society's resources wasted by producing goods that they don't want.

How do producers know what goods consumers want? Consumers buy the goods they want and vote with their dollar spending. A desirable good, one that consumers want, earns profits. A good that incurs losses is a good that society doesn't want its resources wasted on. This shows the producer that society wants their resources used in another way.

SKILL 6.3 Identify the underlying philosophies and characteristics of various economic systems, including that of the U.S. economy

A **TRADITIONAL ECONOMY** is one based on custom that usually exists in less developed countries. The people do things the way their ancestors did and technology and equipment are viewed as a threat to the old way of doing things and to their tradition.

The model of capitalism is based on private ownership of the means of production and operates on the basis of free markets, on both the input and output side. The free markets function to coordinate market activity and to achieve an efficient allocation of resources. **LAISSEZ-FAIRE CAPITALISM** is based on the premise of no

TRADITIONAL ECON-OMY: one based on custom that usually exists in less developed countries

LAISSEZ-FAIRE CAPITALISM: no government intervention in the economy

government intervention in the economy. According to this idea, the market will eliminate any unemployment or inflation that occurs. Government needs only to provide the framework for the functioning of the economy and to protect private property.

A COMMAND ECONOMY is almost the opposite of a market economy. A command economy is based on government ownership of the means of production and the use of planning to take the place of the market. Instead of the market determining the output mix and the allocation of resources, the bureaucracy fulfills this role by determining the output mix and establishing production targets for the enterprises, which are publicly owned.

A MIXED ECONOMY uses a combination of markets and planning, with the degree of each varying according to country. Most countries today have mixed economies.

Economic systems refer to the arrangements a society has devised to answer what are known as the Three Questions: What goods to produce, how to produce the goods, and for whom the goods are being produced (or how is the allocation of the output determined). Different economic systems answer these questions in different ways.

A market economy answers these questions in terms of supply and demand and the use of markets. Consumers vote for the products they want with their dollar spending. Goods acquiring enough dollar votes are profitable, signaling to the producers that society wants their scarce resources used in this way. This is how the "What" question is answered. The producer then hires inputs in accordance with the goods consumers want, looking for the most efficient or lowest cost method of production. The lower the firm's costs for any given level of revenue, the higher the firm's profits. This is the way in which the "How" question is answered in a market economy.

The "For Whom" question is answered in the marketplace by the determination of the equilibrium price. Price serves to ration the good to those that can and will transact at the market price or better. Those who can't or won't are excluded from the market. The United States has a market economy.

The opposite of the market economy is called the centrally planned economy. This used to be called Communism, even though the term in not correct in a strict Marxian sense. In a planned economy, the means of production are publicly owned with little, if any, public ownership. Instead of the Three Questions being solved by markets, a planning authority makes the decisions. The planning authority decides what will be produced and how. Since some planned economies direct resources into the production of capital and military goods, there can be

COMMAND ECONOMY: based on government ownership of the means of production and the use of planning to take the place of the market

MIXED ECONOMY: uses a combination of markets and planning, with the degree of each varying according to country

little remaining for consumer goods and the result may be chronic shortages. Price functions as an accounting measure and does not reflect scarcity. The former Soviet Union and most of the Eastern Bloc countries were planned economies of this sort.

In between the two extremes is market socialism. This is a mixed economic system that uses both markets and planning. Planning is usually used to direct resources at the upper levels of the economy, with markets being used to determine prices of consumer goods and wages. This kind of economic system answers the three questions with planning and markets. The country of Vietnam has a market socialist system.

SKILL 6.4 Identify the role of government and institutions in an economy, and ways in which the U.S. economy relates to and interacts with the economies of other nations

Government policies, whether they are federal, state or local, affect economic decision-making and, in many cases, the distribution of resources. This is the purpose of most economic policies imposed at the federal level. Governments don't implement monetary and fiscal policy at the state or local level, only at the national level. Most state and local laws that affect economic decision-making and the distribution of resources have to do with taxation. If taxes are imposed or raised at the state or local level, the effect is less consumer spending. The purpose of these taxes is to raise revenues for the state and local government, not to affect the level of aggregate demand and inflation. At the federal level, the major purpose of these policies is to affect the level of aggregate demand and the inflation rate or the unemployment rate.

Government at all three levels affects the distribution of resources and economic decision-making through transfer payments. This is an attempt to bring about a redistribution of income and to correct the problem of income inequality. Programs like Food Stamps, AFDC (welfare), unemployment compensation, and Medicaid all fall into this category. Technically, these government transfer programs result in a rearrangement of private consumption, not a real reallocation of resources. Price support programs in agriculture also result in a redistribution of income. The imposition of artificially high prices results in too many resources going into agriculture and leads to product surpluses.

Government at all three levels affects the distribution of resources and economic decision-making through transfer payments.

Laws can be enacted at all three levels to correct for the problem of externalities. An externality occurs when uninvolved third parties are affected by some market activity, like pollution. Dumping poisonous wastes into the air and water means that the air and water are being treated as a free input by the firm. The market does not register all of the costs of production because the firm does not have to pay to use the air or water. The result of the free inputs is lower production costs for the firm and an overallocation of resources into the production of the good the firm is producing. The role for government here is to redistribute resources by shifting all or part of the cost of environmental cleanup on to the offending firm. They can impose fines, taxes, require pollution abatement equipment, sell pollution permits, etc. Whatever method they choose, this raises the costs of production for the offending firms and forces them to bear some of the cost.

Policies can be enacted in order to encourage labor to migrate from one sector of the economy to another. This is primarily done at the national level. The United States economy is so large that it is possible to have unemployment in different areas while the economy is at full employment. State unemployment and labor agencies provide the information for these people.

> **GLOBALIZATION:** the complex of social, political, technological, and economic changes that result from increasing contact, communication, interaction, integration and interdependence of peoples of disparate parts of the world

GLOBALIZATION refers to the complex of social, political, technological, and economic changes that result from increasing contact, communication, interaction, integration and interdependence of peoples of disparate parts of the world. The term is generally used to refer to the process of change or the cause of turbulent change. Globalization may be understood in terms of positive social and economic change, as in the case of a broadening of trade resulting in an increase in the standard of living for developing countries. Globalization may also be understood negatively in terms of the abusive treatment of workers in developing countries in the interest of cultural or economic imperialism. These negative effects can include cultural assimilation, plunder and profiteering, the destruction of the local culture and economy, and ecological indifference.

Globalization also involves exchange of money, commodities, information, ideas, and people. Much of this has been facilitated by the great advances in technology in the last 150 years. The effects of globalization can be seen across all areas of social and cultural interaction. Economically, globalization brings about broader and faster trade and flow of capital, increased outsourcing of labor, the development of global financial systems (such as the introduction of the Euro), the creation of trade agreements, and the birth of international organizations to moderate the agreements. In theory, globalization is creating a new international society. Globalization is occurring at a rapid pace. It is changing the composition of individual societies as it is creating a new international society.

SKILL Identify the knowledge and skills necessary to make reasoned and
6.5 responsible financial decisions as a consumer, producer, saver, and investor in a market economy

Economics is the study of how a society allocates its scarce resources to satisfy what are basically unlimited and competing wants. Economics can also be defined as a study of the production, consumption and distribution of goods and services. Both of these definitions are the same. A fundamental fact of economics is that resources are scarce and that wants are infinite. The fact that scarce resources have to satisfy unlimited wants means that choices have to be made, whether the entity is a consumer, producer, saver or investor. If society uses its resources to produce good A then it doesn't have those resources to produce good B. More of good A means less of good B. This trade-off is referred to as the opportunity cost, or the value of the sacrificed alternative.

A fundamental fact of economics is that resources are scarce and that wants are infinite.

The price of an input or output allocates that input or output to those who are willing and able to transact at the market price. Those who can transact at the market price or better are included in the market; those that can't or won't transact at the market price are excluded from the market.

The fundamental characteristics of the U.S. economic system are the uses of competition and markets. Profit and competition go together in the U.S. economic system. Competition is determined by market structure. Since the cost curves are the same for all the firms, the only difference comes from the revenue side. Each firm maximizes profit by producing at the point where marginal cost equals marginal revenue. The existence of economic profits, an above–normal rate of return, attracts capital to an industry and results in expansion. Whether or not new firms can enter depends on barriers to entry. Firms can enter easily in perfect competition and the expansion will continue until economic profits are eliminated and firms earn a normal rate of return. The significant barriers to entry in monopoly serve to keep firms out so the monopolist continues to earn an above–normal rate of return. Some firms will be able to enter in monopolistic competition but won't have a monopoly over the existing firm's brand name.

The competitiveness of the market structure determines whether new firms or capital can enter in response to profits.

Profit functions as a financial incentive for individuals and firms. The possibility of earning profit is why individuals are willing to undertake entrepreneurial ventures and why firms are willing to spend money on research and development and innovation. Without these kinds of financial incentives, there wouldn't be new product development or technological advancement.

Savings represents delayed consumption. Savers must be paid a price for delaying consumption. This price is called the interest rate. Savers will save more money at higher interest rates than at lower interest rates. The interest rate is the price of borrowing to the investor. Investors will borrow more funds at lower interest rates than at higher interest rates. The equilibrium rate of interest is the rate at which the amount savers want to save is equal to the amount borrowers want to borrow for investment purposes.

Also refer to Skill 6.1 for further discussion of the consumer.

The equilibrium rate of interest is the rate at which the amount savers want to save is equal to the amount borrowers want to borrow for investment purposes.

COMPETENCY 7
UNDERSTAND IMPORTANT THEORIES, CONCEPTS, AND TERMINOLOGY RELATED TO GEOGRAPHY

SKILL 7.1 Apply knowledge of spatial concepts of geography *(e.g., location, distance, direction, scale, region)*

In the context of geography, spatial organization refers to how objects are arranged on Earth's surface. At its most simplistic level, humans' spatial organization is where they live, whether in villages, towns or cities. Four geometric concepts (points, lines, areas and volume) are frequently used to describe spatial organization. Spatial organization can also be described in terms of location, distance, direction and arrangement.

For instance, every point on Earth has a specific location defined by its geographic coordinates, latitude and longitude. Thinking of Earth as a sphere spinning on an axis, latitude is the measurement from the Equator, the starting point, to a distance north or south, with the North and South Poles being the farthest ends of the axis. Longitude lines, also referred to as meridians, are perpendicular to latitude lines and pass through both poles. According to The National Atlas of the United States (a trademark of the United States Department of the Interior), unlike latitude, there is no 0-degree of longitude; however, current international agreement notes Greenwich, England as 0 degrees longitude. This point is known as the Prime Meridian and measures coordinates running east or west. Geographers as well as many other professionals such as pilots and boat captains use latitude and longitude to determine absolute locations on Earth's surface.

Understanding the exact location is only a portion of spatial organization; it is also important to understand how a given place relates to other places on Earth.

Where absolute location involves latitude and longitude measurements, relative location focuses on points of interest, time, direction or distance between or among multiple points. For example, New York's relative location could be described as north of Florida. Relative location establishes a relationship or connection between two places.

Another way geographers identify places on Earth is by physical, human or cultural characteristics. Physical characteristics are naturally occurring features such as the terrain and animal life, whereas human characteristics are man-made and include architecture, land use and ownership, as well as communication and transportation systems. Cultural characteristics such as languages, religions, economies and political philosophies also distinguish places. Integrating physical, human and cultural characteristics into geography lessons can help students distinguish various places on Earth and understand each location's unique traits.

A REGION is one of the major themes and basic organizational units in geography. It is defined as an area of Earth's surface unified by physical, human or cultural characteristics. Geographers can map and analyze a region to determine how it changes over time. Regions can be divided into various units for manageable study plans. For example, the United States is often referred to in terms of cultural regions (New England, the South) influenced by history, geography and economics, instead of governmental regions or specific states. Regions enable geographers to organize the world into manageable study units, achieving an understanding of the identity and characteristics of a specific area.

> **REGION:** an area of Earth's surface unified by physical, human or cultural characteristics

---

SKILL 7.2 Apply knowledge of the purpose of maps, globes, and geographic tools, and locating major physical and human-constructed features of the earth

We use illustrations of various sorts because it is often easier to demonstrate a given idea visually instead of orally. Sometimes it is even easier to do so with an illustration than a description. This is especially true in the areas of education and research, because humans are visual learners. It is a fact that any idea presented visually in some manner is always easier to understand and to comprehend than one that is only written or spoken. Among the more common illustrations used are various types of maps, graphs and charts.

Photographs and globes are useful as well, but because they are limited in what kind of information that they can show, they are rarely used. Although maps have advantages over globes and photographs, they do have a major disadvantage that

DISTORTION: it is impossible to reproduce exactly on a flat surface an object shaped like a sphere; in order to put the Earth's features onto a map they must be stretched in some way

CARTOGRAPHERS: mapmakers

PROJECTION: the process of putting the features of the Earth onto a flat surface

must be considered. The major problem with maps is that they are flat and the Earth is a sphere. It is impossible to reproduce exactly on a flat surface an object shaped like a sphere. In order to put the earth's features onto a map they must be stretched in some way. This stretching is called DISTORTION.

Distortion does not mean that maps are wrong; it simply means that they are not perfect representations of the Earth or its parts. CARTOGRAPHERS, or mapmakers, understand the problems of distortion. They try to design them so that there is as little distortion as possible. The process of putting the features of the Earth onto a flat surface is called PROJECTION. All maps are really map projections. There are many different types. Each one deals in a different way with the problem of distortion.

To properly analyze a given map, one must be familiar with the various parts and symbols that most modern maps use. For the most part, this is standardized, with different maps using similar parts and symbols. These can include:

- The Legend: Most maps have a legend. A legend tells the reader about the various symbols that are used on that particular map and what the symbols represent (also called a map key).

- The Grid: A grid is a series of lines that are used to find exact places and locations on the map. There are several different kinds of grid systems in use; however, most maps use the longitude and latitude system, known as the Geographic Grid System.

- Directions: Most maps have some directional system to show which way the map is being presented. Often, a small compass will be present, with arrows showing the four basic directions: north, south, east, and west.

- The Scale: This is used to show the relationship between a unit of measurement on the map versus the real measure on the Earth. Maps are drawn to many different scales. Some maps show a lot of detail for a small area. Others show a greater span of distance. One must always be aware of what scale is being used. For instance, the scale might be something like 1 inch = 10 miles for a small area, but a map showing the whole world might have a scale in which 1 inch = 1,000 miles. The point is that one must look at the map key in order to see what units of measurement the map is using.

Maps have four main properties:

1. The size of the areas shown on the map

2. The shapes of the areas

3. Consistent scales

4. Straight line directions

A map can be drawn so that it is correct in one or more of these properties. No map can be correct in all of them.

Maps showing physical features often try to show information about the elevation, or relief, of the land. ELEVATION is the distance above or below the sea level. The elevation is usually shown with colors; for instance, all areas on a map which are at a certain elevation will be shown in the same color.

ELEVATION: also called the relief, is the distance above or below sea level

---

SKILL 7.3 **Apply knowledge of physical and population characteristics of places and regions, the processes that have shaped them, and their geographic significance**

See also Skill 7.4

DEMOGRAPHY is the branch of science of statistics most concerned with the composition of social groups. Demographic tables may include:

DEMOGRAPHY: the branch of science of statistics most concerned with the composition of social groups

1. Analysis of the population on the basis of age, parentage, physical condition, race, occupation and civil position, giving the actual size and the density of each separate area

2. Changes in the population as a result of birth, marriage, and death

3. Statistics on population movements and their effects and relations to given economic, social and political conditions

4. Statistics of crime, illegitimacy and suicide

5. Levels of education and economic and social statistics

Another area of science known as vital statistics is indispensable in studying social trends and making important legislative, economic, and social decisions. Such demographic information is gathered from census and registrar reports. By state laws, such information, especially the vital kind, is kept by physicians, attorneys, funeral directors, member of the clergy, and similar professional people. In the United States such demographic information is compiled, kept and published by the Public Health Service of the United States Department of Health, Education, and Welfare.

The most important element of this information is the so-called rate, which customarily represents the average of births and deaths for a unit of 1000 population over a given calendar year. These general rates are called crude rates, which are then sub-divided into *sex, color, age, occupation, locality, etc*. They are then known as refined rates.

In examining statistics and the sources of statistical data, one must be aware of the methods of statistical information gathering. For instance, there are many good sources of raw statistical data. Books such as *The Statistical Abstract of the United States,* published by the United States Chamber of Commerce, *The World Fact Book,* published by the Central Intelligence Agency, or *The Monthly Labor Review* published by the United States Department of Labor are excellent examples that contain much raw data. Many such yearbooks and the like on various topics are readily available from any library, or from the government itself.

SKILL 7.4 **Describe the distribution and movement of people, ideas, and products, and evaluating the consequences of population changes resulting from economic, political, cultural, and/or environmental factors** *(e.g., globalization)*

POPULATION: a group of people living within a certain geographic area

A **POPULATION** is a group of people living within a certain geographic area. Populations are usually measured on a regular basis by census, which also measures age, economic, ethnic and other data. Populations change over time due to many factors, and these changes can have significant impact on cultures.

When a population grows in size, it becomes necessary for it to either expand its geographic boundaries to make room for new people or to increase its density. Population density is the number of people in a population divided by the geographic area in which they live. Cultures with a high population density are likely to have different ways of interacting with one another than those with low density, because people live in closer to proximity to one another.

As a population grows, its economic needs change. More basic needs are required and more workers are needed to produce them. If a population's production or purchasing power does not keep pace with its growth, its economy can be adversely affected. The age distribution of a population can impact the economy as well, if the number of young and old people who are not working is disproportionate to those who are.

Growth in some areas may spur migration to other parts of a population's geographic region that are less densely populated. This redistribution of population also places demands on the economy, because infrastructure is needed to connect these new areas to older population centers, and land is put to new use.

Populations can grow naturally, when the rate of birth is higher than the rate of death, or by adding new people from other populations through immigration. Immigration is often a source of societal change when people from other cultures bring their institutions and language to a new area. Immigration also impacts a population's educational and economic institutions when immigrants enter the workforce and place their children in schools.

Populations can also decline in number, when the death rate exceeds the birth rate or when people migrate to another area. War, famine, disease and natural disasters can also dramatically reduce a population. The economic problems from population decline can be similar to those from overpopulation because economic demands may be higher than can be met. In extreme cases, a population may decline to the point where it can no longer perpetuate itself and its members and their culture either disappear or are absorbed into another population.

Also refer to Skill 6.4 for globalization.

> **SKILL 7.5** **Identify how humans affect physical environments, and how physical characteristics and changes in the environment affect human activities**

How Environments Affect Humans

One example of how the physical characteristics of an environment can affect humans is in urban growth and development. The growth of urban areas is often linked to the advantages provided by geographic location. Before the advent of efficient overland routes of commerce, such as railroads and highways, water provided the primary means for the transportation of commercial goods. Most large cities are thus situated along bodies of water.

As transportation technology advanced, supporting infrastructure was built to connect cities with one another and to connect remote areas to larger communities. The railroad, for example, allowed for the quick transport of agricultural products from rural areas to urban centers. This newfound efficiency not only further fueled the growth of urban centers, but it also changed the economy of rural America. Where once farmers had practiced only subsistence farming—growing enough to support one's own family—the new infrastructure meant that one could convert agricultural products into cash by selling them at market.

For urban dwellers, improvements in building technology and advances in transportation allowed for larger cities. Growth brought with it new problems unique to each location. The bodies of water that had made the development of cities possible also formed natural barriers to growth. Further infrastructure in the form of bridges, tunnels, and ferry routes were needed to connect central urban areas to outlying communities.

By nature, people are social creatures. They generally live in communities or settlements of some kind and of some size. Settlements are the cradles of culture, political structure, education, and the management of resources. The relative placement of these settlements or communities is shaped by proximity to natural resources.

How Humans Affect Environments

Because humans, both individually and in community, rely upon the environment to sustain human life, they draw heavily upon the natural resources of the Earth and affect the environment in many ways.

Natural resources are often classified into renewable and nonrenewable resources. Renewable resources are generally living resources (fish, coffee, forests, etc.), which can restock (renew) themselves if they are not overharvested. Renewable resources can restock themselves and be used indefinitely if they are sustained. Once renewable resources are consumed at a rate that exceeds their natural rate of replacement, the standing stock will diminish and eventually run out.

In an age of global warming, unprecedented demand on natural resources, and a shrinking planet due to a growing population, social and environmental policies must become increasingly interdependent if the planet is to continue to support life and human civilization.

COMPETENCY 8
UNDERSTAND IMPORTANT EVENTS, CONCEPTS, AND TERMINOLOGY RELATED TO WORLD HISTORY

SKILL 8.1 **Recognize chronological relationships and patterns of change and continuity over time in world history**

The practice of dividing time into a number of discrete periods or blocks of time is called "periodization." Because history is continuous, all systems of periodization are arbitrary to some degree. However, dividing time into segments facilitates understanding of changes that occur over time and identifying similarities of events, knowledge, and experience within the defined period. Some divisions of time into these periods apply only under specific circumstances.

Divisions of time may be determined by date, by cultural advances or changes, by historical events, by the influence of particular individuals or groups, or by geography. Speaking of the World War II era defines a particular period of time in which key historical, political, social, and economic events occurred. Speaking of the Jacksonian Era, however, has meaning only in terms of American history. Defining the "Romantic period" makes sense only in England, Europe, and countries under their direct influence. Many of the divisions of time that are commonly used are open to some controversy and discussion. The use of BCE and CE dating, for example, has clear reference only in societies that account time according to the Christian calendar. Similarly, speaking of "the year of the pig" has greatest meaning in China.

SKILL 8.2 Demonstrate knowledge of early civilizations, including the development of empires and kingdoms (e.g., Africa, Imperial China, feudal Japan, the Americas)

China is considered by some historians to be the oldest uninterrupted civilization in the world and was in existence around the same time as the ancient civilizations founded in Egypt, Mesopotamia, and the Indus Valley. The early Chinese studied nature and weather; stressed the importance of education, family, and a strong central government; followed the religions of Buddhism, Confucianism, and Taoism; and invented such things as gunpowder, paper, printing, and the magnetic compass. China began building the Great Wall; practiced crop rotation and terrace farming; increased the importance of the silk industry, and developed caravan routes across Central Asia for extensive trade. They also increased proficiency in rice cultivation and developed a written language based on drawings or pictographs. Chinese people became very proficient at producing beautiful artworks and exporting them, along with silk, to the rest of the world along the Silk Road.

In India, culture was shaped and influenced by Hinduism as well as Buddhism. Industry and commerce developed from extensive trading with the Near East. Outstanding early advances were made in the fields of science and medicine, as well as significant contributions to navigation and maritime enterprises. In India, the caste system was developed, the principle of zero in mathematics was discovered, and the major religion of Hinduism began.

In Africa, the preponderance of deserts and other inhospitable lands restricted African settlements to a few select areas. The city of Zimbabwe became a trading center in south-central Africa in the fifth century but didn't last long. More successful was Ghana, a Muslim-influenced kingdom that arose in the ninth century and lasted for nearly 300 years. Ghanaians were accomplished farmers and also raised cattle and elephants. They traded with people from Europe and the Middle East. Eventually overrunning Ghana was Mali, whose trade center, Timbuktu, survived its own empire's demise and blossomed into one of the world's caravan destinations. The civilizations in Africa south of the Sahara were developing the refining and use of iron, especially for farm implements and later for weapons. Trading was done overland, using camels, and at important seaports. The Arab influence was extremely important, as was their later contact with Indians, Christian Nubians, and Persians. In fact, their trading activities were probably the most important factor in the spread of and assimilation of different ideas and stimulation of cultural growth.

Native Americans in early North America were attuned to nature and had a keen appreciation of the ways of woodworking and metalworking. Various tribes dotted the landscape of what is now the U.S. The North Americans mastered the art of growing many crops and, to their credit, were willing to share that knowledge with the various Europeans who colonized the land.

The most well-known empires of South America were the Aztec, Inca, and Maya. Each of these empires had a central capital where the emperor lived, who controlled all aspects of the lives of his subjects. The empires traded with other peoples. If the relations soured, the results were usually absorption of the trading partners into the empire. These empires, especially the Aztecs, had access to large amounts of metals and jewels, and they created weapons and artwork that continue to impress historians. The Inca Empire stretched across a vast territory down the western coast of South America and was connected by a series of roads. The Mayans are most well-known for their famous pyramids and calendars, as well as their language, which remains only partially understood.

The early civilization in Japan borrowed much of their culture from China. It was the last of these classical civilizations to develop. Although they used, accepted, and copied Chinese art, law, architecture, dress, and writing, the Japanese refined these into their own unique way of life, including incorporating the religion of Buddhism into their culture. Early Japanese society focused on the emperor and the farm, in that order. The power of the emperor declined when it was usurped by the era of the Daimyo and his loyal soldiers, the Samurai. Japan flourished economically and culturally during these early years, although the policy of isolation the country developed limited the influence of its advancements.

Recognize the importance and lasting influence of events (e.g., *the development of major world religions, the Industrial Revolution*)**, issues** (e.g., *colonialism, imperialism, nationalism*)**, and developments** (e.g., *the Renaissance the Cold War*) **in world history**

In the Middle Ages, FEUDALISM was a dominant feature of the economic and social system in Europe. It was a system in which the strong protected the weak, who returned the service with farm labor, military service, and loyalty. Life was lived on a vast estate, owned by a nobleman and his family, called a "manor." It was a complete village supporting a few hundred people, mostly peasants. Improved tools and farming methods made life more bearable, although most never left the manor or traveled from their village during their lifetime. This system would last for many centuries. In Russia, it would last until the 1860s.

The end of the feudal manorial system was sealed by the outbreak and spread of the infamous BLACK DEATH, the waves of bubonic plague that killed over one-third of the total population of Europe. Those who survived and were skilled in any job or occupation were in demand, and many serfs or peasants found freedom and, for that time, a decidedly improved standard of living.

Sharpened skills, development of more sophisticated tools, commerce with other communities, and increasing knowledge of their environment, the resources available to them, and responses to the needs to share good, orderly community life and protect their possessions from outsiders led to further division of labor and community development.

As trade routes developed and travel between cities became easier, trade led to specialization. Trade enables a people to obtain the goods they desire in exchange for the goods they are able to produce. This, in turn, leads to increased attention to refinements of technique and the sharing of ideas. A new discovery or invention provides knowledge and technology that increases the ability to produce goods for trade.

The Agricultural Revolution, initiated by the invention of the plow, led to a thorough transformation of human society by making large-scale agricultural production possible and facilitating the development of agrarian societies. During the period when the plow was invented, the wheel, numbers, and writing were also invented. Coinciding with the shift from hunting wild game to the domestication of animals, this period was one of dramatic social and economic change.

Numerous changes in lifestyle and thinking accompanied the development of stable agricultural communities. Rather than gathering a wide variety of plants as hunter-gatherers, agricultural communities become dependent on a limited

> **FEUDALISM:** a system in which the strong protected the weak, who returned the service with farm labor, military service, and loyalty

> **BLACK DEATH:** waves of bubonic plague that killed over one-third of the total population of Europe

number of plants or crops. Subsistence becomes vulnerable to the weather and dependent upon planting and harvesting times. Agriculture also required a great deal of physical labor and the development of a sense of discipline. Agricultural communities became sedentary, or stable, in terms of location. This made the construction of dwellings appropriate. It also became necessary to maintain social and political stability to ensure that planting and harvesting times were not interrupted by internal discord or a war with a neighboring community.

The ability to produce surplus crops creates the opportunity to trade or barter with other communities in exchange for desired goods. Traders and trade routes begin to develop between villages and cities. The domestication of animals expands the range of trade and facilitates an exchange of ideas and knowledge.

The Scientific Revolution and the Enlightenment were two of the most important movements in the history of civilization, resulting in a new sense of self-examination and a wider view of the world than ever before. The Scientific Revolution was, above all, a shift in focus from belief to evidence. Scientists and philosophers wanted to see the proof, not just believe what other people told them. It was an exciting time for forward-looking thinkers.

A Polish astronomer, Nicolaus Copernicus, began the Scientific Revolution. He crystallized a lifetime of observations into a book that was published about the time of his death. In this book, Copernicus argued that the Sun, not the Earth, was the center of the solar system and that other planets revolved around the Sun, not the Earth. This flew in the face of established doctrine. The Church still wielded tremendous power at this time, including the power to banish people or sentence them to prison or even death.

The Danish astronomer Tycho Brahe was the first to catalog his observations of the night sky, of which he made thousands. Building on Brahe's data, German scientist Johannes Kepler instituted his theory of planetary movement, embodied in his famous Laws of Planetary Movement. Using Brahe's data, Kepler also confirmed Copernicus's observations and argument that the Earth revolved around the Sun.

The most famous defender of this idea was Galileo Galilei, an Italian scientist who conducted many famous experiments in the pursuit of science. He is most well-known, however, for his defense of the heliocentric (sun-centered) idea. He wrote a book comparing the two theories, but most readers could tell easily that he favored the new one. He had used the relatively new invention of the telescope to see four moons of Jupiter. They certainly did not revolve around the Earth, so why should everything else? His ideas angered Church leadership, which continued to assert its authority in this and many other matters.

Galileo died under house arrest, but his ideas didn't die with him. Picking up the baton was an English scientist named Isaac Newton, who became perhaps the most famous scientist of all. He is known as the discoverer of gravity and a pioneering voice in the study of optics (light), calculus, and physics.

More than any other scientist, Newton argued for (and proved) the idea of a mechanistic view of the world: You can see how the world works and prove how the world works through observation; if you can see these things with your own eyes, they must be so. Up to this time, people accepted traditional beliefs, most of which were sanctioned and promoted by the Church. Newton, following in the footsteps of Copernicus and Galileo, changed this.

The Age of Exploration had its beginnings centuries before exploration actually took place. The rise and spread of Islam in the seventh century and its subsequent control over the holy city of Jerusalem led to the European so-called holy wars, the Crusades, to free Jerusalem and the Holy Land from this control. Even though the Crusades were not a success, those who survived and returned to their homes and countries in Western Europe brought back with them new luxuries such as silks, spices, perfumes, and new and different foods.

New ideas, new inventions, and new methods also went to Western Europe with the returning Crusaders. These new influences helped provide the intellectual stimulation that led to the period known as the Renaissance. The revival of interest in classical Greek art, architecture, literature, science, astronomy, medicine, increased trade between Europe and Asia, and also the invention of the printing press helped to push the spread of knowledge and the start of exploration.

Advances made during the Age of Exploration included not only the discovery and colonization of the New World, but also better maps and charts, newer, more accurate navigational instruments, increased knowledge, and great wealth. There were new and different foods and items previously unknown in Europe, and a new hemisphere as a refuge from poverty, persecution, and a place to start a new and better life. The proof that Asia could be reached by sea and that the earth was round were key elements that allowed this exploration.

With the increase in trade and travel, cities sprang up and began to grow. Craft workers in the cities developed their skills to a high degree, eventually organizing guilds to protect the quality of the work and to regulate the buying and selling of their products. City government developed and flourished, centered on strong town councils. Active in city government and the town councils were the businessmen who made up the growing middle class.

This led to the Enlightenment, a period of intense self-study that focused on ethics and logic. More so than at any time before, scientists and philosophers questioned cherished truth and widely held beliefs in an attempt to discover why the world worked—from within. "I think, therefore I am" was one of the famous sayings of that day. It was uttered by Rene Descartes, a French scientist-philosopher whose dedication to logic and the rigid rules of observation was a blueprint for the thinkers who came after him.

One of the giants of the era was England's David Hume. A pioneer of the doctrine of empiricism (believing things only when you've seen the proof for yourself), Hume was also a prime believer in the value of skepticism; in other words, he was naturally suspicious of things that other people told him to be true and constantly set out to discover the truth for himself.

The Enlightenment thinker who might be the most famous is Immanuel Kant of Germany. He was both a philosopher and a scientist, and he took a definite scientific view of the world. He wrote the movement's most famous essay, "Answering the Question: What Is Enlightenment?" and he answered his famous question with the motto "Dare to Know." For Kant, the human being was a rational being capable of hugely creative thought and intense self-evaluation. He encouraged all to examine themselves and the world around them.

SOCIAL CONTRACT: the belief that government existed because people wanted it to, that the people had an agreement with the government that they would submit to it as long as it protected them and didn't encroach on their basic human rights

Also prevalent during the Enlightenment was the idea of the SOCIAL CONTRACT, the belief that government existed because people wanted it to, that the people had an agreement with the government that they would submit to it as long as it protected them and didn't encroach on their basic human rights. This idea was first made famous by the Frenchman Jean-Jacques Rousseau but was also adopted by England's John Locke and America's Thomas Jefferson.

John Locke was one of the most influential political writers of the seventeenth century. He put great emphasis on human rights and put forth the belief that when governments violate those rights people should rebel. He wrote the book *Two Treatises of Government* in 1690, which had tremendous influence on political thought in the American colonies and helped shape the U.S. Constitution and Declaration of Independence.

RENAISSANCE: literally means "rebirth," and signaled the rekindling of interest in ancient classical Greek and Roman civilizations. It was the period in human history marking the start of many ideas and innovations leading to our modern age

The word RENAISSANCE literally means "rebirth," and signaled the rekindling of interest in ancient classical Greek and Roman civilizations. It was the period in human history marking the start of many ideas and innovations leading to our modern age. The Renaissance began in Italy, with many of its ideas starting in Florence, controlled by the Medici family. Education, especially for some of the merchants, required reading, writing, and math, the study of law, and the writings of classical Greek and Roman writers.

Most famous are the Renaissance artists, first and foremost Leonardo da Vinci, Michelangelo, and Raphael, but also Titian, Donatello, and

Rembrandt. All of these men pioneered a new method of painting and sculpture—that of portraying events and people as they really looked, not as the artists imagined them to be. One needs look no further than Michelangelo's *David* to illustrate this.

Literature was a focus as well during the Renaissance. Humanists Petrarch, Boccaccio, Erasmus, and Sir Thomas More advanced the idea of being interested in life here on earth and the opportunities it can bring, rather than constantly focusing on heaven and its rewards. The monumental works of Shakespeare, Dante, and Cervantes found their origins in these ideas as well as those that drove the painters and sculptors. All of these works, of course, owe much of their existence to the invention of the printing press, which occurred during the Renaissance.

The Renaissance changed music as well. No longer just a religious experience, music could be fun and composed for its own sake, to be enjoyed in fuller and more humanistic ways than in the Middle Ages. Musicians could work for themselves, rather than only for the churches, as before, and so could command good money for their work, which increased their prestige.

The INDUSTRIAL REVOLUTION of the eighteenth and nineteenth centuries resulted in even greater changes in human civilization and even greater opportunities for trade, increased production, and the exchange of ideas and knowledge.

> **INDUSTRIAL REVOLUTION:** the mechanization of industry

The first phase of the Industrial Revolution (1750–1830) saw the mechanization of the textile industry, vast improvements in mining, the invention of the steam engine, and numerous improvements in transportation, including the development and improvement of turnpikes, canals, and the invention of the railroad.

The second phase (1830–1910) resulted in vast improvements in a number of industries that had already been mechanized through such inventions as the Bessemer steel process and the invention of steam ships. New industries, such as photography, electricity, and chemical processes, arose as a result of the new technological advances. New sources of power were harnessed and applied, including petroleum and hydroelectric power. Precision instruments were developed and engineering was launched. It was during this second phase that the industrial revolution spread to other European countries, to Japan, and to the United States.

The direct results of the Industrial Revolution, particularly as they affected industry, commerce, and agriculture, included:

- Enormous increase in productivity

- Huge increase in world trade

- Specialization and division of labor

- Standardization of parts and mass production

- Growth of giant business conglomerates and monopolies

- A new revolution in agriculture facilitated by the steam engine, machinery, chemical fertilizers, processing, canning, and refrigeration

The political results included:

- Growth of complex government by technical experts

- Centralization of government, including regulatory administrative agencies

- Advantages to democratic development, including extension of franchise to the middle class, and later to all elements of the population, mass education to meet the needs of an industrial society, and the development of media of public communication, including radio, television, and cheap newspapers

- Dangers to democracy, including the risk of manipulation of the media of mass communication, facilitation of dictatorial centralization and totalitarian control, and subordination of the legislative function to administrative directives

The economic results and conflicts were numerous:

- The conflict between free trade and low tariffs and protectionism

- The issue of free enterprise versus government regulation

- Struggles between labor and capital, including the trade-union movement

- The rise of socialism

The social results of the Industrial Revolution include:

- Increase of population, especially in industrial centers

- Advances in science applied to agriculture, sanitation and medicine

- Growth of great cities

- Disappearance of the difference between city dwellers and farmers

- Faster tempo of life and increased stress from the monotony of the work routine

- The emancipation of women

- The decline of religion

- Rise of scientific materialism

- Darwin's theory of evolution

Things changed in the worlds of literature and art as well. The main development in the nineteenth century was ROMANTICISM, an emphasis on emotion and the imagination that was a direct reaction to the logic and reason so stressed in the preceding Enlightenment. Famous Romantic authors included John Keats, William Wordsworth, Victor Hugo, and Johann Wolfgang von Goethe. The negative aspects of the Industrial Revolution gave rise to the famous realists Charles Dickens, Fyodor Dosteovsky, Leo Tolstoy, and Mark Twain, who described life as they saw it, for better or for worse.

During the eighteenth and especially the nineteenth centuries, NATIONALISM emerged as a powerful force in Europe and elsewhere in the world. Strictly speaking, nationalism is a belief in one's own nation, country, or people. More so than in previous centuries, the people of the European nations began to think in terms of a nation of people who had similar beliefs, concerns, and needs. This was partly a reaction to a growing discontent with the autocratic governments of the day and also a general realization that there was more to life than the individual. People could feel a part of something like their nation, making themselves more than just an insignificant soul struggling to survive.

An additional reason for European imperialism was the harsh, urgent demand for the raw materials needed to fuel and feed the great Industrial Revolution. These resources were not available in the huge quantity so desperately needed, which necessitated (and rationalized) colonizing and partitioning the continent of Africa and parts of Asia. In turn, these colonial areas would purchase the finished manufactured goods. Europe in the nineteenth century was a crowded place. Populations were growing but resources were not. The peoples of many European countries were also agitating for rights as never before. To address these concerns, European powers began to look elsewhere for relief.

The Cold War was, more than anything else, an ideological struggle between proponents of democracy and those of communism. The two major players were the United States and the Soviet Union, but other countries were involved as well. It was a "cold" war because no large-scale fighting took place directly between the two big protagonists.

The Soviet Union rigidly controlled supporting countries, including all of Eastern Europe, which made up a military organization called the Warsaw Pact. The Western nations responded with a military organization of their own, NATO. Another prime battleground was Asia, where the Soviet Union had allies in China, North Korea, and North Vietnam, and the U.S. had allies in Japan, South Korea, Taiwan, and South Vietnam. The Korean War and Vietnam War were major conflicts in which both big protagonists played major roles but didn't directly fight each other. The main symbol of the Cold War was the arms race, a continual buildup of missiles, tanks, and other weapons that became ever more

ROMANTICISM: an emphasis on emotion and the imagination that was a direct reaction to the logic and reason so stressed in the preceding Enlightenment

NATIONALISM: a belief in one's own nation, country, or people

technologically advanced and increasingly more deadly. The ultimate weapon, which both sides had in abundance, was the nuclear bomb. Spending on weapons and defensive systems eventually consumed great percentages of the budgets of the U.S. and the USSR, and some historians argue that this high level of spending played a large part in the end of the Cold War.

The Cold War continued to varying degrees from 1947 to 1991, when the Soviet Union collapsed. Other Eastern European countries had seen their communist governments overthrown by this time as well, marking the fall of the "Iron Curtain."

Growth of Religion

Hinduism was begun by people called Aryans around 1500 BCE and spread into India. The Aryans blended their culture with the culture of the Dravidians, natives they conquered. Today it has many sects, and promotes worship of hundreds of gods and goddesses and the belief in reincarnation. Though forbidden today by law, a prominent feature of Hinduism in the past was a rigid adherence to and practice of the infamous caste system.

Buddhism developed in India from the teachings of Prince Gautama and spread to most of Asia. Its beliefs opposed the worship of numerous deities, the Hindu caste system, and the supernatural. Worshippers must be free of attachment to all things worldly and devote themselves to finding release from life's suffering.

Confucianism is a Chinese religion based on the teachings of the Chinese philosopher Confucius. There is no clergy, no organization, and no belief in a deity or in life after death. It emphasizes political and moral ideas and respect for authority and ancestors. Rulers were expected to govern according to high moral standards.

Taoism is a native Chinese religion with worship of more deities than almost any other religion. It teaches all followers to make the effort to achieve the two goals of happiness and immortality. Practices and ceremonies include meditation, prayer, magic, reciting scriptures, special diets, breath control, beliefs in witchcraft, fortune telling, astrology, and communicating with the spirits of the dead.

Shinto is the native religion of Japan, developed from native folk beliefs worshipping spirits and demons in animals, trees, and mountains. According to its mythology, deities created Japan and its people, which resulted in worshipping the emperor as a god. Shinto was strongly influenced by Buddhism and Confucianism but never had strong doctrines on salvation or life after death.

The ancient Israelites created a powerful legacy of political, legal, religious, and philosophical traditions, much of which survives to this day. Israel was not the first ancient civilization to have a series of laws for its people to follow, but such commandments as the ones that prohibit stealing and killing were revolutionary in their day because they applied to everyone, not just the disadvantaged. In many ancient cultures, the rich and powerful were above the law because they could buy their way out of trouble and because it wasn't always clear what the laws were. Echoing the Code of Hammurabi and preceding Rome's Twelve Tables, the Ten Commandments provided a written record of laws, so all knew what was prohibited.

The civilization of Israel is also known as the first to assume a worship of just one god. The Christian religion built on this tradition, and both Christianity and Judaism exist and are expanding today, especially in Western countries. Rather than a series of gods, each of which was in charge of a different aspect of nature or society, the ancient Israelites and Christians believed in just one god, called Yahweh or God, depending on which religion you look at. This divine being was, these peoples believed, the "one, true God," lord over all. This worship of just one god had more of a personal nature to it, and the result was that the believers thought themselves able to talk (or, more properly, pray) directly to their god, whereas the peoples of Mesopotamia and Egypt thought the gods distant and unapproachable.

A few years after the death of the Emperor Justinian, Mohammed was born (570 CE) in a small Arabian town near the Red Sea. Arabia was a vast desert of rock and sand, except the coastal areas on the Red Sea. It was populated by nomadic wanderers called Bedouin, who lived in scattered tribes near oases where they watered their herds. Tribal leaders engaged in frequent war with one another. The family or tribe was the social and political unit, under the authority of the head of the family.

In about 610 CE, a prophet named Mohammed came to some prominence. He called his new religion Islam (submission [to the will of God]) and his followers were called Moslems—those who had surrendered themselves. His first converts were members of his family and his friends. As the new faith began to grow, it remained a secret society. When they began to make their faith public, they met with opposition and persecution from the pagan Arabians who feared the new religion and the possible loss of the profitable trade with the pilgrims who came to the Kaaba every year. Islam slowly gained ground, and the persecutions became more severe around Mecca. In 622 CE, Mohammed and his close followers fled the city and found refuge in Medina to the North. His flight is called the Hegira. This event marks the beginning of the Moslem calendar. Mohammed took advantage of the ongoing feuds between Jews and Arabs in the city and became the ruler of Medina, making it the capital of a rapidly growing state.

SKILL Recognize the importance and lasting influence of major world
8.4 conflicts

World War I—1914 to 1918

In Europe, war broke out in 1914, eventually involving nearly 30 nations, and ended in 1918. One of the major causes of the war was the tremendous surge of nationalism during the 1800s and early 1900s. People of the same nationality or ethnic group sharing a common history, language, or culture began uniting or demanding the right of unification, especially in the empires of Eastern Europe, such as the Russian Ottoman and Austrian-Hungarian Empires. Getting stronger and more intense were the beliefs of these peoples in loyalty to common political, social, and economic goals. Other causes included the increasing strength of military capabilities, massive colonization for raw materials needed for industrialization and manufacturing, and military and diplomatic alliances. The initial spark, which started the conflagration, was the assassination of Austrian Archduke Francis Ferdinand and his wife in Sarajevo.

In Europe, Italy and Germany were each united into one nation from many smaller states. There were revolutions in Austria and Hungary, the Franco-Prussian War, the dividing of Africa among the strong European nations, interference and intervention of Western nations in Asia, and the breakup of Turkish dominance in the Balkans. France, Great Britain, Italy, Portugal, Spain, Germany, and Belgium controlled the entire continent of Africa, except Liberia and Ethiopia. In Asia and the Pacific Islands, only China, Japan, and present-day Thailand kept their independence. The other countries were controlled by the strong European nations.

World War I saw advent of mechanized warfare, with the use of weapons such as tanks, airplanes, machine guns, submarines, poison gas, and flame throwers. Fighting on the Western front was characterized by a series of trenches that were used throughout the war until 1918. U.S. involvement in the war did not occur until 1916. When the war began in 1914, President Woodrow Wilson declared that the U.S. was neutral and most Americans were opposed to any involvement. In 1916, Wilson was reelected to a second term based on the slogan proclaiming his efforts at keeping America out of the war. For a few months after, he put forth most of his efforts to stopping the war, but German submarines began attacking American merchant ships.

Ironically, the Treaty of Paris, the peace treaty ending World War I, ultimately led to the Second World War. Countries that fought in the first war were either dissatisfied over the "spoils" of war, or were punished so harshly that resentment continued building to an eruption twenty years later.

The economic problems of both winners and losers of the first world war were never resolved, and the worldwide Great Depression of the 1930s dealt the final blow to any immediate recovery. Democratic governments in Europe were severely strained and weakened, which, in turn gave strength and encouragement to those political movements that were extreme and made promises to end the economic chaos in their countries.

Nationalism, which was a major cause of World War I, grew even stronger and seemed to feed the feelings of discontent, which became increasingly rampant. Because of unstable economic conditions and political unrest, harsh dictatorships arose in several countries, especially where there was no history of democratic government. Countries such as Germany, Japan, and Italy began to aggressively expand their borders and acquire additional territory.

World War II—1939 to 1945

In all, 59 nations became embroiled in World War II, which began September 1, 1939 and ended September 2, 1945. These dates include both the European and Pacific Theaters of war. The tragic results of this second global conflagration were more deaths and more destruction than in any previous armed conflict. It completely uprooted and displaced millions of people. The end of the war brought renewed power struggles, especially in Europe and China, with many Eastern European nations as well as China coming under complete control and domination of the Communists, supported and backed by the Soviet Union. With the development and two-time deployment of an atomic bomb against Japan, the world found itself in the nuclear age. The peace settlement established the United Nations Organization, still existing and operating today.

Internment of people of Japanese ancestry

Some authorities in the United States feared sabotage of both civilian and military facilities within the country. By February 1942, Presidential Executive Orders had authorized the arrest of all aliens suspected of subversive activities and the creation of exclusion zones where people could be isolated from the remainder of the population and kept where they could not damage national infrastructure. These War Relocation Camps were used to isolate about 120,000 Japanese and Japanese Americans (62% were citizens) during World War II.

Allied response to the Holocaust

International organizations received sharp criticism during WWII for their failure to act to save the European Jews. The Allied Powers, in particular, were accused of gross negligence. Many organizations and individuals did not believe reports of the abuse and mass genocide that was occurring in Europe. Many nations did not want to accept Jewish refugees. Critics have claimed that even if Allied bombs killed all inmates at Auschwitz at the time, the destruction of the camp would have saved thousands of other Jews. The usual response was that, had the Allies destroyed the camp, the Nazis would have turned to other methods of extermination.

The role of women and minorities

Within the military theater, women and minorities filled a number of new roles. Women served in the military as drivers, nurses, communications operators, and clerks. The Flight Nurses corps was created at the beginning of the war. Among the most notable minority groups in the military were:

The Tuskegee Airmen

The first African-American pilots to fly for the military, the Tuskegee Airmen made a major contribution to the war effort. Although they were not considered eligible for the gold wings of a Navy Pilot until 1948, these men completed standard Army flight classroom instruction and the required flying time. They flew more than 15,000 missions, destroyed over 1,000 German aircraft, and earned more than 150 Distinguished Flying Crosses and hundreds of Air Medals.

The 442nd Regimental Combat Team

Composed of Japanese Americans who fought in Europe, the 442nd Regimental Combat Team was the most highly decorated unit of its size and length of service in the history of the U.S. Army. This self-sufficient force served with great distinction in North Africa, Italy, southern France, and Germany. The medals earned by the group include 21 Congressional Medals of Honor (the highest award given). The unit was awarded 9,486 purple hearts (for being wounded in battle). The casualty rate, combining those killed in action, missing in action, and wounded and removed from action, was 93%.

The Navajo Code Talkers

The Navajo Code Talkers have been credited with saving countless lives and accelerating the end of the war. There were over 400 Navajo Indians who served in all six Marine divisions from 1942 to 1945. At the time of WWII, less than 30 non-Navajo people understood the Navajo language. Because it was a very complex language and because it was not a code, it was unbreakable by the Germans or the Japanese. The job of these men was to talk and transmit information on tactics, troop movements, orders and other vital military information. Not only was the enemy unable to understand the language, but it was far faster than translating messages into Morse code. It is generally accepted that without the Navajo Code Talkers, Iwo Jima could not have been taken.

The Role of Women and Minority Groups at Home

Most able-bodied men of appropriate age were called up for military service. Minorities were generally not drafted. Yet many critical functions remained to be fulfilled by those who remained at home, and women and minorities overturned many expectations and assumptions.

To a greater extent than any previous war, WWII required industrial production. Those who remained at home needed to build the planes, tanks, ships, bombs, torpedoes, etc. The men who remained at home were working, but more labor was desperately needed. In particular, a call went out to women to join the effort and enter the industrial work force. By the middle of 1944, more than 19 million women had entered the work force. Women worked building planes and tanks. Some operated large cranes to move heavy equipment; some loaded and fired machine guns and other weapons to ensure that they were in working order; some operated hydraulic presses; some were volunteer fire fighters; some were welders, riveters, drill press operators, and cab drivers. Women worked all manufacturing shifts, making everything from clothing to fighter jets. Most women and their families tended "Victory Gardens" to produce food items that were in short supply.

Military Technology

Major developments in aviation, weaponry, communications, and medicine were achieved during the war. The years between WWI and WWII produced significant advancement in aircraft technology, but the pace of aircraft development and production was dramatically increased during WWII.

Major developments included:

- Flight-based weapon delivery systems

- The long-range bomber

- The first jet fighter

- The first cruise missile

- The first ballistic missile

Although they were invented, the cruise and ballistic missiles were not widely used during the war. Glider planes were heavily used in WWII because they were silent upon approach. Another significant development was the broad use of paratrooper units. Finally, hospital planes were used to extract the wounded from the front and transport them to hospitals for treatment.

The years between WWI and WWII produced significant advancement in aircraft technology, but the pace of aircraft development and production was dramatically increased during WWII.

The war began with essentially the same weaponry that had been used in WWI.

Weapons and technology in other areas also improved rapidly during the war. These advances were critical in determining the outcome of the war. Used for the first time were: radar, electronic computers, nuclear weapons, and new tank designs. More new inventions were registered for patents than ever before. Most of these new ideas were aimed to either kill or prevent killing. The aircraft carrier joined the battleship; the Higgins boat, the primary landing craft, was invented; light tanks were developed to meet the needs of a changing battlefield; and other armored vehicles were developed. Submarines were also perfected during this period. Numerous other weapons were also developed or invented to meet the needs of battle during WWII: the bazooka, the rocket propelled grenade, anti-tank weapons, assault rifles, mine-clearing Flail tanks, Flame tanks, submersible tanks; cruise missiles, rocket artillery and air launched rockets; guided weapons, self-guiding weapons and Napalm.

The development of the atomic bomb was probably the most profound military development of the war years. This invention made it possible for a single plane to carry a single bomb that was sufficiently powerful to destroy an entire city. It was believed that possession of the bomb would serve as a deterrent to any nation because it would make aggression against a nation with a bomb a decision for mass suicide. The United States dropped two nuclear bombs in 1945 on the cities of Nagasaki and Hiroshima. They caused the immediate deaths of 100,000 to 200,000 people, and far more deaths over time. This was (and still is) a controversial decision. Those who opposed the use of the atom bomb argued that was an unnecessary act of mass killing, particularly of non-combatants. Proponents argued that it ended the war sooner, thus resulting in fewer casualties on both sides.

The development and use of nuclear weapons marked the beginning of a new age in warfare that created greater distance from the act of killing and eliminated the ability to minimize the effect of war on non-combatants. The introduction and possession of nuclear weapons by the United States quickly led to the development of similar weapons by other nations, proliferation of the most destructive weapons ever created, and massive fear of the effects of the use of these weapons, including radiation poisoning and acid rain, and led to the Cold War.

See Skill 8.3 for additional discussion on the Cold War.

SKILL 8.5 **Analyze cause-and-effect relationships in world history**

HISTORIC CAUSATION is the concept that events in history are linked to one another by an endless chain of cause and effect. The root causes of major historical events cannot always be seen immediately, and are only apparent when looking back many years later.

When Columbus landed in the New World in 1492, the full effect of this event could not have been measured at that time. By opening the Western Hemisphere to economic and political development by Europeans, Columbus changed the face of the world. The native populations that had existed before Columbus arrived were quickly decimated by disease and warfare. Over the following century, the Spanish conquered most of South and Central America, and English and French settlers arrived in North America, eventually displacing the native people. This gradual displacement took place over many years and could not have been foreseen by those early explorers. Looking back, it can be said that Columbus caused a series of events that greatly impacted world history.

In some cases, individual events can have an immediate, clear effect. In 1941, Europe was embroiled in war. On the Pacific Rim, Japan was engaged in military occupation of Korea and other Asian countries. The United States took a position of isolation, choosing not to become directly involved in the conflicts.

This position changed rapidly, however, on the morning of December 7, 1941, when Japanese forces launched a surprise attack on the U.S. naval base at Pearl Harbor in Hawaii. The United States immediately declared war on Japan and became involved in the war in Europe shortly afterwards. The entry of the United States into the Second World War undoubtedly contributed to the eventual victory of the Allied forces in Europe and the defeat of Japan. The surprise attack on Pearl Harbor affected the outcome of the war and the shape of the modern world.

Interaction between cultures, either by exploration, migration, or war, often contributes directly to major historical events, but other forces can influence the course of history as well. Religious movements, such as the rise of Catholicism in the Middle Ages, created social changes throughout Europe and culminated in the Crusades and the expulsion of Muslims from Spain. Technological developments led to major historical events, as in the case of the Industrial Revolution which was driven by the replacement of water power with steam power.

Social movements can also cause major historical shifts. Between the Civil War and the early 1960s in the United States, racial segregation was practiced legally in many parts of the country through "Jim Crow" laws. Demonstrations and activism opposing segregation began to escalate during the late 1950s and early 1960s, eventually leading to the passage in the Congress of the Civil Rights Act of 1964, which ended legal segregation in the United States.

> **HISTORIC CAUSATION:** the concept that events in history are linked to one another by an endless chain of cause and effect

SKILL 8.6 Analyze various perspectives and interpretations of events, issues, and developments in world history

ETHNOCENTRISM:
the belief that one's own culture is the central and usually superior culture

Humans are social animals who naturally form groups based on familial, cultural, national and other lines. One source of differing views among groups is ethnocentrism. ETHNOCENTRISM, as the word suggests, is the belief that one's own culture is the central and usually superior culture. An ethnocentric view usually considers different practices in other cultures as inferior or even "savage."

Psychologists have suggested that ethnocentrism is a naturally occurring attitude. For the large part, people are most comfortable among other people who share their same upbringing, language, and cultural background, and are likely to judge other cultural behaviors as alien or foreign.

Historical developments are likely to affect different groups in different ways, some positively and some negatively. These effects can strengthen the ties an individual feels to the group he belongs to, and solidify differences between groups.

History is an integral part of every other discipline in the social sciences. Knowing the historical background of a topic goes a long way towards explaining how what happened in the past led up to and explains the present.

See also Skills 8.3, 8.4, and 8.5

COMPETENCY 9
UNDERSTAND IMPORTANT EVENTS, CONCEPTS, AND TERMINOLOGY RELATED TO THE HISTORY OF THE UNITED STATES AND THE STATE OF OREGON

SKILL 9.1 Recognize chronological relationships and patterns of change and continuity over time in U.S. and Oregon history

By the 1750s in Europe, Spain was no longer the most powerful nation. The remaining rivalry was between Britain and France. For nearly 25 years, between 1689 and 1748, a series of "armed conflicts" involving these two powers took place. These conflicts had spilled over into North America. The War of the League of Augsburg in Europe, 1689 to 1697, had been King William's War. The War of the Spanish Succession, 1702 to 1713, had been Queen Anne's War. The War of the Austrian Succession, 1740 to 1748, was called King George's War in the colonies. The two nations fought for possession of colonies, especially in Asia and North America, and for control of the seas, but none of these conflicts was decisive.

The final conflict, which decided once and for all who was the most powerful, began in North America in 1754, in the Ohio River Valley. It was known in America as the French and Indian War and in Europe as the Seven Years' War, since it began there in 1756.

In 1763, Spain, France, and Britain met in Paris to draw up a treaty. Great Britain got most of India and all of North America east of the Mississippi River, except for New Orleans. Britain received control of Florida from Spain and returned Cuba and the islands of the Philippines, taken during the war, to Spain. France lost nearly all of its possessions in America and India but was allowed to keep four islands: Guadeloupe, Martinique, Haiti on Hispaniola, and Miquelon and St. Pierre. France gave Spain New Orleans and the vast territory of Louisiana, west of the Mississippi River. Britain was now the most powerful nation in the world.

Causes for the War for Independence

With the end of the French and Indian War (The Seven Years' War), England decided to reassert control over the colonies in America. England particularly needed the revenue from the control of trade to pay for the recent war and to defend the new territory obtained as a result of the war.

English leaders decided to impose a tax that would pay for the military defense of the American lands. The colonists rejected this idea for two reasons: (1) they were undergoing an economic recession, and (2) they believed it unjust to be taxed unless they had representation in the Parliament.

England passed a series of laws that provoked fierce opposition. Opposition melded in Massachusetts. Leaders denounced "taxation without representation" and a boycott was organized against imported English goods. The movement spread to other colonies rapidly.

The situation in the colonies between colonists and British troops was becoming increasingly strained. Despite a skirmish in New York and the Boston Massacre in 1770, tensions abated over the next few years.

The Tea Act of 1773 gave the British East India Company a monopoly on sales of tea. The colonists responded with the "Boston Tea Party." England responded with the "Coercive Acts" (called the "Intolerable Acts" by the colonists) in 1774. This closed the port of Boston, changed the charter of the Massachusetts colony, and suppressed town meetings.

> **DECLARATION OF INDE-PENDENCE:** the founding document of the United States of America

The DECLARATION OF INDEPENDENCE was the founding document of the United States of America. The Articles of Confederation were the first attempt of the newly independent states to reach a new understanding among themselves. The Declaration was intended to demonstrate the reasons that the colonies were seeking separation from Great Britain. Conceived by and written for the most part by Thomas Jefferson, it is not only important for what it says, but also for how it is written. The Declaration is in many respects a poetic document. Instead of a simple recitation of the colonists' grievances, it set out clearly the reasons why the colonists were seeking their freedom from Great Britain. They had tried all means to resolve the dispute peacefully. It was the right of a people, when all other methods of addressing their grievances have been tried and failed, to separate themselves from that power that was keeping them from fully expressing their rights to "life, liberty, and the pursuit of happiness."

The Declaration of Independence was drafted and declared on July 4, 1776. George Washington labored against tremendous odds to wage a victorious war. The turning point in the Americans' favor occurred in 1777 with the American victory at Saratoga. After this victory, the French decided to align themselves with the Americans against the British. With the aid of Admiral deGrasse and French warships blocking the entrance to Chesapeake Bay, British General Cornwallis, trapped at Yorktown, Virginia, surrendered in 1781 and ended the war. The Treaty of Paris, officially ending the war, was signed in 1783.

The Articles of Confederation was the first political system under which the newly independent colonies tried to organize themselves. It was drafted after the Declaration of Independence, in 1776, and was passed by the Continental Congress on November 15, 1777, ratified by the thirteen states, and took effect on March 1, 1781.

The newly independent states were unwilling to give too much power to a national government. They were already fighting Great Britain. They did not want to replace one harsh ruler with another. After many debates, the form of the Articles was accepted. Each state agreed to send delegates to the Congress. Each state had one vote in the Congress. The Articles gave Congress the power to declare war, appoint military officers, and coin money. The Congress was also responsible for foreign affairs. The Articles of Confederation limited the powers of Congress by giving the states final authority. Although Congress could pass laws, at least nine of the thirteen states had to approve a law before it went into effect. Congress could not pass any laws regarding taxes. To get money, Congress had to ask each state for it; no state could be forced to pay.

This weak national government might have worked if the states were able to cooperate. However, many different disputes arose and there was no way of settling them. Thus, the delegates went to meet again to try to fix the Articles. Instead, they ended up creating a new Constitution revised in light of these earlier mistakes.

Ratification of the U.S. Constitution was by no means a foregone conclusion. The representative government had powerful enemies, especially those who had seen firsthand the failure of the Articles of Confederation. The strong central government had powerful enemies, including some of the guiding lights of the American Revolution.

Those who wanted to see a strong central government were called FEDERALISTS, because they wanted a strong, central federal government. Among the leaders of the Federalists were Alexander Hamilton and John Jay. These two, along with James Madison, wrote a series of letters to New York newspapers, urging that that state ratify the Constitution. These became known as the *Federalist Papers*.

> **FEDERALISTS:** individuals who believed in a strong central government

In the Anti-Federalist camp were Thomas Jefferson and Patrick Henry. These men and many others like them were worried that a strong national government would descend into the kind of tyranny that they had just worked so hard to abolish. In the same way that they took their name from their foes, they wrote a series of arguments against the Constitution called the *Anti-Federalist Papers*.

In the end, both sides got most of what they wanted. The Federalists got their strong national government, which was held in place by "checks and balances." The Anti-Federalists got the BILL OF RIGHTS, the first ten Amendments to the Constitution and a series of laws that protect some of the most basic of human rights. The states that were unsure about ratifying the Constitution signed on when the Bill of Rights was promised.

> **BILL OF RIGHTS:** the first ten Amendments to the Constitution

Americans had good reason to fear the emergence of political parties. They had witnessed how parties worked in Great Britain. Parties, called "factions" in Britain, were made up of a few people who schemed to win favors from the government. It was, ironically, disagreements between two of Washington's chief advisors, Thomas Jefferson and Alexander Hamilton, that spurred the formation of the first political parties in the newly formed United States of America.

By the time Washington retired from office in 1796, the new political parties would come to play an important role in choosing his successor: For the first time, each party would put up its own candidates for office. By the beginning of the

1800s, the Federalist Party, torn by internal divisions, began suffering a decline. The election in 1800 of Thomas Jefferson, Hamilton's bitter rival, as President, and after its leader Alexander Hamilton was killed in 1804 in a duel with Aaron Burr, the Federalist Party began to collapse.

By 1816, after losing a string of important elections, (Jefferson was reelected in 1804, and James Madison, a Democratic-Republican was elected in 1808), the Federalist Party ceased to be an effective political force, and soon passed off the national stage.

By the late 1820s, new political parties had emerged. The Democratic-Republican Party, or simply the Republican Party, had been the major party for many years, but differences within it about the direction the country was going caused a split after 1824. Those who favored strong national growth took the name Whigs after a similar party in Great Britain and united around then President John Quincy Adams. Many business people in the Northeast, as well as some wealthy planters in the South, supported it.

The Indian Removal Act of 1830 authorized the government to negotiate treaties with Native Americans to provide land west of the Mississippi River in exchange for lands east of the river. This policy resulted in the relocation of more than 100,000 Native Americans. Theoretically, the treaties were expected to result in voluntary relocation of the native people. In fact, however, many of the native chiefs were forced to sign the treaties.

This forced migration of the Native Americans to lands that were deemed marginal, combined with the near-extermination of the buffalo, caused a downturn in Prairie Culture that relied on the horse for hunting, trading, and traveling.

One of the worst examples of "removal" was the Treaty of New Echota. This treaty was signed by a faction of the Cherokees rather than the actual leaders of the tribe. When the leaders attempted to remain on their ancestral lands, the treaty was enforced by President Martin Van Buren. The removal of the Cherokees came to be known as "The Trail of Tears" and resulted in the deaths of more than 4,000 Cherokees, mostly due to disease. Numerous conflicts, often called the "Indian Wars," broke out between the U.S. army and many different native tribes. Many treaties were signed with the various tribes, but most were broken by the government for a variety of reasons. Two of the most notable battles were the Battle of Little Bighorn in 1876, in which native people defeated General Custer and his forces, and the massacre of Native Americans in 1890 at Wounded Knee. In 1876, the U.S. government ordered all surviving Native Americans to move to reservations.

Civil War and Reconstruction

At the Constitutional Convention, one of the slavery compromises concerned how slaves should be counted to decide the number of representatives for the House and the amount of taxes to be paid. Southerners pushed for counting the slaves for representation but not for taxes. The Northerners pushed for the opposite. The resulting compromise, sometimes referred to as the "three-fifths compromise," stated that three-fifths of the slaves would be counted for both taxes and representation.

The other compromise over slavery was part of the disputes over how much regulation the central government would have over commercial activities such as trade with other nations and the slave trade. It was agreed that Congress would regulate commerce with other nations, including taxing imports. Southerners were worried about the potential taxes on slaves coming into the country, and the possibility of Congress prohibiting the slave trade altogether. The agreement reached allowed the states to continue importation of slaves for the next 20 years until 1808, at which time Congress would make a decision as to the future of the slave trade. During the 20-year period, no more than $10 could be levied on each slave coming into the country.

An additional provision of this compromise was that, with the admission of Missouri to the U.S., slavery would not be allowed in the rest of the Louisiana Purchase territory north of latitude 36 degrees 30'. This was acceptable to the Southern Congressmen, because it was not profitable to grow cotton on land north of this latitude line. It was thought that the crisis had been resolved, but, in the next year, it was discovered that in its state constitution, Missouri discriminated against free blacks. Anti-slavery supporters in Congress went into an uproar, determined to exclude Missouri from the Union. Henry Clay, known as the Great Compromiser, then proposed a second Missouri Compromise, which was acceptable to everyone. His proposal stated that the Constitution of the United States guaranteed protections and privileges to citizens of states and Missouri's proposed constitution could not deny these to any of its citizens. The acceptance in 1820 of this second compromise opened the way for Missouri's statehood—a temporary reprieve only.

The doctrine of nullification says that the states have the right to "nullify"—declare invalid—any act of Congress they believe to be unjust or unconstitutional. The nullification crisis of the mid–nineteenth century climaxed over a new tariff on imported manufactured goods that was enacted by the Congress in 1828. While this tariff protected the manufacturing and industrial interests of the North, it placed an additional burden of cost on the South, the consumers of manufactured goods.

This issue of disagreement reached its climax when John C. Calhoun, Jackson's vice president, led South Carolina to adopt the Ordinance of Nullification which declared the tariff null and void within state borders. Although this issue came to the brink of military action, it was resolved by the enactment of a new tariff in 1832.

When economic issues and the issue of slavery came to a head, the North declared slavery illegal. The South acted on the principles of the doctrine of nullification, declared the new laws null, and acted upon their presumed right as states to secede from the union and form their own government. The North saw secession as a violation of the national unity and contract.

It is ironic that South Carolina was the first state to secede from the Union and that the first shots of the war were fired on Fort Sumter in Charleston Harbor. Both sides quickly prepared for war. The North had more in its favor: a larger population; superiority in finances and transportation facilities; and more manufacturing, agricultural, and natural resources. The North possessed most of the nation's gold, had about 92 percent of all industries, and almost all known supplies of copper, coal, iron, and various other minerals. Since most of the nation's railroads were in the North and Midwest, men and supplies could be moved wherever needed; food could be transported from the farms of the Midwest to workers in the East and to soldiers on the battlefields. Trade with nations overseas could go on as usual due to Northern control of the navy and the merchant fleet. The Northern states numbered twenty-four and included western (California and Oregon) and border (Maryland, Delaware, Kentucky, Missouri, and West Virginia) states.

The Southern states numbered eleven and included South Carolina, Georgia, Florida, Alabama, Mississippi, Louisiana, Texas, Virginia, North Carolina, Tennessee, and Arkansas, making up the Confederacy. Although outnumbered in population, the South was confident of victory. They knew that all they had to do was fight a defensive war, protecting their own territory, until the North, who had to invade and defeat an area almost the size of Western Europe, tired of the struggle and gave up. Another advantage the South had was that a number of its best officers had graduated from the U.S. Military Academy at West Point and had long years of army experience, some even exercising varying degrees of command in the Indian Wars and the war with Mexico.

The South had specific reasons and goals for fighting the war. The major aim of the Confederacy never wavered: to win independence, to govern themselves as they wished, and to preserve slavery. The Northerners were not as clear in their reasons for conducting war. At the beginning, most believed, along with Lincoln, that preservation of the Union was paramount. Only a few abolitionists looked on the war as a way to end slavery. However, by war's end, more and more Northerners had come to believe that freeing the slaves was just as important as restoring the Union.

The major military and political turning points of the war

The war strategies for both sides were relatively clear and simple. The South planned a defensive war, wearing down the North until it agreed to peace on Southern terms. The only exceptions were to gain control of Washington, D.C., go north through the Shenandoah Valley into Maryland and Pennsylvania in order to drive a wedge between the Northeast and Midwest, interrupt the lines of communication, and end the war quickly.

The North had three basic strategies:

1. Blockade the Confederate coastline in order to cripple the South

2. Seize control of the Mississippi River and interior railroad lines to split the Confederacy in half

3. Seize the Confederate capital of Richmond, Virginia, and drive southward to join Union forces coming east from the Mississippi Valley

The Civil War took more American lives than any other war in history, the South losing one-third of its soldiers in battle and the North losing about one-sixth. More than half of the total deaths were caused by disease and the horrendous conditions of field hospitals. Both armies paid a tremendous economic price but the South suffered more severely from direct damages. Towns, farms, trade, industry, lives and homes of men, women, and children were all destroyed, and an entire Southern way of life was lost. The deep resentment, bitterness, and hatred that remained for generations gradually lessened as the years went by, but legacies of it surface and remain to this day. The South had no voice in the political, social, and cultural affairs of the nation, lessening the influence of traditional Southern ideals.

The Civil War took more American lives than any other war in history.

The effects of the Civil War were tremendous. It changed the methods of waging war and has been called the first modern war. It introduced weapons and tactics that, when improved later, were used extensively in wars of the late 1800s and 1900s. Civil War soldiers were the first to fight in trenches, first to fight under a unified command, and first to wage a defense called "major cordon defense," a strategy of advance on all fronts. They were also the first to use repeating and breech loading weapons. Observation balloons were first used during the war, along with submarines, ironclad ships, and mines.

Telegraphy and railroads were first put to use in the Civil War. It was considered "total war," involving the use of all the resources of the opposing sides. There was probably no way it could have ended other than the total defeat and unconditional surrender of one side or the other.

By executive proclamation and constitutional amendment, slavery was officially ended, although deep prejudice and racism remained. The Union was preserved and the states were united.

Plans for Reconstruction and its implementation

Following the Civil War, the nation was faced with repairing the torn Union and readmitting the Confederate states. RECONSTRUCTION refers to this period between 1865 and 1877 when the federal and state governments debated and implemented plans to provide civil rights to freed slaves and to set the terms under which the former Confederate states might once again join the Union.

> **RECONSTRUCTION:** the period between 1865 and 1877 when the federal and state governments debated and implemented plans to provide civil rights to freed slaves and to set the terms under which the former Confederate states might once again join the Union

Planning for Reconstruction began early in the war, in 1861. Abraham Lincoln's Republican Party in Washington favored the extension of voting rights to black men, but was divided as to how far to extend the right. Moderates, such as Lincoln, wanted only literate blacks and those who had fought for the Union to be allowed to vote. Radical Republicans wanted to extend the vote to all black men. Conservative Democrats did not want to give black men the vote at all. In the case of former Confederate soldiers, moderates wanted to allow all but former leaders to vote, while the radicals wanted to require an oath from all eligible voters that they had never borne arms against the U.S., which would have excluded all former rebels. On the issue of readmission into the Union, moderates favored a much lower standard, with the radicals demanding nearly impossible conditions for rebel states to return.

Lincoln's moderate plan for Reconstruction was actually part of his effort to win the war. Lincoln and the moderates felt that if it remained easy for states to return to the Union, and if moderate proposals on black suffrage were made, that Confederate states involved in the hostilities might be swayed to rejoin the Union rather than continue fighting. The radical plan was to ensure that Reconstruction did not actually start until after the war was over.

In 1863, Abraham Lincoln was assassinated, leaving his Vice President Andrew Johnson to oversee the beginning of the actual implementation of Reconstruction. Johnson took a moderate position, and was willing to allow former confederates to keep control of their state governments. These governments quickly enacted Black Codes that denied the vote to blacks and granted them only limited civil rights.

In 1866, the radical Republicans won control of Congress and passed the Reconstruction Acts, which placed the governments of the Southern states under the control of the federal military. With this backing, the Republicans began to implement their radical policies, such as granting all black men the vote and denying the vote to former Confederate soldiers. Congress had passed the 13th, 14th and 15th amendments, granting citizenship and civil rights to blacks, and made ratification of these amendments a condition of readmission into the Union for the rebel states. The Republicans found support in the South among Freedmen, as former slaves were called, white Southerners who had not supported the Confederacy, called Scalawags, and Northerners who had moved to the South, known as Carpetbaggers.

Federal troops were stationed throughout the South and protected Republicans who took control of Southern governments. Bitterly resentful, white Southerners fought the new political system by joining a secret society called the Ku Klux Klan, using violence to keep black Americans from voting and getting equality. However, before being allowed to rejoin the Union, the Confederate states were required to agree to all federal laws. Between 1866 and 1870, all of them had returned to the Union, but Northern interest in Reconstruction was fading. Reconstruction officially ended when the last Federal troops left the South in 1877. It can be said that Reconstruction had a limited success, because it set up public school systems and expanded the legal rights of black Americans. Nevertheless, racism and discrimination have continued to this day.

The rise of the Redeemer governments marked the beginning of the Jim Crow laws and official segregation. Blacks were still allowed to vote, but ways were found to make it difficult for them to do so, such as literacy tests and poll taxes. Reconstruction, which had set as its goal the reunification of the South with the North and civil rights for freed slaves was a limited success, at best, and in the eyes of blacks was considered a failure.

Segregation laws were foreshadowed in the Black Codes, strict laws proposed by some Southern states during the Reconstruction Period that sought to essentially recreate the conditions of pre-war servitude. Under these codes, blacks were to remain subservient to their white employers, and were subject to fines and beatings if they failed to work. Freedmen, as newly freed slaves were called, were afforded some civil rights protection during the Reconstruction period; however, beginning around 1876, so–called Redeemer governments began to take office in Southern states after the removal of Federal troops that had supported Reconstruction goals. The Redeemer state legislatures began passing segregation laws, which came to be known as Jim Crow laws.

The Jim Crow laws varied from state to state, but the most significant of them required separate school systems and libraries for blacks and whites and separate ticket windows, waiting rooms and seating areas on trains and, later, other public transportation. Restaurant owners were permitted or sometimes required to provide separate entrances, tables, and counters for blacks and whites, so that the two races would not interact while dining. Public parks and playgrounds were constructed for each race. Landlords were not allowed to mix black and white tenants in apartment houses in some states.

The Jim Crow laws were given credibility in 1896 when the Supreme Court handed down its decision in the case *Plessy vs. Ferguson*. In 1890, Louisiana had

The Jim Crow laws varied from state to state, but the most significant of them required separate school systems and libraries for blacks and whites and separate ticket windows, waiting rooms and seating areas on trains and, later, other public transportation.

passed a law requiring separate train cars for blacks and whites. To challenge this law, in 1892 Homer Plessy, a man who had a black great–grandparent and so was considered legally "black" in that state, purchased a ticket in the white section and took his seat. Upon informing the conductor that he was black, he was told to move to the black car. He refused and was arrested. His case was eventually presented to the Supreme Court.

Foreign Policy

In the early years of the American nation, three primary ideas determined American foreign policy:

1. Isolationism: The founding fathers and the earliest Americans (after the Revolution) tended to believe that the U.S. had been created and destined for a unique role as what Thomas Jefferson called the "City on the Hill." They understood personal and religious freedom as a unique blessing given by God to the people of the nation. Although many hoped the nation would grow, this expectation did not extend to efforts to plant colonies in other parts of the world.

2. "No Entangling Alliances": George Washington's farewell address had initially espoused the intention of avoiding permanent alliances in any part of the world. This was echoed in Jefferson's inaugural address. In fact, when James Madison led the nation into the war of 1812, he refrained from entering an alliance with France, which was also at war with England at the time.

3. Nationalism: The American experience had created a profound wariness of any encroachment onto the continent by European countries. The Monroe Doctrine was a clear warning: No new colonies in the Americas. Nationalism found individual expression in Regionalism (the political division of an area into partially autonomous regions or loyalty to the interests of a particular region) and Sectionalism (excessive devotion to local interests and customs).

In the United States, territorial expansion occurred in the expansion westward under the banner of MANIFEST DESTINY, the belief in the divinely given right of the nation to expand westward and incorporate more of the continent into the nation. This belief had been expressed at the end of the Revolutionary War, in the demand that Britain cede all lands east of the Mississippi River to America.

> **MANIFEST DESTINY:** the belief in the divinely given right of the nation to expand westward and incorporate more of the continent into the nation

The Mexican-American War

The goal of expanding westward was further confirmed with the Northwest Ordinance (1787) and the Louisiana Purchase (1803). Manifest Destiny was the justification of the Mexican-American War (1846–48), which resulted in the annexation of Texas and California, as well as much of the southwest. Due to the U.S. involvement in the War with Mexico, the Spanish-American War, and support of the Latin American colonies of Spain in their revolt for independence, the Spanish colonies were successful in their fight for independence and self-government.

After the U.S. purchased the Louisiana Territory, Jefferson appointed Captains Meriwether Lewis and William Clark to explore it, to find out exactly what had been bought. The Corps of Discovery went all the way to the Pacific Ocean, returning two years later with maps, journals, and artifacts. This led the way for future explorers to learn and share more about the territory and resulted in the Westward Movement and the later belief in the doctrine of Manifest Destiny. The U.S. and Britain had shared the Oregon country. By the 1840s, with the increase in the free and slave populations and the demand of the settlers for control and government by the U.S., the conflict had to be resolved. In a treaty, signed in 1846 by both nations, Britain gave up its claims south of the 49th parallel.

The Mexican government encouraged and allowed extensive trade and settlement, especially in Texas. Many of the new settlers were southerners and brought their slaves with them. Slavery was outlawed in Mexico and technically illegal in Texas, although the Mexican government looked the other way.

Friction increased between land-hungry Americans swarming into western lands and the Mexican government, which controlled these lands. The clash was not only political but also cultural and economic. The Spanish influence permeated all parts of southwestern life: law, language, architecture, and customs. By this time, the doctrine of Manifest Destiny was in the hearts and on the lips of those seeking new areas of settlement and a new life. Americans were demanding U.S. control of not only the Mexican Territory but also of Oregon. Peaceful negotiations with Great Britain secured Oregon, but it took two years of war to gain control of the southwestern U.S.

In addition, the Mexican government owed debts to U.S. citizens whose property was damaged or destroyed during its struggle for independence from Spain. By the time war broke out in 1845, Mexico had not paid its war debts. The government was weak, corrupt, irresponsible, torn by revolutions, and in poor financial shape. Mexico was also bitter over American expansion into Texas and the 1836 revolution, which resulted in Texas independence. In the 1844 Presidential election, the Democrats pushed for annexation of Texas and Oregon and, after winning, they started the procedure to admit Texas to the Union. When statehood was granted, diplomatic relations between the U.S. and Mexico ended.

President Polk wanted U.S. control of the entire southwest, from Texas to the Pacific Ocean. He sent a diplomatic mission with an offer to purchase New

Mexico and Upper California, but the Mexican government refused to even receive the diplomat. Consequently, in 1846, each nation claimed aggression on the part of the other and war was declared. The treaty signed in 1848 and a subsequent one in 1853 established the southwestern boundary of the United States, reaching to the Pacific Ocean, as President Polk wished.

Religion in America

THE SECOND GREAT AWAKENING was an evangelical Protestant revival that preached personal responsibility for one's actions both individually and socially. This movement was led by preachers such as Charles Finney who traveled the country preaching the gospel of social responsibility. This point of view was taken up by the mainline Protestant denominations (Episcopal, Methodist, Presbyterian, Lutheran, and Congregational). Part of the social reform movement that led to an end to child labor, to better working conditions, and to other changes in social attitudes arose from this new recognition that the Christian faith should be used for the good of society. Closely allied to the Second Great Awakening was the temperance movement. This movement to end the sale and consumption of alcohol arose from religious beliefs, the violence many women and children experienced from heavy drinkers, and from the effect of alcohol consumption on the workforce.

Utopianism is the dream of or the desire to create the perfect society. However, by the nineteenth century few believed this was possible. One of the major causes of utopianism is the desire for moral clarity. Against the backdrop of the efforts of a young nation to define itself and to ensure the rights and freedoms of its citizens, and within the context of the Second Great Awakening, it becomes quite easy to see how the reform movements, the religious sentiment, and the gathering national storm would lead to the rise of expressions of desire to create the perfect society.

> **THE SECOND GREAT AWAKENING:** an evangelical Protestant revival that preached personal responsibility for one's actions both individually and socially

The United States as a World Power

When revolution began in Cuba, it aroused the interest and concern of Americans who were aware of what was happening just to the south of their borders. When the Spanish attempted to put down the revolt, the women and children of Cuba were treated with great cruelty. They were gathered into camps surrounded by armed guards and given little food. President McKinley had refused to recognize the rebellion, but had affirmed the possibility of American intervention. Spain resented this.

In February 1898, the American battleship *Maine* was blown up in Havana harbor. Although there was no incontrovertible evidence that the Spanish were responsible, popular sentiment accused Spanish agents and war became inevitable. Two months later, Congress declared war on Spain and the U.S. achieved a quick victory. The peace treaty gave the U.S. possession of Puerto Rico, the Philippines, Guam and Hawaii, which was annexed during the war.

Although the idea of a canal in Panama goes back to the early sixteenth century, work did not begin until 1880 by the French. The effort collapsed and the U.S. completed the task, opening the Panama Canal in 1914. Construction was an enormous task of complex engineering. The canal connects the Gulf of Panama in the Pacific Ocean with the Caribbean Sea and the Atlantic Ocean. It eliminated the need for ships to skirt the southern boundary of South America, effectively reducing the sailing distance from New York to San Francisco by 8,000 miles (over half of the total distance). The Canal results in a shorter and faster voyage, thus reducing shipping time and cost. The U.S. helped Panama win independence from Colombia in exchange for control of the Panama Canal Zone. A large investment was made in eliminating disease from the area, particularly yellow fever and malaria.

After WWII, control of the canal became an issue of contention between the U.S. and Panama. Negotiations toward a settlement began in 1974, resulting in the Torrijos-Carter Treaties of 1977. These treaties began the process of handing the canal over to Panama. On December 31, 1999, control of the canal was handed over to the Panama Canal Authority.

The Open Door Policy refers to maintaining equal commercial and industrial rights for the people of all countries in a particular territory. The Open Door Policy generally refers to China, but it has also been applied to the Congo basin. The essential purpose of the policy was to permit equal access to trade for all nations with treaties with China while protecting the integrity of the Chinese empire. This policy was in effect from about 1900 until the end of WWII.

Big Stick Diplomacy was a term adopted from an African proverb, "speak softly and carry a big stick," to describe President Theodore Roosevelt's policy of the U.S. as an international police power in the Western Hemisphere. The phrase implied the power to retaliate if necessary. The intention was to safeguard American economic interests in Latin America. The policy led to the expansion of the U.S. Navy and to greater involvement in world affairs. Should any nation in the Western Hemisphere become vulnerable to European control because of political or economic instability, the U.S. had both the right and the obligation to intervene.

Dollar Diplomacy describes U.S. efforts under President Taft to extend its foreign policy goals in Latin America and East Asia via economic power. The designation derives from Taft's claim that U.S. interests in Latin America had changed from "warlike and political" to "peaceful and economic." Taft justified this policy in terms of protecting the Panama Canal. The practice of dollar diplomacy was occasionally violent, particularly in Nicaragua. When revolts or revolutions occurred, the U.S. sent troops to resolve the situation. Immediately upon resolution, bankers were sent in to loan money to the new regimes. The policy persisted until the election of Woodrow Wilson to the Presidency in 1913.

Wilson repudiated the dollar diplomacy approach to foreign policy within weeks of his inauguration. Wilson's "moral diplomacy" became the model for American foreign policy to this day. Wilson envisioned a federation of democratic nations, believing that democracy and representative government were the foundation of world stability. Specifically, he saw Great Britain and the United States as the champions of self-government and the promoters of world peace. Wilson's beliefs and actions set in motion an American foreign policy that was dedicated to the interests of all humanity rather than merely national interests. Wilson promoted the power of free trade and international commerce as the key to enlarging the national economy into world markets as a means of acquiring a voice in world events.

The 1920s were a period of relative prosperity under the leadership of Warren G. Harding and Calvin Coolidge. Harding had promised a return to "normalcy" in the aftermath of World War I. During most of the decade, the output of industry boomed and the automobile industry put almost 27 million cars on the road. Per capita income rose for almost everyone except farmers.

A huge wave of labor strikes sought a return to wartime working conditions when the work day was shorter, wages were higher, and conditions were better. Occasionally, these labor strikes turned violent. Many Americans viewed the early strikes as the work of radicals, who were labeled "reds" (communists).

At this time, some Americans feared a Bolshevik-type revolution in America. As a result, many individuals were jailed for expressing views that were considered anarchist, communist or socialist. In an attempt to control the potential for revolution, civil liberties were ignored and thousands were deported. Several state and local governments passed a variety of laws designed to reduce what they considered to be radical speech and activity.

The Ku Klux Klan (KKK) is a name that has been used by several white supremacist organizations through history. Their beliefs encompass white supremacy, anti-Semitism, racism, anti-Catholicism and nativism. Their typical methods of intimidation have included terrorism, violence, and cross burning. The birth of the organization was in 1866. At that time, members were veterans of the Confederate Army seeking to resist Reconstruction.

The Klan entered a second period beginning in 1915. Using the new film medium, this group tried to spread its message with *The Birth of a Nation*. They also published a number of anti-Semitic newspaper articles. The group became a structured membership organization. Its membership did not begin to decline until the Great Depression. Although the KKK began in the South, its membership at its peak extended into the Midwest, the Northern states, and even into Canada. Membership during the 1920s reached approximately 4 million—20 percent of the adult white male population in many regions, and as high as 40 percent in some areas. The political influence of the group was significant; the Klan they essentially controlled the governments of Tennessee, Indiana, Oklahoma and Oregon as well as some Southern legislatures.

The National Association for the Advancement of Colored People (NAACP) was founded in 1909 to assist African Americans. In the early years, the work of the organization focused on working through the courts to overturn "Jim Crow" statutes that legalized racial discrimination. The group organized voters to oppose Woodrow Wilson's efforts to weave racial segregation into federal government policy. Between WWI and WWII, much energy was devoted to stopping the lynching of blacks throughout the country.

The Anti-Defamation League was created in 1913 to stop discrimination against the Jewish people. The organization has historically opposed all groups considered anti-Semitic or racist. This has included the Ku Klux Klan, the Nazis, and a variety of others.

Innovation

Although the British patent for the radio was awarded in 1896, it was not until WWI that the equipment and capability of the use of radio was recognized. The first radio program was broadcast on August 31, 1920. The first entertainment broadcasts began in 1922 from England. One of the first developments in the twentieth century was the use of commercial AM radio stations for aircraft navigation. In addition, radio was used to communicate orders and information between army and navy units on both sides of the war during WWI. Broadcasting became practical in the 1920s. Radio receivers were introduced on a wide scale.

Another innovation of the 1920s was the introduction of MASS PRODUCTION. This is the production of large amounts of standardized products on production lines. The method became very popular when Henry Ford used mass production to build the Model T Ford. The process facilitates high production rates per worker and thereby creates very inexpensive products. The process is, however, capital intensive. It requires expensive machinery in proportion to the number of workers needed to operate it.

MASS PRODUCTION: the production of large amounts of standardized products on production lines

The Great Depression and the New Deal

The 1929 stock market crash was the powerful event that is generally interpreted as the beginning of the Great Depression in America. Although the crash of the stock market was unexpected, it was not without identifiable causes. The 1920s had been a decade of social and economic growth and hope. But the attitudes and actions of the 1920s regarding wealth, production, and investment created several trends that quietly set the stage for the 1929 disaster.

Another factor contributing to the Great Depression was the economic conditions in Europe. The U.S. was lending money to European nations to rebuild. Many of these countries used this money to purchase U.S. food and manufactured goods. But they were not able to pay off their debts.

Several other factors may have contributed to the Great Depression. First, in 1929, the Federal Reserve increased interest rates. Second, as interest rates rose and the stock market began to decline, people began to hoard money. This was certainly the case after the crash.

In September 1929, stock prices began to slip, yet people remained optimistic. On Monday, October 21, prices began to fall quickly. The volume traded was so high that the tickers were unable to keep up. Investors were frightened, and they started selling very quickly. This caused further collapse. For the next two days prices stabilized somewhat. On Black Thursday, October 24, prices plummeted again. By this time investors had lost confidence. On Friday and Saturday an attempt to stop the crash was made by some leading bankers. But on Monday the 28th, prices began to fall again, declining by 13% in one day. The next day, Black Tuesday, October 29, saw 16.4 million shares traded. Stock prices fell so far that at many times no one was willing to buy at any price.

> More than 100,000 businesses failed between 1929 and 1932.

Unemployment quickly reached 25% nationwide. People thrown out of their homes created makeshift domiciles of cardboard, scraps of wood and tents. With unmasked reference to President Hoover, who was quite obviously overwhelmed by the situation and incompetent to deal with it, these communities were called Hoovervilles. Families stood in bread lines, rural workers left the dust bowl of the plains to search for work in California, and banks failed. The despair that swept the nation left an indelible scar on all who endured the Depression.

When the stock market crashed, businesses collapsed. Without demand for products, other businesses and industries collapsed. This, in turn, brought down the businesses and industries that provided raw materials or components to these industries. Hundreds of thousands of Americans lost their jobs.

Hoover's bid for reelection in 1932 failed. The new president, Franklin D. Roosevelt, won the White House on his promise of a "New Deal." Upon assuming the office, Roosevelt and his advisers immediately launched a massive program of innovation and experimentation to try to bring the Depression to an end. Congress gave the President unprecedented power to act to save the nation. During the next eight years, the most extensive and broadly-based legislation in the nation's history was enacted. The legislation was intended to accomplish three goals: relief, recovery, and reform.

The first step in the New Deal was to relieve suffering. This was accomplished through a number of job-creation projects. The second step, the recovery aspect, was to stimulate the economy. The third step was to create social and economic change through innovative legislation.

Congress passed the Glass-Steagall Act, which separated banking and investing. The Securities and Exchange Commission was created to regulate dangerous speculative practices on Wall Street. The Wagner Act guaranteed a number of rights to workers and unions in an effort to improve worker-employer relations. The SOCIAL SECURITY ACT OF 1935 established pensions for the aged and infirm as well as a system of unemployment insurance.

> **SOCIAL SECURITY ACT OF 1935:** established pensions for the aged and infirm as well as a system of unemployment insurance

By far the worst natural disaster of the decade came to be known as the Dust Bowl. Due to severe and prolonged drought in the Great Plains and previous reliance on inappropriate farming techniques, a series of devastating dust storms occurred in the 1930s that resulted in destruction, economic ruin for many, and dramatic ecological change.

Crops were ruined, the land was destroyed, and people either lost or abandoned homes and farms. Fifteen percent of Oklahoma's population left. Because so many of the migrants were from Oklahoma, the migrants came to be called Okies no matter where they came from. Estimates of the number of people displaced by this disaster range from 300,000 or 400,000 to 2.5 million.

In the aftermath of the Second World War, with the Soviet Union having emerged as a competing power, the United States embarked on a policy known as Containment of the Communist menace. This involved what came to be known as the Marshall Plan and the Truman Doctrine. The Marshall Plan involved the economic aid that was sent to Europe in the aftermath of the Second World War aimed at preventing the spread of communism.

Harry S. Truman became president near the end of WWII. He is credited with some of the most important decisions in history. When Japan refused to surrender, Truman authorized dropping atomic bombs on Japanese cities dedicated to war support: Hiroshima and Nagasaki. He took to the Congress a 21-point plan that came to be known as the Fair Deal. It included:

- Expansion of Social Security

- A full-employment program

- Public housing and slum clearance

- A permanent Fair Employment Practices Act

The Truman Doctrine provided support for Greece and Turkey when they were threatened by the Soviet Union. The Marshall Plan (named after his Secretary of State) stimulated economic recovery for Western Europe. Truman participated in the negotiations that resulted in the formation of the North Atlantic Treaty Organization. He and his administration believed it necessary to support South Korea when it was threatened by the communist government of North Korea. But he contained American involvement in Korea so as not to risk conflict with China or Russia.

Dwight David Eisenhower succeeded Truman. Eisenhower obtained a truce in Korea and worked during his two terms to mitigate the tension of the Cold War. When Stalin died, he was able to negotiate a peace treaty with Russia that neutralized Austria. His domestic policy was moderate. He continued most of the programs introduced under both the New Deal and the Fair Deal. When desegregation of schools began, he sent troops to Little Rock, Arkansas to enforce desegregation. He ordered the complete desegregation of the military. During his administration, the Department of Health, Education and Welfare was established and the National Aeronautics and Space Administration was formed.

John F. Kennedy is widely remembered for his Inaugural Address in which he asked, "Ask not what your country can do for you—ask what you can do for your country." His campaign pledge was to get America moving again. During his brief presidency, his economic programs created the longest period of continuous expansion in the country since WWII. He wanted the U.S. to again take up the mission as the first country committed to the preservation of human rights. Through the Alliance for Progress and the Peace Corps, the nation reached out to assist developing nations. He was deeply and passionately involved in the cause of equal rights for all Americans and he drafted new civil rights legislation. He also drafted plans for a broad attack on the systemic problems of privation and poverty.

In 1962, during the administration of President John F. Kennedy, Premier Khrushchev and the Soviets decided to install nuclear missiles on the island of Cuba as a protective measure against an American invasion. In October, American U-2 spy planes photographed what were identified as missile bases under construction. The White House needed to decide how to handle the situation without starting a war.

The only recourse was removal of the missile sites. Kennedy announced that the U.S. had set up a "quarantine" of Soviet ships heading to Cuba. It was in reality a blockade, but the word itself could not be used publicly because a blockade was considered an act of war.

Lyndon B. Johnson assumed the presidency after the assassination of Kennedy. His vision for America was called A Great Society. He won support in Congress for the largest group of legislative programs in the history of the nation. These included programs Kennedy had been working on at the time of his death, including a new civil rights bill and a tax cut. He defined the great society as "a place where the meaning of man's life matches the marvels of man's labor." The legislation enacted during his administration included: an attack on disease, urban renewal, Medicare, aid to education, conservation and beautification, development of economically depressed areas, a war on poverty, voting rights for all, and control of crime and delinquency. Johnson managed an unpopular military action in Vietnam and encouraged the exploration of space. During his administration the Department of Transportation was formed and the first African American, Thurgood Marshall, was nominated and confirmed to the Supreme Court.

Richard Nixon inherited racial unrest and the Vietnam War, from which he extracted the American military. His administration is probably best known for improved relations with both China and the USSR. However, the Watergate scandal divided the country and led to his resignation. His major domestic achievements were: the appointment of conservative justices to the Supreme Court, new anti-crime legislation, a broad environmental program, revenue sharing legislation, and ending the draft.

Gerald Ford was the first vice president selected under the 25th Amendment. The challenges that faced his administration were a depressed economy, inflation, energy shortages, and the need to champion world peace. Once inflation slowed and recession was the major economic problem, he instituted measures that would stimulate the economy. He tried to reduce the role of the federal government. He reduced business taxes and lessened the controls on business. His international focus was on preventing a major war in the Middle East. He negotiated limitations on nuclear weapons with Russia.

Jimmy Carter strove to make the government "competent and compassionate" in response to the American people and their expectations. Although significant progress was made by his administration in creating jobs and decreasing the budget deficit, inflation and interest rates were near record highs.

Some of Carter's notable achievements are: establishment of a national energy policy to deal with the energy shortage, decontrolling petroleum prices to stimulate production, civil service reform that improved government efficiency, deregulation of the trucking and airline industries, the creation of the Department of Education, negotiating the framework for peace in the Middle East, leading in the establishment of diplomatic relations with China, and reaching a Strategic Arms

Limitation Agreement with the Soviet Union. He expanded the national park system, supported the Social Security system, and appointed a record number of women and minorities to government jobs.

Iran's Ayatollah Khomeini's extreme hatred for the U.S. was the result of the 1953 overthrow of Iran's Mossadegh government, sponsored by the CIA. To make matters worse, the CIA proceeded to train the Shah's ruthless secret police force. So when the terminally ill exiled Shah was allowed into the U.S. for medical treatment, a mob supported and encouraged by Khomeini stormed into the American embassy, taking the 53 Americans as prisoners.

President Carter froze all Iranian assets in the U.S., set up trade restrictions, and approved a risky rescue attempt, which failed. He had appealed to the UN for aid in gaining release for the hostages and to European allies to join the trade embargo on Iran. Khomeini ignored UN requests for releasing the Americans and Europeans refused to support the embargo so as not to risk losing access to Iran's oil. American prestige was damaged and Carter's chances for reelection were doomed. The hostages were released on the day of Ronald Reagan's inauguration as President when Carter released Iranian assets as ransom.

Ronald Reagan introduced an innovative program that came to be known as the Reagan Revolution. The goal of this program was to reduce the reliance of the American people upon government. His legislative accomplishments include stimulating economic growth, curbing inflation, increasing employment, and strengthening the national defense. He won Congressional support for a complete overhaul of the income tax code in 1986 in favor businesses and the upper and middle classes. By the time he left office there was prosperity in peacetime with no depression or recession. His foreign policy was "peace through strength." Reagan nominated Sandra Day O'Connor as the first female justice on the Supreme Court.

George H. W. Bush, a Republican, was responsible for anti-drug programs and Federal deregulation during the Reagan administration. When the Cold War ended and the Soviet Union broke apart, he supported the rise of democracy, but took a position of restraint toward the new nations. Bush also dealt with defense of the Panama Canal and Iraq's invasion of Kuwait, which led to the first Gulf War, known as Desert Storm. Although his international affairs record was strong, he was not able to turn around increased violence in the inner cities and a struggling economy.

William Clinton led the nation in a time of greater peace and economic prosperity than has been experienced at any other time in history. His domestic accomplishments include: the lowest inflation in 30 years, the lowest unemployment rate in modern days, the highest home ownership rate in history, lower crime rates in many places, and smaller welfare rolls. He proposed and achieved a balanced budget and achieved a budget surplus.

George W. Bush was serving his first term in office when the most devastating act of terrorism on American soil occurred—the bombing of the World Trade Center and the Pentagon on September 11, 2001. Tasked with Americans' safety and peace of mind, Bush arranged the most dramatic reorganization of the federal government since the Cold War, restructuring the nation's intelligence community and implementing new organizations like the Department of Homeland Security. In addition to his role in the Iraq and Afghanistan Wars, Bush's two-term tenure included the No Child Left Behind Act, a bipartisan measure intended to raise school standards and accountability in exchange for federal funding; federal income tax cuts, which lead to an unprecedented 52 straight months of job creation; and a new Medicare prescription drug benefit, which benefited 40 million seniors and other recipients. Bush was also responsible for appointing a new Chief Justice, John Roberts and Justice Samuel Alito to the U.S. Supreme Court. One of Bush's most criticized initiatives while in office surrounded his response to the 2005 Hurricane Katrina disaster in New Orleans. Federal, state, and local governments' inability to respond fast enough and with the proper resources garnered negative media attention for months following the catastrophe.

Barack Obama made history in 2008 when he was elected as the first African-American president. Since then, Obama has continued to make history by signing into law health care and financial reforms. The health care reform was developed to make health care more affordable, hold health insurance companies accountable, and extend health coverage to all Americans. The Dodd-Frank Wall Street Reform and Consumer Protection Act encompasses numerous financial reforms including an independent watchdog housed at the Federal Reserve, measures to limit large financial companies, an advanced warning system, investor protection measures, and other fiscal stabilization policies. While Obama has made improvement in foreign relations, especially with the Muslim community, he has had the challenge of high unemployment rates, an unstable housing market, and failing businesses, the result of some of the hardest economic times since the Great Depression. Additionally, Obama has had to oversee clean-up and political criticism for one of the world's most devastating disasters, the BP oil spill in the Gulf of Mexico in 2010.

The History of Oregon

The history of Oregon is closely tied to the history of western expansion and has parallels with other periods of American growth. Just as American pioneers slowly pushed westward toward the Mississippi River, establishing a foothold in the Midwest, so did pioneers expand the American settlement into the Oregon

Territory. Just as in California and much of the Midwest, Oregon was claimed by another country when settlers started moving in, making American expansion an international matter. The U.S. went to war with Mexico over land claims, which resulted in the annexation of California, and was at the brink of war with Britain over the border each claimed between their shares of the Oregon Territory.

Growth in Oregon followed a similar pattern to the rest of the country. The Native American population was slowly absorbed or removed to reservations and communities of mainly white settlers were established. Just as the conditions during World Wars spurred the migration of African–Americans from the south to northern cities, they also brought African–Americans to Oregon to work in war-related industries such as shipbuilding. The Dust Bowl of the 1930s contributed to Oregon's growth as many farmers moved west to find agricultural work.

SKILL 9.2 Recognize the importance and lasting influence of people, events, issues, and developments in Oregon history (e.g., indigenous peoples of the region, the Lewis and Clark Expedition, nineteenth-century westward migration, human rights policies and practices, the use and conservation of natural resources)

Several Native American groups thrived in Oregon. Europeans exploring the West Coast of North America found them living along the sea and many rivers and inlets, fishing and hunting. These natives had already developed a complex trading system with natives that lived further inland, and began trading with the newcomers as well. The trappers that were drawn to the area learned from the natives and also traded with them. Thus the Natives Americans facilitated the economic drive that would eventually lead to the westward expansion of the U.S. into the Oregon Territory.

In 1803, under President Thomas Jefferson, the U.S. purchased a large section of what is now the central United States from France. Called the Louisiana Purchase, this acquisition nearly doubled the area of the young country. In 1804, Jefferson dispatched Meriwether Lewis and William Clark to explore the newly purchased land, to report back on what they found, and, if possible, to seek out the fabled Northwest Passage—a water route to the Pacific Ocean.

Lewis and Clark assembled a group of explorers that included a young Native American woman named Sacagawea, who would act as guide and interpreter. The band traveled up the Missouri River as far as possible and turned west, eventually making their way to the Columbia River, which they followed to the Pacific.

Lewis and Clark's expedition was a turning point in Oregon's history. The region had been partly explored by water, but now a land route was opened that connected the area to the United States. News of the abundance of fur animals brought trappers and other explorers, and within a decade a permanent settlement was established, paving the way for future American settlement.

The Oregon Trail defines American westward expansion and was named so because the Oregon territory was the final destination of many settlers in the 1840s and 1850s. The first permanent American settlement west of the Rocky Mountains was in Oregon, at Fort Astoria at the mouth of the Columbia River. As news of Oregon's rich natural resources spread to the east, more families came to settle on the rich soil of western Oregon's river valleys, or to carve out a homestead in its wide forests. The Columbia, one of the great rivers of North America, provided Oregonians with transportation for their goods as industry grew. As the railroad expanded into the region, economic opportunity increased.

Oregon was admitted as a state shortly before the Civil War broke out, and took the side of the Union. It has developed a reputation for taking a liberal stance on human rights policies and practices over the years, although conservative movements among smaller town residents have often come into conflict with the more liberal views of people in the larger cities. Oregon has been in the forefront of the national debate over the right to assisted suicide and was the first state to make assisted suicide legal.

Oregon has always been rich in natural resources. The native people had an abundance of food available in the form of fish and game animals and used timber for shelter, tools and boats. With the increase of the fur trade, the number of fur animals began to decline. Timber became a dominant source of growth in the region beginning in the late nineteenth century, and increased as logging methods and transportation improved. Loggers found a seemingly endless supply of huge old-growth trees to feed their mills and provide lumber to a growing market. A conservation movement began in the 1960s and grew in strength through the 1970s as old-growth forests became scarcer and some woodland species began to lose habitat. Conservation became a popular ethic in Oregon, which began to clean up many of its polluted areas, including the Willamette River, which runs through Portland. Oregon was one of the first states to encourage recycling by passing a bottle deposit law. This conservation movement has often conflicted with logging companies and the communities that they supported. This, along with other economic factors, brought economic difficulty to many Oregonians. Similar conflicts are also taking place between conservationists and cattle grazers over water quality and water usage issues.

SKILL **Recognize the importance and lasting influence of events, 9.3 issues, and developments in U.S. history** *(e.g., American Revolution, Constitutional Convention, European immigration, Irish Potato Famine, Mexican War, slavery, the Civil War, Asian migration, child labor laws, women's suffrage, territorial expansion and imperialism, the Great Depression, the civil rights movement)*

See also Skill 9.1

The Irish Potato Famine

IRISH FAMINE OF 1845-1849: the cause of the famine was the appearance of "the blight;" this was the destruction of the potato crops due to a fungus

The IRISH FAMINE OF 1845-1849 is alternately referred to as the Irish Potato Famine, The Great Famine or the Great Hunger. The immediate cause of the famine was the appearance of "the blight." This was the destruction of the potato crops due to a fungus. The potato was the primary food source for much of the population of Ireland at the time. Deaths were not officially recorded, but are believed to be in the 500,000 to one million range during the five years from 1846 to 1851. Although estimates vary, the number of people who emigrated from Ireland is in the neighborhood of two million.

The famine was more than potato blight. It was the culmination of a biological, political, social, and economic catastrophe that can be attributed to both the British and the Irish. The famine essentially changed Irish culture and tradition forever.

POPERY ACT: prohibited Irish Catholics from passing family landholdings to a single son

The food value of the potato made it the single staple in the Irish food system. British laws (the POPERY ACT) prohibited Irish Catholics from passing family landholdings to a single son. This meant that land was subdivided among the male descendents in the family. The number of surviving male heirs was increasing, and this, combined with the opportunity to own land, led to sons marrying earlier and producing large families. With the legal restrictions on inheritance of land, this eventually meant that at the time when family size was increasing, the size of the land available to them was decreasing.

Ireland's economic and social vehicle for assistance to the poor was inadequate to meet the needs of the starving thousands. The program was funded by taxes charged to landholders on the basis of the number of tenants on the estate. As poverty and starvation increased, so did the financial need. This resulted in increasing tax rates on the landholders. To remain solvent, many landowners evicted tenants in an effort to reduce the tax bill. But this left more people poor and in need of assistance, which led to another increase in tax rates. In an effort to find an escape route from this vicious circle, some landowners paid passage to other countries rather than evict tenants. The ships on which they took passage came to be called "coffin ships," becuase many of these emigrants died during the voyage to North America. Many of the landowners who attempted to care for their tenants went bankrupt in the process. Ten percent of the estates were bankrupt by 1850. There were many charitable donations from around the world, but they were not adequate to solve such a large problem.

The responses of those leading the government of the United Kingdom were inadequate. It is believed that in 1851 the population of Ireland was 6.6 million. By 1911, it was only 4.4 million.

Civil Rights Movement

The phrase the CIVIL RIGHTS MOVEMENT generally refers to the nationwide effort made by black people and those who supported them to gain equal rights and to eliminate segregation. Discussion of this movement is generally understood in terms of the period of the 1950s and 1960s.

> **CIVIL RIGHTS MOVEMENT:** the nationwide effort made by black people and those who supported them to gain equal rights and to eliminate segregation

Key people in the Civil Rights Movement

Rosa Parks: A black seamstress from Montgomery Alabama who, in 1955, refused to give up her seat on the bus to a white man. This event is generally understood as the spark that lit the fire of the Civil Rights Movement. She has been called the "mother of the Civil Rights Movement."

Martin Luther King, Jr.: The most prominent member of the Civil Rights movement, King promoted nonviolent methods of opposition to segregation. The "Letter from Birmingham Jail" explained the purpose of nonviolent action as a way to make people notice injustice. He led the march on Washington in 1963, at which he delivered the "I Have a Dream" speech. He received the 1968 Nobel Prize for Peace.

James Meredith: The first African American to enroll at the University of Mississippi.

Emmett Till: A teenage boy who was murdered in Mississippi while visiting from Chicago. The crime of which he was accused was "whistling at a white woman in a store." He was beaten and murdered, and his body was dumped in a river. His two white abductors were apprehended and tried. They were acquitted by an all-white jury. After the acquittal, they admitted their guilt, but remained free because of double jeopardy laws.

Ralph Abernathy: A major figure in the Civil Rights Movement who succeeded Martin Luther King, Jr. as head of the Southern Christian Leadership Conference.

Malcolm X: A political leader and part of the Civil Rights Movement. He was a prominent Black Muslim.

Stokely Carmichael: One of the leaders of the Black Power movement that called for independent development of political and social institutions for blacks. Carmichael called for black pride and maintenance of black culture. He was head of the Student Nonviolent Coordinating Committee.

Key events of the Civil Rights Movement

Brown vs. Board of Education, 1954: The Supreme Court declared that Plessy v. Ferguson was unconstitutional. This was the ruling that had established Separate but Equal as the basis for segregation. With this decision, the Court ordered immediate desegregation.

Rosa Parks and the Montgomery Bus Boycott, 1955–56: After refusing to give up her seat on a bus in Montgomery, Alabama, Parks was arrested, tried, and convicted of disorderly conduct and violating a local ordinance. When word reached the black community, a bus boycott was organized to protest the segregation of blacks and whites on public buses. The boycott lasted 381 days, until the ordinance was lifted.

Strategy shift to "direct action": Nonviolent resistance and civil disobedience, 1955–1965. This action consisted mostly of bus boycotts, sit-ins, and freedom rides.

Formation of the Southern Christian Leadership Conference, 1957: This group, formed by Martin Luther King, Jr., John Duffy, Rev. C. D. Steele, Rev. T. J. Jemison, Rev. Fred Shuttlesworth, Ella Baker, A. Philip Randolph, Bayard Rustin, and Stanley Levison, provided training and assistance to local efforts to fight segregation. Non-violence was its central doctrine and its major method of fighting segregation and racism.

The Desegregation of Little Rock, 1957: Following up on the decision of the Supreme Court in Brown vs. Board of Education, the Arkansas school board voted to integrate the school system. The NAACP chose Arkansas as the place to push integration because it was considered a relatively progressive Southern state. However, the governor called up the National Guard to prevent nine black students from attending Little Rock's Central High School.

Sit-ins: In 1960, students began to stage "sit-ins" at local lunch counters and stores as a means of protesting the refusal of those businesses to desegregate. The first was in Greensboro, NC. This led to a rash of similar campaigns throughout the South. Demonstrators began to protest at parks, beaches, theaters, museums, and libraries. When arrested, the protesters made "jail-no-bail" pledges. This called attention to their cause and put the financial burden of providing jail space and food on the cities.

Freedom Rides: Activists traveled by bus throughout the Deep South to desegregate bus terminals (required by federal law). These protesters undertook extremely dangerous protests. Many buses were firebombed, attacked by the KKK, and riders were beaten. They were crammed into small, airless jail cells and mistreated in many ways. Key figures in this effort included John Lewis, James Lawson, Diane Nash, Bob Moses, James Bevel, Charles McDew, Bernard Lafayette, Charles Jones, Lonnie King, Julian Bond, Hosea Williams, and Stokely Carmichael.

The Birmingham Campaign, 1963–64: A campaign was planned to use sit-ins, kneel-ins in churches, and a march to the county building to launch a voter registration campaign. The City obtained an injunction forbidding all such protests. The protesters, including Martin Luther King, Jr., believed the injunction was unconstitutional, and defied it. They were arrested. While in jail, King wrote his famous "Letter from Birmingham Jail." When the campaign began to falter, the "Children's Crusade" called on students to leave school and join the protests. The events became news when more than 600 students were jailed. The next day more students joined the protest. The media was present, and broadcast to the nation vivid pictures of fire hoses being used to knock down children and dogs attacking some of them. The resulting public outrage led the Kennedy administration to intervene. About a month later, a committee was formed to end hiring discrimination, arrange for the release of jailed protesters, and establish normative communication between blacks and whites. Four months later, the KKK bombed the Sixteenth Street Baptist Church, killing four girls.

The March on Washington, 1963: This was a march on Washington for jobs and freedom. It was a combined effort of all major civil rights organizations. The goals of the march were: meaningful civil rights laws, a massive federal works program, full and fair employment, decent housing, the right to vote, and adequate integrated education. It was at this march that Martin Luther King, Jr. made the famous "I Have a Dream" speech.

Mississippi Freedom Summer, 1964: Students were brought from other states to Mississippi to assist local activists in registering voters, teaching in "Freedom schools" and in forming the Mississippi Freedom Democratic Party. Three of the workers disappeared; they were murdered by the KKK. It took six weeks to find their bodies. The national uproar forced President Johnson to send in the FBI. Johnson was able to use public sentiment to effect passage of the Civil Rights Act of 1964 in Congress.

Selma to Montgomery marches, 1965: Attempts to obtain voter registration in Selma, Alabama had been largely unsuccessful due to opposition from the city's sheriff. M.L. King came to the city to lead a series of marches. He and over 200 demonstrators were arrested and jailed. Each successive march was met with violent resistance by police. In March, a group of over 600 intended to walk from Selma to Montgomery (54 miles). News media were on hand when, 6 blocks into the march, state and local law enforcement officials attacked the marchers with billy clubs, tear gas, rubber tubes wrapped in barbed wire and bull whips. They were driven back to Selma. National broadcast of the footage provoked a nation-wide response. President Johnson again used public sentiment to achieve passage of the Voting Rights Act of 1965. This law changed the political landscape of the South irrevocably.

Key policies, legislation, and court cases of the Civil Rights Movement

Civil Rights Act of 1964: Bars discrimination in public accommodations, employment and education.

Voting Rights Act of 1965: Suspended poll taxes, literacy tests and other voter tests for voter registration.

Since 1941, a number of anti-discrimination laws have been passed by Congress. These acts have protected the civil rights of several groups of Americans. These laws include:

- Fair Employment Act of 1941
- Civil Rights Act of 1964
- Immigration and Nationality Services Act of 1965
- Voting Rights Act of 1965
- Civil Rights Act of 1968
- Age Discrimination in Employment Act of 1967
- Age Discrimination Act of 1975
- Pregnancy Discrimination Act of 1978
- Americans with Disabilities Act of 1990
- Civil Rights Act of 1991
- Employment Non-Discrimination Act

Minority Rights

The concept of minority rights encompasses two ideas: the first is the normal individual rights of members of ethnic, racial, class, religious or sexual minorities; the second is collective rights of minority groups. Various civil rights movements have sought to guarantee that the individual rights of persons are not denied on the basis of being part of a minority group. The effects of these movements may be seen in guarantees of minority representation, equal housing acts, and equal opportunity employment laws.

The disability rights movement was a successful effort to guarantee access to public buildings and transportation, equal access to education and employment, equal protection under the law in terms of access to insurance, and other basic rights of American citizens. As a result of these efforts, public buildings and public transportation must be accessible to persons with disabilities, and discrimination in hiring or housing on the basis of disability is also illegal.

A prisoners' rights movement has been working for many years to ensure the basic human rights of persons incarcerated for crimes.

Immigrant rights movements have worked for employment and housing rights, as well as preventing abuse of immigrants through hate crimes. In some states, immigrant rights movements have led to bilingual education and public information access.

Another group movement to obtain equal rights is the lesbian, gay, bisexual and transgender social movement. This movement seeks equal housing, freedom from social and employment discrimination, and equal recognition of relationships under the law.

The women's rights movement is concerned with the freedoms of women as differentiated from broader ideas of human rights. These issues are generally different from those that affect men and boys because of biological conditions or social constructs. The rights the movement has sought to protect throughout history include:

- The right to vote
- The right to work
- The right to fair wages
- The right to bodily integrity and autonomy
- The right to own property
- The right to an education
- The right to hold public office

> *The concept of minority rights encompasses two ideas: the first is the normal individual rights of members of ethnic, racial, class, religious or sexual minorities; the second is collective rights of minority groups.*

- Marital rights

- Parental rights

- Religious rights

- The right to serve in the military

- The right to enter into legal contracts

Some of the most famous leaders in the women's movement throughout American history are:

- Abigail Adams

- Susan B. Anthony

- Gloria E. Anzaldua

- Betty Friedan

- Olympe de Gouges

- Gloria Steinem

- Harriet Tubman

- Mary Wollstonecraft

- Virginia Woolf

- Germaine Greer

SKILL 9.4 **Analyze cause-and-effect relationships in the history of the United States and Oregon**

See also Skill 8.5

A chain of causes and effects can be traced through the early history of Oregon. The Louisiana Purchase led to the official exploration of the Oregon region by Lewis and Clark, who, upon their return, made known the abundance of fur-bearing animals there. This in turn led to the increase in trapping activity and the founding of a trading post at the mouth of the Columbia River, and eventually to the further settlement of the area.

SKILL 9.5 **Analyze various perspectives and interpretations of issues and events in U.S. and Oregon history**

See also Skills 9.1, 9.3, and 9.4

Prior to becoming an official part of the United States, Oregon was an international territory shared with the British. When the U.S. and Britain went to war in 1812, the permanent Oregon residents at Fort Clatsop had a unique perspective.

While they were sponsored by an American, John Jacob Astor, and worked for his American fur company, many of the men were British. Their solution was to keep an American and British flag handy, intending to fly whichever one was being flown by a visiting ship.

It seems Oregonians have shown a similar independent streak ever since, probably made possible at first by its remoteness from the eastern U.S. Oregon became a state just as the country was descending into the Civil War, but the war had very little direct effect on the new state, except to deprive it temporarily of federal troops. Oregon was more directly affected by World War II, which was fought partly against Japan. The coast of Oregon was the only place in the continental U.S. fired upon during WWII when a Japanese battleship launched a brief, unsuccessful attack on Battery Russell on the Oregon coast.

Many Americans of Japanese descent had settled in Oregon, and the United States adopted a policy of containing them out of fear that they would support Japan in the war. Many Japanese-American families were placed in large detainment centers, some of them located in Oregon. They were detained based solely on their heritage and not out of any specific belief that they might help Japan in the war. This policy was supported by many Americans and Oregonians at the time, but has left a lasting impact on the families that were detained.

As American trade with Japan and other Asian countries has increased, Oregon has benefited, owing to its large port and connections to other markets on the Pacific. The balance of trade with these other markets is an important national issue. Because Oregon itself is a provider of exports such as raw lumber, the trade balance is important to Oregon as a state. Because Oregon is also the point of entry for many Asian products, such as automobiles, it can benefit from increased trade regardless of the relative balance. Oregon is like most states in this way, having a perspective that must take in both national and state interests.

SKILL 9.6 Demonstrate knowledge of strategies for interpreting events, issues, and developments in local history

Research into local history usually requires local sources, such as newspapers, family histories, memoirs and oral interviews with local residents. Local records of births, deaths, land holdings, etc., can often be found at local courthouses and city halls.

Historical events can affect local communities in significant ways. A factory closing may not have a large impact on a state's economy, for instance, but might be

Interpreting the local historical events, issues and developments of a specific locality requires a sharp focus on how relatively small groups of people are affected by larger historical forces.

devastating for the town in which the factory was located. Interpreting the local historical events, issues and developments of a specific locality requires a sharp focus on how relatively small groups of people are affected by larger historical forces.

COMPETENCY 10
UNDERSTAND METHODS OF SOCIAL SCIENCE RESEARCH AND ANALYSIS

SKILL 10.1 Recognize methods for analyzing an event, issue, problem, or phenomenon and its significance to society

Sociologists and anthropologists are social scientists who study the issues, problems, and phenomena of societies.

In measuring the social significance of an event or issue, one of the first questions to ask is how many people are affected. Sweeping events such as wars, natural disasters, and revolutions are significant partly because they can change the way of life for many people in a short time.

Sometimes significant changes take place over long periods of time, however, so it is also important to look at long-term effects of an event or phenomenon, following the chain of causes and effects. In this way, sometimes events that seem insignificant at the time they occur, or which initially affect only a small number of people, can be linked directly to large societal changes.

SOCIOLOGY: the study of human society through the individuals, groups, and institutions that make it up

SOCIOLOGY is the study of human society through the individuals, groups, and institutions that make it up. Sociology includes every feature of human social conditions. It deals with the predominant behaviors, attitudes, and types of relationships within a society as defined by a group of people with a similar cultural background living in a specific geographical area. Sociology is divided into five major areas of study:

- Population studies: General social patterns of groups of people living in a certain geographical area

- **Social behaviors**: Changes in attitudes, morale, leadership, conformity, and other areas
- **Social institutions**: Organized groups of people performing specific functions within a society such as churches, schools, hospitals, business organizations, and governments
- **Cultural influences**: Customs, knowledge, arts, religious beliefs, and language
- **Social change**: Wars, revolutions, inventions, fashions, and other events or activities

Sociologists use three major methods to test and verify theories:

- Surveys
- Controlled experiments
- Field observations

ANTHROPOLOGY is the scientific study of human culture and humanity and the relationship between man and culture. Anthropologists study similarities and difference among different groups, how they relate to other cultures, and patterns of behavior. Their research is two-fold: cross-cultural and comparative. A major method of study is referred to as "participant observation." The anthropologist studies the people of a culture by living among them and participating with them in their daily lives. Other methods may be used, but this method is most characteristic.

> **ANTHROPOLOGY:** the scientific study of human culture and humanity and the relationship between man and culture

There are four types of anthropology:

Archaeology	Study of material remains of humans
Social-cultural	Study of norms, values, standards
Biological	Study of genetic characteristics
Linguistics	Study of the historical development of language

SKILL 10.2 Identify strategies for gathering, using, and evaluating information to support analysis and conclusions

Primary Sources

Primary sources include numerous kinds of materials; they are documents that reflect the immediate, everyday concerns of people. Some examples are:

- Memoranda
- Bills
- Deeds
- Charters
- Newspaper reports
- Pamphlets
- Graffiti
- Popular writings
- Journals or diaries
- Records of decision-making bodies
- Letters
- Receipts
- Snapshots

Other primary sources are theoretical writings that reflect care and consideration in composition and are an attempt to convince or persuade. These may include newspaper or magazine editorials, sermons, political speeches, philosophical writings, or narrative accounts of events, ideas, and trends, written by someone contemporary with the events described.

Literature and nonverbal materials, novels, stories, poetry and essays from the period, as well as coins, archaeological artifacts, and art produced during the period are also primary sources.

Guidelines for the use of primary resources

- Be certain that you understand how language was used at the time of writing and that you understand the context in which it was produced

- Do not read history blindly; be certain that you understand both explicit and implicit references in the material

- Read the entire text you are reviewing; do not simply extract a few sentences to read

- Although anthologies of materials may help you identify primary source materials, the full original text should be consulted

Secondary Sources

- Books written on the basis of primary materials about the period of time

- Books written on the basis of primary materials about persons who played a major role in the events under consideration

- Books and articles written on the basis of primary materials about the culture, the social norms, the language, and the values of the period

- Quotations from primary sources

- Statistical data on the period

- The conclusions and inferences of other historians

- Multiple interpretations of the ethos of the time

Guidelines for the use of secondary sources

- Do not rely upon a single secondary source

- Check facts and interpretations against primary sources whenever possible

- Do not accept the conclusions of other historians uncritically

- Place greatest reliance on secondary sources created by the most respected scholars

- Do not use the inferences of other scholars as if they were facts.

- Ensure that you recognize any bias the writer brings to his/her interpretation of history

- Understand the primary point of the book as a basis for evaluating the value of the material presented in it

---

SKILL 10.3 Identify approaches for analyzing an event, issue, problem, or phenomenon from multiple perspectives

Analyzing an event or issue from multiple perspectives involves seeking out sources that advocate or express those perspectives and comparing them with one another. Listening to the speeches of Martin Luther King, Jr. provides insight into the perspective of one group of people on the issue of civil rights in the U.S. in the 1950s and 1960s. Public statements of George Wallace, an American governor opposed to desegregation, provide another perspective from the same time period. Looking at the legislation that was proposed at the time and how it came into effect offers a window into the political thinking of the day.

Comparing these perspectives on the topic of civil rights provides information on the key issues, and gives a fuller picture of the societal changes that were occurring at that time. Analysis of any social event, issue, problem, or phenomenon requires that various perspectives be taken into account.

SKILL 10.4 Recognize methods for analyzing characteristics, causes, and consequences of an event, issue, problem, or phenomenon

Historic events and social issues cannot be considered in isolation. People and their actions are connected in many ways, and events are linked through cause and effect over time. Identifying and analyzing these social and historic links is a primary goal of the social sciences.

The methods used to analyze social phenomena borrow from several of the social sciences. Interviews, statistical evaluation, observation and experimentation are just some of the ways that people's opinions and motivations can be measured. From these opinions, larger social beliefs and movements can be interpreted, and events, issues and social problems can be placed in context to provide a fuller understanding of their importance.

SKILL 10.5 Recognize ways of comparing and evaluating outcomes, responses, or solutions, and using the results to reach conclusions and drive further inquiry

Human societies can differ in an infinite number of ways, but all are faced with similar problems as they develop and change. Identifying how different peoples cope with and solve these challenges illustrates differences between cultures, as well as the common traits they share.

By identifying and analyzing these different approaches to social challenges, one can draw conclusions about the societal sources and causes of these differences that may be unique to each society. These conclusions can then be examined further, which may lead to the discovery of other social phenomena.

DOMAIN III
THE ARTS

Available for purchase at www.XAMonline.com:

eFlashcards: a digital representation of a card represented with words, numbers or symbols or any combination of each and briefly displayed as part of a learning drill. eFlashcards takes away the burden of carrying around traditional cards that could easily be disarranged, dropped, or soiled. Available at www.XAMonline.com/flashcards

More Sample Tests: more ways to assess how much you know and how much further you need to study. Ultimately, makes you more prepared and attain mastery in the skills and techniques of passing the test the FIRST TIME! Available at www.XAMonline.com/sampletests

PERSONALIZED STUDY PLAN

KNOWN MATERIAL/ SKIP IT

PAGE	COMPETENCY AND SKILL	
131	**11: Understand techniques and materials associated with the visual arts and the cultural, political, and historical significance of the visual arts**	☐
	11.1: Recognize basic terms and elements of the visual arts	☐
	11.2: Identify media, techniques, and processes used in the visual arts	☐
	11.3: Identify how cultural, political, and historical contexts influence works from the visual arts	☐
135	**12: Understand techniques and materials associated with theatre and dance and the cultural, political, and historical significance of theatre and dance**	☐
	12.1: Identify the basic nature, materials, elements, and means of communicating in the visual arts	☐
	12.2: Identify elements and skills in performing dance	☐
	12.3: Recognize the role of theatre, film, television, and electronic media in the past and the present	☐
	12.4: Recognize elements of dance from different styles or traditions	☐
	12.5: Identify connections among dance, theatre, and other disciplines taught in school	☐
141	**13: Understand techniques and materials associated with music and the cultural, political, and historical significance of musical genres and styles**	☐
	13.1: Recognize basic principles of music	☐
	13.2: Identify distinguishing characteristics of musical genres and styles from various cultures	☐
	13.3: Recognize the roles and functions of music in different cultures	☐
	13.4: Identify connections between music and other arts and disciplines taught in school	☐

COMPETENCY 11

UNDERSTAND TECHNIQUES AND MATERIALS ASSOCIATED WITH THE VISUAL ARTS AND THE CULTURAL, POLITICAL, AND HISTORICAL SIGNIFICANCE OF THE VISUAL ARTS

SKILL 11.1 Recognize basic terms and elements of the visual arts

These standards provide a framework for helping students learn the characteristics of the visual arts by using a wide range of subject matter, symbols, meaningful images, and visual expressions to reflect their ideas, feelings, and emotions; and to evaluate the merits of their efforts. The standards address these objectives in ways that promote acquisition of and fluency in new ways of thinking, working, communicating, reasoning, and investigating. They emphasize student acquisition of the most important and enduring ideas, concepts, issues, dilemmas, and knowledge offered by the visual arts. They present new techniques, approaches, and habits for applying knowledge and skills in the visual arts to the world beyond school.

Some of the expectations for students' progress include:

- Experimenting and creating of art works in a variety of mediums (drawing, sculpting, ceramics, printmaking, video, and computer graphics)

- Developing their own ideas and images through exploration and collaboration based on themes

- Understanding the use of the elements and principles of art ideas (line, color, shape)

- Revealing through their own art work an understanding of how art mediums and techniques influence their creative ideas

- Identifying and using, in both individual and group experiences, roles such as designing, producing and exhibiting art works

Some examples in the classroom could include, but are not limited to, the following:

- Painting a picture in tempera or watercolor depicting an experience they recall

- Make a ceramic design that they decorate with symbols

- Making a drawing with three-dimensional space

- Selecting a medium for a work based on an experience

- Working with others to plan and produce a group project

- Using primary colors to paint a picture from nature

SKILL 11.2 Identify media, techniques, and processes used in the visual arts

The visual arts are extremely rich. They range from drawing, painting, sculpture, and design to architecture, film, video, and folk arts. They involve a wide variety of tools, techniques, and processes. Examples of assorted techniques and the tools they require include:

- **Sculpting:** A sand castle is a type of sculpture that resembles a building, often a castle. In the process of sculpting the building, two basic building ingredients are used, sand and water, which are available in abundance on a beach or in a sandpit. The main tools for construction are a bucket and shovel, although using the hands alone is also quite common. Sand sculpting has been around for decades and has become very popular recently, with hundreds of competitions held all over the world every year.

- **Mosaic:** Decorating with small pieces of colored glass, stone or other material. Small tiles or fragments of colored glass are used to create a pattern or picture. Mosaic was used across the ancient world for interior decoration.

- **Painting by numbers:** A popular coloring book-style hobby. Students are given a piece of detailed art in which every shape, shadow, and toned area of the picture is drawn with a number placed inside. The student matches each number with the intended color listed on an instruction sheet. When completed, the coloring-in process will create a detailed, attractive painting. The idea is to allow youngsters, who may not be artistically talented on their own, to participate in painting as a leisure activity. In children's activity books, simpler activities are often done with crayons and are called color by numbers.

- **Drawing:** the act of making marks on a surface to create a visual image of a perceived form or shape. The image produced may be defined as a sketch. Drawing involves the choice of a tool (or medium) and the choice of a surface. To produce a drawing, the tool needs to be moved across the surface or used in such a way as to create marks on the surface. Common tools for drawing include pencils, pens, crayons, pastels, or markers, and common surfaces include paper, tablets, or a sketchbook.

The standards are structured to recognize that many elements from this broad array can be used to accomplish specific educational objectives. For example, drawing can be used as the basis for creative activity, historical and cultural investigation, or analysis, as can any other field within the visual arts. The standards present educational goals. It is the responsibility of practitioners to choose appropriately from this rich array of content and processes to fulfill these goals in specific circumstances and to develop the curriculum. To meet the standards, students must learn vocabularies and concepts associated with various types of work in the visual arts and must exhibit their competence at various levels in visual, oral, and written form.

Creation is at the heart of this instruction. Students learn to work with various tools, processes, and media. Some examples of media can include crayons, markers, glue, clay, paints, and various types of woods, metals, etc. They learn to coordinate their hands and minds in explorations of the visual world. They learn to make choices that enhance communication of their ideas. Their natural inquisitiveness is promoted, and they learn the value of perseverance.

In Kindergarten–grade 4, young children experiment enthusiastically with art materials and investigate the ideas presented to them through visual arts instruction. They exhibit a sense of joy and excitement as they make and share their artwork with others.

SKILL 11.3 Identify how cultural, political, and historical contexts influence works from the visual arts

Although the elements of design have remained consistent throughout history, the emphasis on specific aesthetic principles has periodically shifted. Aesthetic standards or principles vary from time period to time period and from society to society.

Aesthetic standards or principles vary from time period to time period and from society to society.

There are obvious differences in the aesthetic principles of works created by Eastern and Western cultures. In attempting to convey reality, Eastern artists generally prefer to use line, simple color, and a minimalist view. Western artists tend toward a literal use of line, shape, color, and texture to convey a concise, detailed, complicated view. Eastern artists portray the human figure with symbolic meanings and little regard for muscle structure, resulting in a mystical view of the human experience. Western artists use the "principle of pondering," which requires the knowledge of both human anatomy and an expression of the human spirit.

In attempts to convey the illusion of depth or visual space in a work of art, Eastern and Western artists use different techniques. Eastern artists prefer a diagonal projection of eye movement into the picture plane, and often leave large areas of the surface untouched by detail. The result is the illusion of vast space. Western artists rely on several techniques, such as overlapping planes, variation of object size, object position on the picture plane, linear and aerial perspective, color change, and various points of perspective to convey the illusion of depth. The result is space that is limited and closed.

An interesting change in aesthetic principles occurred between the Renaissance and Baroque periods in Europe.

The Renaissance period was concerned with the rediscovery of the works of classical Greece and Rome.

The Renaissance period was concerned with the rediscovery of the works of classical Greece and Rome. The art, literature, and architecture was inspired by classical style, which tended to be formal, simple, and concerned with the ideal human proportions. This means that the painting, sculpture, and architecture was of a closed nature, composed of forms that were restrained and compact. For example, consider the visual masterpieces of the period: Raphael's painting *The School of Athens*, with its precise use of space; Michelangelo's sculpture *David*, with its compact mass; and the facade of the Palazzo Strozzi, with its defined use of the rectangle, arches, and rustication of the masonry.

The Baroque period was concerned with imagination and human fancy.

Compare the Renaissance characteristics to those of the Baroque period. The word *Baroque* means grotesque, which was the contemporary criticism of the new style. In comparison to the styles of the Renaissance, the Baroque was concerned with imagination and human fancy. The painting, sculpture, and architecture were of an open nature, composed of forms that were whimsical and free-flowing. Consider again the masterpieces of the period: Ruben's painting *The Elevation of the Cross*, with its turbulent forms of light and dark tumbling diagonally through space; Puget's sculpture *Milo of Crotona*, with its use of open space and twisted forms; and Borromini's *Chapel of St. Ivo*, with a facade that plays convex forms against concave ones.

Although artists throughout time have used the same elements of design to create their works, the emphasis on specific aesthetic principles has periodically shifted. Aesthetic principles vary from time period to time period and from society to society.

In the 1920s and 1930s, the German art historian Professor Wolfflin outlined these shifts in aesthetic principles in his influential book *Principles of Art History*. He arranged these changes into five categories of "visual analysis," sometimes referred to as the "categories of stylistic development." Wolfflin was careful to point out that no style is inherently superior to any other. They are simply indicators of the phase of development of that particular time or society. However, Wolfflin goes on to state, correctly or not, that once an evolution occurs, it is impossible to regress. These modes of perception apply to drawing, painting, sculpture, and architecture.

COMPETENCY 12

UNDERSTAND TECHNIQUES AND MATERIALS ASSOCIATED WITH THEATRE AND DANCE AND THE CULTURAL, POLITICAL, AND HISTORICAL SIGNIFICANCE OF THEATRE AND DANCE

SKILL **Identify the basic nature, materials, elements, and means of**
12.1 **communicating in theatre** *(e.g., dramatic media, musical theatre, dance, music)*

See Skill 12.3

SKILL **Identify elements and skills in performing dance** *(e.g., balance,*
12.2 *articulation of isolated body parts, weight shift)*

Dance is an artistic form of self expression that uses various elements such as space, time, levels, and force, which form a composition.

Students in the primary grades have a gross understanding of their motor movements, whereas older children have a more refined concept of their bodies. Individual movements are developed by the instructor with attention to various aspects such as:

- The range of movement or gestures through space
- The direction of the action or imaginary lines the body makes through space
- The timing of movements to form dramatic effects
- The planes formed by any two areas, such as height and width or width and depth
- Levels are introduced so that the composition incorporates sitting, standing, and kneeling, etc.
- Elevation is the degree of lift created by movements like leaping, which creates the illusion of suspension and gives character to the dance

- The force and energy of dance can be a reflection of the music, such as adagio (slow music) or allegro (quickening steps)

- Balance is important to the movement and flow of dance

- Articulation of isolated body parts requires dancers to moves only selected body parts (arms and legs) while mastering other movements at the same time

- Dancers must be able to control weight shift during specific movements that may require physical strength and control of a variety of muscles

---

SKILL 12.3 **Recognize the role of theatre, film, television, and electronic media in the past and the present**

Theatre

The history of theatre can be dated back to early sixth century BCE in Greece. The Greek theatre was the earliest known theatre experience. Drama was expressed in many Greek spiritual ceremonies. There are two main forms of drama that have evolved over time:

- Tragedy: Typically depicts conflict between characters

- Comedy: Typically depicts paradoxical relationships between humans and gods such as Sophocles and Euripides

Comedies were designed to entertain and contained little violence.

Roman history

Roman theatre developed times was discovered in the third century. These theatre shows were based on religious aspects of the lives of Roman gods and goddesses. By the end of the sixth century drama was nearly a dead art form in Rome.

Medieval drama

Medieval theatre was a new revelation of drama that appeared around the tenth century CE. In the church itself, drama was used in many troupes that toured churches, presenting religious narratives and life stories of moral deeds. Over time the once small traveling productions grew into full sized plays, presentations, and elaborate passions. Performances became spectacles at outdoor theatres, market-places, and any place large audiences could gather. The main focus of these presentations was to glorify God and humanity, and to celebrate local artisan trades.

Puritan Commonwealth

The Puritan Commonwealth was ruled by Oliver Cromwell outlawed dramatic performances. That ban lasted for nearly twenty years. Following the Puritan era was the restoration of the English monarchy and new, more well-rounded, plays became the focus of art. For the first time in history women were allowed to perform on stage.

Melodrama

In melodramas, good always triumph over evil. This form of theatre was pleasing to the audience but usually unrealistic.

Serious drama

Serious drama emerged late in the nineteenth and twentieth centuries following the movement of realism. Realism attempted to combine nature with realistic and ordinary situations on stage.

Realism

Today realism is the most common form of theatre. The techniques used today to stage drama combine many of the past elements and conventions of drama.

Film

Beginning with silent films in the 1920s, cinema has a rich history that includes numerous technological advances, studio conglomerates, government attention in the form of Communist Party accusations, and industry monopolization. From incorporating sound and color to 3-D technology, which emerged in the 1950s, film has evolved to include a variety of genres such as action, comedy, thriller, and documentary. Beyond its 3-D technology, which quickly lost consumer interest, the 1950s also brought a drastic decrease in attendance due to the introduction of television. It wasn't until the 1980s that attendance rates rose into the double digits with hits such as *E.T.: The Extra-Terrestrial* and *Batman*.

The "blockbuster" of today emerged in the 1970s and is frequently associated with *Jaws*, which used thrilling special effects such as a large mechanical shark. Audiences were familiar with special effects, but *Jaws* elevated the level of realism and captivated audiences. This was demonstrated once again a few years later by the classic movie *Star Wars*. Advertising and a new business model were in place, and remain in place today, ending the challenges faced by the industry in the 1960s. From the first piano- or organ-accompanied show, film has grown into a multibillion dollar industry and remains one of Americans' favorite pastimes.

Television

Dating back to the late 1880s, television existed as an idea long before the accompanying technology was available. Following many inventors' technological advances, work began on two TV models: the mechanical and the electronic. Regardless of the patent battles that ensued, according to the Federal Communications Commission's (FCC) history of TV, the device as it is known today emerged thanks to the 1939 World's Fair showcase by David Sarnoff of Radio Corporation of America (RCA). Shortly after, the electronic system won the development race and the number of commercial TV stations grew rapidly. By 1960, 85 percent of U.S. households owned a TV. Nielsen, the leading provider of television audience measurement, estimated there were 114.9 million households with TVs in 2009.

The TV industry has progressed to include cable television, videotape, satellite, digital video disc (DVD) fiber optics, and high definition. As with the film industry, regulations have been put into place by the FCC to limit monopolization and set quality standards. From Sarnoff's broadcast of the first presidential speech, TV has completely altered the way Americans receive news, consume entertainment and interact with advertisers, as is the case with new digital video recording (DVR) devices. TV enables viewers to receive instant breaking news, experience places and events thousands of miles away, and get a behind-the-scenes look at everything from current international politics to the real lives of brides-to-be. Just as technology has changed, the type of programming available continues to evolve and now includes everything from sports and scripted dramas to music television and reality shows.

Electronic media

Telegraphs, facsimiles, radios, video games and the Internet—all of these forms of electronic media have had a huge impact on the way Americans communicate in both business and their personal lives. Developed from initial transmission experiments in the early 1800s, the electronic media field has experienced vast growth throughout the last century. Electronic media, especially the Internet, has infiltrated nearly every aspect of life. From digital presentations in the classroom to video games at home, students are continually surrounded by electronic media. However, as with other media forms, regulations and protective measures are being developed to ensure the safety of all people, especially children. While some critics claim that too much media exposure can harm youth, many teachers have embraced the technology and used it to enhance their lessons or offer students another way to communicate. Advances in electronic media occur so frequently that even the most diligent media follower can lose track. The key is to stay informed and knowledgeable on not only the new electronic media, but also the rules and regulations surrounding those technologies.

SKILL 12.4 Recognize elements of dance from different styles or traditions

There are seven primary styles of dance:

- Creative dance
- Structured dance
- Modern dance
- Ritual dance
- Social dance
- Ballet
- Dance of other cultures

Creative dance is the one that is most natural to a young child. Creative dance depicts feelings through movement. It is the initial reaction to sound and movement. The older elementary student will incorporate mood and expressiveness into creative dance.

Isadora Duncan is considered the mother of modern dance. Modern dance portrays opposites such as fast–slow and contract–release and vary height and level to fall and recover. Modern dance is based on four principles: substance, dynamism, kinesis, and form.

Social dance refers to a cooperative form of dance between partners or larger groups. Social dance may be in the form of marches, waltzes, line dancing, or salsa.

The upper level elementary student can learn simple social dances such as the minuet. The minuet was introduced to the court in Paris in 1650, and it dominated the ballroom until the end of the eighteenth century. The pomp and ceremony of social dance makes for fun classroom experiences. Dance is central to many cultures, and teaching history can include dances such as Native American dance or the Mexican hat dance.

Structured dances are composed of particular patterns, such as the tango or waltz, and are popular in dance studios and gym classes alike.

Ritual dances are often of a religious nature that celebrate a significant life event, such as a harvest season or the rainy season, asking for favors in hunting, and birth or death. In Africa, traditional dances and chants summoned the gods and sometimes produced trance-like states.

Dancing at weddings today is an example of ritual dance. The father dances with the bride. Then the husband dances with the bride. The two families then dance with each other.

In ballet a barre is used for balance to practice the five basic positions. Various parts of the dancer's body are in line with one another while the dancer is moving. It is a very precise dance form and executed with grace and form. The mood and expressions of the music are very important to ballet and form the canvas upon which the dance is performed.

SKILL 12.5 Identify connections among dance, theatre, and other disciplines taught in school

Dance is a product of the creative impulse. One of the earliest structured uses of dance may have been in the performed retelling of stories. Indeed, before the introduction of written languages, dance was one of the primary methods of passing these stories down from generation to generation.

In sixteenth and seventeenth century England, many plays were written in verse. Shakespeare was a prominent playwright during this period and wrote plays that used rhyming schemes and specialized roles. Folk tales are an example of traditional narratives. The telling of stories appears to be universal, common to basic and complex societies alike. Folk tales are often similar from culture to culture, and studies of common themes have been successful in showing these relationships.

Drama has a unique ability to allow us to play, allowing us to be another person or experience a situation that we would not normally encounter. Play allows students to act out new situations, try out new ways of doing things, and learn by doing.

COMPETENCY 13

UNDERSTAND TECHNIQUES AND MATERIALS ASSOCIATED WITH MUSIC AND THE CULTURAL, POLITICAL, AND HISTORICAL SIGNIFICANCE OF MUSICAL GENRES AND STYLES

SKILL 13.1 Recognize basic principles of music (e.g., meter, rhythm, chords, melody)

METER is the division of a musical line into measures of stressed and unstressed "beats." Rhythms are usually arranged by using a time signature, signifying a meter. The top number of the time signature reflects the number of beats in each measure, whereas the bottom number reflects which type of note uses a single beat (e.g., 1 on the bottom reflects a whole note, 2 on the bottom reflects a half note, 4 reflects a quarter note, etc.). Rhythmic notation refers to the exact rhythm in which the indicated notes or chords are played or sung. The speed of the underlying beat is the tempo (e.g., Allegro, Allegretto, Presto, Moderato, Lento, Largo), used singly or in combination within a selection. Some music makes different use of rhythm than others. Most Western music is based on DIVISIVE RHYTHM, while non-Western music uses ADDITIVE RHYTHM. In music, a divisive rhythm is when a larger period of time is divided into smaller units. Additive rhythms are when larger periods of time are made from smaller units of time added together.

Any single strike or series of beats on a percussion instrument creates a rhythmic pattern, sometimes called a "drum beat." Percussion instruments are sometimes referred to as nonpitched, or untuned. Untuned instruments have no pitch that can be heard by the ear. Examples of percussion instruments that are nonpitched are the snare drum, cymbals, and bass drum.

Melodic music is music that is characterized by a single, strong melody line. The melody line, or tune, is easily memorized and followed. Melodic music may be performed by a singer, and orchestra, a single instrument, or any combination of the three. Operas, operettas, and musicals are all examples of melodic music.

A chord consists of three or more notes or pitches played simultaneously and is created by the combination of notes making intervals. An interval is the relationship between two separate musical pitches. There are twelve pitches in the musical scale, with each pitch a degree of the scale. A chord is the harmonic function of a group of notes, but it is unnecessary for all the notes to be played together. For example, "broken chords" or "arpeggios" are ways of playing notes in succession.

> **METER:** the division of a musical line into measures of stressed and unstressed "beats"

> **DIVISIVE RHYTHM:** when a larger period of time is divided into smaller units

> **ADDITIVE RHYTHM:** when larger periods of time are made from smaller units of time added to a previous unit

Performing, creating, and responding to music are fundamental music processes in which humans engage. Students, particularly in grades K–4, learn by doing. Singing, playing instruments, moving to music, and creating music enable them to acquire musical skills and knowledge. Learning to read and notate music gives them a skill with which to explore music independently and with others. Listening to, analyzing, and evaluating music are important building blocks of musical learning.

Students are expected to display the following skills:

- Sing independently, on pitch and in rhythm, with appropriate timbre, diction, and posture, and maintain a steady tempo

- Sing expressively, with appropriate dynamics, phrasing, and interpretation

- Sing from memory a varied repertoire of songs representing genres and styles from diverse cultures

- Sing ostinatos, partner songs, and rounds

- Sing in groups, blending vocal timbres, matching dynamic levels, and responding to the cues of a conductor

SKILL 13.2 Identify distinguishing characteristics of musical genres and styles from various cultures

CLASSICAL MUSIC: based on European secular and religious music from the ninth century to the present; the term itself is generally understood to refer to the "golden age" of composers from Johann Sebastian Bach (1685–1750) to Ludwig van Beethoven (1770–1827)

CLASSICAL MUSIC is a type of music based on European secular and religious music from the ninth century to the present. The term itself is generally understood to refer to the "golden age" of composers from Johann Sebastian Bach (1685–1750) to Ludwig van Beethoven (1770–1827). Classical music is composed and written using musical notation and, as a rule, is performed exactly as written. Classical music often refers to instrumental music in general.

A BALLAD is a song that contains a story. Any story form can be a ballad, such as fairy tales or historical accounts. It usually has simple repeating rhymes and often contains a refrain (or repeating section) that is played or sung at regular intervals throughout. Ballads are called hymns when they are based on religious themes. In the twentieth century, "ballad" took on the meaning of a popular song, especially of a romantic or sentimental nature.

BALLAD: a song that contains a story

FOLK MUSIC is music that has endured and been passed down by oral tradition among ordinary people. In early societies, it arose in areas that were not yet affected by mass communication. It was normally shared by the entire community and was transmitted by word of mouth. A folk song is usually seen as an expression of a way of life now past, or about to disappear. In the 1960s folk songs were sung as a means of political protest.

CALL-AND-RESPONSE SONGS are a form of interaction between a singer and a listener, in which the listener sings a response to the singer. In West African cultures, call-and-response songs were used in religious rituals, gatherings, and are now used in other forms such as gospel, blues, and jazz. In certain Native American tribes, call-and-response songs are used to preserve and protect the tribe's cultural heritage and can be seen and heard at modern-day pow-wows. The men begin the song as the speaker with singing and drumming and the women respond with singing and dancing.

The WORK SONG is typically a song sung a cappella by people working on a physical and often repetitive task. It was probably intended to reduce feelings of boredom. Rhythms of work songs also serve to synchronize physical movement in a gang or the movement in marching. Frequently, the verses of work songs are improvised and sung differently each time. Examples of work songs could be heard among slaves working in the field, prisoners on chain gangs, and soldiers in the military.

JAZZ is a form of music that grew out of a combination of folk music, ragtime, and band music. It has been called the first native art form to develop in the United States. Jazz music has gone through a series of developments since its inception.

BLUES is a vocal and instrumental music form that developed from West African spirituals, work songs, and chants. This musical form has been a major influence on later American popular music, finding expression in jazz, rock and roll, and country music. Due to its powerful influence, blues can be regarded as the root of pop as well as American music in general. Elvis Presley and Eric Clapton were greatly influenced by their predecessors in the blues industry.

ROCK AND ROLL, in its broadest sense, can refer to almost all pop music recorded since the early 1950s. Its main features include an emphasis on rhythm and the use of percussion and amplified instruments like the bass and guitar. In the 1950s Elvis Presley shocked the nation with his rhythm and gyrating hips. Starting the mid-1960s, a group of British bands, sometime referred to as the British Invasion, formed folk rock, as well as a variety of less popular genres.

FOLK MUSIC: music that has endured and been passed down by oral tradition among ordinary people

CALL-AND-RESPONSE SONGS: a form of interaction between a singer and a listener, in which the listener sings a response to the singer

WORK SONG: a song sung a cappella by people working on a physical and often repetitive task

JAZZ: a form of music that grew out of a combination of folk music, ragtime, and band music

BLUES: a vocal and instrumental music form that developed from West African spirituals, work songs, and chants; it has been a major influence on later American popular music, finding expression in jazz, rock and roll, and country music

ROCK AND ROLL: broadly, this can refer to almost all pop music recorded since the early 1950s; its main features include an emphasis on rhythm, and the use of percussion and amplified instruments

SKILL 13.3 Recognize the roles and functions of music in different cultures

See Skill 13.2

SKILL 13.4 Identify connections between music and other arts and other disciplines taught in school

Experience with and knowledge of the arts is a vital part of a complete education. The arts are rich disciplines that include a vibrant history, an exemplary body of work to study, and compelling cultural traditions. An education in the arts is an essential part of the academic curriculum.

The education of our students in the disciplines of dance, music, theatre, and visual art is critical to their personal success and to the success of all students. The arts offer tools for development. They enable personal, intellectual, and social development for each individual. Teaching in and through the arts within the context of the total school curriculum, especially during the formative years of an elementary K-6 education, is key to maximizing the benefits of the arts in education.

For students, an education in the arts provides:

- The ability to be creative and inventive decision-makers

- An enhanced sense of poise and self-esteem

- The confidence to undertake new tasks

- An increased ability to achieve across the curriculum

- A framework that encourages teamwork and fosters leadership skills

- Knowledge of the less recognized experiences of aesthetic engagement and intuition

- Increased potential for life success

- An enriched quality of life

Recent studies such as *Critical Links and Champions of Change* provide evidence of the positive correlations between regular, sequential instruction in the arts and improved cognitive capacities and motivations to learn. These often result in improved academic achievement through near and far transfer of learning (i.e., music and spatial reasoning, visual art and reading readiness, dance and non-verbal reasoning and expressive skills, theatre and reading comprehension, writing proficiency, and increased peer interaction). Additionally, the arts are uniquely qualified to cultivate a variety of multiple intelligences.

The student educated in the arts is:

- Equipped with essential technical skills and abilities significant to many aspects of life and work

- Aware of the increasingly complex technological environment around us

- Cognizant of social, cultural, and intellectual interplay, among men and women of different ethnic, racial, and cultural backgrounds

- Is critically empowered to create, reshape, and fully participate in the enhancement of the quality of life for all

DOMAIN IV
READING INSTRUCTION

Available for purchase at www.XAMonline.com:

eFlashcards: a digital representation of a card represented with words, numbers or symbols or any combination of each and briefly displayed as part of a learning drill. eFlashcards takes away the burden of carrying around traditional cards that could easily be disarranged, dropped, or soiled. Available at www.XAMonline.com/flashcards

More Sample Tests: more ways to assess how much you know and how much further you need to study. Ultimately, makes you more prepared and attain mastery in the skills and techniques of passing the test the FIRST TIME! Available at www.XAMonline.com/sampletests

PERSONALIZED STUDY PLAN

PERSONALIZED STUDY PLAN

KNOWN MATERIAL/ SKIP IT

PAGE	COMPETENCY AND SKILL	
182	**17: Understand reading comprehension and fluency**	☐
	17.1: Demonstrate knowledge of literal and inferential comprehension, and evaluative comprehension	☐
	17.2: Apply knowledge of strategies for promoting literal, inferential, and evaluative comprehension	☐
	17.3: Demonstrate knowledge of reading phrasing, rate, and expression as part of fluency	☐
	17.4: Recognize the role of automatic word recognition and the relationship between reading fluency and reading comprehension	☐
	17.5: Apply knowledge of strategies for promoting students' reading comprehension	☐
	17.6: Demonstrate knowledge of curriculum materials and instruction in reading comprehension and fluency	☐
212	**18: Understand reading comprehension strategies for literary and informational text**	☐
	18.1: Recognize how to apply reading comprehension strategies to promote understanding of literary and informational text	☐
	18.2: Demonstrate knowledge of literary response skills	☐
	18.3: Demonstrate knowledge of common patterns of organization in informational text	☐
	18.4: Describe the use of writing activities to promote comprehension of informational text	☐
	18.5: Demonstrate knowledge of curriculum materials and instruction in comprehension of literary and informational text	☐

COMPETENCY 14
UNDERSTAND PHONOLOGICAL AND PHONEMIC AWARENESS

SKILL Demonstrate knowledge of phonological awareness *(i.e., the*
14.1 *awareness that oral language comprises units such as spoken words and syllables)*

Phonological Awareness

PHONOLOGICAL AWARENESS is the ability of the reader to recognize the sounds of spoken language. This recognition includes how these sounds can be blended together, segmented (divided up), and manipulated (switched around). This awareness then leads to phonics, a method for teaching children to read. It helps them "sound out words."

Development of phonological skills may begin during pre-K years. Indeed, by the age of five, a child who has been exposed to rhyme can recognize a rhyme. Such a child can demonstrate phonological awareness by filling in the missing rhyming word in a familiar rhyme or rhymed picture book.

You teach children phonological awareness when you teach them the sounds made by the letters and the sounds made by various combinations of letters, as well as how to recognize individual sounds in words.

> **PHONOLOGICAL AWARENESS:** the ability of the reader to recognize the sounds of spoken language

> *Phonological awareness skills:*
> - *Rhyming and syllabification*
> - *Blending sounds into words—such as pic-tur-bo-k*
> - *Identifying the beginning or starting sounds of words and the ending or closing sounds of words*
> - *Breaking words down into sounds, also called "segmenting" words*
> - *Recognizing other smaller words in a big word by removing starting sounds—such as hear to ear*

SKILL Demonstrate knowledge of phonemic awareness *(i.e., a specific type of*
14.2 *phonological awareness involving the ability to distinguish the individual sounds that make up a spoken word)*

Phonemic Awareness

> *The two best predictors of early reading success are alphabetic recognition and phonemic awareness.*
>
> *—Marilyn Jager Adams*

> *In order to benefit from formal reading instruction, children must have a certain level of phonemic awareness. . . phonemic awareness is both a prerequisite for and a consequence of learning to read.*
>
> —*Hallie Kay Yopp*

Phonemic Awareness

PHONEMIC AWARENESS is understanding that words are composed of sounds. To be phonemically aware means that the reader and the listener can recognize and manipulate specific sounds in spoken words.

PHONEMIC AWARENESS: understanding that words are composed of sounds

Phonemic awareness deals with sounds in words that are spoken. The majority of phonemic awareness tasks, activities, and exercises are oral.

Theorist Marilyn Jager Adams, who researches early reading, has outlined five basic phonemic awareness tasks:

Task 1: Ability to hear rhymes and alliteration. Children listen to a poem, rhyming picture book, or song and identify the rhyming words heard, which the teacher might then record or list on an experiential chart.

Task 2: Ability to do oddity tasks (recognize the member of a set that is different, or odd, among the group). Children look at the pictures of a blade of grass, a garden, and a rose, and identify which starts with a different sound.

Task 3: Ability to orally blend words and split syllables. Children say the first sound of a word and then the rest of the word and put it together as a single word.

Task 4: Ability to orally segment words. The ability to count sounds. Children would be asked as a group to count the sounds in "hamburger."

Task 5: Ability to do phonics manipulation tasks. Children replace the "r" sound in rose with a "p" sound.

Because the ability to distinguish between individual sounds, or phonemes, within words is a prerequisite to association of sounds with letters and manipulating sounds to blend words—a fancy way of saying "reading"—the teaching of phonemic awareness is crucial to EMERGENT LITERACY (early childhood K–2 reading instruction). Children need a strong background in phonemic awareness in order for phonics instruction (sound-spelling relationship printed materials) to be effective.

EMERGENT LITERACY: early childhood K–2 reading instruction

Instructional methods that may be effective for teaching phonemic awareness include:

- Clapping out syllables in words

- Distinguishing between a word and a sound

- Using visual cues and movements to help children understand when the speaker goes from one sound to another

- Incorporating oral segmentation activities that focus on easily distinguished syllables rather than sounds

- Singing familiar songs (e.g., Happy Birthday, Knick Knack Paddy Wack) and replacing key words in them with words with a different ending or middle sound (oral segmentation)

- Dealing children a deck of picture cards and having them sound out the words for the pictures on their cards or calling for a picture by asking for its first and second sound

---

SKILL 14.3 Demonstrate knowledge of the significance of phonological and phonemic awareness in emergent literacy development and strategies for promoting students' phonological and phonemic awareness

The Role of Phonological Awareness in Reading Development

Instructional methods to teach phonological awareness may include any or all of the following:

- Auditory games and drills during which children recognize and manipulate the sounds of words, separate or segment the sounds of words, take out sounds, blend sounds, add in new sounds, or take apart sounds to recombine them in new formations.

- Snap game: The teacher says two words. The children snap their fingers if the two words share a sound, which might be at the beginning, middle or end of the word. Silence occurs if the words share no sounds. Children love this simple game and it also helps with classroom management.

- Language games model identification of rhyming words and inspire children to create their own rhymes.

- Word strip activities and experiences help children concretely experience how words are made up of syllables and that words can be broken down into separate sounds. Word strips help kinesthetic and spatial learners work to enhance this auditory skill.

- Read books that rhyme such as *Sheep in Jeep* by Nancy Shaw or *The Fox on a Box* by Barbara Gregorich.

- Share books with children that use alliteration (words that all begin with the same sound) such as *Avalanche, A to Z*.

Assessment of phonological awareness

These skills can be assessed by having the child listen to the teacher say two words. Then ask the child to decide if these two words are the same word repeated twice or two different words.

When you make this assessment, if you do use two different words, make certain that they only differ by one phoneme, such as /d/ and /g/.

Children can be assessed on words that are not real words. Words used can be make-believe words.

The Role of Phonological Processing in the Reading Development of Individual Students

English Language Learners (ELL)

Children who are raised in homes where English is not the first language or where standard English is not spoken may have difficulty with hearing the difference between similar sounding words like "send" and "sent." Any child who is not in a home, day care, or preschool environment where English phonology operates may have difficulty perceiving and demonstrating the differences between English language phonemes. If children cannot hear the difference between words that sound the same like "grow" and "glow," they will be confused when these words appear in a print context. This confusion will impact their comprehension.

Research recommends that ELL children initially learn to read in their first language. It has been found that a priority for ELL should be learning to speak English before being taught to read English. Research supports oral language development, since it lays the foundation for phonological awareness.

All phonological instruction programs must be tailored to the children's learning backgrounds. Rhymes and alliteration introduced to ELL children should be read or shared with them in their first language, if possible. If you do not speak the student's first language, get a paraprofessional or an available ELL educator to support your instruction in the first language.

The teacher must realize that what works for the English-speaking child from an English-speaking family does not necessarily work for children who do not come from English-speaking families.

Struggling readers

Students who cannot read by age 9 are unlikely to become fluent readers and have a greater tendency to drop out.

—*Beth Antunez*

Among the causes that make reading a struggle for some children (and adults) are auditory trauma or ear infections that affect their ability to hear speech. Such children need one-on-one support with articulation and perception of different sounds. When a child says a word, for example, "parrot," incorrectly, repeat it back as a question with the correct pronunciation of the sounds that were incorrectly uttered. If the child "gets" the sound correctly after your question, all is well. If the child still has difficulty with pronunciation, consult a speech therapist or audiologist. Early identification of medical conditions that affect hearing is crucial to reading development. As a teacher/educator, you need to make time to sit with struggling readers and play games such as "same or different" to identify those children who may be struggling due to a hearing difficulty.

Points to ponder

- Phonological awareness is auditory

- Phonological awareness does not involve print

- Phonological awareness must start before children have learned letter-sound correlations

- Phonological awareness is the basis for the successful teaching of phonics and spelling

- Phonological awareness can and must be taught and nurtured

- Phonologic activities can and may be done with the children's eyes closed

- Phonologic awareness must be in place before the alphabetic principle can be taught

The role of phonemic awareness in reading development

Children who have problems with phonics generally have not acquired or been exposed to phonemic awareness activities usually fostered at home and in pre-school. These include extensive songs, rhymes and read–alouds.

Consideration for ELL students

As a conscientious educator, it is important that you understand the special factors involved in supporting ELL development, which include fostering progress in native language literacy as a perquisite for second language reading progress.

> *Not all English phonemes are present in various ELL native languages. Some native language phonemes conflict with English phonemes.*

It is recommended that all teachers of reading and particularly those who are working with ELL students use meaningful, student-centered, and culturally appropriate activities. These activities may include: language games, word walls, and poems. Some of these activities might also, if possible, be initiated in the child's first language and then reiterated in English.

Reading and the ELL student

Research has shown that there is a positive and strong correlation between a child's literacy in her native language and her learning of English. The degree of native language proficiency and literacy is a strong predictor of English language development. Children who are literate and engaged readers in their native language can easily transfer their skills to a second language (i.e., English).

What this means is that educators should not approach the needs of all ELL learners in the same way. Those whose families are not from a focused oral literacy and reading culture in the native language will need additional oral language rhymes, read-alouds, and singing as supports for reading skills development in both their native and the English language.

Assessment of phonemic awareness

Teachers can maintain ongoing logs and rubrics for assessment throughout the year of phonemic awareness for individual children. Such assessments identify particular stated reading behaviors or performance standards, the date of observation of the child's behavior (in this context, phonemic activity or exercise), and comments.

The rubric or legend for assessing these behaviors might include the following descriptors: demonstrates or exhibits reading behavior consistently, making progress toward this reading behavior, and has not yet demonstrated or exhibited this behavior.

Depending on the particular phonemic task you are modeling, the performance task might include:

- Saying rhyming words in response to an oral prompt
- Segmenting a word spoken by the teacher into its beginning, middle and end sounds
- Counting correctly the number of syllables in a spoken word

SKILL 14.4 Demonstrate knowledge of phonemic awareness skills *(e.g., segmenting a spoken word into phonemes, blending phonemes to form a spoken word, deleting or substituting phonemes)*

See Skills 14.2 and 15.4

COMPETENCY 15
UNDERSTAND THE USE OF PHONICS AND OTHER WORD-IDENTIFICATION STRATEGIES

SKILL 15.1 Recognize how beginning readers learn to apply knowledge of letter-sound correspondence to decode simple words

PHONOLOGICAL AWARENESS involves the recognition that spoken words are composed of a set of smaller units including syllables and sounds.

PHONEMIC AWARENESS is a specific type of phonological awareness that focuses on the ability to distinguish, manipulate, and blend specific sounds or phonemes within a given word.

PHONICS deals with printed words and learning sound–spelling correlations, while phonemic awareness activities are for the most part oral.

In reading theory, these distinctions are semantic; sometimes accepted and respected theories can change over time.

PHONOLOGICAL AWARENESS: recognition that spoken words are composed of a set of smaller units including syllables and sounds

PHONEMIC AWARENESS: a specific type of phonological awareness that focuses on the ability to distinguish, manipulate, and blend specific sounds or phonemes within a given word

PHONICS: printed words and learning sound–spelling correlations

Blending letter sounds prompts for graphophonic cues

You said [the child's incorrect attempt]. Does that match the letters you see?

If it were the word you just said, [the child's incorrect attempt], what would it have to start with?

If it were the word you just said [the child's incorrect attempt], what would it have to end with?

Look at the first letter/s . . . look at the middle letter/s . . . the last letter. What could it be?

If you were writing [the child's incorrect attempt], what letter would you write first? What letters would go in the middle?

What letters would go last?

A good strategy to use in working with individual children is to have them explain how they correctly identified a word that was troubling them. If prompted and habituated through one-on-one tutoring conversations, they can be quite clear about what they did to "get" the word.

If the children are already writing their own stories, the teacher might say to them: "You know when you write your own stories you would never write a story that did not make sense. This writer probably didn't either. If you read something that does make sense, but doesn't match the letters, then it's probably not what the author wrote. This is the author's story, not yours, so go back to the work and see if you can find out the author's story. Later on, you might write your own story."

Letter/sound correspondence and beginning decoding

Use this procedure for letter-sound investigations that support beginning decoding.

First, focus on a particular letter or letters that you want the child to investigate. It is good to choose one from a shared text with which the children are familiar with. Make certain that the teachers' directions to the children are clear and either focuses them on looking for a specific letter or listening for sounds.

Next, begin a list of words that meet the task given to the children. Use chart paper to list the words that the children identify. This list can be continued into the next week as long as the children's focus is maintained on the list. This can be easily done by challenging the children to identify a specific number of letters or sounds and "daring" them as a class team to go beyond those words or sounds.

Third, continue to add to the list. Focus the children at the beginning of the day on the goal of their individually adding to the list. Give them an adhesive note (sticky pad sheet) on which they can individually write down the words they find. Then they can attach their newly found words with their names on them to the chart. This provides the children with a sense of ownership and pride in their letter-sounding abilities. During shared reading, discuss the children's proposed additions and have the group decide if these meet the directed category. If all the children agree that they meet the category, include the words on the chart.

Fourth, do a word sort from all the words generated and have the children put the words into categories that demonstrate similarities and differences. They can be prompted to see if the letter appeared at the beginning of the word, or in the middle of the word. They might also be prompted to see that one sound could have two different letter representations. The children can then "box" the word differences and similarities by drawing colors established in a chart key.

Finally, before the children go off to read, ask them to look for new words in the texts that they can now recognize because of the letter sound relationships on their chart. During shared reading, make certain that they have time to share these words they were able to decode because of their explorations.

Explicit and implicit strategies for teaching phonics

The CVC Phonic Card game developed by Jackie Montierth, a computer teacher in San Diego, for use with fifth and sixth grade students, is a good one to adapt to the needs of any group with appropriate modification for age, grade level, and language needs.

The children use the vehicle of the card game to practice and enhance their use of consonants and vowels. Their fluency in this will increase their ability to decode words.

Potential uses beyond whole classroom instruction include use as part of the small group word work and as part of cooperative team learning. This particular strategy also is particularly helpful for grade four and beyond English Language Learners who are in a regular English language classroom setting.

The card game works well because the practice of the content is implicit for transfer as the children continue to improve their reading skills. In addition, the card game format allows "instructional punctuation" using a student-centered exploration.

Teachers of ELL learners can do this game in the native language first and then transition it into English, facilitating native language reading skills and second language acquisition. They can develop their own appropriate decks to meet the vocabulary needs of their children and to complement the curricula.

For a complete description and rules, see Jackie Montierth's CVC Phonetic Card Game page at:

http://edweb.sdsu.edu/ courses/edtec670 /cardboard/Card/C /c-v-c_game.html

Role of phonics in developing rapid, automatic word recognition

Decoding and reading comprehension

DECODE: to change com-munication signals into messages

To **DECODE** means to change communication signals into messages. Reading com-prehension requires that the reader learn the code in which a message is written and be able to decode it to get the message.

Although effective reading comprehension requires identifying words automati-cally (Adams, 1990, Perfetti, 1985), children do not have to be able to identify every single word or know the exact meaning of the every word in a text to understand the text. Indeed, Nagy (1988) says that children can read with a high level of comprehension even if they do not fully know as many as 15 percent of the words within a given text.

Children develop the ability to decode and recognize words automatically. They can then extend their ability to decode to multi-syllabic words.

J. David Cooper (2004), and other advocates of the Balanced Literacy Approach, feel that children become literate, effective communicators and able to compre-hend by learning phonics and other aspects of word identification through the use of engaging reading texts. Engaging texts, as defined by the balanced literacy group, are those texts that contain highly predictable elements of rhyme, sound patterns, and plot. Researchers, such as Chall (1983) and Flesch (1981), support a phonics-centered foundation before the use of engaging reading texts. This is at the crux of the Phonics versus Whole Language /Balanced Literacy/ Integrated Language Arts controversy.

It is important for the new teacher/educator or teacher candidate to be informed about both sides of this controversy, as well as the work of theorists who attempt to reconcile these two perspectives, such as Kenneth Goodman (1994).

As far as the examinations go, all that is asked of you is the ability to demonstrate that you are familiar with these varied perspectives. If asked on a constructed response question, you need to be able to show that you can talk about teaching some aspect of reading using strategies from one or the other or a combination of both approaches.

This guide is designed to provide you with numerous strategies representing both approaches.

The working teacher/educator can, depending on the perspective of the school administration and the needs of the particular children, choose the strategies and approaches that work best for the children concerned.

SKILL 15.2 **Describe how beginning readers use knowledge of common consonant-vowel patterns in single-syllable words to decode unfamiliar words through analogy with known words**

Using Phonics to Decode Words in Connected Text

Some strategies to share with children during conferences or as part of shared reading include the following prompts:

- *Look at the beginning letter/s... What sound do you hear?*
- *Stop to think about the text or story. What word with this beginning letter would make sense here?*
- *Look at the book's illustrations. Do they help you figure out the new word?*
- *Think of what word would make sense, sound right, and match the letters that you see. Start the sentence over, making your mouth ready to say that word.*
- *Skip the word, read to the end of the sentence, and then come back to the word. How does what you've read help you with the word?*
- *Listen to whether what you are reading makes sense and matches the letters [this is asking the child to self-monitor]. If it doesn't make sense, see if you can correct it on your own.*
- *Look for spelling patterns you know from the spelling pattern wall.*
- *Look for smaller words you might know within the larger word.*
- *Think of any place you may have seen this word before.*
- *Read on a little, and then return to the part that confused you.*

Phases of Phonics Learning

Uta Frith has done work on the sequence of children's phonic learning.

Frith has identified three phases that describe the progression of children's phonic learning from ages four through eight. These are:

1. Logographic Phase: Children recognize whole words that have significance for them, such as their own names, the names of stores they frequent, or products that their parents buy.

   - Strategies that nurture development in this phase can include explicit labeling in the classroom using the children's names and those of classroom objects, components, furniture and materials. In addition, during snack time and lunch time, explicit attention and talk can be focused on new brands of foods and drink.

   - Toward the end of this phase children start to notice initial letters in words and the sounds that they represent.

2. Analytic Phase: During this phase the children make associations between the spelling patterns in the words that they know and the new words that they encounter.

3. Orthographic Phase: In this phase children recognize words almost automatically. They can rapidly identify an increasing number of words because they know a good deal about the structure of words and how they are spelled.

To best support these phases and the development of emergent and early readers, teachers should focus on elements of phonics learning, which help children analyze words for their letters, spelling patterns, and structural components. The children need to be involved in activities where they can use what they know about words to learn new ones.

The teacher needs to build on what the children know to introduce new spelling patterns, vowel combinations, and short and long vowel investigations. The teacher must do this and be aware that these will be reintroduced again and again as needed.

Keep in mind that children's learning of phonics and other key components of reading is not linear, but rather falls back to review and then flows forward to build new understandings.

Strategies

Sorting words

This activity allows children to focus closely on the specific features of words and to begin to understand the basic elements of letter sound relationships.

Start with monosyllabic words. Have the children group them by their length, common letters, sound, or spelling pattern.

Prepare for the activity by writing ten to fifteen words on oaktag strips and place them randomly on the sentence strip holder. These words should come from a book previously shared in the classroom or a language experience chart.

Next, begin to sort out the words with the children, perhaps by where a particular letter appears in a word. While the children sort the place of a particular letter in a given word, they should also be coached (or facilitated) by the teacher to recognize that sometimes a letter in the middle of the word can still be the last sound that we hear and that some letters at the end of a word are silent (such as "e").

Children should be encouraged to make their own categories for word sorts and to share their own discoveries as they do the word sorts. The children's discoveries should be recorded and posted in the room with their names so they have owner-ship of their phonics learning.

Spelling pattern word wall

One of the understandings emergent readers come to about a word is that if they know how to read, write, and spell one word, they can write, read, and spell many other words as well.

Create a spelling pattern word wall in your classroom. Wylie and Durrell have identified spelling patterns that are in their classic thirty-seven "dependable" rimes. The spelling word wall can be created by stapling a piece of 3" by 5" butcher block paper to the bulletin board. Then attach spelling pattern cards around the border with thumbtacks, so that the cards can be easily removed to use at the meeting area.

Once you decide on a spelling pattern for instruction, remove the correspond-ing card from the word wall. Then take a 1" by 3" piece of a contrasting color of butcher block paper and tape the card to the top end of a sheet the children will use for their investigation. Next, read one of Wylie and Durrell's short rimes with the children and have them identify the pattern.

After the pattern is identified, the children can try to come up with other words that have the same spelling pattern. The teacher can write these on the spelling pattern sheet, using a different color marker to highlight the spelling pattern within the word. The children have to add to the list until the sheet is full, which might take two days or more.

After the sheet is full, the completed spelling pattern is attached to the wall.

Letter holder making words

Use a 2" by 3" piece of foam board to make a letter holder. On the front of the board, attach 16 library pockets—one for each letter from A to P. Use the back of the board to attach another 10 pockets for the rest of the alphabet.

Write the letter name on each pocket and use clear bookbinding tape to secure each row of cards with clear tape. Make twelve cards for each letter. On the front of each 2" by 6" strip, make a capital letter and on its back write that letter in lower case. Write consonants in, say, black marker and vowels in red marker.

Through use of this letter holder, children can experience how letters can be rearranged, added, or removed to make new words. They can also use these cards to focus on letter sequences and to support them in recognizing spelling patterns in words.

The words you choose to use for this activity can be selected from Patricia Cunningham and Dorothy P. Hall's Making Words (1994).

Select a word that is called the "SECRET WORD." Build up toward the creation of that word through a focus on the smaller words within it. Words should be chosen that reflect the spelling patterns being studied by the class.

You can create letter holders for the children by folding up the bottom third of a used manila file folder and taping the ends to form a shallow pocket. Give them letter cards that are made of 2" by 6" oaktag. So, for example, if the secret word is *bicycle*, the children would be given the separate letter cards that make up that word. The children keep the letters on the floor in front of them and only place them in the holder when they are actually making a word.

Making words should begin with making two letter words and then progress as per the individual child's progress to making larger words. The teacher tells the children which two letters to use to make a word. Then the children select the correct letters and make the word in their folders. The teacher then writes the word down and the children check their letter holder words against it. The teacher goes around checking through and reviewing the letter holders to see which children have formed the word correctly and then continues to build up words with more letters if the children are ready.

Splitting compound words

Through working with compound words, children can actually experience bigger words that are made up of smaller words. By working with five to ten compound words on oaktag cards, children can analyze letter-sound relationships and meaning.

Before children meet in a group, write five to ten words on oaktag cards and arrange them on the sentence strip holder. After the words have been read, cut each of the words into its two smaller words and randomly arrange them on the sentence strip holder. Allow the children to randomly take turns arranging the small words back into the original compound words. Also, encourage them to form new compound words. For example, if one of two original compound words is "rainbow" and the other is "dropping," the children should be able to come with "raindrop." The new words the children come up with should be written on blank oaktag cards with the names of the children who came up with them attached. In this way the children can add to their growing bank of new words and have ownership in the words that they have added.

See also Skill 15.7

Word Study Group

This involves the teacher taking time to meet with children from grades 3-6 in a small group of no more than six children for a word study session. Taberski suggests that this meeting take place next to the Word Wall. The children selected for this group are those who need to focus more on the relationship between spelling patterns and their consonant sounds.

It is important that this not be a formalized traditional reading group that meets at a set time each week or biweekly. Rather, the group should be spontaneously formed by the teacher based on a quick inventory of the selected children's needs at the start of the week. Taberski has templates in her book of *Guided Reading Planning Sheets*. These sheets are essentially targeted word and other skills sheets with her written dated observations of children who are in need of support to develop a given skill.

The teacher should try to meet with this group for at least two consecutive twenty minute periods per day. Over those two meetings, the teacher can model a Making Words Activity. Once the teacher has modeled making words the first day, the children then make their own words. On the second day, the children "sort" their words.

Other topics for a word study group within the framework of the Balanced Literacy Approach that Taberski advocates are: inflectional endings, prefixes and suffixes, and/or common spelling patterns.

It should be noted that this activity would be classified by theorists as a structural analysis activity because the structural components (i.e., prefixes, suffixes, and spelling patterns) of the words are being studied.

Use of Syllabification as a Word Identification Strategy

Taberski, S., and Harwayne, S. On Solid Ground: Strategies for Teaching Reading K-3. *Heinemann Educational Books, 2000.*

The objective of this activity is for children to understand that every syllable in a polysyllabic word can be studied for its spelling patterns in the same way that monosyllabic words are studied for their spelling patterns.

The easiest way for the K-3 teacher to introduce this activity to the children is to share a familiar poem from the poetry chart (or to write out a familiar poem on a large experiential chart).

First, the teacher reads the poem with the children. As they are reading it aloud, the children clap the beats of the poem and the teacher uses a colored marker to place a tic (/) above each syllable.

Next, the teacher takes letter cards and selects one of the polysyllabic words from the poem that the children have already clapped out.

The children use letter cards to spell that word on the sentence strip holder, or it can be placed on a felt board or up against a window on display. Together the children and teacher divide the letters into syllables and place blank letter cards between the syllables. The children identify spelling patterns they know.

Finally, and as part of continued small group syllabification study, the children identify other polysyllabic words they clapped out from the poem. They make up the letter combinations of these words. Then they separate them into syllables with blank letter cards between the syllables.

Children who require special support in syllabification can be encouraged to use lots of letter cards to create a large butcher paper syllabic (in letter cards with spaces) representation of the poem or at least a few lines of the poem. They can be told that this is for use as a teaching tool for others. In this way, they authenticate their study of syllabification with a real product that can be referenced by peers.

Relationship Between Word Analysis Skills and Reading Comprehension

The explicit teaching of word analysis requires that the teacher preselect words from a given text for vocabulary learning.

These words should be chosen based on the storyline and main ideas of the text. The educator may even want to create a story map for a narrative text or develop a graphic organizer for an expository text.

Once the story mapping and/or graphic organizing have been done, the educator can compile a list of words that relate to the storyline and/or main ideas.

Next, the educator should decide which key words are already well-defined in the text. Obviously, these will not need explicit class review.

Identify the words that the children can determine through use of prefixes, suffixes or base words. Again, these words will not require direct teaching.

Then reflect on the words in relation the children's background, prior knowledge base and language experiences (including native language/dialect words).

Based on the above steps, decide which words need to be taught.

The number of words that require explicit teaching should only be two or three. If the number is higher than that, the children need guided reading and the text needs to be broken down into smaller sections for teaching. When broken down into smaller sections, each text section should only have two to three words that need explicit teaching.

Some researchers, including Tierney and Cunningham, believe that a few words should be taught as a means of improving comprehension.

It is up to the educator whether the vocabulary selected for teaching needs review before reading, during reading, or after reading.

Introduce vocabulary BEFORE READING if . . .

- Children are having difficulty constructing meaning on their own or if the children themselves have previewed the text and indicated words they want to know

- The teacher has seen that there are words within the text that are definitely necessary for reading comprehension

- The text itself, in the judgment of the teacher, contains difficult concepts for the children to grasp

Introduce vocabulary DURING READING if . . .

- The children are already doing guided reading

- The text has words that are crucial to its comprehension and the children will have trouble comprehending it if they are not helped with the text

Introduce vocabulary AFTER READING if . . .

- The children themselves have shared words that they found difficult or interesting

- The children need to expand their vocabulary

- The text itself is one that is particularly suited for vocabulary building

Strategies that use word analysis to build reading comprehension include:

- Use of a graphic organizer such as a word map

- Semantic mapping

- Semantic feature analysis

- Hierarchical and linear arrays
- Preview in context
- Contextual redefinition
- Vocabulary self-collection

> **SKILL 15.4** **Apply knowledge of structural analysis as a word-identification strategy** *(e.g., identifying base words, roots, and inflections; identifying prefixes and suffixes)*

Structural Analysis—Memorizing the Definitions of These Structural Word Components

Learning how to distinguish among and to correctly define these structural word components can seem daunting to young children. Actually, they can accomplish memorizing these set definitions, which is the first necessary step for correctly using them as they construct the meaning, quite easily. Pleasure in structural analysis is just a melodic song away.

Use a familiar song, which is actually a definition, such as "Do-Re-Mi" from *The Sound of Music*, or any children's song that is regularly used in the classroom. Model for the children how this familiar song can be "changed" to be the "sung" definitions of these structural components.

> *"re" this prefix means again*
> *"pre" like "re" but means before*
> *"de" means down, away, remove*
> *"ex" when something is no more*
> *"sub" means underneath or less*
> *"semi" half or only part*
> *"trans" across beyond or changed*
> *That will bring us back to "re"!*
> *Re pre de ex sub semi trans, re, trans!*

Once the teacher does the opening stanza, the children can then be challenged to come up with the next stanza's lines. The teachers will set the structural component for the line; let's say "compound words." Then the children, either as a whole class, in small groups, or as a guided writing activity, will author a line to share a compound word and explain what it is. Once this is successfully done the child or group of children who wrote the correct lyric can select another structural component. They can challenge other class members to complete the next line and the structural song writing can continue for the time allotted to vocabulary development or writing workshop.

This activity can develop into a structural song writing lyric wall, center, or sound recording. The teacher or one of the children (if the children are on grade three level or above), can write down each lyric line contributed and then routinely sing it with small groups or the whole class as practice for reviewing structural components. The songs can be shared with other classes. They can also be used as student-centered (written by and for students) exercises for a Structural Analysis center where peers will do activities in word study using work done by their classmates.

ELL students can do these activities using songs that are familiar to them from their native language or in a dual language version.

Using singing to help support children in necessary structural analysis definitions also differentiates instruction and helps the teacher to draw children whose learning styles and strengths are auditory and musical into the circle of engaged readers and writers.

Identification of Common Morphemes, Prefixes, and Suffixes

This aspect of vocabulary development helps children look for structural elements within words that they can use independently to help them determine meaning.

Some teachers choose to teach structural analysis directly. In particular, those who teach by following the phonics-centered approach for reading do this.

Other teachers, who follow the balanced literacy approach, introduce the structural components as part of mini lessons that are focused on the students' reading and writing.

Structural analysis of words, as defined by J. David Cooper (2004), involves the study of significant word parts. This analysis can help the child with pronunciation and constructing meaning.

Key Structural Analysis Components

A ROOT WORD is a word from which another word is developed. The second word can be said to have its "root" in the first. This structural component lends itself nicely to a tree with roots illustration that can illustrate this idea for children. Children may also want to construct root words using cardboard trees and roots to create word family models.

ROOT WORD: a word from which another word is developed

ELL students can construct these models for their native language root word families as well for the English language words they are learning. ELL learners in the fifth and sixth grade may even appreciate analyzing the different root structures for contrasts and similarities between their native language and English.

Special needs learners can work in small groups or with a paraprofessional on building root word models.

A base word is a stand-alone linguistic unit that cannot be deconstructed or broken down into smaller words. For example, in the word "retell," the base word is "tell."

A contraction is a shortened form of two words in which a letter or letters have been deleted and replaced by an apostrophe.

Prefixes are beginning units of meaning that can be added, or affixed, to a base word or root word. They cannot stand alone. They are also known as "bound morphemes."

Suffixes are ending units of meaning which can be affixed or added on to the ends of root or base words. Suffixes transform the original meanings of base and root words. Like prefixes, they are also known as "bound morphemes," because they cannot stand alone.

Compound words occur when two or more base words are connected to form a new word. The meaning of the new word is in some way connected with that of one or both the base words.

Inflectional endings are suffixes that impart a new meaning to the base or root word. These endings may change the gender, number, tense, or form of the base or root words. Just like other suffixes, these are also termed bound morphemes.

SKILL 15.5 Recognize strategies for identifying high-frequency sight words with irregular spellings

Spelling instruction should include words misspelled in daily writing, generalized spelling knowledge, and objectives in progressive phases of development. The developmental stages of spelling are:

1. Pre-phonemic spelling: Children know that letters stand for a message, but they do not know the relationship between spelling and pronunciation.

2. Early phonemic spelling: Children are beginning to understand spelling. They usually write the beginning letter correctly.

3. **Letter-name spelling:** Some words are consistently spelled correctly. The student is developing a sight vocabulary and a stable understanding of letters as representing sounds. Long vowels are usually used accurately, but silent vowels are omitted. Unknown words are spelled by attempting to match the name of the letter to the sound.

4. **Transitional spelling:** This phase is typically entered in late elementary school. Short vowel sounds are mastered and some spelling rules are known. Students are developing a sense of which spellings are correct and which are not.

5. **Derivational spelling:** This is the stage from high school to adulthood. This is the stage where spelling rules are being mastered.

Recognizing sight words is an essential component of good reading. Many of these words do not sound like their spellings might suggest, so sounding them out would be unproductive. Sight words are usually not decodable and must be memorized by the student in the earliest years of school.

Recognizing sight words is an essential component of good reading.

50 to 75 percent of all words used in schoolbooks, library books, newspapers, and magazines are in the Dolch Basic Sight Vocabulary of 220 words. They are pronouns, adjectives, adverbs, prepositions, conjunctions, and verbs that cannot be learned by sounding them out or by decoding.

Studies show that the 100 most common sight words, also known as high-frequency words, actually make up about 50 percent of the material we read.

The following 50 most common words make up about one third of written material for elementary readers.

a	for	it	pretty	to
and	funny	like	ride	too
are	get	little	run	two
at	go	look	said	up
big	have	me	see	want
can	help	my	that	we
did	here	new	the	will

Continued on next page

down	I	on	they	with
find	in	one	this	what
fly	is	play	three	you

Adapted from Fry, E. B., Kress, J. E., & Fountoukidis, D. L. The Reading Teacher's Book of Lists. *Prentice Hall. 1993.*

Students can create their own class version of this list with illustrations and even write their comments about why they have nominated certain words for the list.

SKILL 15.6 Recognize how readers use context, including semantic and syntactic clues, to help identify words, including words with multiple meanings

Semantic Feature Analysis

This technique for enhancing vocabulary skills by using semantic cues is based on the research of Johnson and Pearson (1984) and Anders and Bos (1986). It involves setting up a feature analysis grid of various subject content words that is an outgrowth of their discussion about these words.

For instance, Cooper (2004) includes a sample of a Semantic Features Analysis Grid for Vegetables.

Vegetables	Green	Have Peels	Eat Raw	Seeds
Carrots	−	+	+	−
Cabbage	+	−	+	−

Note that the use of the + for yes, − for no. Make this grid very accessible for young readers and very easy for them to do as part of their independent word analysis.

Teachers of children in grade one and beyond can design their own semantic analysis grids to meet their students' needs and to align with the topics the kids are learning.

1. Select a category or class of words (for example, planets, rodent family members, winter words, weather words).

2. Use the left side of the grid to list at least three if not more items that fit this category. The number of actual items listed will depend on the age and grade level of the children, with three or four items fine for K–1 and up to fifteen items for grades 5 and 6.

3. Brainstorm with the children to list features that the items have in common. As can be noted from the example excerpted from *Cooper's Literacy—Helping Children Construct Meaning* (2004), these common features such as green color, peels, and seeds are usually easy to identify.

4. Show the children how to insert +, −, and even ? (if they are not certain) notations on the grid. The teacher might also explore the possibility that an item could get both a + and a −. For example, a vegetable like broccoli might be eaten cooked or raw depending on taste.

Whatever the length of the grid when first presented to the children, make certain that the grid as presented and filled out is not the end of the activity. Children can use it as a model for developing their own semantic features grid and share them with the whole class. Child-developed grids can become part of a Word Work center in the classroom or even be published in a WORD STUDY GAMES book by the class as a whole. Such a publication can be shared with parents during open school week and evening visits and with peer classes.

Contextual Redefinition

This strategy helps children to use context more effectively by presenting them with sufficient context before they begin reading. It models the use of contextual clues so the children can make informed guesses about word meanings.

To apply this strategy, the teacher should first select unfamiliar words for teaching. No more than two or three words at a time should be selected for direct teaching. The teacher should then write a sentence in which there are sufficient clues supplied for the child to successfully figure out the meaning. Among the types of context clues the teacher can use are compare/contrast, synonyms, and direct definition.

The teacher should present the words on the experiential chart or as letter cards. Have the children pronounce the words. As they pronounce them, challenge them to come up with a definition for each word. After more than one definition is offered, encourage the children to decide as a whole group what the definition is. Write down their definition with no comment as to the word's true meaning.

Next, share the contexts (sentences the teacher wrote with the words and explicit context clues) with the children. Ask that the children read the sentences aloud. Then have them come up with a definition for each word. Make certain that, as they present their definitions, the teacher does not comment. Ask that they justify their definitions by making specific references to the context clues in the sentences. As the discussion continues, direct the children's attention to their previously agreed upon definition of the word. Help them discuss the differences between their guesses about the word when they saw only the word itself and their guesses about the word when they read it in context. Finally, have the children check their use of context skills to correctly define the word by using a dictionary.

This type of direct teaching of word definitions is useful when the children have dictionary skills and the teacher is aware of the fact that there are not sufficient clues about the words in the context to help the students define it. In addition, struggling readers and students from ELL backgrounds may benefit tremendously from being walked through this process, which highly proficient and successful readers apply automatically.

By using this strategy, the teacher can note the students' prior knowledge as they guess the word's meaning in isolation. The teacher can also witness and hear how various students use context skills.

> *Through their involvement in this strategy, struggling readers gain a feeling of community as they experience the ways in which their struggles and guesses resonate in other peer's responses to the text. Students also learn how to use context clues in order to navigate potential mazes of meaning themselves.*

> *Knowledge of vocabulary will not guarantee vocabulary success, but lack of vocabulary knowledge can ensure failure.*
>
> *—Andrew Biemiller (2003)*

SKILL 15.7 Demonstrate knowledge of curriculum materials and effective instruction in word-identification strategies for learners at various stages of literacy and from different cultural and language backgrounds

Many factors can affect someone's ability to pick up a second or third language. Age is one common factor. It is said that after a certain age (usually seven), learning a second language becomes dramatically more difficult. But there are also many social factors, such as anxiety, that influence language learning. Often, informal social settings are more conducive to second language learning. Motivation is another factor. A final important factor, particularly for teachers, is the strategies one uses to learn a language. For example, memorizing words out of context is not as effective as using words strategically for real-life purposes.

The most important concept to remember about the difference between learning a first language and a second is that if the learner is approximately age seven or older, learning a second language will occur very differently in the learner's brain than it would if the learner had been younger. The reason for this is that there is a language-learning function that exists in young children that appears to go away as they mature. Learning a language prior to age seven is almost guaranteed with relatively little effort. The mind is like a sponge and it soaks up language very readily.

Some theorists, including the famous linguist Noam Chomsky, argue that the brain has a "universal grammar" and that only vocabulary and very particular grammatical structures, related to specific languages, need to be introduced in order for a child to learn a language. What this really means is that, in essence, there are slots that language fills in a child's mind. This is definitely not the case with learning a second language after about seven years old.

Learning a second language as a pre-adolescent, adolescent or adult requires quite a bit of translation from the first language to the second. Vocabulary and grammar particulars are memorized, not necessarily internalized (at least not as readily as a first language). In fact, many (though not all) people who are immersed in a second language are never fully fluent in the language. They may appear to be totally fluent, but often there will be small traits that are hard to pick up and internalize.

It is clear that learning a second language successfully does require fluency in the first language. This is because, as stated above, the second language is translated from the first in the learner's mind.

> *First language literacy is a crucial factor in second language learning and particularly in second language literacy.*

When helping second language learners make the "cross-over" in language fluency or literacy from first language to second language, it is important to help them identify strategies they use in the first language and apply those to the second language. It is also important to note similarities and differences in phonetic principals in the two languages. Sometimes it is helpful to encourage students to translate; at other times, it is helpful for them to practice production in the target language. In either case, teachers must realize that learning a second language is a slow and complicated process.

Comprehension

COMPREHENSION means that the reader can ascribe meaning to text. Even though students may be good with phonics and even know what many words on a page mean, some of them are not good with comprehension because they do not know the strategies that would help them derive meaning from the text. For example, students should know that stories often have structures (beginning, middle, and end). They should also know that when they are reading something and it does not make sense, they will need to employ "fix-up" strategies where they go back into the text they just read and look for clues. Teachers can use many strategies to teach comprehension, including questioning, asking students to paraphrase or summarize, utilizing graphic organizers, and focusing on mental images.

> **COMPREHENSION:** the reader can ascribe meaning to text

Decoding, Word Recognition, and Spelling

Word analysis (a.k.a. phonics or decoding) is the process readers use to figure out unfamiliar words based on written patterns. Word recognition is the process of automatically determining the pronunciation and some degree of the meaning of an unknown word. In other words, fluent readers recognize most written words easily and correctly, without consciously decoding or breaking them down.

To decode means to change communication signals into messages. Reading comprehension requires that the reader learn the code in which a message is written and be able to decode it to get the message. Encoding involves changing a message into symbols. Some examples are, to encode oral language into writing (spelling), to encode an idea into words, or to encode a mathematical or physical idea into appropriate mathematical symbols.

Although effective reading comprehension requires identifying words automatically (Adams, 1990, Perfetti, 1985), children do not have to be able to identify every single word or know the exact meaning of every word in a text to understand the text. Indeed, Nagy (1988) says that children can read a work with a high level of comprehension even if they do not fully know as many as 15 percent of the words within a given text. Children develop the ability to decode and recognize words automatically.

> Fluent readers recognize most written words easily and correctly, without consciously decoding or breaking them down.

COMPETENCY 16
UNDERSTAND THE DEVELOPMENT OF VOCABULARY KNOWLEDGE AND SKILLS

SKILL 16.1 **Demonstrate knowledge of criteria for selecting appropriate vocabulary words** (e.g., key words, words that are conceptually related, synonyms and antonyms, idioms, colloquial expressions) **to increase students' vocabulary knowledge**

Word meanings in context are definitions that you determine based on information from the surrounding text, such as other words, phrases, sentences and paragraphs. You can use words you already know to piece together possible meanings. You can use root words, antonyms, and word forms to help determine the meaning of an unfamiliar word.

Root Words

Look at word parts to determine the meaning if you are stumped. For example:

> *If you learn that <u>chronological</u> order means arranged by order of occurrence in time, and you know that <u>speedometer</u> measures speed, you know that a chronometer is an instrument for measuring time.*

Antonyms

Sometimes antonyms, opposites or contrasts, can illuminate the meaning of an unfamiliar word. For example:

> *If you know that something <u>delayed</u> arrives late, then you can determine the meaning of <u>expedite</u> in the following sentence:*
>
> *To avoid the delay, Julius sent the package months early to expedite its arrival.*

Word Forms

Sometimes a very familiar word can appear as a different part of speech, as in these examples:

> *You may have heard that <u>fraud</u> involves a criminal misrepresentation, so when it appears as the adjective form <u>fraudulent</u> ("He was suspected of fraudulent activities") you can make an educated guess.*
>
> *You probably know that something out of date is <u>obsolete</u>; therefore, when you read about "built-in <u>obsolescence</u>," you can detect the meaning of the unfamiliar word.*

SKILL 16.2 **Demonstrate knowledge of a range of strategies for promoting and reinforcing students' oral and written vocabulary knowledge** *(e.g., read-alouds, word sorts, word banks, semantic mapping, knowledge of words that form common word roots in English)*

Read-Alouds

Reading aloud brings the class together to listen to, think about, and share a wide range of stories, poems, and informational reading. Listening to books being read aloud by the teacher is a way for children to engage in analytical conversations and to have meaningful discussions about the story.

Reading aloud allows the teacher to:

- Develop print and book concepts
- Instill a love for reading

- Develop students' understanding of poetry and stories
- Develop listening skills

Word Sorts

Word sorts help students to group words by the sounds they hear and the spelling patterns they see in each word.

Strategy

Have the students:

- Look at a list of words on an index card
- Cut apart the words on the card
- Say each word
- Use the sounds the students hear and the spelling patterns they see to match each to a Master Word
- Place the words they do not understand under the Question Mark

Word Banks

Steps to make a word bank:

1. Prepare a series of envelopes or file folders by labeling one for each beginning letter or sound of the alphabet

   - *Variation:* Have just one envelope or file folder for each student to put all their own words into

2. File them in a box or hang them on the wall in alphabetical order

3. When the student learns to read or spell a new word, write the word on a card

   - *Variation:* Have the student write the word

4. Have the student put the card in the appropriate envelope according to the first letter of the word on the card

SEMANTIC MAPS: diagrams that help students see how words or concepts are related to one another

Semantic Mapping

SEMANTIC MAPS are diagrams that help students see how words or concepts are related to one another. In most cases, semantic mapping begins with a brainstorming session in which students are encouraged to make associations to the main word or the concept presented. Students are actively engaged in using their prior knowledge and experiences that the teacher has provided to develop a semantic map. Semantic maps can be accomplished individually or with the whole class.

Semantic mapping strategy

Masters, Mori, and Mori (1993) discuss the use of semantic mapping strategy. They define semantic mapping as a technique being "used to motivate and involve students in the thinking, reading, and writing aspects. It enhances vocabulary development by helping students link new information with previous experience." The instructional sequence of semantic mapping is:

1. Select a word central to the topic

2. Display the target word

3. Invite the students to generate as many words as possible that relate to the target word

4. Have the students write the generated words in categories

5. Have the students label categories

6. From this list, construct a map

7. Lead the class in a discussion that focuses on identifying meanings and uses of words, clarifying ideas, highlighting major conclusions, identifying key elements, expanding ideas, and summarizing information

SKILL **Recognize ways to help students make effective use of reference**
16.3 **sources** (e.g., dictionaries, thesauruses, glossaries) to clarify understanding of a word's denotative and connotative meanings

Semantic Connotations

To effectively teach language, it is necessary to understand that, as human beings acquire language, they realize that words have denotative and connotative meanings. Generally, denotative words point to things and connotative words deal with mental suggestions that the words convey. The word skunk has a denotative meaning if the speaker can point to the actual animal as he speaks the word and intends the word to identify the animal. Skunk has connotative meaning depending upon the tone of delivery, the socially acceptable attitudes about the animal, and the speaker's personal feelings about the animal.

Informative Connotations

Informative connotations are definitions agreed upon by the society in which the learner operates. A skunk is "a black and white mammal of the weasel family with a pair of perineal glands which secrete a pungent odor." *The Merriam Webster Collegiate Dictionary* adds "...and offensive" odor. Identification of the color, species, and glandular characteristics are informative. The interpretation of the odor as offensive is affective.

Affective Connotations

Affective connotations are the personal feelings a word arouses. A child who has no personal experience with a skunk and its odor will feel differently about the word skunk than a child who has smelled the spray or been conditioned vicariously to associate offensiveness with the animal denoted skunk. The very fact that our society views a skunk as an animal to be avoided will affect the child's interpretation of the word. In fact, it is not necessary for one to have actually seen a skunk (that is, have a denotative understanding) to use the word in either connotative expression. For example, one child might call another child a skunk, connoting an unpleasant reaction (affective use) or, seeing another small black and white animal, call it a skunk based on the definition (informative use).

SKILL 16.4 Demonstrate knowledge of the role of vocabulary development in reading comprehension

See Skills 16.5, 17.4, and 17.6

SKILL 16.5 Demonstrate knowledge of curriculum materials and effective instruction in vocabulary knowledge and skills for learners at various stages of literacy and from different cultural and language backgrounds

Students will be better at comprehension if they have a stronger working vocabulary. Research has shown that students learn more vocabulary when it is presented in context rather than in vocabulary lists. Furthermore, the more students get to use particular words in context, the more they will remember each word and utilize it in the comprehension of sentences that contain the words.

The identification of common morphemes, prefixes, and suffixes is an important method of word analysis that students need to know when learning to read. This aspect of vocabulary development helps students look for structural elements in words that they can use to help them determine meaning. (*See Competency 15 for word analysis and word identification strategies.*)

The National Reading Panel (2000) has published the following conclusions about vocabulary instruction.

1. There is a need for direct instruction of vocabulary items required for a specific text.

2. Repetition and multiple exposure to vocabulary items are important. Students should be given items that are likely to appear in many contexts.

3. Learning in rich contexts is valuable for vocabulary learning. Vocabulary words should be those that the learner will find useful in many contexts. When vocabulary items are derived from content learning materials, the learner will be better equipped to deal with specific reading matter in content areas.

4. Vocabulary tasks should be restructured as necessary. It is important to be certain that students fully understand what is asked of them in the context of reading rather than focusing only on the words to be learned.

5. Vocabulary learning is effective when it entails active engagement in learning tasks.

6. Computer technology can be used effectively to help teach vocabulary.

7. Vocabulary can be acquired through incidental learning. Much of a student's vocabulary will have to be learned in the course of doing things other than explicit vocabulary learning. Repetition, richness of context, and motivation may also add to the efficacy of incidental learning of vocabulary.

8. Dependence on a single vocabulary instruction method will not result in optimal learning. A variety of methods can be used effectively, with emphasis on multimedia aspects of learning, richness of context in which words are to be learned, and the number of exposures to words that learners receive.

The panel found that a critical feature of effective classrooms is specific vocabulary instruction including lessons and activities in which students apply their vocabulary knowledge and strategies to reading and writing. Included in the activities were discussions in which teachers and students talked about words, their features, and strategies for understanding unfamiliar words.

COMPETENCY 17
UNDERSTAND READING COMPREHENSION AND FLUENCY

SKILL Demonstrate knowledge of literal comprehension *(e.g., sequence*
17.1 *of events in a narrative),* **inferential comprehension** *(e.g., drawing*
conclusions), **and evaluative comprehension** *(e.g., analyze author's*
motivation and purpose)

Literal comprehension is the ability to identify sequences of events, explicitly stated main ideas, and cause and effect relationships in a written text.

Inferential comprehension is the ability to draw conclusions or generalizations and infer ideas, details, and cause and effect relationships that are not explicitly stated in a written text.

Evaluative comprehension is the ability to distinguish between facts and opinions, detect faulty reasoning, and recognize bias in a written text.

SKILL Apply knowledge of strategies for promoting students' literal,
17.2 inferential, and evaluative comprehension *(e.g., analyze author's*
motivation and purpose)

See also Skills 17.5 and 17.6

Expository texts are full of information that may or may not be factual and that may reflect the bias of the editor or author. As such, they are good resources for practicing the reading skills of literal, inferential, and evaluative comprehension.

Types of expository texts to which children can be introduced are:

Description process text: This type of text usually describes a particular topic or provides the identifying characteristics of a topic. It can be depended upon to be factual. In this type of text, the child reader has to use all of his or her basic reading strategies because these types of expository texts do not have explicit clue words.

Cause and effect text: This type of text may contain faulty reasoning and the child reader has to use inferential and self-questioning skills to assess whether the stated cause-and-effect relationship is a valid and correct one. This type of content can be found in textbooks, newspapers, magazines, advertisements, and general information websites. The reader must note clue words ("therefore," "the reasons for," "as a result of," "because," "in consequence of," and "since") and then decide whether or not the evidence available or presented in the excerpt is sufficient to support the cause-and-effect relationship.

Comparison text: This type of expository text focuses the reader the contrasts and similarities between two or more objects or ideas. Many social studies, art, and science textbooks, as well as nonfiction books and newspaper editorials, include this type of text. Focusing on the clue words will allow the children to identify the comparison and/or contrast and decide if it is accurate. Key clue words include "like," "unlike," "resemble," "different," "different from," "similar to," "in contrast with," "in comparison to," etc.

Collection text: This is an expository text that presents ideas in a group. The writer's goal is to present a set of related points or ideas. The author uses clue words such as "first," "second," "third," "finally," and "next" to alert the reader to the sequence. Depending on how well the writer structures the sequence of points or ideas, the reader should be able to make connections and evaluate their validity.

Response structure text: These expository texts present a question or response followed by an answer or solution. Math, science, and social studies textbooks are filled with these types of questions. Clue words include "the problem is," "the question is," "you need to solve for," "one probable solution would be," "an intervention could be," "the concern is," etc.

Newspapers provide feature articles that can be used to evaluate point of view distinctions. Children can also come to understand the distinction between fact and fiction by examining newspaper advertisements for a product they commonly use, eat, drink, or wear.

SKILL 17.3 **Demonstrate knowledge of reading phrasing, rate, and expression as part of fluency**

FLUENCY is the ability to read a text quickly and with comprehension. It is an important connection between word recognition and reading. Children that can read fluently do not have to spend a lot of time trying to decode words, thereby losing the meaning of the text. The rate at which students read is affected by how

FLUENCY: the ability to read a text quickly and with comprehension

automatically they recognize words. Fluency is not the same as automaticity. Students may be able to automatically identify words in a list, but still not be fluent readers who are able to read sentences quickly with prosody.

The rate at which the students read should be about the same as their rate of speech. Though many students can read rapidly, they may lack the other two components of fluent reading, accuracy and prosody. Accuracy is the number of words a student can read correctly. PROSODY is the ability to read with expression, intoning the words correctly depending on the punctuation and the meaning of the text. When students possess all three of these components when reading a passage, they are fluent readers at their grade level.

In the early stages of reading, students may read slowly because they are focusing on individual words. The rate at which they read changes according to the text, their familiarity with the topic, and the amount of interest that they have in reading. Thus, students may read a familiar rhyme fluently, but have trouble with the same words in a story.

In the instruction of reading, fluent reading has often been an overlooked and under-taught skill in schools. The work of the National Reading Panel brought attention to the importance of fluency. This research has indicated that a child who reads fluently will be more likely to comprehend the text than a child who does not read fluently. Since the end result of all reading is comprehension, this body of research cannot be ignored.

READING FLUENCY is a broad term that is used to describe reading that has a high degree of accuracy, appropriate phrasing, smoothness, and an appropriate pace.

Reading is a complex task that requires many cognitive processes to occur simultaneously. In order to read fluently, students must be able to decode words in a rapid, automatic way. This allows students to free up some of their mental energy to focus on comprehension. Children who struggle with decoding cannot move beyond individual words to the level of comprehension.

This automatic capacity in reading is essential as the amount of information in texts grows and students are required to comprehend more and more information in order to be successful.

There are three components of fluent reading: rate, accuracy, and prosody.

PROSODY: the ability to read with expression

READING FLUENCY: a broad term used to describe reading that has a high degree of accuracy, appropriate phrasing, smoothness, and an appropriate pace

Fluency develops over time and with much repetition and practice.

SKILL 17.4 **Recognize the role of automatic word recognition in reading fluency and the relationship between reading fluency and reading comprehension**

See also Skill 15.7

Fluency

Fluency is the ability to read a text quickly and accurately. When reading silently, fluent readers can recognize words automatically and fully comprehend what they read. If comprehension is not immediate, these readers can use context clues to grasp the meaning of a sentence or paragraph. When reading aloud, fluent readers display confidence and read effortlessly and with expression (prosody).

Fluency allows students to progress from simple word recognition to an understanding of what they read. When students do not have to spend time focusing on reading individual words, they can group words together to form ideas, leading to comprehension. At this point, they can grasp the main idea of the text and can also make connections between the text and prior knowledge and events in their own lives.

Fluency changes over time as readers are exposed to more difficult texts. Readers who are fluent at grade level may read slowly when they are first introduced to a more difficult text because they need time for comprehension.

Some techniques to use when teaching students to read fluently include:

- Repeated reading of the same text
- Oral reading practice using recordings
- Models of what fluent reading looks and sounds like
- Reading to students
- Choral reading
- Partner reading
- Readers' Theatre

Automaticity

Automaticity is not the same as fluency. AUTOMATICITY is the fast and effortless recognition of words that comes through repeated practice. Automaticity refers to accurate reading of words, not to reading with expression or reading with comprehension. It is necessary for fluency, but it is not the only factor that determines whether or not a student can read fluently.

AUTOMATICITY: is the fast and effortless recognition of words that comes through repeated practice

Decoding and Reading Comprehension

See also Skill 15.7

J. David Cooper (2004) and other advocates of the Balanced Literacy Approach feel that children become literate, effective communicators and able to comprehend by learning phonics and other aspects of word identification through the use of engaging reading texts.

Engaging texts, as defined by the balanced literacy group, are those texts containing highly predictable elements of rhyme, sound patterns, and plot. Researchers such as Chall (1983) and Flesch (1981) support a phonics-centered foundation before the use of engaging reading texts. This is at the crux of the Phonics versus Whole Language/Balanced Literacy/Integrated Language Arts teaching of reading controversy.

It is important for the new teacher, educator, or teacher candidate to be informed about both sides of this controversy and the work of theorists who attempt to reconcile these two perspectives, such as Kenneth Goodman (1994).

In the teacher examinations, you will need to demonstrate that you are familiar with these varied perspectives. If asked on a constructed-response question, you need to be able to show that you can talk about teaching some aspect of reading using strategies from one or a combination of these approaches.

Working teachers can, depending on the perspective of their school administration and the needs of the particular children they serve, choose from the varied strategies and approaches.

SKILL 17.5 Apply knowledge of strategies for promoting students' reading comprehension

See also Skill 18.1

Theories and Strategies

Transactional theory

The transactional theory of reading comprehension suggests that there is an interaction between readers and texts. This theory places a great deal of responsibility on teachers for helping the students to make meaning of texts. Students should be encouraged to respond to their reading and reflect upon what they read. The classroom atmosphere must be one of cooperation where all student responses are accepted. Before reading, students should be asked to predict what they think the text is about, look for clues during reading, and confirm or refute their predictions after the reading.

Teachers may need to provide background information for those students who do not have any prior knowledge about the topic of the text. Students also need time to develop their ideas and should to be taught to respect other students' points of view. They should also be directed to connect their reading to other points in their lives; for example, other books they have read, things they have seen, or places they have visited.

Interactive theory

Interactive theory sees reading as the interaction between what readers bring to the text and what they read. According to interactive theory, readers use both top-down and bottom-up skills when reading. The top-down model starts with what the students know: They begin with a hypothesis and prediction and then attempt to verify what they believe to be true. This makes readers active participants in the reading process. According to Goodman (1986), there are five processes that students employ when reading:

- Recognition-initiation

- Prediction

- Confirmation

- Correction

- Termination

According to Stanovich (1980), the top-down approach makes reading easy for readers who have prior knowledge but poor word recognition skills, and the bottom-up approach makes reading easy for those who are skilled at word recognition but do not bring any prior knowledge of the topic to the text.

The bottom-up model suggests that students decode the words of a text by sounding them out when they are reading.

Metacognitive theory

Metacognitive theory focuses on six strategies that students use to make sense of the text when reading. These are:

1. Setting a purpose for reading

2. Activating prior knowledge

3. Paying attention to important ideas in the text

4. Evaluating for consistency and compatibility with prior knowledge

5. Self-monitoring for understanding

6. Making inferences and confirming or denying them

According to this theory, readers learn that the text they are reading is an organization of concepts rather than isolated words or facts. They work to understand what the words and sentences mean and are able to retell the text in their own words and make inferences.

Socio-psycholinguistic theory

The socio-psycholinguistic theory of reading stems from the work of Kenneth Goodman and incorporates both the linguistic nature of reading and the influence that social settings have on language. He states that rules for language differ according to the situation and region, and that this is something that reading specialists and teachers should acknowledge.

According to this theory, students start reading by recognizing what they are reading and going through a series of experiments with letters and words to make meaning of the text. The way they read has a lot to do with what they expect to find in the text. Students will make informed inferences about the words as they use cueing systems to decode them. They are able to recognize when words don't make sense in context and, will go back and make the necessary connections.

In this theory, reading is cyclical rather than linear. Readers constantly use visual, perceptual, syntactic, and semantic cues. Reading is goal-oriented, with the overall meaning of the text as the goal. Students use prediction and inference to help them move toward an understanding of meaning.

Constructivist theory

The constructivist theory is based on the work of Jerome Bruner and suggests that readers, while relying on a cognitive structure, construct new knowledge from the text based on their prior knowledge. Teachers using this theory encourage students to discover things about reading on their own. This means that there is active dialogue in the classroom and that the instruction should be organized in a spiral manner so that students build on what they have learned before.

Application of Theories and Strategies

The instruction teachers provide must be consistent with students' willingness to learn.

The instruction teachers provide must be consistent with students' willingness to learn. It should be easy for the students to grasp and designed to facilitate the acquisition of new knowledge and to fill in any gaps in the learning.

Decoding

In the late 1960s and the 1970s, many reading specialists, most prominently Fries (1962), believed that successful decoding resulted in reading comprehension. This meant that if children could sound out words, they would then automatically be able to comprehend the words. Many teachers of reading and reading texts still subscribe to this theory.

Asking questions

Another approach to the teaching of reading that gained currency in the late 1960s and the early 1970s was the importance of asking inferential and critical thinking questions of readers that would challenge and engage them in the text. This approach to reading went beyond the literal level of what is stated in the text to an inferential level of using text clues to make predictions, and then to a critical level of involving the student in evaluation of the text. While asking engaging and thought-provoking questions is still viewed as part of the teaching of reading, it is currently viewed as only one component of this teaching.

Comprehension skills

As various reading theories, practices, and approaches percolated during the l970s and l980s, many educators and researchers in the field came to believe that the teacher of reading had to teach a set of discrete "Comprehension Skills" (Otto et al, l977). Therefore, the reading teacher became the teacher of each individual comprehension skill. Students in such classrooms came away with concepts like main idea, sequence, cause and effect, and others that were supposed to help them better comprehend what they read. However, did it make them lifelong readers?

Bottom-up, top-down, interactional theories of reading

Bottom-up theories of reading assume that children learn from part to whole, starting with the smallest segments possible. Instruction begins with a strong phonics approach, learning letter-sound relationships, and often basal readers or decodable books. Decodable books are vocabulary-controlled, using language from word families with high predictability, such as "Nan has a tan fan." According to bottom-up theories, reading is skills-based, and the skills are taught one at a time.

Top-down theories of reading suggest that reading begins with the reader's knowledge, not the printed text. These theories state that students are driven to construct meaning. This stance views reading as moving from the whole to the parts.

An early top-down theory was the whole word approach. Children memorized high-frequency words to assist them in reading the Dick and Jane books of the 1930s. A more recent top-down theory is the whole language approach. This approach is influenced by research on how young children learn language, and believes that children can learn to read as naturally as they learn to talk. Children are surrounded by print in their classrooms, and taught using

> *Bottom-up theories of reading assume that children learn from part to whole, starting with the smallest segments possible. According to bottom-up theories, reading is skills-based, and the skills are taught one at a time.*

> *Top-down theories of reading suggest that reading begins with the reader's knowledge, not the printed text.*

quality literature often printed in Big Books. Students are also viewed as writers from the start, and even kindergarteners keep journals.

Interactive theories of reading combine the strengths of both bottom-up and top-down approaches. Teachers need to be able to teach decoding, vocabulary, and comprehension skills (bottom-up skills) to support students' drive for meaning and desire for a stimulating exchange with high-quality literary texts (top-down skills). Strategies include shared, guided, and independent reading, Big Books, and reading and writing workshops. Today this approach is called the balanced literacy approach.

> The balanced literacy approach is considered to be a synthesis of the best of bottom-up and top-down methods.

Factors that affect comprehension

Some of the factors that affect students' reading comprehension include:

- Schema (background knowledge): In order for students to comprehend what they read, they need to have some background knowledge of the subject matter. Sometimes they do have some knowledge, but do not know how to bring it to a conscious level. Through such prereading activities as brainstorming, graphic organizers, questioning, and writing activities, teachers can assess how much prior knowledge the students have and what additional background information they need. Once they determine this, teachers will know how much time they need to allot to the instruction and what activities they need to use to help the students become familiar with the subject matter.

- Lack of vocabulary knowledge: When students do not have the necessary vocabulary knowledge they will not be able to understand what the words in a text mean.

- Fluency difficulties: Students who read slowly because they have to spend time decoding will lose the meaning of a text as they focus on the individual words. They may not put expression into their reading and thus lose the meaning that is conveyed through punctuation and phrasing.

- Lack of word-recognition skills: If students do not have a sight vocabulary at their grade level, they will have difficulty understanding what they read. They will spend most of the time trying to decode the words, and this will hamper their understanding of the text.

- Student motivation: When students are not motivated by the material teachers ask them to read, they will not be able to comprehend the material as easily as they would if it were about a topic they like.

- Syntax and sentence structure: Students need instruction on how connections between words in the text can affect the text's meaning.

- Text structure: Students in the early grades are familiar with narrative writing, but may have difficulty with comprehension when they are introduced to expository writing.

- Strategies: Students need instruction in strategies to help them with comprehension, such as inferring, summarizing, predicting, formulating questions, and visualizing the text.

- Past reading instruction: As students progress through the grades, they have different teachers and therefore different methods of instruction. Reading specialists have to take this into consideration, especially if they are dealing with students who are learning English.

Teachers need to look at flexible grouping within the classroom setting. Although students may be grouped for ability at different times, this should not be the standard. Some of the various instructional grouping strategies that teachers can use in the classroom are:

- Whole class instruction: used to introduce new materials and strategies to the whole class

- Small group instruction: used for small groups of students who need more instruction on an objective

- Students working alone in teacher-directed activities: this enables the teacher to give one-on-one instruction or to assess how students are progressing

- Collaborative groups: students working together on a project

- Circle sharing: student discussion, such as author's chair

- Partner groups: for example, paired reading and think pair share

Awareness of strategies and resources for supporting individual students

Children who come from family backgrounds where English is not spoken lack a solid understanding of its syntactic structure. Therefore, as they are being assessed using the oral running record, they may need additional support from their teacher in examining the structure and meaning of English. A child from a non-native English language speaking background may often pronounce words that make no sense to him or her and just go on reading. These students have to learn to stop reading in order to construct meaning. They may have to be prompted to self-correct.

Students from non-native English language speaking backgrounds can benefit from independent reading opportunities to listen to a familiar story on tape and read along. This also gives them practice in listening to standard English oral

Highly proficient readers can sometimes support early readers through a partner relationship. Some children, particularly the emergent and beginning early readers, benefit from reading books with partners. The partners sit side by side and each one takes a turn reading the entire text.

reading. Often these students can begin to internalize the language structures by listening to a recording of the book several times.

Use of comprehension skills before, during, and after reading

Cooper (2004) advocates that children ask themselves what a text is about both before they read it and as they are in the process of reading it. Further, he asserts that they should note what they think the text is going to be about. While children are reading the text, Cooper feels that they should be continually questioning themselves as to whether the text is confirming their predictions. After completing the text, children can then review their predictions in summary fashion.

Again, within the framework set by Cooper in his work, *Literacy–Helping Children Construct Meaning*, children should be taught to look over the expository text subheads, illustrations, captions, and indices to get an idea about a book. Then children can decide where to look to find the target information. During the reading, children can then ask themselves, "Am I finding the answer to my question?"

After the reading, children can make notes such as, "I have found the answer to my question" or "This book is an excellent source of information for me about my question." If the book does not contain the needed information, the notes would be, "No, I have not found the answer to my question," "This book or is not a good source of information for me about my question," or "I will have to look for other resources."

SKILL 17.6 Demonstrate knowledge of curriculum materials and effective instruction in reading comprehension and fluency for learners at various stages of literacy and from different cultural and language backgrounds

See also Skills 15.3 and 18.5

Readability

To ensure readability, the text for instruction must be on the students' reading level. "Reading level" refers to the ease with which students can read a passage. If the passage is too difficult, students will have trouble reading and understanding the material. When material is presented at the students' reading level, they will recognize 90% of the words and will be able to read fluently without having to stop to decode individual words.

Some of the factors that can affect the readability include:

- Technical material beyond the scope of the students' understanding

- Use of vocabulary with which the students are not familiar

- The length of the text

Visual Representations

Students often refer to pictures when they are reading to help them infer or predict what will come next in the passage they are reading. They use the pictures to help them understand the story. Often teachers have students draw pictures about what they read to help assess whether or not students comprehend the material.

Text Organization

A newspaper is a good way to introduce students to expository text to and provide them with daily, ongoing experiences while they also keep up with real-world events that positively and negatively affect their daily lives.

Students can go on a chronological hunt through the daily newspaper and discover the many formats of schedules contained therein. For instance, some newspapers include a calendar of the week with literary, sports, movies, and other public events. They can also go on scavenger hunts through various sections of the newspaper and on certain days find timelines detailing famous individuals' careers, business histories, milestones in the political history of a nation, or even movies that have been nominated for awards.

In response to the public's need to know the why and wherefore behind natural disasters, company takeovers, and political upheavals, newspapers often represent events graphically and use cause and effect diagramming and comparison and contrast wording.

After reading this material, students can be asked to find additional examples of these text structures in the news or asked to reframe or rewrite familiar stories using these text structures. They can even use desktop publishing to re-author the stories using the same text structures.

If a class participates in a local "Newspapers in Education" program, where the children receive a newspaper in the classroom for free two to three times a week, the teacher can teach index skills by using the index of the newspaper and having children race to find various features.

Map and chart skills take on more relevance and excitement when the children work on these skills using sports charts detailing the batting averages and pass completions of their favorite players or perhaps the box scores of their older siblings' football and baseball games. Maps dealing with upcoming weather become meaningful to children as they anticipate a holiday vacation.

Genre

The genre of a text also affects how well the students can understand the material. Stories are the easiest for early readers to comprehend, and fiction is easier to understand than nonfiction.

Authors tell stories in different ways and employ various literary techniques. If teachers want students to understand these techniques, they need to teach the characteristics of each narrative genre. It may be necessary to draw the students' attention to the elements and structure of narratives as well as the strategies they can use for reading each of the genres. Before students actually read a selection, the teacher can address the literary techniques, forms, and vocabulary of the selections in mini-lessons to provide the students with knowledge about what they will be reading. This will help students become more engaged with the text and give them an idea of what they should think about as they are reading.

Narrative genres

Prose fiction

PROSE FICTION:
literature about imaginary people, places, and events

PROSE FICTION is literature about imaginary people, places, and events. The purpose of this narrative genre is to stimulate the students' imaginations and to present the author's view of the world. This genre includes novels, short stories, and plays, each of which has its own distinctive characteristics. Every piece of prose fiction has a setting, conflict, plot, climax and resolution, in varying degrees.

A short story is a narrative that usually has only one focus and a smaller worldview. The students should determine whether the person telling the story is an outside narrator or a character within the story. They must take note of the central conflict and determine why the characters act as they do. As a response to the story, they can decide how they feel about the characters and their actions and ask questions about the message that the author is trying to convey in the story.

A novel is a longer version of the short story, often with subplots. While reading a novel, the students have to be able to keep the subplots separated and understand their relationship to the main plot. They must be aware of the motives of the various characters and of their own reactions to the characters' actions.

PROSE NONFICTION:
literature that is about real events, times, and places

PROSE NONFICTION is literature that is about real events, times, and places. It includes essays, journals, articles, letters, biographies, and autobiographies. Much of the contemporary nonfiction reads like fiction, with suspense, expression, and ingenuity of style. Because it is vivid and personal, it can provide students with a model for their own writing. When students are reading for information, they need to keep this purpose in mind and may need time and instruction to help them summarize or restate the main ideas.

POETRY is a form of literature that communicates ideas and feelings through an arrangement of words and sounds. Poetry can be used to capture a mood, tell a story, or explore different ideas. There are various literary techniques authors use in writing poetry, which the teacher can discuss with the class through mini-lessons.

PLAYS are works that can be read for the purpose of performance or for literary effect. Students should pay attention to the literary devices that the author uses. When reading a play, students can work on putting expression into their reading so that they can bring the characters to life.

Students should be aware of the purpose for reading so that they know what thinking is expected of them. When reading any text, students need to employ certain strategies. Therefore, teachers need to engage the students in the reading process and model the appropriate strategies of:

- Connecting
- Making meaning
- Questioning
- Predicting
- Making inferences
- Reflecting
- Evaluating

> **POETRY:** a form of literature that communicates ideas and feelings through an arrangement of words and sounds

> **PLAYS:** works that can be read for the purpose of performance or for literary effect

The Relationship Between Oral and Written Vocabulary Development and Reading Comprehension

Biemiller's (2003) research documents that those children entering fourth grade with significant vocabulary deficits demonstrate increasing reading comprehension problems. Evidence shows that these children do not catch up, but rather continue to fall behind.

Strategy One: Word map strategy

This strategy is useful for children grades 3 to 6 and beyond. The target group of children for this strategy includes those who need to improve their independent vocabulary acquisition abilities. The strategy is essentially teacher-directed learning, in which children are "walked through" the process. They are helped by the teacher to identify the type of information that makes a definition. They are also assisted in using context clues and background understanding to construct meaning.

> *Word map templates are available online:*
>
> *www.eduplace.com/ graphicorganizer*
>
> *www.readwritethink.org.*

The word map graphic organizer is the tool teachers use to complete this strategy with children. Word maps help the children to visually represent the elements of a given concept.

The children's articulation of the concept can be prompted by three key questions:

- What is it?

- What is it like?

- What are some examples?

For instance, the word oatmeal might yield a word map with "What?" and, in a rectangular box, the answer might be that it is a hot cereal you eat in the morning, "What is it like?" might produce the answers hot, mushy, salty, "What are some examples?" might produce the response instant oatmeal you make in a minute, apple-flavored oatmeal, Irish Oatmeal.

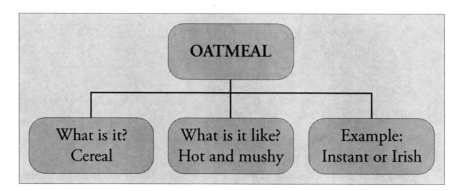

The procedure to be used in sharing this strategy with children is to select three concepts the children are familiar with. Then show them the template of a word map. Tell them that the three questions asked on the map and the boxes to fill in beneath them helps readers and writers to see what they need to know about a word. Next, help the children to complete at least two word maps for two of the three concepts that were preselected. Then have the children select a concept of their own to map either independently or in a small group. As the final task for this first part of the strategy, have the children, working in teams or individually, write a definition for at least one of the concepts using the key things about it listed on the map. Have the children share these definitions aloud and talk about how they used the word maps to help them with the definitions.

For the next part of this strategy, the teacher should pick up an expository text or a textbook the children are already using to study mathematics, science, or social studies. The teacher should either locate a short excerpt where a particular concept is defined or use the content to write model passages of definition.

After the passages are selected or authored, the teacher should duplicate them. Then they should be distributed to the children along with blank word map templates. The children should be asked to read each passage and then to complete the word map for the concept in each passage. Finally, have the children share the word maps they have developed for each passage. Give them a chance to explain how they used the word in the passage to help them fill out their word map. End by telling them that the three components of the concept—class, description, example—are just three of the many components for any given concept.

This strategy has assessment potential because the teacher can see how the students understand specific concepts by looking at their maps and hearing their explanations. The maps the students develop on their own demonstrate whether they have really understood the concepts in the passages. This strategy serves to ready students for inferring word meanings on their own. By using the word map strategy, children develop concepts of what they need to know to begin to figure out an unknown word on their own. It assists children in grades 3 and beyond to connect prior knowledge with new knowledge.

This word map strategy can be adapted by teachers to suit the specific needs and goals of their instruction. Illustrations of the concept and the comparisons to other concepts can be included in the word mapping for children grades 5 and beyond. This particular strategy is also one that can be used with a research theme in other content areas.

Strategy Two: Preview in context

This is a direct teaching strategy that allows the teacher to guide the students as they examine words in context prior to reading a passage. Before beginning the strategy, the teacher selects only two or three key concept words. Then the teacher reads carefully to identify passages within the text that evidence strong context clues for the chosen words.

Then the teacher presents the word and the context to the children. As the teacher reads aloud, the children follow along. Once the teacher has finished the read aloud, the children reread the material silently. After the silent rereading, the children will be coached by the teacher to a definition of one of the key words selected for study. This is done through a child-centered discussion. As part of the discussion, the teacher asks questions that get the children to activate their prior knowledge and to use the contextual clues to figure out the correct meanings of the selected key words. Make certain that the definitions of the key concept words is finally made by the children.

Next, help the children to begin to expand the word's meaning. Do this by having them consider the following for the given key concept word: synonyms, antonyms, and other contexts or other kinds of stories or texts where the word might appear. This is the time to have the children check their responses to the challenge of identifying word synonyms and antonyms by having them go to the thesaurus or the dictionary to confirm their responses. In addition, have the children place the synonyms or antonyms they find in their word boxes or word journals. This record of their findings will guarantee them ownership of the words and deepen their capacity to use contextual clues.

The main point to remember in using this strategy is that it should only be used when the context is strong. It will not work with struggling readers who have less prior knowledge. Through listening to the children's responses as they define the word and its potential synonyms and antonyms, the teacher can assess their ability to successfully use context clues. The key to this simple strategy is that it allows the teacher to draw the child out and to grasp, through the child's responses, the individual child's thinking process. The more talk from the child the better.

The Role of Systematic, Noncontextual Vocabulary Strategies

Strategy One: Hierarchical and linear arrays

The very complexity of the vocabulary used in this strategy description may be unnerving for the teacher, yet this strategy, included in the Cooper (2004) literacy instruction, is really very simple once it is outlined directly for children.

By using the term hierarchical and linear arrays, Cooper really is talking about how some words are grouped based on associative meanings. The words may have a "hierarchical" relationship to one another. For instance, an undergraduate or a first grader is lower in the school hierarchy than the graduate student or second grader. Within an elementary school, the fifth grader is at the top of the hierarchy and the Pre-K or kindergartener is at the bottom of the hierarchy. The term for this strategy obviously need not be explained in detail to K–3 children, but it might be shared with some grade- and age-appropriate modifications with children in grades 3 and beyond. It will enrich their vocabulary development and ownership of arrays they create.

Words can have a linear relationship to one another in that they run a spectrum from bad to good—for example, from K–3 experiences, pleased to happy to overjoyed. These relationships can be displayed in horizontal boxes connected with dashes. The following diagram is another way to display hierarchical relationships.

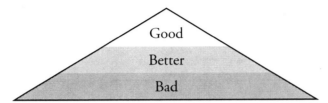

Once you get past the seemingly daunting vocabulary words, the arrays turn out to be another neat, graphic organizer that can help children "see" how words relate to one another.

To use this graphic organizer, the teacher should preselect a group of words from a read-aloud or from the children's writing. Show the children how the array will look using arrows for the linear array and straight lines for the hierarchy. Invite some children up to draw the straight hierarchy lines, so they have a role in developing even the first hierarchical model.

Do one hierarchy array and one linear array with the preselected word with the children. Talk them through filling out (or helping the teacher to fill out) the array. After the children have had their own successful experience with arrays, they can select the words from their independent texts or familiar, previously read favorites to study. They will also need to decide which type of array, hierarchical or linear, is appropriate. For fifth and sixth graders, this choice can and should be voiced using the now familiar vocabulary words hierarchical array and linear array.

This strategy is best used after reading, because it will help the children to expand their word banks.

Strategy Two: Contextual vocabulary strategies

Vocabulary self-collection

This strategy is one in which children, even on the emergent level from grade 2 and up, take responsibility for their learning. It is also, by definition, a student-centered strategy, which demonstrates student ownership of their chosen vocabulary.

This strategy can be introduced by the teacher early in the year, perhaps even the first day or week. The format for self-collection can then be adopted by the children. It may take the form of a journal with photocopied template pages. It can be continued throughout the year.

To start, ask the children to read a required text or story. Invite them to select one word from this text or story for the class to study. The children can work individually, in teams, or in small groups. The teacher can also do the self-collecting so that this becomes the joint effort of the class community of literate readers. Tell the children that they should select words that particularly interest them or that are unique in some way.

After the children have had time to make their selections and to reflect on them, make certain that they have time to share them with their peers as a whole class. When each child shares the selected word, have the class provide a definition for the word. Each word that is given should be listed on a large experiential chart or even in a big book format, if that is age- and grade-appropriate. The teacher should also share the word she selected and provide a definition. The teacher's definition and sharing should fall somewhere in the middle of the children's definitions.

The dictionary should then be used to verify the definitions. When all the definitions have been checked, a final list of child-selected (and the single teacher-selected) words should be made.

Once this final list has been compiled, the children can record it in their word journals, or they may opt to record only those words they find interesting in their individual journals. It is up to the teacher at the onset of the vocabulary self-collection activity to decide whether the children have to record all the words on the final list or can eliminate some. The decision the teacher makes at the outset, however, must be adhered to throughout the year.

> One of the nice things about vocabulary self-selection is that it works equally well with either expository or narrative texts. It also provides children with an opportunity to use the dictionary.

To further enhance this strategy, children—particularly those in grades 3 and beyond—can be encouraged to use their collected words as part of their writings or to record and clip the appearance of these words in newspaper stories or online. This type of additional recording demonstrates that the child has truly incorporated the word into his reading and writing. It also habituates children to be lifelong readers, writers, and researchers.

Assessment is built into this strategy. As the children select the word for the list, they share how they used contextual clues. Through the children's response to the definitions offered by their peers, their prior knowledge can be assessed.

Learn to read and write by reading and writing

In this strategy, children take ownership of the words in their self-collection journals. These can also be the beginning of writer-observation journals if they include their own writings. Children can also use the word lists as a beginning for writers' commonplace books. These books are filled with newspaper, magazine, and functional document clippings using the journal words.

This activity is a good one for demonstrating the balanced literacy belief that vocabulary study works best when the words studied are chosen by the child.

The Relationship Between Oral Vocabulary and the Process of Identifying and Understanding Written Words

One way to explore the relationship between oral vocabulary and the comprehension of written words is through the use of oral records.

In On Solid Ground: Strategies for Teaching Reading K-3, Sharon Taberski (2000) discusses how oral reading records can be used by the K-3 teacher to assess how well children are using cueing systems. She notes that the running record format can also show visual depictions for the teacher of how the child "thinks" as the child reads. The notation of miscues, in particular, shows how a child "walks through" the reading process. They indicate if and in what ways the child may require guided support in understanding the words she reads aloud. Taberski notes that when children read they need to think about several things at once. First, they must consider whether what they are reading makes sense (semantic or meaning cues). Next, they must know whether their reading sounds right in terms of Standard English (syntactic and structural cues). Third, they have to weigh whether their oral language actually and accurately matches the letters the words represent (visual or graphophonic cues).

In taking the running record and having the opportunity to listen first-hand to the children talk about the text, the teacher can analyze the relationship between the child's oral language and word comprehension. Information from the running record provides the teacher with a road map for differentiated cueing system instruction.

For example, when a running record is taken, a child often makes a mistake but then self-corrects. The child may select from various cueing systems when he self-corrects. These include: *M* for meaning, *S* for syntax, and *V* for visual. The use of a visual cue means that the child is drawing on his knowledge of spelling patterns. Of course, Taberski cautions that any relationship between oral language and comprehension that the teacher draws from an examination of the oral-reading records must be drawn using a series of three or more of the child's oral reading records, taken over time, not just on one.

A teacher can review children's running records over time to note their pattern of miscues and which cues they have the greatest tendency to use in their self-corrections. Whichever cueing system the children use to the greatest extent, it is necessary for the teacher to encourage the children to also use the other cueing systems to construct correct meaning. Taberski suggests that, while assessing running records to determine the relationship between oral language and meaning, the children read from "just right" books.

A teacher can review children's running records over time to note their pattern of miscues and which cues they have the greatest tendency to use in their self-corrections.

The classroom library

Taberski generally keeps book crates containing books that are not leveled on tables. Children choose from among these books during the first independent reading session of the day, which is from 8:40-9:00. During the second reading session, from 9:30-10:20, the children select books from the leveled-reading bins, which are stored on the bookcase shelves.

Beyond the leveled books, which have already been discussed, Taberski also maintains a nonleveled, nonfiction library, which includes dictionaries, atlases, almanacs, and informational books related to the themes, projects, and investigations that the children will undertake throughout the year.

Beyond the leveled books and nonfiction books in the classroom, Taberski and other balanced literacy advocates generally include at least ten to fifteen big books that they routinely use to engage children with the text.

Because guided reading with groups of six children is a major part of the balanced literacy approach, Taberski and other disciplined and dedicated teacher/educators bundle up six copies of selected books so that they can distribute them to their guided reading groups whenever they choose to use them. Taberski models the concept of a home library collection for the children by keeping books that she particularly likes in a bookcase behind her chair. She sometimes places "her" books on the easel so that they can be shared by the children and returned to her.

Wall words

Much of creating a family atmosphere lies in the use of the room walls to document the children's learning experiences, skills work, and readings.

Generally at least one wall in a reading classroom is the chart wall. Charts with various spelling patterns discussed in class can be posted. If a child has issues or concerns with that particular pattern, she should be directed to look at and to review the chart.

One of the centerpieces of the K–2 classroom is the high frequency word chart. This is a growing list of commonly used words that the teacher tapes under the appropriate beginning letter according to the children's directions. At the end of each month, the newest high frequency words go into the children's folders and become part of their spelling words. Therefore reading, writing, and spelling are all intricately connected.

Supplies for children K–3 and beyond can include:

- A red plastic double pocket reading folder

- A blue plastic double pocket reading folder

- A four-sectioned pressed board spelling/poetry folder
- A 4" by 6" assessment notebook for reading
- A 4" by 6" assessment notebook for writing
- A reading response notebook (sixty page loose-leaf)
- A handwriting notebook

The reading folder contains the assessment notebooks, the reading response notebooks, a weekly reading log, and the strategy sheets the child may be using that particular week.

The assessment notebook is a key evaluative tool and a recording document for the conscientious balanced literacy specialist. The teacher uses the notebook to record the child's running record and retellings of stories shared by the child, and to summarize talks about leveled books read. Within the assessment books, the teacher also has notes about the child's progress, the strategies the child has learned to use well, the books he or she has read, and those strategies the child still needs to practice. These assessment notebooks must be kept accessible so that the teacher can use them to confer with the child, parents, and administrators as needed.

The reading response notebook is a compilation of reading strategy sheets and children's writings and art in response to literature.

The weekly reading log allows the children to maintain for themselves the titles of books they have read and to write a bit about the narrative, style, and genre of that given book.

Book bags are 10" by 12" heavy duty freezer bags that hold three to ten books that a child is "working on" during his free time. The teacher generally matches the children to the books and changes these books as needed by the children.

Adjustment of Reading Instruction Based on Ongoing Assessment

Children's running records help the teacher learn about the cueing systems that children use. It is important for the teacher to adjust reading instruction based on the pattern of miscues gathered from several successive reading records. When the teacher carefully reviews a given student's substitutions and self-corrections, certain patterns begin to surface. A child may use visual cues as he or she reads and adds meaning to self-correct. To the alert teacher, the reliance on visual miscues indicates that the reader doesn't make sense of what she is reading. This means that the teacher needs to check to see what cueing system the child uses

> Children's running records help the teacher learn about the cueing systems that children use.

when she is reading "just right" books. Children, who use meaning and structure but not visual graphophonic cues, need to be reminded and helped to understand the importance of getting and reconstructing the author's message. They have to be able to share the author's story, not their own.

Instructional Reading Strategies for Promoting the Development of Particular Reading Skills

Phonemic awareness can be developed through using leveled books that deal with rhyming words and segmenting phonemes into words. Children can also work with word or letter strips to continue the poems from the books and create their own "sequels" to the phoneme-filled story. They can also create an in-style rhyming story using some of the same phonemes from the leveled story they have heard.

Word identification: selective cue stage

Sometimes children have not yet experienced an awareness of the conventions of print and labeling in their home environments. The teacher or an aide may have to go on a label adventure and support children in recognizing or affixing labels to parts of the classroom, halls, and school building. A neighborhood walk with a digital or hand held camera may be required to help children identify uses and functions of print in society. A classroom photo essay or bulletin board could be the outgrowth of such an activity.

Uses of Large Group, Small Group, and Individualized Reading Instruction

The framework for organizing the balanced literacy classroom is referred to as the one book–whole class mode. What this means is that everyone in the class has experiences with the same book.

The framework for organizing the balanced literacy classroom is referred to as the one book–whole class mode. What this means is that everyone in the class has experiences with the same book. The teacher begins the discussion by activating prior knowledge and developing the context or background for the text. Some of the children within the class may have less prior knowledge or context within which to frame the book. The teacher will need to provide a preview of the book or develop key concepts to provide a stronger base for what the class will read together.

Some children will have to work with a paraprofessional or with a reading tutor before the class studies the book. Different modes of reading are accommodated within the class, by the books being read as a read-aloud, as part of shared reading, or as guided reading. Student-reader choices can also include: cooperative reading, reading with a partner, or independent reading.

Following the reading, the children respond to what they have read, which can be done through a literature circle, a whole class response, or in writing.

Strategies for Selecting and Using Meaningful Reading Materials at Appropriate Levels of Difficulty

Matching young children with "just right" books fosters their independent reading, no matter how young they are. The teacher needs to have an extensive classroom library of books. Books that emergent readers and early readers can be matched with should have fairly large print and appropriate spacing, so that the reader can easily see where a word begins and ends, and few words on each page so that the young reader can focus on top-to bottom, left-to-right directionality and the one-to-one match of word to print.

Illustrations for young children should support the meaning of the text, and language patterns and predictable text structures should make these texts appealing to young readers. Most important of all, the content of the story should relate to the children's interests and experiences.

Only after all these considerations have been addressed can the teacher select "just right" books from an already leveled bin or list. In a similar fashion, when the teacher is selecting books for transitional and fluent readers, the following ideas need to be taken into account.

The book should take at least two sittings to read so children can get used to reading longer books. The fluent and transitional reader needs to deal with more complex characters and more intricate plots. Look for books that set the stage for plot development with a compelling beginning. Age appropriateness of the concepts, plot, and themes is important so that the child will maintain interest in the book. Look for book features such as a list of chapters to help children navigate through the book. Series books are wonderful to introduce at this point in the children's development.

Creation of an Environment that Promotes Love of Reading

The creation of the meeting area and the reading chair (sometimes a rocking chair) with throw pillows around it promotes a love of reading. Beyond that, some classrooms have adopted an author's hat, decorated with the pictures of famous authors and book characters that children wear when they read from their own works.

Many classrooms also have children's storyboards, artwork, story maps, pop-up books, and "in the style of" writing inspired by specific authors. Some teachers buy calendars for the daily schedule, which celebrate children's authors or types of literature. Children are also encouraged to bring in public library books and

> *The content of the story should relate to the children's interests and experiences.*

> *The creation of the meeting area and the reading chair (sometimes a rocking chair) with throw pillows around it promotes a love of reading.*

special books from their home libraries. The teacher can model this habit of sharing beautiful books and inviting stories from his or her home library.

In addition, news stories about children's authors, series books, television versions of books, theatrical film versions of books, stuffed toy book character decorations, and other memorabilia related to books can be used to decorate the room.

Various chain book stores give out free bookmarks and promotional display materials related to children's books, which can be available in the room for children to use as they read independently or in their guided groups. They might even use these artistic models to inspire their own book-themed artifacts.

Uses of Instructional Technology to Promote Reading Development

One of the most interesting ways in which the Internet complements the reading and writing workshop involves the proliferation of author-specific Web sites. If used judiciously, these resources allow authors to come into the classroom and allow children to write, question, discuss, and share their literacy experiences with the authors themselves. Children can also readily become part of a distance community of peers who are also reading works by a given author.

There are some reader response online resources, such as the spaghetti review Web site, (http://www.book-club-review.com/view.php?cid=1) where young readers can post their response to different books they are reading.

For instance, children who have been introduced to the work of Faith Ringgold, the author of *Tar Beach*, can easily visit her online site, *www.faithringgold.com*. Here they will not only find extensive biographic data on Ringgold, but they will also be able to learn a song inspired by her main character, Cassie. They will be able to help illustrate a new story Ringgold has put up on the site and see if any of the questions they may have generated in their shared or independent reading of her books have already been answered in the "frequently asked questions" section of her site. A few of the author Web sites respond online to individual children's questions.

Knowledge of Reading as a Process to Construct Meaning

If there were two words synonymous with reading comprehension as far as the balanced literacy approach is concerned, they would be constructing meaning.

Cooper, Taberski, Strickland, and other key theorists and classroom teachers conceptualize the reader as interacting with the text and bringing her prior knowledge and experience to it. Writing is interlaced with reading and is a mutually integrative and supportive parallel process. Hence, the division of literacy learning into reading workshop and writing workshop, with the same anchor "readings" or books being used for both.

Consider this sentence:

> *The test booklet was white with black print, but very scary looking.*

According to the idea of constructing meaning, as the reader reads this sentence, the schemata (generic information stored in the mind) of tests the reader has experienced is activated by the author's notion that tests are scary. Therefore, the ultimate meaning that the reader derives from the page is from the reader's own responses and experiences coupled with the ideas the author presents. The reader constructs a meaning that reflects the author's intent and also the reader's response to that intent.

It is important to remember that readings are generally fairly lengthy passages, composed of paragraphs, which in turn are composed of more than one sentence. With each successive sentence, and every new paragraph, the reader refocuses. The schemata are reconsidered and a new meaning is constructed.

Knowledge of Levels of Reading Comprehension and Strategies for Promoting Comprehension of Imaginative Literary Texts at All Levels

Sharon Taberski (2000) recommends that, initially, strategies for promoting comprehension of imaginative literary texts be done with the whole class.

Taberski recommends specific strategies for promoting comprehension of imaginative literary texts. She feels that, if repeated sufficiently during the K–3 years, and even if introduced as late as grade 4, these strategies will serve the adult lifelong reader well.

Strategy One: Stopping to think

In this strategy students reflect on the text as a whole. The reader is challenged to come up with the answer to these three questions:

- What do I think is going to happen? (inferential)

- Why do I think this is going to happen? (evaluative and inferential)

- How can I prove that I am right by going back to the story?"(inferential)

Taberski recommends that teachers introduce these key strategies with books that can be read in one sitting and recommends the use of picture books for these instructive strategies. She also suggests that books that are read aloud and used for this strategy also contain a strong storyline, some degree of predictability, and invite discussion as well as be a narrative with obvious stopping points.

Strategy Two: Story mapping

This strategy promotes comprehension of imaginative literary texts.

For stories to suit this strategy, they should have distinct episodes, few characters, and clear-cut problems to solve. In particular, Taberski tries to use a story where a single, central problem or issue is introduced at the beginning of the story and then resolved or at least followed through by the close of the story. To make a story map of a particular story, Taberski divides the class into groups and asks one group of children to illustrate the characters in the book. Another group of children are asked to draw the setting, while a third and fourth group of children tackle problem and resolution. The story map may also help children hold together their ideas for writing in the writing workshop as they take their reading of an author's story to a new level.

Strategy Three: Character mapping

This strategy focuses the children, as readers, on the ways in which the main character's personal traits can determine what will happen in the story. Character mapping works best when the character is a nonstereotypical individual, has been featured, perhaps, in other books by the same author, has a personality that is somewhat predictable, and is capable of changing behavior as a consequence of what happens.

Teachers who employ a balanced literacy curriculum in their classroom make choices on a daily basis in planning lessons that will benefit the students. This approach to teaching reading integrates all components of language arts and uses multiple strategies to help students develop as fluent readers. The main purpose is to integrate reading, writing, listening, speaking, and viewing so that each is not a separate part of learning to read.

Reading aloud to students is a main part of balanced literacy. However, the focus is on modeling the skills and strategies and then allowing the students time to practice them on their own. The components of a balanced literacy curriculum are:

- Shared reading
- Shared writing
- Guided reading
- Guided writing
- Independent reading
- Independent writing

Discussion circles and literature circles is another strategy by which students can be involved in reading and writing in a balanced literacy framework. J David Cooper believes that children should not be "taught" vocabulary and structural analysis skills. Flesch and E.D. Hirsch , who are key theorist of the Phonics approach and advocates of Cultural Literacy (a term coined and associated with E. D. Hirsch), believe that specific vocabulary words at various grade and age levels need to be mastered and *must* be explicitly taught in schools. As far as Cooper is concerned, it isn't possible to teach all the necessary and meaningful (for the child and, ultimately, adult reader) vocabulary in schools. To Cooper it is far more important that the children be made aware of and become interested in learning words by themselves. Cooper feels that, through reading and writing, children develop a love for and a sense of "ownership" of words. All of Cooper's suggested structural analysis word strategies are, therefore, designed to foster children's love of words and a desire to "own" more of them through reading and writing.

Discussion circle is an activity that fits nicely into the Balanced Literacy Lesson Format as part of a SHARE. After the children (and this activity works well from grades 3 to 6 and beyond) conclude a particular text, Cooper suggests that they get together in discussion circles to respond to the book. Among the prompts, the teacher might suggest that the children focus on words of interest that they encountered in the text. These can also be words that they heard if the text was read aloud. Children can be asked to share something funny or upsetting or unusual about the words they have read. Through this focus on children's response to words as the center of the discussion circle, peers become more interested in word study.

Strategic reading occurs when students are reading for information. The purpose for reading is simply to learn. Typically, strategic reading occurs in nonfiction or expository texts. The students are generally given some guidance on what information they are to find.

Strategic reading, however, is not a simple recall of facts. This is not literal comprehension. The students are required to read a great deal of information about a topic. Then they need to then take all of that information and build their own foundation of knowledge. Constructing knowledge is what makes strategic reading different than simple literal recall. It is through this process that information is connected to prior knowledge.

These connections are key factors in the success of comprehension. Strategic reading requires the reader to be able to tie new and old learning together to compound it into useful information. This process of thinking about reading and manipulating all that was learned is known as METACOGNITION.

> **METACOGNITION:** the process of thinking about reading and manipulating all that was learned

Metacognition presents a complex set of variables for the reader. The reader needs to be aware of the reading process and be able to recognize when information does not make sense. At this point, he needs to adjust the things he is doing in order to clarify and make the necessary connections. Throughout this process, the reader must continue to integrate the new and old.

Strategic readers use their metacognitive capacities as they analyze texts so that they are aware of the skills needed to construct meaning from the text structure.

When reading strategically, students need to keep in mind several factors.

- Self-Monitoring: When students self-monitor, they are able to keep track of all the factors involved in the process. In this way, they are able to process the information in the manner that is best for them.

- Setting the Purpose for Reading: In strategic reading, children have a specific reason for reading the text. There is information they need to gain and teachers should make that clear to the students. If it is unclear, the students will not be successful.

- Rereading: Rereading is probably one of the most-used methods for taking in initially overwhelming information. By revisiting the text, the students are able to take in smaller pieces of information that they missed in the first read through.

- Adjusting Reading Rates and Strategies: This is similar to self-monitoring; the students must be able to understand that sometimes it will be necessary to read more slowly than at other times. Sometimes they will need to make adjustments to the way they are reading in order to be successful at gaining the information they want to gain.

- Text Factors: Understanding the arrangement of nonfiction text with section titles and other unique organizational devices can provide the students with important tools leading to success. Knowing the structure of the text can save valuable time and decrease the need for rereading.

Consideration for the planning of reading can be a complex task. It is important to base the information you are relaying to the students on the appropriate grade-level standards and grade-level curriculum for the students with whom you are working.

A dilemma comes into play when the students are not functioning at grade level or are not demonstrating grade-level skills. This means that reading specialists must find yet another balance in their planning and later in their instructional methodologies. Finding the right combination of skills to teach requires much planning.

Because teachers will be working with students across grade levels or with the same skill at various grade levels, it is necessary to be familiar with the appropriate standards and curriculum at the various grade levels. In this manner, teachers can sit down and look at the standards, curriculum, and needs of the students and find the correct approach.

It is also important that all students, no matter how far behind, be exposed to grade-level standards and curriculum. The question for teachers, then, becomes how to deliver that information. When planning instruction, reading specialists must think carefully about what strategies will allow the students to gain the most benefit.

From here, it is simply determining the techniques or modifications that will need to be made to deliver this instruction:

- Will the vocabulary work well if you introduce some synonyms that the students have already learned successfully?

- Would this story work better if taught in smaller chunks so that the students can better manage the information?

- Is there a piece of information that needs to be taught first in order for the students to be successful with the material?

Ultimately, these types of questions must be considered prior to teaching in order for the information to be presented correctly to students. Sometimes this planning phase requires tremendous thought and effort in order to determine the appropriate method to help the students be successful.

General expectations for grade levels include phonemic awareness for kindergarten and grade one, and phonics is the emphasis through grade one and grade two. Fluency, comprehension, and vocabulary then become the focus as reading shifts from learning to read in the early primary grades to reading to learn in the late elementary grades and onward. Keep in mind, however, that all general areas can certainly be worked on outside of these general guidelines.

COMPETENCY 18
UNDERSTAND READING COMPREHENSION STRATEGIES FOR LITERARY AND INFORMATIONAL TEXT

> **SKILL 18.1** **Recognize how to apply comprehension strategies before reading** *(e.g., making predictions, previewing)*, **during reading** *(e.g., self-questioning to monitor understanding, skimming, scanning)*, **and after reading** *(e.g., retelling, summarizing)* **to promote understanding of literary and informational text**

There are five key strategies for child reading of informational/expository texts.

INFERENCING: making a reasonable judgment based on the information given

INFERENCING is an evaluative process that involves the reader making a reasonable judgment based on the information given and engages children in constructing meaning. In order to develop and enhance this key skill in children, they might have a mini lesson where the teacher demonstrates this key skill by reading an expository book aloud (i.e., one about skyscrapers for young children) and then demonstrates for them the following reading habits: looking for clues, reflecting on what the reader already knows about the topic ("activating prior knowledge" in a teacher's jargon), and using the clues in the expository text to figure out what the author means or intends.

Identifying main ideas in an expository text can be improved when the children have an explicit strategy for identifying important information. They can be assisted in making this strategy part of their everyday reading style by being focused and "walked" through the following exercises as a part of a series of guided reading sessions. The child should read the passage so that the topic is readily identifiable to him or her.

Next, the child should be asked to be on the lookout for a sentence within the expository passage that summarizes key information in the paragraph or in the lengthier excerpt. Then the child should read the rest of the passage or excerpt in light of this information and also note which information in the paragraph is not important. The important information the child has identified in the paragraph can be used by the child reader to formulate the author's main idea. The child reader may even want to use some of the author's own language in formulating that idea.

MONITORING means self-clarifying. As a reader reads, the reader often realizes that what he or she is reading is not making sense. The reader then has to have a plan for making sensible meaning out of the excerpt. Cooper and other balanced literacy advocates have a stop and think strategy that they use with children. The child reflects, "Does this make sense to me?" When the child concludes that it does not, the child then rereads, reads ahead in the text, looks up unknown words, or asks for help from the teacher.

> **MONITORING:** a plan for making sensible meaning out of the excerpt

What is important about monitoring is that some readers ask these questions and try these approaches without ever being explicitly taught them in school by a teacher. However, the key philosophy of the foundations of reading theorists mentioned here is that these strategies need to be explicitly modeled and practiced under the guidance of the teacher by most, if not all, child readers.

SUMMARIZING engages the reader in pulling together the essential bits of information within a longer passage or excerpt of text into a cohesive whole. Children can be taught to summarize informational or expository text by following these guidelines. First, they should look at the topic sentence of the paragraph or the text and delete the trivial information. Then they should search for information that has been mentioned more than once and make sure it is included only once in their summary. Find related ideas or items and group them under a unifying heading. Search for and identify a main idea sentence. Finally, put the summary together using all these guidelines.

> **SUMMARIZING:** pulling together the essential bits of information within a longer passage or excerpt of text

Use of Reading Strategies for Different Texts

As children progress to the older grades (3-6), it is important for the teacher to model for them that, in research on a social studies or science exploration, it may not be necessary to read every single word of a given expository text. For instance, if the child is trying to find out about hieroglyphics, he or she might only read through those sections of a book on Egyptian or Sumerian civilization that deal with picture writing. The teacher should model how to go through the table of contents and the index of the book to identify only those pages which deal with picture writing. In addition, other children should come to the front of the room or to the center of the area where the reading group is meeting. They should then, with the support of the teacher, skim through the book for illustrations or diagrams of picture writing, the focus of their need.

> *Children need to understand and to be comfortable with the fact that not every single expository text is meant to be read thoroughly and completely.*

Children can practice the skills of skimming texts and scanning for particular topics that connect with their grade social studies, science, and mathematics content area interests.

SKILL 18.2 Demonstrate knowledge of literary response skills (e.g., connecting elements in a literary text to personal experience and other text)

> When texts relate to a student's life or other reading materials or areas of study, they become more meaningful and relevant to students' learning.

Students enjoy seeing reading material connect to their life, other subject areas, and other reading material.

Teachers should realize that historically, there are two broad theories about the construction of meaning. One is behavioral learning. Behavioral learning theory suggests that people learn socially or through some sort of stimulation or repetition. For example, when we touch a hot stove, we learn not to do that again. We can also learn to produce something by watching someone do the same thing.

The other broad theory is cognitive. Cognitive learning theories suggest that learning takes place in the mind, and that the mind processes ideas through brain mapping and connections with other material and experiences. In other words, learning is somewhat external. We see something, for example, and then we copy it. With cognitive theories, learning is internal. For example, we see something, analyze it in our minds, and make sense of it for ourselves. Then, if we choose to copy it, we do so having internalized (or thought about) the process.

Today, most educators believe that children learn cognitively. So, for example, when teachers introduce new topics by relating those topics to information students are already familiar with or exposed to, they are expecting that students will be able to better integrate new information into their memories by attaching it to something that is already there. Or, when teachers apply new learning to real-world situations, they are expecting that the information will make more sense when it is applied to a real situation.

In all of the examples given in this standard, the importance is the application of new learning to something concrete. Cognitively, this makes a great deal of sense. Think of a file cabinet. When we already have files for certain things, it's easy for us to find a file and store new information in it. When we're given something that doesn't fit into one of the pre-existing files, we struggle to know what to do with it. The same is true with human minds.

SKILL 18.3 Demonstrate knowledge of common patterns of organization in informational text (e.g., chronological, compare-and-contrast, cause-and-effect)

Authors use a particular organization to best present the concepts they are writing about. Teaching students to recognize organizational structures helps them to understand authors' intentions, and helps them in deciding which structure to use in their own writing.

- Cause and Effect: When writing about why things happen, as well as what happens, authors commonly use the cause and effect structure. For example, when writing about how he became so successful, a CEO might talk about how he excelled in math in high school, moved to New York after college, and stuck to his goals even after multiple failures. These are all causes that lead to the effect, or result, of him becoming a wealthy and powerful businessman.

- Compare and Contrast: When examining the merits of multiple concepts or products, compare and contrast lends itself easily to the organization of ideas. For example, a person writing about foreign policy in different countries will describe them in relation to each other to point out differences and similarities, highlighting the concepts the author wishes to emphasize.

- Problem and Solution: This structure is used in a lot of handbooks and manuals. Anything organized around procedure-oriented tasks, such as a computer repair manual, gravitates toward a problem and solution format, because it offers clear, sequential text organization.

SKILL 18.4 **Describe the use of writing activities** (e.g., note taking, outlining, summarizing, semantic maps, K-W-L charts) **to promote comprehension of informational text**

KWL CHARTS aid reading comprehension by outlining what readers *KNOW*, what they *WANT* to know, and what they've *LEARNED* after reading. Students are asked to activate prior knowledge about a topic and further develop their knowledge about it using this organizer. Teachers often opt to display and maintain KWL charts throughout the reading of a text to continually record pertinent information about a student's reading.

KWL CHARTS: outline what readers KNOW, what they WANT to know, and what they've LEARNED after reading

When the teacher first introduces the KWL strategy, the children should be allowed sufficient time to brainstorm in response to the first question, listing what all of them in the class or small group actually know about the topic. The children should have a three-columned KWL worksheet template for their journals and the teacher should use a KWL chart to record the responses from class or group discussion. The children can write under each column in their own journal and should also help the teacher with notations on the chart. This strategy allows the children to gain experience in note taking and in creating a concrete record of new data and information they have gleaned from the passage about the topic.

Depending on the grade level of the participating children, the teacher may also want to ask them to consider categories of information they hope to find out from the expository passage. For instance, they may be reading a book about animals to find out more about animals' habitats during the winter or about the animals' mating habits.

For example, use this chart during your study of spiders. First write what you know about spiders. Then write what you would like to know about spiders. At the end of your study write the most important things you learned.

SPIDER KWL		
What I know	**What I want to know**	**What I have learned**
•	•	•
•	•	•
•	•	•

The most interesting fact I learned was:

_____

_____

When children are working on the middle section of their KWL strategy sheet— What I want to know—the teacher may want to give them a chance to share what they would like to learn further about the topic and help them to express it in question format.

KWL is useful and can even be introduced as early as grade 2 with extensive teacher discussion support. It not only serves to support the child's comprehension of a particular expository text, but also models a format for note taking for children. Beyond note taking, when the teacher wants to introduce report writing, the KWL format provides excellent outlines and question introductions for at least three paragraphs of a report.

Cooper (2004) recommends this strategy for use with thematic units and with reading chapters in required science, social studies, or health text books.

In addition to its usefulness with thematic unit study, KWL is wonderful for providing the teacher with a concrete format to assess how well children have absorbed pertinent new knowledge within the passage by looking at the third section—What I have learned. Ultimately, it is hoped that students will learn to use this strategy, not only under explicit teacher direction with templates of KWL sheets, but also on their own by informally writing questions they want to explore in their journals and then going back to their own questions and answering them after the reading.

> *KWL is useful and can even be introduced as early as grade 2 with extensive teacher discussion support.*

SKILL Demonstrate knowledge of curriculum materials and effective 18.5 instruction in reading comprehension of literary and informational text for learners at various stages of literacy and from different cultural and language backgrounds

While all child readers can benefit from explicit expository reading strategies, the English Language Learner can truly get a gateway for understanding second language materials by working with a native English language speaking partner on the question generating strategy. Both the partner (a peer) and the teacher should demonstrate how much of a resource illustrations and pictures can be for constructing meaning.

If the teacher has time to work individually with the English Language Learner, the daily newspaper, which is replete with graphics, photos and text, is a wonderful tool for honing expository reading skills using these strategies.

The five strategies for enhancing expository reading skills are not beyond use with special needs learners. However, rather than be offered in an array, these strategies would have to be presented one at a time, probably one-on-one with explicit teacher modeling, and then done as shared reading and shared writing with the specific child.

Highly proficient readers might enjoy sharing their skills with peers and could serve as the newspaper reading buddies for special needs students. They might not only support special needs grade level or younger peers in reading through a designated newspaper section every day, but might also collaborate with their peers or younger peers in designing a word search or crossword puzzle based on that particular section of the newspaper.

Use of editorial sports page cartoons is a good way to give special needs learners opportunities for identifying point of view. They can also create their own takes on the topics of the editorial cartoons using an accessible, nonthreatening storyboard format for their commentary.

DOMAIN V
MATHEMATICS

Available for purchase at www.XAMonline.com:

 eFlashcards: a digital representation of a card represented with words, numbers or symbols or any combination of each and briefly displayed as part of a learning drill. eFlashcards takes away the burden of carrying around traditional cards that could easily be disarranged, dropped, or soiled. Available at www.XAMonline.com/flashcards

 More Sample Tests: more ways to assess how much you know and how much further you need to study. Ultimately, makes you more prepared and attain mastery in the skills and techniques of passing the test the FIRST TIME! Available at www. XAMonline.com/sampletests

PERSONALIZED STUDY PLAN

![X] **KNOWN MATERIAL/ SKIP IT**

PAGE	COMPETENCY AND SKILL	KNOWN MATERIAL/ SKIP IT
223	**19: Understand mathematical communication**	☐
	19.1: Interpret mathematical terminology, symbols, and representations	☐
	19.2: Connect everyday language to mathematical language and symbols	☐
	19.3: Use visual, numeric, and symbolic representations to communicate mathematical concepts	☐
	19.4: Convert among visual, numeric, and symbolic representations	☐
226	**20: Understand numbers, number theory, and numeration**	☐
	20.1: Demonstrate knowledge of the concepts of place value, prime numbers, multiples, factors, and integers	☐
	20.2: Recognize numbers represented by exponential and scientific notation in context	☐
	20.3: Apply concepts of numbers and numeration to compare, order, and round up or down	☐
	20.4: Identify equivalent forms of fractions, decimals, and percentages	☐
236	**21: Understand mathematical problem solving**	☐
	21.1: Make use of pictures, models, charts, graphs, and symbols as tools of mathematical problem solving	☐
	21.2: Identify and use relevant information in a problem to solve it	☐
	21.3: Recognize and apply multiple solution strategies to problem solving	☐
	21.4: Evaluate calculations and problem-solving strategies to verify the accuracy of the results	☐
239	**22: Understand methods of mathematical operations, calculation, and estimation**	☐
	22.1: Use the basic four operations with variables and numbers	☐
	22.2: Recognize relationships among mathematical operations	☐
	22.3: Apply properties of real numbers and the number system	☐
	22.4: Make calculations with whole numbers, decimals, fractions, and integer numbers	☐
	22.5: Apply methods of approximation and estimation	☐
	22.6: Identify strategies for estimating solutions and for evaluating the accuracy of estimated solutions	☐
	22.7: Recognize methods and tools for computing with numbers	☐
257	**23: Understand and apply concepts and methods of measurement**	☐
	23.1: Identify procedures and units of measurement for problems involving length, area, volume, weight, angles, time, and temperature	☐
	23.2: Identify and use measurement tools	☐
	23.3: Demonstrate knowledge of conversions within and between measurement systems	☐
	23.4: Identify approaches to direct measurement units and indirect measurement	☐

PERSONALIZED STUDY PLAN

KNOWN MATERIAL/ SKIP IT

PAGE	COMPETENCY AND SKILL	
270	**24: Understand patterns, relationships, and algebraic concepts**	☐
	24.1: Define and describe patterns and relationships using various representations	☐
	24.2: Solve linear and nonlinear equations and inequalities	☐
	24.3: Identify algebraic concepts of relation and function	☐
	24.4: Represent relationships among variables using words, tables, graphs, and rules	☐
	24.5: Make use of algebraic functions to plot points, describe graphs, determine slope, and extrapolate	☐
282	**25: Understand and apply principles and properties of geometry**	☐
	25.1: Recognize the geometric properties of and relationships between two- and three-dimensional figures	☐
	25.2: Apply knowledge of basic geometric concepts	☐
	25.3: Identify and measure component parts of geometric figures	☐
	25.4: Apply knowledge of symmetry and transformations	☐
	25.5: Make use of geometric models and properties of figures to solve problems	☐
295	**26: Understand concepts and applications of probability**	☐
	26.1: Recognize real-world applications of probabilities and their consequences	☐
	26.2: Recognize expressions of probabilities as fractions, ratios, and decimals	☐
	26.3: Determine theoretical probabilities and make predications based on them	☐
	26.4: Determine probabilities of dependent and independent events	☐
	26.5: Make use of tools to estimate probabilities	☐
301	**27: Understand concepts and applications of statistics**	☐
	27.1: Apply knowledge of methods for organizing data in a variety of formats	☐
	27.2: Interpret statistical data expressed in various formats	☐
	27.3 Identify assumptions, trends, and patterns in data	☐
	27.4: Recognize limitations of data and models	☐
	27.5: Describe data using standard measures	☐
311	**28: Understand the nature and histories of mathematics**	☐
	28.1: Recognize the histories and importance of mathematical ideas	☐
	28.2: Identify inherent values of mathematics	☐
	28.3: Identify the roles and importance of mathematics in everyday life	☐

COMPETENCY 19
UNDERSTAND MATHEMATICAL COMMUNICATION

SKILL Interpret mathematical terminology, symbols, and representations
19.1

Students of mathematics must be able to recognize and interpret the different representations of arithmetic operations.

First, there are many different verbal descriptions for the operations of addition, subtraction, multiplication, and division. The table below identifies several words and phrases that are often used to denote the different arithmetic operations.

Operation	Descriptive Words
Addition	plus, combine, sum, total, put together
Subtraction	minus, less, take away, difference
Multiplication	product, times, groups of
Division	quotient, into, split into equal groups

Second, diagrams of arithmetic operations can present mathematical data in visual form. For example, we can use the number line to add and subtract.

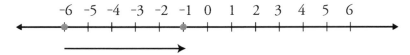

The addition of 5 to -6 on the number line; -6 + 5 = -1.

Finally, as shown in the examples below, we can use pictorial representations to explain arithmetic processes.

Two groups of four equals eight or $2 \times 4 = 8$ shown in picture form.

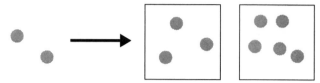

Adding three objects to two or $3 + 2 = 5$ shown in picture form.

SKILL 19.2 Connect everyday language to mathematical language and symbols

In real situations, relationships can be described mathematically. The function, $y = x + 1$, can be used to describe the idea that people age one year on their birthday. To describe the relationship in which a person's monthly medical costs are 6 times a person's age, we could write $y = 6x$. The monthly cost of medical care could be predicted using this function. A 20 year-old person would spend $120 per month ($120 = 20 \times 6$). An 80 year-old person would spend $480 per month ($480 = 80 \times 6$). Therefore, one could analyze the relationship by saying that as you get older, medical costs increase $6 each year.

SKILL 19.3 Use visual (e.g., graphs, drawings), numeric, and symbolic representations to communicate mathematical concepts

A relationship between two quantities can be shown using a table, graph or rule. In this example, the rule $y = 9x$ describes the relationship between the total amount earned, y, and the total number of pairs of $9 sunglasses sold, x.

A table using this data would appear as:

Number of Sunglasses Sold	1	5	10	15
Total Dollars Earned	9	45	90	135

Each (x,y) relationship between a pair of values is called the coordinate pair and can be plotted on a graph. The coordinate pairs (1,9), (5,45), (10,90), and (15,135) are plotted on the graph below.

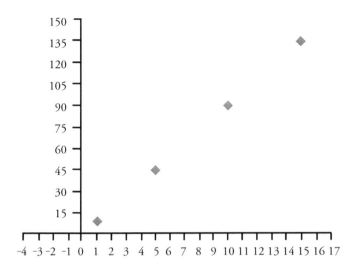

The graph above shows a linear relationship. A linear relationship is one in which two quantities are proportional to each other. Doubling x also doubles y. On a graph, a straight line depicts a linear relationship.

> On a graph, a straight line depicts a linear relationship.

The relationship between two or more variables can be analyzed using a table, graph, written description or symbolic rule. The function, $y = 2x + 1$, is written as a symbolic rule. The same relationship is also shown in the table below:

x	0	2	3	6	9
y	1	5	7	13	19

A relationship could be written in words by saying the value of y is equal to two times the value of x, plus one. This relationship could be shown on a graph by plotting given points such as the ones shown in the table above.

Another way to describe a function is as a process in which one or more numbers are input into an imaginary machine that produces another number as the output. If 5 is input, (x), into a machine with a process of $x + 1$, the output, (y), will equal 6.

SKILL **Convert among visual** (e.g., graphs, drawings), **numeric, and symbolic**
19.4 **representations**

Mathematical concepts and procedures can take many different forms. Students of mathematics must be able to recognize different forms of equivalent concepts.

For example, the slope of a line can be represented graphically, algebraically, verbally, and numerically. A line drawn on a coordinate plane will show the slope. In the equation of a line, $y = mx + b$, the term m represents the slope. The slope of a line can be defined in several different ways; it is the change in the value of y divided by the change in the value of x over a given interval. Alternatively, the slope of a line is the ratio of "rise" to "run" between two points. The numerical value of the slope can be calculated by using the verbal definitions and the algebraic representation of the line.

In order to understand mathematics and to solve problems, it is important to know the definitions of basic mathematic terms and concepts. Additionally, one must use the language of mathematics correctly and precisely to communicate concepts and ideas.

For example, the statement "minus 10 times minus 5 equals plus 50" is incorrect because "minus" and "plus" are arithmetic operations, not numerical modifiers. The statement should read "negative 10 times negative 5 equals positive 50."

> *For a list of definitions and explanations of basic math terms, visit this Web site:*
>
> *http://home.blarg.net /~math/deflist.htm*

COMPETENCY 20
UNDERSTAND NUMBERS, NUMBER THEORY, AND NUMERATION

SKILL 20.1 Demonstrate knowledge of the concepts of place value, prime numbers, multiples, factors, and integer numbers

---

Whole Number Place Value

Consider the number 792. We can assign a place value to each digit.

Reading from left to right, the first digit (7) represents the hundreds place. The hundreds place tells us how many sets of 100 the number contains. Thus, there are seven sets of 100 in the number 792.

The second digit (9) represents the tens place. The tens place tells us how many sets of 10 the number contains. Thus, there are nine sets of 10 in the number 792.

The last digit (2) represents the ones place. The ones place tells us how many 1s the number contains. Thus, there are two sets of 1 in the number 792.

Therefore, there are seven sets of 100, plus nine sets of 10, plus two 1s in the number 792.

Decimal Place Value

More complex numbers have additional place values to both the left and right of the decimal point. Consider the number 374.8.

Reading from left to right, the first digit (3) is in the hundreds place and tells us the number contains three sets of 100.

The second digit (7) is in the tens place and tells us the number contains seven sets of 10.

The third digit, 4, is in the ones place and tells us the number contains four 1s.

Finally, the number after the decimal (8) is in the tenths place and tells us the number contains eight tenths.

Place Value for Older Students

Each digit to the left of the decimal point increases progressively in powers of 10. Each digit to the right of the decimal point decreases progressively in powers of 10.

Example: 12345.6789 occupies the following power-of-10 positions:

10^4	10^3	10^2	10^1	10^0	0	10^{-1}	10^{-2}	10^{-3}	10^{-4}
1	2	3	4	5	$\times$	6	7	8	9

NAMES OF POWER OF 10 POSITIONS			
10^0	=	ones (note that any nonzero base raised to the power zero is 1)	
10^1	=	tens	number 1 and 1 zero or 10
10^2	=	hundreds	number 1 and 2 zeros or 100
10^3	=	thousands	number 1 and 3 zeros or 1000

Continued on next page

10^4	$=$	ten thousands	number 1 and 4 zeros, or 10000
10^{-1}	$=$	$\frac{1}{10^1} = \frac{1}{10} =$ tenths	1st digit after decimal point, or 0.1
10^{-2}	$=$	$\frac{1}{10^2} = \frac{1}{100} =$ hundredths	2nd digit after decimal point, or 0.01
10^{-3}	$=$	$\frac{1}{10^3} = \frac{1}{1000} =$ thousandths	3rd digit after decimal point, or 0.001
10^{-4}	$=$	$\frac{1}{10^4} = \frac{1}{10000} =$ ten thousandths	4th digit after decimal point, or 0.0001

Example: Write 73169.00537 in expanded form.

We start by listing all the power of 10 positions.

10^4	10^3	10^2	10^1	10^0	$\times$	10^{-1}	10^{-2}	10^{-3}	10^{-4}	10^{-5}

Multiply each digit by its power of 10. Add all the results.

Thus $73169.00537 = (7 \times 10^4) + (3 \times 10^3) + (1 \times 10^2) + (6 \times 10^1)$
$+ (9 \times 10^0) + (0 \times 10^{-1}) + (0 \times 10^{-2}) + (5 \times 10^{-3})$
$+ (3 \times 10^{-4}) + (7 \times 10^{-5})$

Example: Determine the place value associated with the underlined digit in 3.16<u>9</u>5.

10^0	$\times$	10^{-1}	10^{-2}	10^{-3}	10^{-4}
3	$\times$	1	6	9	5

The place value for the digit 9 is 10^{-3} or $\frac{1}{1000}$.

Example: Find the number that is represented by (7 × 10³) + (5 × 10⁰) + (3 × 10⁻³).

$= 7000 + 5 + 0.003$
$= 7005.003$

Example: Write 21 × 10³ in standard form.

$= 21 \times 1000 = 21,000$

Example: Write 739 × 10⁻⁴ in standard form.

$= 739 \times \frac{1}{1000} = \frac{739}{10000} = 0.0739$

Greatest Common Factor

GCF is the abbreviation for GREATEST COMMON FACTOR. The GCF is the largest number that is a factor of all the numbers given in a problem. The GCF can be no larger than the smallest number given in the problem. If no other number is a common factor, then the GCF will be the number 1.

To find the GCF, list all possible factors of the smallest number (including the number itself). Starting with the largest factor (which is the number itself), determine if that factor is also a factor of all the other given numbers. If so, that factor is the GCF. If that factor doesn't divide evenly into the other given numbers, try the same method on the next smaller factor. Continue until a common factor is found. That factor is the GCF.

Note: There can be other common factors in addition to the GCF.

Example: Find the GCF of 12, 20, and 36.
The smallest number in the problem is 12. The factors of 12 are 1, 2, 3, 4, 6, and 12. 12 is the largest of these factors, but it does not divide evenly into 20. Neither does 6. However, 4 will divide into both 20 and 36 evenly. Therefore, 4 is the GCF.

Example: Find the GCF of 14 and 15.
The factors of 14 are 1, 2, 7 and 14. 14 is the largest factor, but it does not divide evenly into 15. Neither does 7 or 2. Therefore, the only factor common to both 14 and 15 is the number 1, the GCF.

> **GREATEST COMMON FACTOR:** the largest number that is a factor of all the numbers in a problem

Least Common Multiple

LCM is the abbreviation for LEAST COMMON MULTIPLE. The least common multiple of a group of numbers is the smallest number that all of the given numbers will divide into. The LCM will always be the largest of the given numbers or a multiple of the largest number.

Example: Find the LCM of 20, 30, and 40.
The largest number given is 40, but 30 will not divide evenly into 40. The next multiple of 40 is 80 (2 × 40), but 30 will not divide evenly into 80 either. The next multiple of 40 is 120 (3 × 40). 120 is divisible by both 20 and 30, so 120 is the LCM.

Example: Find the LCM of 96, 16, and 24.
The largest number is 96. 96 is divisible by both 16 and 24, so 96 is the LCM.

> **LEAST COMMON MULTIPLE:** the smallest number of a group of numbers that all the given numbers will divide into evenly

Example: Elly Mae can feed the animals in 15 minutes. Jethro can feed them in 10 minutes. How long will it take them to feed the animals if they work together?

If Elly Mae can feed the animals in 15 minutes, then she could feed $\frac{1}{15}$ of them in 1 minute, $\frac{2}{15}$ of them in 2 minutes, and $\frac{x}{15}$ of them in x minutes. In the same fashion, Jethro could feed $\frac{x}{10}$ of them in x minutes. Together they complete 1 job. The equation is:

$$\frac{x}{15} + \frac{x}{10} = 1$$

Multiply each term by the LCD (least common denominator) of 30:

$$2x + 3x = 30$$
$$x = 6 \text{ minutes}$$

Factors

COMPOSITE NUMBERS are whole numbers that have more than two different factors. For example, 9 is composite because, in addition to the factors of 1 and 9, 3 is also a factor. 70 is composite because, in addition to the factors of 1 and 70, the numbers 2, 5, 7, 10, 14, and 35 are also factors.

PRIME NUMBERS are whole numbers greater than 1 that have only two factors: 1 and the number itself. Examples of prime numbers are 2, 3, 5, 7, 11, 13, 17, and 19. Note that 2 is the only even prime number. When factoring into prime factors, all the factors must be numbers that cannot be factored again (without using 1). Initially, numbers can be factored into any two factors. Check each resulting factor to see whether it can be factored again. Continue factoring until all remaining factors are prime. This is the list of prime factors. Regardless of what way the original number was factored, the final list of prime factors will always be the same.

Remember that the number 1 is neither prime nor composite.

Example:

Factor 30 into prime factors.
Factor 30 into any two factors.

5 × 6	Now factor the 6.
5 × 2 × 3	These are all prime factors.

Or:

Factor 30 into any two factors.

3 × 10	Now factor the 10.
3 × 2 × 5	These are the same prime factors, even though the original factors were different than those in the previous example.

COMPOSITE NUMBERS: whole numbers that have more than two different factors

PRIME NUMBERS: whole numbers greater than 1 that have only two factors: 1 and the number itself

Example:

Factor 240 into prime factors.

Factor 240 into any two factors.

24×10	Now factor both 24 and 10.
$4 \times 6 \times 2 \times 5$	Now factor both 4 and 6.
$2 \times 2 \times 2 \times 3 \times 2 \times 5$	These are the prime factors.

This can also be written as $2^4 \times 3 \times 5$.

**SKILL Recognize numbers represented by exponential and scientific
20.2 notation in context**

The **EXPONENT FORM** is a shortcut method to write repeated multiplication. The basic form is b^n, where b is called the **BASE** and n is the **EXPONENT**. Both b and n are real numbers. The b^n implies that the base b is multiplied by itself n times.

Examples:

$3^4 = 3 \times 3 \times 3 \times 3 = 81$

$2^3 = 2 \times 2 \times 2 = 8$

$(-2)^4 = (-2) \times (-2) \times (-2) \times (-2) = 16$

$-2^4 = -(2 \times 2 \times 2 \times 2) = -16$

Caution: The exponent does not affect the sign unless the negative sign is inside the parentheses and the exponent is outside the parentheses.

$(-2)^4$ implies that -2 is multiplied by itself 4 times.

-2^4 implies that 2 is multiplied by itself 4 times, then the answer is negated.

EXPONENT FORM: a shorthand way of writing repeated multiplication

BASE: the number to be multiplied as many times as indicated by the exponent

EXPONENT: tells how many times the base is multiplied by itself

KEY EXPONENT RULES: FOR 'a' NONZERO AND 'm' AND 'n' REAL NUMBERS	
Product Rule	$a^m \times a^n = a^{(m+n)}$
Quotient Rule	$\dfrac{a^m}{a^n} = a^{(m-n)}$
Rule of Negative Exponents	$\dfrac{a^{-m}}{a^{-n}} = \dfrac{a^n}{a^m}$

KEY EXPONENT RULES: FOR 'a' AND 'b' NONZERO AND 'm' AND 'n' REAL NUMBERS		
Product Rule	$a^m \times a^n = a^{(m+n)}$	$(3^4)(3^5) = 3^9$
	$a^m \times b^m = (ab)^m$	$(4^2)(5^2) = 20^2$
	$(a^m)^n = a^{mn}$	$(2^3)^2 = 2^6$
Quotient Rule	$\dfrac{a^m}{a^n} = a^{(m-n)}$	$2^5 \div 2^5 = 2^2$
Rule of Negative Exponents	$a^{-m} = \dfrac{1}{a^m}$	$2^{-2} = \dfrac{1}{2^2}$

When 10 is raised to any power, the exponent tells the numbers of zeros in the product.

Example:
$$10^7 = 10,000,000$$

Scientific Notation

SCIENTIFIC NOTATION: a convenient method for writing very large and very small numbers

SCIENTIFIC NOTATION is a convenient method for writing very large and very small numbers. It employs two factors. The first factor is a number between 1 and 10. The second factor is a power of 10. This notation is considered "shorthand" for expressing very large numbers (such as the weight of 100 elephants) or very small numbers (such as the weight of an atom in pounds).

Recall that:

10^n	$=$	Ten multiplied by itself n times
10^n	$=$	Any nonzero number raised to the power of zero is 1
10^1	$=$	10
10^2	$=$	$10 \times 10 = 100$
10^3	$=$	$10 \times 10 \times 10 = 1000$
10^{-1}	$=$	$\dfrac{1}{10}$ (deci)
10^{-2}	$=$	$\dfrac{1}{100}$ (centi)
10^{-3}	$=$	$\dfrac{1}{1000}$ (milli)
10^{-6}	$=$	$\dfrac{1}{1,000,000}$ (micro)

Example: Write 46,368,000 in scientific notation.

1. Introduce a decimal point and decimal places.
   $$46,368,000 = 46,368,000.0000$$

2. Make a mark between the two digits that give a number between -9.9 and 9.9.
   $$4 \wedge 6,368,000.0000$$

3. Count the number of digit places between the decimal point and the $\wedge$ mark. This number is the nth power of ten.
   So, $46,368,000 = 4.6368 \times 10^7$.

Example: Write 0.00397 in scientific notation.

1. Decimal place is already in place.

2. Make a mark between 3 and 9 to obtain a number between -9.9 and. 9.9.

3. Move decimal place to the mark (three hops).
   $$0.003 \wedge 97$$
   Motion is to the right, so n on 10^n is negative.
   Therefore, $0.00397 = 3.97 \times 10^{-3}$.

SKILL 20.3 Apply concepts of numbers and numeration to compare, order, and round up or down

$$1 > \frac{7}{8} > 0.65 > 60\% > 2^{-2} > 10^{-2}$$

The **DENSENESS PROPERTY** of real numbers states that if all real numbers are ordered from least to greatest on a number line, there is an infinite set of real numbers between any two given numbers on the line.

Example: Between 7.6 and 7.7, there is the rational number 7.65 in the set of real numbers.

Between 3 and 4 there exists no other natural number.

ROUNDING NUMBERS is a form of estimation that is very useful in many mathematical operations. For example, when estimating the sum of two three-digit numbers, it is helpful to round the two numbers to the nearest hundred prior to addition. We can round numbers to any place value.

> **DENSENESS PROPERTY:** states that if all real numbers are ordered from least to greatest on a number line, there is an infinite set of real numbers between any two given numbers on the line

> **ROUNDING NUMBERS:** a form of estimation that is very useful in many mathematical operations

Rounding Whole Numbers

To round whole numbers, first find the place value you want to round to (the rounding digit). Look at the digit directly to the right. If the digit is less than 5, do not change the rounding digit and replace all numbers after the rounding digit with zeros. If the digit is greater than or equal to 5, increase the rounding digit by 1, and replace all numbers after the rounding digit with zeros.

Example: Round 517 to the nearest ten.

1 is the rounding digit because it occupies the tens place. 517 rounded to the nearest ten = 520; because 7 > 5, we add 1 to the rounding digit.

Example: Round 15,449 to the nearest hundred.

The first 4 is the rounding digit because it occupies the hundreds place. 15,449 rounded to the nearest hundred = 15,400; because 4 < 5, we do not add to the rounding digit.

Rounding Decimals

Rounding decimals is identical to rounding whole numbers except that you simply drop all the digits to the right of the rounding digit.

Example: Round 417.3621 to the nearest tenth.

3 is the rounding digit because it occupies the tenths place. 417.3621 rounded to the nearest tenth = 417.4; because 6 > 5, we add 1 to the rounding digit.

SKILL 20.4 **Identify equivalent forms of fractions, decimals, and percentages**

If we compare numbers in various forms, we see that:

The integer $400 = \frac{800}{2}$ (fraction) $= 400.0$ (decimal) $= 400\%$ (percent).

From this, you should be able to determine that fractions, decimals, and percents can be used interchangeably within problems.

- To change a percent into a decimal, move the decimal point two places to the left and drop the percent sign.

- To change a decimal into a percent, move the decimal two places to the right and add a percent sign.

- To change a fraction into a decimal, divide the numerator by the denominator.

- To change a decimal into an equivalent fraction, write the decimal part of the number as the fraction's numerator. As the fraction's denominator, use the place value of the last column of the decimal. Reduce the resulting fraction as far as possible.

Example: J.C. Nickels has Hunch jeans for sale at $\frac{1}{4}$ off the usual price of $36.00. Shears and Roadster have the same jeans for sale at 30% off their regular price of $40. Find the cheaper price.

$\frac{1}{4} = .25$ so $.25(36) = \$9.00$ off; $\$36 - 9 = \$27$ sale price

$30\% = .30$ so $.30(40) = \$12$ off; $\$40 - 12 = \$28$ sale price

The price at J.C Nickels is actually $1 lower.

To convert a fraction to a decimal, as we did in the example above, simply divide the numerator (top) by the denominator (bottom). Use long division if necessary.

If a decimal has a fixed number of digits, the decimal is said to be a TERMINATING DECIMAL. To write such a decimal as a fraction, first determine the place value of the digit farthest to the right (for example: tenths, hundredths, thousandths, ten-thousandths, hundred-thousandths, etc.). Then drop the decimal point and place the string of digits over the number given by the place value.

> **TERMINATING DECIMAL:** a decimal that has a fixed number of digits

If a decimal continues forever by repeating a string of digits, the decimal is said to be a REPEATING DECIMAL. To write a repeating decimal as a fraction, follow these steps.

> **REPEATING DECIMAL:** a decimal that continues forever by repeating a string of digits

1. Let $x =$ the repeating decimal. ($x = 0.716716716...$)

2. Multiply x by the multiple of 10 that will move the decimal just to the right of the repeating block of digits. ($1000x = 716.716716...$)

3. Subtract the first equation from the second. ($1000x - x = 716.716.716... - .716716...$)

4. Simplify and solve this equation. The repeating block of digits will subtract out. ($999x = 716$ so $x = \frac{716}{999}$)

5. The solution will be the fraction for the repeating decimal.

COMPETENCY 21
UNDERSTAND MATHEMATICAL PROBLEM SOLVING

> **SKILL 21.1** Make use of pictures, models, charts, graphs, and symbols as tools of mathematical problem solving

Drawing pictures or diagrams can also help to make relationships in a problem clearer.

Example: In a women's marathon, the first five finishers (in no particular order) were Frieda, Polly, Christa, Betty, and Dora. Frieda finished 7 seconds before Christa. Polly finished 6 seconds after Betty. Dora finished 8 seconds after Betty. Christa finished 2 seconds before Polly. In what order did the women finish the race?

Drawing a picture or diagram will help to illustrate the answer more easily.

From the diagram, we can see that the women finished in the following order: 1st – Frieda, 2nd – Betty, 3rd – Christa, 4th – Polly, and 5th – Dora.

Sometimes, using a model is the best way to see the solution to a problem, as in the case of fraction multiplication.

Example: Model $\frac{5}{6} \times \frac{2}{3}$:

Draw a rectangle. Divide it vertically into 6 equal sections (the denominator of the first number).

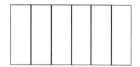

Divide the rectangle horizontally into 3 equal sections (the denominator of the second number).

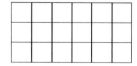

Color in a number of vertical strips equal to the numerator of the first number.

Use a different color to shade a number of horizontal strips equal to the numerator of the second number.

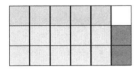

By describing the area where both colors overlap, we have the product of the two fractions. The answer is $\frac{10}{18}$.

SKILL 21.2 Identify and use relevant information in a problem to solve it

Many times, the description of a problem may contain more information than is needed to solve the problem. Some of the information may actually be irrelevant. It is important to focus on what information is relevant to the problem.

Example: Jonathan went to the mall and bought a baseball cap for $14, gloves for $10, a stocking cap for $8, a headband for $7, and an umbrella for $15. What was the average price of the headwear that Jonathan bought?

In this problem, we are interested only in the items Jonathan bought that could be worn on the head: a baseball cap, a stocking cap, and a headband. We are not interested in the gloves or the umbrella. Therefore, we average $14, $8, and $7 to get $9.67.

SKILL 21.3 Recognize and apply multiple solution strategies to problem solving

Successful math teachers introduce their students to multiple problem-solving strategies. They create classroom environments where free thought and experimentation are encouraged. Teachers can promote problem solving among their students by allowing them to make multiple attempts at solving problems, giving credit for reworking test or homework problems, and encouraging them to share their ideas through class discussion. To maximize efficacy, there are several specific problem-solving skills with which teachers should be familiar.

GUESS-AND-CHECK STRATEGY: calls for students to make an initial guess at the solution, check the answer, and use that outcome to guide the next guess

The GUESS-AND-CHECK STRATEGY calls for students to make an initial guess at the solution, check the answer, and use that outcome to guide the next guess. With each successive guess, the student should get closer to the correct answer. Constructing a table from the guesses can help to organize the data.

Example: There are 100 coins in a jar. 10 are dimes. The rest are pennies and nickels. There are twice as many pennies as nickels. How many pennies and nickels are in the jar?

There are 90 total nickels and pennies in the jar (100 coins—10 dimes).

There are twice as many pennies as nickels. Students can take guesses that fulfill the criteria and adjust these guesses based on the answer found. They can continue until they find the correct answer: 60 pennies and 30 nickels.

Number of Pennies	40	80	70	60
Number of Nickels	20	40	35	30
Total Number of Pennies and Nickels	60	120	105	90

WORKING BACKWARD STRATEGY: requires students to determine a starting point when solving a problem where the final result and the steps to reach the result are given

The WORKING BACKWARD STRATEGY requires students to determine a starting point when solving a problem where the final result and the steps to reach the result are given.

Example: John subtracted 7 from his age and then divided the result by 3. The final result was 4. What is John's age?

Work backwards by reversing the operations.

$4 \times 3 = 12$;

$12 + 7 = 19$

John is 19 years old.

ESTIMATING AND TESTING FOR REASONABLENESS: related skills that students should employ before and after solving a problem

The strategy of ESTIMATING AND TESTING FOR REASONABLENESS draws on related skills that students should employ prior to and after solving a problem. These skills are particularly important when students use calculators to find answers.

Example: Find the sum of 4387 + 7226 + 5893.

$4300 + 7200 + 5800 = 17300$ Estimation.

$4387 + 7226 + 5893 = 17506$ Actual sum.

By comparing their estimate to the sum that they actually computed, students can determine whether their answer is reasonable.

SKILL Evaluate calculations and problem-solving strategies to verify the
21.4 accuracy of the results

The QUESTIONING TECHNIQUE is a mathematic process in which students devise questions to clarify the problem, eliminate possible solutions, and simplify the problem-solving process. By developing and attempting to answer simple questions, students can tackle difficult and complex problems.

> **QUESTIONING TECH-NIQUE:** a mathematic process in which students devise questions to clarify the problem, eliminate possible solutions, and simplify the problem-solving process

COMPETENCY 22
UNDERSTAND METHODS OF MATHEMATICAL OPERATIONS, CALCULATION, AND ESTIMATION

SKILL Use the basic four operations with variables and numbers
22.1

When simplifying algebraic expression, we must use the following order:

1. Perform operations within parentheses

2. Evaluate exponents

3. Multiply and divide from left to right.

4. Add and subtract when possible to produce a final answer

Example: $3^3 - 5(b + 2)$
$$= 3^3 - 5b - 10$$
$$= 27 - 5b - 10 = 17 - 5b$$

Example: $2 - 4 \times 2^3 \; 2(4 - 2 \times 3)$

$$= 2 - 4 \times 2^3 - 2(4 - 6) = 2 - 4 \times 2^3 - 2(\text{-}2)$$

$$= 2 - 4 \times 2^3 + 4 = 2 - 4 \times 8 + 4$$

$$= 2 - 32 + 4 = 6 - 32 = \text{-}26$$

SKILL 22.2 Recognize relationships among mathematical operations

Many algebraic procedures are similar to and rely upon number operations and algorithms. Two examples of this similarity are the adding of rational expressions and division of polynomials.

Addition of rational expressions is similar to fraction addition. The basic algorithm of addition for both fractions and rational expressions is the common denominator method. Consider an example of the addition of numerical fractions.

$$\frac{3}{5} + \frac{2}{3} = \frac{3(3)}{3(5)} + \frac{5(2)}{5(3)} = \frac{9}{15} + \frac{10}{15} = \frac{19}{15}$$

To complete the sum, we first find the least common denominator (15).

Now, consider an example of rational expression addition.

$$\frac{(x + 5)}{(x + 1)} + \frac{2x}{(x + 3)} = \frac{(x + 3)\,(x + 5)}{(x + 3)\,(x + 1)} + \frac{(x + 1)2x}{(x + 1)\,(x + 3)}$$

$$= \frac{x^2 + 8x + 15}{(x + 3)\,(x + 1)} + \frac{2x^2 + 2x}{(x + 3)\,(x + 1)} = \frac{3x^2 + 10x + 15}{(x + 3)(x + 1)}$$

Note the similarity to fractional addition. The basic algorithm, finding a common denominator and adding numerators, is the same.

Division of polynomials follows the same algorithm as numerical long division. Consider an example of numerical long division.

$$6\overline{)4321} \quad \begin{array}{l} 720 \\ 42 \\ \,12 \\ \,12 \\ \,\,01 \end{array} \qquad \rightarrow 720\,\tfrac{1}{6} = \text{final quotient}$$

Compare the process of numerical long division to polynomial division.

$$\begin{array}{r} x - 9 \\ x + 1 \overline{)x^2 - 8x - 9} \\ \underline{^{-}x^2 - x} \quad\quad \rightarrow x - 9 = \text{final quotient} \\ -9x - 9 \\ \underline{+9x + 9} \\ 0 + 0 \end{array}$$

Note that the step-by-step process is identical in both cases.

SKILL **Apply properties of real numbers and the number system** *(e.g.,* 22.3 *commutative, associative)*

PROPERTIES: rules that
apply for addition, sub-
traction, multiplication, or
division of real numbers

PROPERTIES are rules that apply for addition, subtraction, multiplication, or division of real numbers. These properties are:

Commutative	You can change the order of the terms or factors as follows.
	For addition: $a + b = b + a$
	For multiplication: $ab = ba$
	Since addition is the inverse operation of subtraction and multiplication is the inverse operation of division, no separate laws are needed for subtraction and division.
	Example: $5 + 8 = 8 + 5 = 13$
	Example: $2 \times 6 = 6 \times 2 = 12$
Associative	You can regroup the terms as you like.
	For addition: $a + (b + c) = (a + b) + c$
	For multiplication: $a(bc) = (ab)c$
	This rule does not apply for division and subtraction.
	Example: $(2 + 7) + 5 = 2 + (7 + 5)$ $9 + 5 = 2 + 12 = 14$
	Example: $(3 \times 7) \times 5 = 3 \times (7 \times 5)$ $21 \times 5 = 3 \times 35 = 105$

Continued on next page

Identity	Finding a number that, when added to a term, results in that number (additive identity); finding a number that, when multiplied by a term, results in that number (multiplicative identity).
	For addition: $a + 0 = a$ (zero is additive identity)
	For multiplication: $a \times 1 = a$ (one is multiplicative identity)
	Example: 17 + 0 = 17
	Example: 34 × 1 = 34
	The product of any number and one is that number.
Inverse	Finding a number that, when added to the number, results in zero; or when multiplied by the number, results in 1.
	For addition: $a - a = 0$
	For multiplication: $a \times \left(\frac{1}{a}\right) = 1$
	$(-a)$ is the additive inverse of a; $\left(\frac{1}{a}\right)$, also called the reciprocal, is the multiplicative inverse of a.
	Example: 25 − 25 = 0
	Example: $5 \times \frac{1}{5} = 1$
	The product of any number and its reciprocal is one.
Distributive	This technique allows us to operate on terms within parentheses without first performing operations within the parentheses. This is especially helpful when terms within the parentheses cannot be combined.
	$a(b + c) = ab + ac$
	Example: 6 × (4 + 9) = (6 × 4) + (6 × 9)
	6 × 13 = 24 + 54 = 78
	To multiply a sum by a number, multiply each addend by the number, then add the products.

SUMMARY OF THE PROPERTIES OF OPERATION		
Property	**Of Addition**	**Of Multiplication**
Commutative	$a + b = b + a$	$ab = ba$
Associative	$a + (b + c) = (a + b) + c$	$a(bc) = (ab)c$
Identity	$a + 0 = a$	$(a)(1) = a$
Inverse	$a + (-a) = 0$	$a \times \left(\frac{1}{a}\right) = 1$

Use your knowledge of the properties to answer the following questions.

1. What property is illustrated by $\frac{1}{(x^2 + 4)} \times \frac{(x^2 + 4)}{1} = 1$?

   Because multiplying by the reciprocal $= 1$, the answer is the inverse property of multiplication.

2. What properties are illustrated in the following examples?

   $3x + (5y + 2z) = (3x + 5y) + 2z$
   $(3x + 6y) + 2z = 3(x + 2y) + 2z$

   The first example shows that the order of grouping does not matter, therefore the answer is the associative property of addition.

   The second example is pulling the common factor 3 outside the parentheses. This is applying the distributive property of multiplication over addition in reverse.

SKILL 22.4 Make calculations with whole numbers, decimals, fractions, and integer numbers

Addition of Whole Numbers

Example: At the end of a day of shopping, a shopper had $24 remaining in his wallet. He spent $45 on various goods. How much money did the shopper have at the beginning of the day?

The total amount of money the shopper started with is the sum of the amount spent and the amount remaining at the end of the day.

$$\begin{array}{r} \$\ 24 \\ +\ 45 \\ \hline \$\ 69 \end{array}$$ The original total was $69.

Example: A race took the winner 1 hr. 58 min. 12 sec. on the first half of the race and 2 hr. 9 min. 57 sec. on the second half. How much time did the entire race take?

$$\begin{array}{l} 1\ \text{hr}\ 58\ \text{min}\ 12\ \text{sec} \\ +\ 2\ \text{hr}\ \ \ 9\ \text{min}\ 57\ \text{sec} \\ \hline 3\ \text{hr}\ 67\ \text{min}\ 69\ \text{sec} \end{array}$$ Add these numbers.

$$\begin{array}{l} \qquad\qquad +\ 1\ \text{min}\ -\ 60\ \text{sec} \\ \hline 3\ \text{hr}\ 68\ \text{min}\ \ \ 9\ \text{sec} \end{array}$$ Change 60 sec. to 1 min.

$$\begin{array}{l} +\ 1\ \text{hr}\ -\ 60\ \text{min} \\ \hline 4\ \text{hr}\ 8\ \text{min}\ 9\ \text{sec} \end{array}$$ Change 60 min. to 1 hr.
   Final answer.

Subtraction of Whole Numbers

Example: At the end of his shift, a cashier has $96 in the cash register. At the beginning of his shift, he had $15. How much money did the cashier collect during his shift?

The total collected is the difference between the ending amount and the starting amount.

$$\begin{array}{r} \$\,96 \\ -15 \\ \hline \$\,81 \end{array}$$ The total collected was $81.

Multiplication of Whole Numbers

Multiplication is one of the four basic number operations. In simple terms, multiplication is the addition of a number to itself a certain number of times. For example, 4 multiplied by 3 is equal to $4 + 4 + 4$ or $3 + 3 + 3 + 3$. Another way of conceptualizing multiplication is to think in terms of groups. For example, if we have 4 groups of 3 students, the total number of students is 4 multiplied by 3. We call the solution to a multiplication problem the PRODUCT.

The basic algorithm for whole number multiplication begins with aligning the numbers by place value, with the number containing more places on top.

$$\begin{array}{r} 172 \\ \times\, 43 \end{array}$$ Note that we placed 172 on top because it has more places than 43 does.

Next, we multiply the ones place of the bottom number by each place value of the top number sequentially.

$$\begin{array}{r} (2) \\ 172 \\ \times\, 43 \\ \hline 516 \end{array}$$ $\{3 \times 2 = 6; 3 \times 7 = 21; 3 \times 1 = 3\}$
Note that we had to carry a 2 to the hundreds column because $3 \times 7 = 21$. Note also that we add carried numbers to the product.

Next, we multiply the number in the tens place of the bottom number by each place value of the top number sequentially. Because we are multiplying by a number in the tens place, we place a zero at the end of this product.

$$\begin{array}{r} (2) \\ 172 \\ \times\, 43 \\ \hline 516 \\ 6880 \end{array}$$ $\{4 \times 2 = 8; 4 \times 7 = 28; 4 = 1 = 4\}$

Finally, to determine the final product, we add the two partial products.

$$
\begin{array}{r}
172 \\
\times\ 43 \\
\hline
516 \\
+\ 6880 \\
\hline
7396
\end{array}
$$
The product of 172 and 43 is 7,396.

Example: A student buys 4 boxes of crayons. Each box contains 16 crayons. How many total crayons does the student have?

The total number of crayons is 16×4.

$$
\begin{array}{r}
16 \\
\times\ 4 \\
\hline
64
\end{array}
$$
The total number of crayons equals 64.

Division of Whole Numbers

Division, the inverse of multiplication, is another of the four basic number operations. When we divide one number by another, we determine how many times we can multiply the divisor (number divided by) before we exceed the number we are dividing (dividend). For example, 8 divided by 2 equals 4 because we can multiply 2 four times to reach 8 ($2 \times 4 = 8$ or $2 + 2 + 2 + 2 = 8$). Using the grouping conceptualization we used with multiplication, we can divide 8 into 4 groups of 2 or 2 groups of 4. We call the answer to a division problem the QUOTIENT.

If the divisor does not divide evenly into the dividend, we express the leftover amount either as a remainder or as a fraction with the divisor as the denominator. For example, 9 divided by 2 equals 4 with a remainder of 1, or $4\frac{1}{2}$.

QUOTIENT: the answer to a division problem

The basic algorithm for division is long division. We start by representing the quotient as follows.

$14\overline{)293}$ → 14 is the divisor and 293 is the dividend. This represents $293 \div 14$.

Next, we divide the divisor into the dividend, starting from the left.

$14\overline{)293}^{\ \ 2}$ → 14 divides into 29 two times with a remainder.

Next, we multiply the partial quotient by the divisor, subtract this value from the first digits of the dividend, and bring down the remaining dividend digits to complete the number.

$$
\begin{array}{r}
2 \\
14\overline{)293} \\
-28\downarrow \\
\hline
13
\end{array}
$$
$\rightarrow 2 \times 14 = 28; \, 29 - 28 = 1$, and bringing down the 3 yields 13.

Finally, we divide again (the divisor into the remaining value) and repeat the preceding process. The number left after the subtraction represents the remainder.

$$
\begin{array}{r}
20 \\
14\overline{)293} \\
-28 \\
\hline
13 \\
-0 \\
\hline
13
\end{array}
$$
$\rightarrow$ The final quotient is 20 with a remainder of 13. We can also represent this quotient as $20\frac{13}{14}$.

Example: Each box of apples contains 24 apples. How many boxes must a grocer purchase to supply a group of 252 people with one apple each?

The grocer needs 252 apples. Because he must buy apples in groups of 24, we divide 252 by 24 to determine how many boxes he needs to buy.

$$
\begin{array}{r}
10 \\
24\overline{)252} \\
-24 \\
\hline
12 \\
-0 \\
\hline
12
\end{array}
$$
$\rightarrow$ The quotient is 10 with a remainder of 12.

Thus, the grocer needs 10 boxes plus 12 more apples. Therefore, the minimum number of boxes the grocer can purchase is 11.

Example: At his job, John gets paid $20 for every hour he works. If John made $940 in a week, how many hours did he work?

This is a division problem. To determine the number of hours John worked, we divide the total amount made ($940) by the hourly rate of pay ($20). Thus, the number of hours worked equals 940 divided by 20.

$$
\begin{array}{r}
47 \\
20\overline{)940} \\
-80 \\
\hline
140 \\
-140 \\
\hline
0
\end{array}
$$
$\rightarrow 20$ Divides into 940 a total of 47 times with no remainder.

John worked 47 hours.

Addition and Subtraction of Decimals

When adding and subtracting decimals, we align the numbers by place value as we do with whole numbers. After adding or subtracting each column, we bring the decimal down, placing it in the same location as in the numbers added or subtracted.

> *When adding and subtracting decimals, align the numbers by place value as we do with whole numbers.*

Example: Find the sum of 152.3 and 36.342.

```
  152.300
+  36.342
  188.642
```

Note that we placed two zeros after the final place value in 152.3 to clarify the column addition.

Example: Find the difference of 152.3 and 36.342.

```
    2 9 10        (4)11(12)
  152.300         152.300
−  36.342        −  36.342
       58         115.958
```

Note how we borrowed to subtract from the zeros in the hundredths and thousandths places of 152.300.

Multiplication of Decimals

When multiplying decimal numbers, we multiply exactly as with whole numbers and place the decimal in from the right the total number of decimal places contained in the two numbers multiplied. For example, when multiplying 1.5 and 2.35, we place the decimal in the product 3 places in from the right (3.525).

Example: Find the product of 3.52 and 4.1.

```
     3.52          Note that there are three decimal places in total
   × 4.1           in the two numbers.
     352
+ 14080
  14.432           We place the decimal three places in from the right.
```
Thus, the final product is 14.432.

Example: A shopper has 5 one-dollar bills, 6 quarters, 3 nickels, and 4 pennies in his pocket. How much money does he have?

```
                        1 3      1
                      $0.25   $0.05   $0.01
5 × $1.00 = $5.00      × 6     × 3     × 4
                      $1.50   $0.15   $0.04
```

Note the placement of the decimals in the multiplication products. Thus, the total amount of money in the shopper's pocket is:

$5.00
1.50
0.15
+ 0.04
_____
$6.69

Division of Decimals

When dividing decimal numbers, we first remove the decimal in the divisor by moving the decimal in the dividend the same number of spaces to the right. For example, when dividing 1.45 into 5.3, we convert the numbers to 145 and 530 and perform normal whole-number division.

Example: Find the quotient of 5.3 divided by 1.45.
Convert to 145 and 530.

Divide.

$$
\begin{array}{r}
3 \\
145\overline{)530} \\
-435 \\
\hline
95
\end{array}
\qquad
\begin{array}{r}
3.65 \\
145\overline{)530.00} \\
-435 \\
\hline
950 \\
-870 \\
\hline
800
\end{array}
$$

Note that we insert the decimal to continue division.

Because one of the numbers divided contained one decimal place, we round the quotient to one decimal place. Thus, the final quotient is 3.7.

Operating with Percents

Example: 5 is what percent of 20?

This is the same as converting $\frac{5}{20}$ to percent (%) form.

$$\frac{5}{20} = \frac{x}{100} = \frac{5 \times 5}{100} = \frac{25}{100} = 25\%$$

Example: There are 64 dogs in the kennel. 48 are collies. What percent are collies?

Restate the problem.	48 is what percent of 64?
Write an equation.	$48 = n \times 64$
Solve.	$\frac{48}{64} = n$

$n = \frac{3}{4} = 75\%$

75% of the dogs are collies.

Example: The auditorium was filled to 90% capacity. There were 558 seats occupied. What is the capacity of the auditorium?

Restate the problem.	90% of what number is 558?
Write an equation.	$0.9n = 558$
Solve.	$n = \frac{558}{.09}$
	$n = 620$

The capacity of the auditorium is 620 people.

Example: A pair of shoes costs $42.00. The sales tax is 6%. What is the total cost of the shoes?

Restate the problem.	What is 6% of 42?
Write an equation.	$n = 0.06 \times 42$
Solve.	$n = 2.52$
Add the sales tax to the cost.	$42.00 + $2.52 = $44.52

The total cost of the shoes, including sales tax, is $44.52.

Addition and Subtraction of Fractions

Key points

1. You need a common denominator in order to add and subtract reduced and improper fractions.

   Example:
   $$\frac{1}{3} + \frac{7}{3} = \frac{1+7}{3} = \frac{8}{3} = 2\frac{2}{3}$$

   Example:
   $$\frac{4}{12} + \frac{6}{12} - \frac{3}{12} = \frac{4+6-3}{12} = \frac{7}{12}$$

2. Adding an integer and a fraction of the same sign results directly in a mixed fraction.

   Example:
   $$2 + \frac{2}{3} = 2\frac{2}{3}$$

   Example:
   $$-2 - \frac{2}{3} = -2\frac{2}{3}$$

3. Adding an integer and a fraction with different signs involves the following steps.

   - Get a common denominator

   - Add or subtract as needed

   - Change to a mixed fraction if possible

Example:
$$2 - \frac{1}{3} = \frac{2 \times 3 - 1}{3} = \frac{6 - 1}{3} = \frac{5}{3} = 1\frac{2}{3}$$

Example:

Add $7\frac{3}{8} + 5\frac{2}{7}$

Add the whole numbers, add the fractions, and combine the two results:

$$7\frac{3}{8} + 5\frac{2}{7} = (7 + 5) + \left(\frac{3}{8} + \frac{2}{7}\right)$$

$$= 12 + \frac{(7 \times 3) + (8 \times 2)}{56} \qquad \text{(LCM of 8 and 7)}$$

$$= 12 + \frac{21 + 16}{56} = 12 + \frac{37}{56} = 12\frac{37}{56}$$

Example: Perform the operation.

$$\frac{2}{3} - \frac{5}{6}$$

We first find the LCM of 3 and 6, which is 6.

$$\frac{2 \times 2}{3 \times 2} - \frac{5}{6} \rightarrow \frac{4 - 5}{6} = \frac{-1}{6} \qquad \text{(Using method A)}$$

Example:

$$-7\frac{1}{4} + 2\frac{7}{8}$$

$$-7\frac{1}{4} + 2\frac{7}{8} = (-7 + 2) + \left(\frac{-1}{4} + \frac{7}{8}\right)$$

$$= (-5) + \frac{-2 + 7}{8} = (-5) + \left(\frac{5}{8}\right)$$

$$= (-5) + \frac{5}{8} = \frac{-5 \times 8}{1 \times 8} + \frac{5}{8} = \frac{-40 + 5}{8}$$

$$= \frac{-35}{8} = -4\frac{3}{8}$$

Divide 35 by 8 to get 4, remainder 3.

Example:

Caution: A common error would be

$$-7\frac{1}{4} + 2\frac{7}{8} = -7\frac{2}{8} + 2\frac{7}{8} = -5\frac{9}{8} \text{ Wrong.}$$

It is correct to add -7 and 2 to get -5, but adding $\frac{2}{8} + \frac{7}{8} = \frac{9}{8}$ is wrong. It should have been $\frac{-2}{8} + \frac{7}{8} = \frac{5}{8}$. Then, $-5 + \frac{5}{8} = -4\frac{3}{8}$ as before.

Multiplication of Fractions

Using the following example: $3\frac{1}{4} \times \frac{5}{6}$

1. Convert each number to an improper fraction

$$3\frac{1}{4} = \frac{(12 + 1)}{4} = \frac{13}{4} \qquad \frac{5}{6} \text{ is already in reduced form.}$$

2. Reduce (cancel) common factors of the numerator and denominator if they exist

$\frac{13}{4} \times \frac{5}{6}$ No common factors exist.

3. Multiply the numerators by each other and the denominators by each other

$\frac{13}{4} \times \frac{5}{6} = \frac{65}{24}$

4. If possible, reduce the fraction to its lowest terms

$\frac{65}{24}$ Cannot be reduced further.

5. Convert the improper fraction back to a mixed fraction by using long division

$$\frac{65}{24} = 24\overline{)65} \quad = 2\frac{17}{24}$$
$$\underline{48}$$
$$17$$

Summary of sign changes for multiplication

1. $(+) \times (+) = (+)$

2. $(-) \times (+) = (-)$

3. $(+) \times (-) = (-)$

4. $(-) \times (-) = (+)$

Example: $7\frac{1}{3} \times \frac{5}{11} = \frac{22}{3} \times \frac{5}{11}$
Reduce like terms (22 and 11).
$= \frac{2}{3} \times \frac{5}{1} = \frac{10}{3} = 3\frac{1}{3}$

Example: $-6\frac{1}{4} \times \frac{5}{9} = \frac{-25}{4} \times \frac{5}{9}$
$= \frac{-125}{36} = -3\frac{17}{36}$

Example: $\frac{-1}{4} \times \frac{-3}{7}$
A negative times a negative equals a positive.
$= \frac{1}{4} \times \frac{3}{7} = \frac{3}{28}$

Division of Fractions

1. Change mixed fractions to improper fractions

2. Change the division problem to a multiplication problem by using the reciprocal of the number after the division sign

3. Find the sign of the final product

4. Cancel if common factors exist between the numerator and the denominator

5. Multiply the numerators together and the denominators together

6. Change the improper fraction to a mixed number

Example: $3\frac{1}{5} \div 2\frac{1}{4} = \frac{16}{5} \div \frac{9}{4}$

$= \frac{16}{5} \times \frac{4}{9}$ The reciprocal of $\frac{9}{4}$ is $\frac{4}{9}$.

$= \frac{64}{45} = 1\frac{19}{45}$

Example: $7\frac{3}{4} \div 11\frac{5}{8} = \frac{31}{4} \div \frac{93}{8}$

$= \frac{31}{4} \times \frac{8}{93}$ Reduce like terms.

$= \frac{1}{1} \times \frac{2}{3} = \frac{2}{3}$

Example: $\left(-2\frac{1}{2}\right) \div 4\frac{1}{6} = \frac{-5}{2} \div \frac{25}{6}$

$= \frac{-5}{2} \times \frac{6}{25}$ Reduce like terms.

$= \frac{-1}{1} \times \frac{3}{5} = \frac{-3}{5}$

Example: $\left(-5\frac{3}{8}\right) \div \left(\frac{7}{16}\right) = \frac{-43}{8} \div \frac{27}{16}$

$= \frac{-43}{8} \times \frac{-16}{7}$ Reduce like terms.

$= \frac{43}{1} \times \frac{2}{7}$ A negative times a negative equals a positive.

$= \frac{86}{7} = 12\frac{2}{7}$

Converting Decimals, Fractions, and Percents

A decimal can be converted to a percent by multiplying by 100 or by merely moving the decimal point two places to the right. A percent can be converted to a decimal by dividing by 100 or by moving the decimal point two places to the left.

Examples:

$0.375 = 37.5\%$

$0.7 = 70\%$

$0.04 = 4\%$

$3.15 = 315\%$

$84\% = 0.84$

$3\% = 0.03$

$60\% = 0.6$

$110\% = 1.1$

$\frac{1}{2}\% = 0.5\% = 0.005$

A percent can be converted to a fraction by placing it over 100 and reducing to its simplest terms.

Example: Convert 50% to a fraction.

$50\% = \frac{50}{100} = \frac{1}{2}$

A decimal can be converted to a fraction by multiplying by a number that will remove the decimal point and reducing the result to its simplest terms.

Example: Convert 0.056 to a fraction.

Multiply 0.056 by $\frac{1000}{1000}$ to get rid of the decimal point:

$$0.056 \times \frac{1000}{1000} = \frac{56}{1000} = \frac{7}{125}$$

Example: Convert 6.25% to a decimal and to a fraction.

$$6.25\% = 0.0625 = 0.0625 \times \frac{1000}{1000} = \frac{625}{10000} = \frac{1}{16}$$

An example of a type of problem involving fractions is the conversion of recipes. For example, if a recipe serves eight people and we want to make enough to serve only four, we must determine how much of each ingredient to use. The conversion factor, or the number we multiply each ingredient by, is:

$$\text{Conversion Factor} = \frac{\text{Number of Servings Needed}}{\text{Number of Servings in Recipe}}$$

Example: Consider the following recipe.

3 cups flour

$\frac{1}{2}$ tsp. baking powder

$\frac{2}{3}$ cups butter

2 cups sugar

2 eggs

If this recipe serves eight, how much of each ingredient do we need to serve only four people?

First, determine the conversion factor.

Conversion Factor $= \frac{4}{8} = \frac{1}{2}$

Next, multiply each ingredient by the conversion factor.

$3 \times \frac{1}{2} = $ $1\frac{1}{2}$ cups flour

$\frac{1}{2} \times \frac{1}{2} = $ $\frac{1}{4}$ tsp. baking powder

$\frac{2}{3} \times \frac{1}{2} = \frac{2}{6}$ $\frac{1}{3}$ cup butter

$2 \times \frac{1}{2} = $ 1 cup sugar

$2 \times \frac{1}{2} = $ 1 egg

SKILL 22.5 Apply methods of approximation and estimation (e.g., rounding)

Estimation and approximation may be used to check the reasonableness of answers.

Example: Estimate the answer.

$$\frac{58 \times 810}{1989}$$

58 becomes 60, 810 becomes 800, and 1989 becomes 2000.

$$\frac{60 \times 800}{2000} = 24$$

For word problems, an estimate may sometimes be all that is needed to find the solution.

Example: Janet goes into a store to purchase a CD that is on sale for $13.95. While shopping, she sees two pairs of shoes priced at $19.95 and $14.50. She only has $50. Can she purchase everything?

Solve by rounding:

$19.95 \rightarrow$ $20.00

$14.50 \rightarrow$ $15.00

$13.95 \rightarrow$ $14.00

            $49.00   Yes, she can purchase the CD and the shoes.

SKILL 22.6 Identify strategies for estimating solutions and for evaluating the accuracy of estimated solutions

To estimate measurement of familiar objects, it is first necessary to determine the units to be used.

LENGTH	
The coastline of Florida	miles or kilometers
The width of a ribbon	inches or millimeters
The thickness of a book	inches or centimeters
The length of a football field	yards or meters
The depth of water in a pool	feet or meters

WEIGHT OR MASS	
A bag of sugar	pounds or grams
A school bus	tons or kilograms
A dime	ounces or grams

CAPACITY	
Paint to paint a bedroom	gallons or liters
Glass of milk	cups or liters
Bottle of soda	quarts or liters
Medicine for child	ounces or milliliters

Example: Estimate the measurements of the following objects:

Length of a dollar bill	6 inches
Weight of a baseball	1 pound
Distance from New York to Florida	1100 kilometers
Volume of water to fill a medicine dropper	1 milliliter
Length of a desk	2 meters
Temperature of water in a swimming pool	80° F

Depending on the degree of accuracy needed, an object may be measured to different units. For example, a pencil may be 6 inches to the nearest inch, or $6\frac{3}{8}$ inches to the nearest eighth of an inch. Similarly, it might be 15 cm to the nearest centimeter or 154 mm to the nearest millimeter.

When one is given a set of objects and their measurements, it is often helpful to attempt to round to the nearest given unit. When rounding to a given place value, it is necessary to look at the number in the next smaller place. If this number is 5 or more, the number in the place being rounded to is increased by 1, and all numbers to the right are changed to 0. If the number is less than 5, the number in the place being rounded to stays the same, and all numbers to the right are changed to 0.

Some methods of rounding measurements can require an additional step. First, the measurement must be converted to a decimal number. Then the rules for rounding can be applied.

Example: Round the measurements to the given units.

MEASUREMENT	ROUND TO NEAREST	ANSWER
1 foot 7 inches	foot	2 feet
5 pound 6 ounces	pound	5 pounds
$5\frac{9}{16}$ inches	inch	6 inches

Convert each measurement to a decimal number. Then apply the rules for rounding.

1 foot 7 inches = $1\frac{7}{12}$ ft = 1.58333 ft, round up to 2 ft.

5 pounds 6 ounces = $5\frac{6}{16}$ pounds = 5.375 pound, round to 5 pounds.

$5\frac{9}{16}$ inches = 5.5625 inches, round up to 6 inches.

Calculators are important tools. Their use should be encouraged in the classroom and at home. They do not replace basic knowledge but they can relieve the tedium of mathematical computations, allowing students to explore more challenging mathematical directions. Students will be able to use calculators more intelligently if they are taught how. Students need to always check their work by estimating. The goal of mathematics is to prepare the child to survive in the real world. Technology is a reality in today's society.

Computers cannot replace teachers. However, they can be used to enhance the curriculum. They may be used thoughtfully to help students practice basic skills. Many excellent programs exist to encourage higher-order thinking skills, creativity, and problem solving. Learning to use technology appropriately is an important preparation for adulthood. Computers can also show the connections between mathematics and the real world.

COMPETENCY 23

UNDERSTAND AND APPLY CONCEPTS AND METHODS OF MEASUREMENT

SKILL **Identify and use appropriate procedures and units of measurement
23.1 for problems involving length, area, volume, weight, angles, time,
and temperature**

MEASUREMENTS OF LENGTH (ENGLISH SYSTEM)		
12 inches (in)	=	1 foot (ft)
3 ft	=	1 yard (yd)
1760 yd	=	1 mile (mi)

MEASUREMENTS OF LENGTH (METRIC SYSTEM)

kilometer (km)	=	1000 meters (m)
hectometer (hm)	=	100 meters (m)
decameter (dam)	=	10 meters (m)
meter (m)	=	0 decimeter (dm)
decimeter (dm)	=	$\frac{1}{10}$ meter (m)
centimeter (cm)	=	$\frac{1}{100}$ meter (m)
millimeter (mm)	=	$\frac{1}{1000}$ meter (m)

CONVERSION OF LENGTH FROM ENGLISH TO METRIC

1 inch	=	2.54 centimeters
1 foot	$\approx$	30 centimeters
1 yard	$\approx$	0.9 meters
1 mile	$\approx$	1.6 kilometers

MEASUREMENTS OF WEIGHT (ENGLISH SYSTEM)

28 grams (g)	=	1 ounce (oz)
16 ounces (oz)	=	1 pound (lb)
2000 pounds (lb)	=	1 ton (t) (short ton)
1.1 ton (t)	=	1 ton (t)

MEASUREMENTS OF WEIGHT (METRIC SYSTEM)

kilogram (kg)	=	1000 grams (g)
gram (g)	=	1000 (mg)
milligram (mg)	=	$\frac{1}{1000}$ gram (g)

CONVERSION OF WEIGHT FROM ENGLISH TO METRIC		
1 ounce	≈	28 grams
1 pound	≈ ≈	0.45 kilogram 454 grams

MEASUREMENT OF VOLUME (ENGLISH SYSTEM)		
8 fluid ounces (oz)	=	1 cup (c)
2 cups (c)	=	1 pint (pt)
2 pints (pt)	=	1 quart (qt)
4 quarts (qt)	=	1 gallon (gal)

MEASUREMENT OF VOLUME (METRIC SYSTEM)		
kiloliter (kL)	=	1000 liters (L)
liter (L)	=	1 liter (L)
milliliter (mL)	=	$\frac{1}{1000}$ liters (mL)

CONVERSION OF VOLUME FROM ENGLISH TO METRIC		
1 teaspoon (tsp)	≈	5 milliliters
1 fluid ounce	≈	15 milliliters
1 cup	≈	0.24 liters
1 pint	≈	0.47 liters
1 quart	≈	0.95 liters
1 gallon	≈	3.8 liters

MEASUREMENT OF TIME		
1 minute	=	60 seconds
1 hour	=	60 minutes
1 day	=	24 hours
1 week	=	7 days
1 year	=	365 days
1 century	=	100 years

Square Units

Square units can be derived with knowledge of basic units of length by squaring the equivalent measurements.

> 1 square foot (sq. ft.) = 144 sq. in.
>
> 1 sq. yd. = 9 sq. ft.
>
> 1 sq. yd. = 1296 sq. in.

Example:
14 sq. yd. = _____ sq. ft.
14 × 9 = 126 sq. ft.

Weight

Example: Kathy has a bag of potatoes that weighs 5 lbs., 10 oz. She uses one third of the bag to make mashed potatoes. How much does the bag weigh now?

1 lb. = 16 oz.
5(16 oz.) + 10 oz.
= 80 oz + 10 oz = 90 oz
$90 - (\frac{1}{3})90$ oz
= 90 oz − 30 oz
= 60 oz
60 ÷ 16 = 3.75 lb
.75 = 75%
$75\% = \frac{75}{100} = \frac{3}{4}$
$\frac{3}{4} \times 16$ oz = 12 oz

The bag now weighs 3 lbs. 12 oz.

Example: The weight limit of a playground merry-go-round is 1000 pounds. There are 11 children on the merry-go-round. 3 children weigh 100 pounds. 6 children weigh 75 pounds. 2 children weigh 60 pounds. George weighs 80 pounds. Can he get on the merry-go-round?

$$3(100) + 6(75) + 2(60)$$
$$= 300 + 450 + 120$$
$$= 870$$
$$1000 - 870$$
$$= 130$$

George weighs less than 130 pounds, so he can get on the merry-go-round.

Perimeter and Area

The PERIMETER of any polygon is the sum of the lengths of the sides.

The AREA of a polygon is the number of square units covered by the figure.

PERIMETER: the sum of the lengths of the sides of any polygon

AREA: the number of square units covered by a polygon

FIGURE	AREA FORMULA	PERIMETER FORMULA
Rectangle	LW	$2(L + W)$
Triangle	$\frac{1}{2} bh$	$a + b + c$
Parallelogram	bh	sum of lengths of sides
Trapezoid	$\frac{1}{2} h(a + b)$	sum of lengths of sides

Example: A farmer has a piece of land shaped as shown below. He wishes to fence this land at an estimated cost of $25 per linear foot. What is the total cost of fencing this property to the nearest foot?

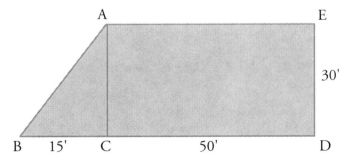

From the right triangle *ABC*, *AC* = 30 and *BC* = 15.

Since $(AB) = (AC)^2 + (BC)^2$
$(AB) = (30)^2 + (15)^2$
So feet $\sqrt{(AB)^2} = AB = \sqrt{1125} = 33.5410$ feet
To the nearest foot, $AB = 34$ feet.

Perimeter of the piece of land is $= AB + BC + CD + DE + EA$
$= 34 + 15 + 50 + 30 + 50 = 179$ feet
Cost of fencing $= \$25 \times 179 = \$4,475.00$

Example: What will be the cost of carpeting a rectangular office that measures 12 feet by 15 feet if the carpet costs \$12.50 per square yard?

12 ft

15 ft

The problem is asking you to determine the area of the office. The area of a rectangle is *length* × *width* = *A*.

Substitute the given values in the equation $A = lw$.
$A = (12 \text{ ft})(15 \text{ ft})$
$A = 180 \text{ ft}^2$

The problem asked you to determine the cost of carpet at \$12.50 per square yard.

First, you need to convert 180 ft^2 into yards².
1 yd $= 3$ ft
$(1 \text{ yd})(1 \text{ yd}) = (3 \text{ ft})(3 \text{ ft})$
$1 \text{ yd}^2 = 9 \text{ ft}^2$
$\frac{180 \text{ ft}^2}{9 \text{ ft}^2} = 20 \text{ yd}^2$.

The carpet costs \$12.50 per square yard; thus the cost of carpeting the office described is $\$12.50 \times 20 = \$250.00$.

Example: Find the area of a parallelogram if its base is 6.5 cm long and the height is 3.7 cm.

6.5 cm

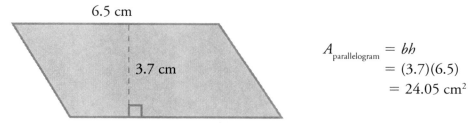

3.7 cm

$$A_{\text{parallelogram}} = bh$$
$$= (3.7)(6.5)$$
$$= 24.05 \text{ cm}^2$$

Example: Find the area of this triangle.

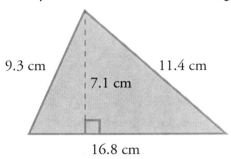

9.3 cm   11.4 cm

7.1 cm

16.8 cm

$$A_{\text{triangle}} = \tfrac{1}{2}bh$$
$$= 0.5(16.8)(7.1)$$
$$= 59.64 \text{ cm}^2$$

Example: Find the area of this trapezoid.

17.5 cm

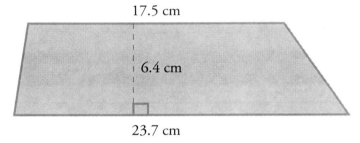

6.4 cm

23.7 cm

The area of a trapezoid equals one-half the sum of the bases times the height.

$$A_{\text{trapezoid}} = \tfrac{1}{2}h(b_1 + b_2)$$
$$A_{\text{trapezoid}} = 0.5(6.4)(17.5 + 23.7)$$
$$A_{\text{trapezoid}} = 131.84 \text{ cm}^2$$

Circles

The distance around a circle is the CIRCUMFERENCE. The ratio of the circumference to the diameter is represented by the Greek letter pi, $\pi \sim 3.14 \sim \tfrac{22}{7}$.

The circumference of a circle is found by the formula $C = 2\pi r$ or $C = \pi d$, where r is the radius of the circle and d is the diameter.

The area of a circle is found by the formula $A = \pi r^2$.

CIRCUMFERENCE: the distance around a circle

The area of a circle is found by the formula $A = \pi r^2$.

Example: Find the circumference and area of a circle whose radius is 7 meters.

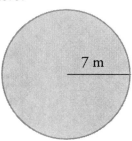

7 m

$$C = \pi r$$
$$= 2(3.14)(7)$$
$$= 43.96 \text{ m}$$

$$A = \pi r^2$$
$$= 3.14(7)(7)$$
$$= 153.86 \text{ m}^2$$

Volume and Surface Area

We use the following formulas to compute volume and surface area:

FIGURE	VOLUME	TOTAL SURFACE AREA
Right Cylinder	$\pi r^2 h$	$2\pi rh + 2\pi r^2$
Right Cone	$\dfrac{\pi r^2 h}{3}$	$\pi r \sqrt{r^2 + h^2} + \pi r^2$
Sphere	$\dfrac{4}{3}\pi r^3$	$4\pi r^2$
Rectangular Solid	LWH	$2LW + 2WH + 2LH$

FIGURE	LATERAL AREA	TOTAL AREA	VOLUME
Regular Pyramid	$\dfrac{1}{2}Pl$	$\dfrac{1}{2}Pl + B$	$\dfrac{1}{3}Bh$

P = Perimeter, h = height, B = Area of Base, l = slant height

Example: What is the volume of a shoe box with a length of 35 cm, a width of 20 cm, and a height of 15 cm?

Volume of a rectangular solid = Length × Width × Height
$$= 35 \times 20 \times 15$$
$$= 10500 \text{ cm}^3$$

Example: A water company is trying to decide whether to use traditional cylindrical paper cups or to offer conical paper cups, since both cost the same. The traditional cups are 8 cm wide and 14 cm high. The conical cups are 12 cm wide and 19 cm high. The company will use the cup that holds the most water.

Draw and label a sketch of each.

$V = \pi r^2 h$ $V = \frac{\pi r^2 h}{3}$ 1. Write a formula.

$V = \pi(4)^2(14)$ $V = \frac{1}{3}\pi(6)^2(19)$ 2. Substitute.

$V = 703.717$ cm³ $V = 716.283$ cm³   3. Solve.

The choice should be the conical cup since its volume is more.

Example: How much material is needed to make a basketball that has a diameter of 15 inches? How much air is needed to fill the basketball?

Draw and label a sketch:

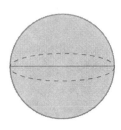

$D = 15$ inches

Total surface area   Volume

TSA $= 4\pi r^2$ $V = \frac{4}{3}\pi r^3$ 1. Write a formula.

    $= 4\pi(7.5)^2$ $= \frac{4}{3}\pi(7.5)^3$ 2. Substitute.

    $= 706.858$ in² $= 1767.1459$ in³   3. Solve.

SKILL 23.2 Identify and use appropriate measurement tools in various situations

When reading inches on a ruler, the student needs to understand that each inch is divided into halves by the longest mark in the middle; into fourths by the next-longest marks; into eighths by the next; and into sixteenths by the shortest marks. When the measurement falls between two "inch marks," they can give the whole number of inches, count the additional fractional marks, and give the answer as the number and fraction of inches. Remind students that the convention is always to express a fraction with its lowest possible denominator.

If students are using the metric system on a ruler, have them focus on the marks between the whole numbers (centimeters). Point out that each centimeter is broken into tenths, with the mark in the middle being longer to indicate a halfway mark. Students should learn to measure things accurately to the nearest tenth of a centimeter, then the nearest hundredth, and finally the nearest thousandth. Measurements using the metric system should always be written using the decimal system—for example, 3.756 centimeters.

When reading a thermometer, one should hold it vertically at eye level. Students should check the scale of the thermometer to make certain that they read as many significant digits as possible. Thermometers with heavy or extended lines that are marked 10, 20, 30, and so on should be read to the nearest 0.1 degree. Thermometers with fine lines every two degrees should be read to the nearest 0.5 degree.

In order to get an accurate reading in a liquid measuring cup, students should set the cup on a level surface and read it at eye level. The measurement should be read at the bottom of the concave arc at the liquid's surface (the meniscus line). When measuring dry ingredients, dip the appropriately sized measuring cup into the ingredient, and sweep away the excess across the top with a straight-edged object.

Protractors measure angles in degrees. To measure accurately, students must find the center hole on the straight edge of the protractor and place it over the vertex of the angle they wish to measure. They should line up the zero on the straight edge with one of the sides of the angle and then find the point where the second side of the angle intersects the curved edge of the protractor. They can then read the number that is written at the point of intersection.

When one is reading an instrument such as a rain gauge, it is important to read at eye level and at the base of the meniscus. The measuring tube is divided, marked, and labeled in tenths and hundredths. The greatest number of decimal places there will be is two.

Most numbers in mathematics are "exact" or "counted," but measurements are "approximate." They usually involve interpolation, or figuring out which mark on the ruler is closest. Any measurement acquired with a measuring device is approximate. These variations in measurement are called precision and accuracy.

A measurement's PRECISION tells us how exactly a measurement is made, without reference to a true or real value. If a measurement is precise, it can be made again and again with little variation in the result. The precision of a measuring device is the smallest fractional or decimal division on the instrument. The smaller the unit or fraction of a unit on the measuring device, the more precisely it can measure.

The greatest possible error of measurement is always equal to one-half the smallest fraction of a unit on the measuring device.

A measurement's ACCURACY tells us how close the result of measurement comes to the "true" value.

In the game of throwing darts, the true value is the bull's eye. If the three darts land on the bull's eye, the dart thrower is both precise (all the darts land near the same spot) and accurate (the darts all land on the "true" value).

The greatest measure of error allowed is called the TOLERANCE. The least acceptable limit is called the LOWER LIMIT, and the greatest acceptable limit is called the UPPER LIMIT. The difference between the upper and lower limits is called the TOLERANCE INTERVAL. For example, a specification for an automobile part might be 14.625 ± 0.005 mm. This means that the smallest acceptable length of the part is 14.620 mm and the largest acceptable length is 14.630 mm. The tolerance interval is 0.010 mm. One can see how it would be important for automobile parts to be within a set of limits in terms of length. If the part is too long or too short, it will not fit properly, and vibrations will occur that weaken the part and may eventually cause damage to other parts.

> **PRECISION:** tells us how exact a measurement is

> **ACCURACY:** how close a measurement comes to the "true" value

> **TOLERANCE:** the greatest measure of error allowed

> **LOWER LIMIT:** the least acceptable measure of error

> **UPPER LIMIT:** the greatest acceptable measure of error

> **TOLERANCE INTERVAL:** the difference between the lower and upper levels of tolerance

---

SKILL 23.3 **Demonstrate knowledge of conversions within and between measurement systems**

Length

Example: A car skidded 170 yards on an icy road before coming to a stop. How long is the skid distance in kilometers?

Since 1 yard 0.9 meter, multiply 170 yards by 0.9.

$$170 \times 0.9 = 153 \text{ meters}$$

Since 1000 meters = 1 kilometer, divide 153 by 1000.

$$\frac{153}{1000} = 0.153 \text{ kilometer.}$$

Example: The distance around a race course is exactly 1 mile, 17 feet, and $9\frac{1}{4}$ inches. Approximate this distance to the nearest tenth of a foot.

Convert the distance to feet.

$$1 \text{ mile} = 1760 \text{ yards} = 1760 \times 3 \text{ feet} = 5280 \text{ feet}$$
$$9\tfrac{1}{4} \text{ inches} = \tfrac{37}{4} \times \tfrac{1}{12} = \tfrac{37}{48} \approx 0.77083 \text{ foot}$$

So 1 mile, 17 feet, and $9\frac{1}{4}$ inches $= 5280 + 17 + 0.77083$ feet
$$= 5297.\underline{7}7083 \text{ feet}.$$

Now, we need to round to the nearest tenths digit. The underlined 7 is in the tenths place. The digit in the hundredths place, also a 7, is greater than 5, so the 7 in the tenths place must be rounded up to 8 to get a final answer of 5297.8 feet.

Weight

Example: Zachary weighs 150 pounds. Tom weighs 153 pounds. What is the difference in their weights in grams?

$$153 \text{ pounds} - 150 \text{ pounds} = 3 \text{ pounds}$$
$$1 \text{ pound} = 454 \text{ grams}$$
$$3(454 \text{ grams}) = 1362 \text{ grams}$$

Capacity

Example: Students in a fourth grade class want to fill a 3-gallon jug using cups of water. How many cups of water are needed?

$$1 \text{ gallon} = 16 \text{ cups of water}$$
$$3 \text{ gallons} \times 16 \text{ cups} = 48 \text{ cups of water are needed.}$$

Time

Example: It takes Cynthia 45 minutes to get ready each morning. How many hours does she spend getting ready each week?

$$45 \text{ minutes} \times 7 \text{ days} = 315 \text{ minutes}$$
$$\frac{315 \text{ minutes}}{60 \text{ minutes in an hour}} = 5.25 \text{ hours}$$

SKILL **Identify approaches to direct measurement through standard and**
23.4 **nonstandard units and indirect measurement through the use of**
algebra or geometry

There are two types of measurement: direct measurement and indirect measurement. As the name implies, **DIRECT MEASUREMENT** is the action of measuring something directly. For example, the length of a boat can be measured with a measuring tape, and elapsed time can be measured with a stopwatch.

INDIRECT MEASUREMENT is measurement that is not done with a tool such as a ruler or watch. Instead, other mathematical approaches are used to derive the desired measurement. Using similar triangles is an example of indirect measurement. Similar triangles have the same angles and proportionate sides, but they are different sizes. They can be used to determine the distance from one point to another without measuring it directly. In the diagram below, X represents the distance between two points with an unknown length.

> **DIRECT MEASURE-MENT:** measuring something directly

> **INDIRECT MEASURE-MENT:** using an alternate method for measuring, such using scale drawings

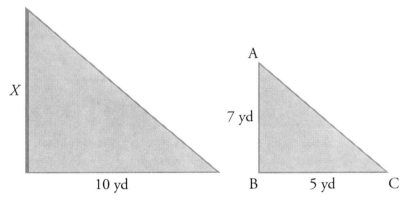

The problem can be addressed by setting up the following proportion and solving for X.

$$\frac{X}{10 \text{ yd}} = \frac{7 \text{ yd}}{5 \text{ yd}}$$

After cross-multiplying, the equation can be written as $5X = 70$; X equals 14 yards. Without actually measuring the distance with a measuring tape or other tool, the distance between the points is determined.

Indirect measurement also occurs in instances other than simply measuring length. The area of a room can be measured using a scale drawing. It is possible to determine the weight of the moon by using the measurable effects the moon exerts on the earth, such as the changes in tides. Another familiar indirect measurement is the Body Mass Index (BMI), which indicates body composition. BMI uses height and weight measurements to measure health risks.

COMPETENCY 24
UNDERSTAND PATTERNS, RELATIONSHIPS, AND ALGEBRAIC CONCEPTS

> **SKILL** **Define and describe patterns and relationships using various**
> **24.1** **representations** (e.g., numbers, symbols, variables, visual representations)

Example: Conjecture about pattern presented in tabular form.

Kepler discovered a relationship between the average distance of a planet from the sun and the time it takes the planet to orbit the sun.

The following table shows the data for the six planets closest to the sun:

	Mercury	Venus	Earth	Mars	Jupiter	Saturn
Average distance, x	0.387	0.723	1	1.523	5.203	9.541
x^3	0.058	0.378	1	3.533	140.852	868.524
Time, y	0.241	0.615	1	1.881	11.861	29.457
y^2	0.058	0.378	1	3.538	140.683	867.715

Looking at the data in the table, we see that $x^3 \simeq y^2$. We can conjecture the following function for Kepler's relationship:

$$y = \sqrt{x^3}.$$

Example: Find the recursive formula for the sequence 1, 3, 9, 27, 81...

We see that any term other than the first term is obtained by multiplying the preceding term by 3. Thus, we can express the formula in symbolic notation as

$$a_n = 3a_{n-1}, \, a_1 = 1,$$

where a represents a term, the subscript n denotes the place of the term in the sequence, and the subscript $n - 1$ represents the preceding term.

A **LINEAR FUNCTION** is a function defined by the equation $f(x) = mx + b$.

> **LINEAR FUNCTION:** a function defined by the equation $f(x) = mx + b$

Example: A model for the distance traveled by a migrating monarch butterfly looks like f(t) = 80t, *where* t *represents time in days. We interpret this to mean that the average speed of the butterfly is 80 miles per day and distance traveled may be computed by substituting the number of days traveled for* t. *In a linear function, there is a* constant rate of change.

The standard form of a QUADRATIC FUNCTION is $f(x) = ax^2 + bx + c$.

Example: What patterns appear in a table for y = x² − 5x + 6?

X	0	1	2	3	4	5
Y	6	2	0	0	2	6

We see that the values for *y* are symmetrically arranged.

An EXPONENTIAL FUNCTION is a function defined by the equation $y = ab^x$, where *a* is the starting value, *b* is the growth factor, and *x* tells how many times to multiply by the growth factor.

Example: y = 100(1.5)ˣ

X	0	1	2	3	4
Y	100	150	225	337.5	506.25

This is an exponential or multiplicative pattern of growth.

The iterative process involves repeated use of the same steps. A recursive function is an example of the iterative process. A recursive function is a function that requires the computation of all previous terms in order to find a subsequent term. Perhaps the most famous recursive function is the Fibonacci sequence. This is the sequence of numbers 1, 1, 2, 3, 5, 8, 13, 21, 34 … for which the next term is found by adding the previous two terms.

> **QUADRATIC FUNCTION:** the standard form of a quadratic function is $f(x) = ax^2 + bx + c$

> **EXPONENTIAL FUNCTION:** a function defined by the equation $y = ab^x$, where *a* is the starting value, *b* is the growth factor, and *x* tells how many times to multiply by the growth factor

---

SKILL 24.2 **Solve linear and nonlinear equations and inequalities**

Procedure for Solving Algebraic Equations

Example: 3(x + 3) = -2x + 4

Solve for *x*.

1. Expand to eliminate all parentheses.

   $3x + 9 = -2x + 4$

2. Multiply each term by the LCD to eliminate all denominators.

3. Combine like terms on each side when possible.

4. Use the properties to put all variables on one side and all constants on the other side.

   $\rightarrow 3x + 9 - 9 = -2x + 4 - 9$ Subtract nine from both sides.

   $\rightarrow 3x = -2x - 5$

   $\rightarrow 3x + 2x = -2x + 2x - 5$ Add $2x$ to both sides.

   $\rightarrow 5x = -5$

   $\rightarrow \frac{5x}{5} = \frac{-5}{5}$ Divide both sides by 5.

   $\rightarrow x = -1$

Example: Solve: $3(2x + 5) - 4x = 5(x + 9)$

$6x + 15 - 4x = 5x + 45$

$2x + 15 = 5x + 45$

$-3x + 15 = 45$

$-3x = 30$

$x = -10$

Example: Mark and Mike are twins. Three times Mark's age, plus 4, equals 4 times Mike's age minus 14. How old are the boys?

Because the boys are twins, their ages are the same. "Translate" the English into algebra. Let $x = $ their age.

$3x + 4 = 4x - 14$

$18 = x$

The boys are both 18 years old.

Procedure for Solving Algebraic Inequalities

We use the same procedure we used above for solving linear equations, but the answer is either represented in graphical form on the number line or in interval form.

Example: Solve the inequality, show its solution using interval form, and graph the solution on the number line.

$\frac{5x}{8} + 3 \geq 2x - 5$

$8\left(\frac{5x}{8}\right) + 8(3) \geq 8(2x) - 5(8)$ Multiply by LCD = 8.

$5x + 24 \geq 16x - 40$

$5x + 24 - 24 - 16x \geq 16x - 16x - 40 - 24$

Subtract 16x and 24 from both sides of the equation.

$-11x \geq -16$

$\frac{-11x}{-11} \leq \frac{-64}{-11}$

$x \leq \frac{64}{11}$ $\qquad$ $x \leq 5\frac{9}{11}$

Solution in interval form: $\left(-\infty, 5\frac{9}{11}\right]$

Note: " $]$ " means $5\frac{9}{11}$ is included in the solution.

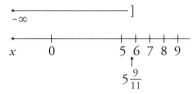

Example: Solve the following inequality, and express your answer in both interval and graphical form.

$3x - 8 < 2(3x - 1)$

$3x - 8 < 6x - 2$ $\qquad$ Distributive property.

$3x - 6x - 8 + 8 < 6x - 6x - 2 + 8$

Add 8 and subtract 6x from both sides of the equation.

$-3x < 6$

$\frac{-3x}{-3} > \frac{6}{-3}$ $\qquad$ Note the change in direction of the equality.

$x > -2$

Graphical form:

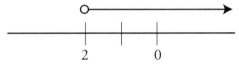

or

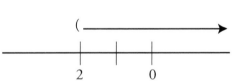

Interval form: $(-2, \infty)$

Recall:

A. Using a parenthesis or an open circle implies that the point is not included in the answer.

B. Using a bracket or a closed circle implies that the point is included in the answer.

Example: Solve:

$6x + 21 < 8x + 31$

$-2x + 21 < 31$

$-2x < 10$

$x > -5$

Note that the inequality sign has changed.

Absolute Value Equations and Equalities

If a and b are real numbers, and k is a non-negative real number, the solution of

$|ax + b| = k$ is $ax + b = k$ or $ax + b = -k$

$|ax + b| > k$ is $ax + b > k$ or $ax + b < -k$

Example: Solve for x.

$|2x + 3| = 9$

$2x + 3 = 9$	or	$2x + 3 = -9$
$2x + 3 - 3 = 9 - 3$	or	$2x + 3 - 3 = -9 - 3$
$2x = 6$	or	$2x = -12$
$\frac{2x}{2} = \frac{6}{2}$	or	$\frac{2x}{2} = \frac{-12}{2}$
$x = 3$	or	$x = -6$

Therefore, the solution is $x = \{3, -6\}$.

Example: Solve

$|7x + 3| < 25$

$-25 < (7x + 3) < 25$ Subtract 3 from each side.

$(-25 - 3) < (7x) < (25 - 3)$

$-28 < 7x < 22$

$-4 < x < \frac{22}{7}$ Divide all terms by 7.

Solution in interval form is $(-4, \frac{22}{7})$.

Solution in graphical form:

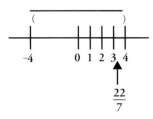

An algebraic formula is an equation that describes a relationship among variables. While it is not often necessary to derive the formula, one must know how to rewrite a given formula in terms of a desired variable.

Example: Given that the relationship of voltage, V, applied across a material with electrical resistance, R, when a current, I, is flowing through the material is represented by the formula V = IR, find the resistance of the material when a current of 10 milliamps is flowing, when the applied voltage is 2 volts.

$V = IR$ Solve for R.

$IR = V; R = \frac{V}{I}$ Divide both sides by I.

When $V = 2$ volts; $I = 10 \times 10^{-3}$ amps;

$R = \frac{2}{10^1 \times 10^{-3}}$

$R = \frac{2}{10^{-2}}$ Substituting $R = \frac{V}{I}$, we get

$R = 2 \times 10^2$

$R = 200$ ohms

Example: Given that temperature in Celsius (C), and Fahrenheit (F) are related by the formula: $C = \frac{5}{9}(F - 32)$, solve for F.

$\frac{C}{1} = \frac{5(F - 32)}{9} \rightarrow 9C = 5F - 160$

$5F = 9C + 160$

$5F = \frac{9C + 160}{5} = \frac{9C}{5} + \frac{160}{5}$

$F = \frac{9C}{5} + 32$

SKILL 24.3 **Identify algebraic concepts of relation and function** *(e.g., domain, range)* **to analyze mathematical relationships**

A RELATION is any set of ordered pairs. The DOMAIN of a relation is the set containing all the first coordinates of the ordered pairs, and the RANGE of a relation is the set containing all the second coordinates of the ordered pairs.

A FUNCTION is a relation in which each value in the domain corresponds to only one value in the range. It is notable, however, that a value in the range may correspond to any number of values in the domain. Thus, although a function is necessarily a relation, not all relations are functions, since a relation is not bound by this rule.

On a graph, use the vertical line test to check whether a relation is a function. If any vertical line intersects the graph of a relation in more than one point, then the relation is not a function.

RELATION: any set of ordered pairs

DOMAIN: the set containing all the first coordinates of the ordered pairs

RANGE: the set containing all the second coordinates of the ordered pairs

FUNCTION: a relation in which each value in the domain corresponds to only one value in the range

ONE-TO-ONE: a relationship in which each value in the domain corresponds to only one value in the range, and each value in the range corresponds to only one value in the domain

A relation is considered ONE-TO-ONE if each value in the domain corresponds to only one value in the range, and each value in the range corresponds to only one value in the domain. Thus, a one-to-one relation is also a function, but has an additional condition.

In the same way that the graph of a relation can be examined using the vertical line test to determine whether it is a function, the horizontal line test can be used to determine if a function is a one-to-one relation. If no horizontal lines superimposed on the plot intersect the graph of the relation in more than one place, then the relation is one-to-one (assuming it also passes the vertical line test and, therefore, is a function).

A mapping is essentially the same as a function. Mappings (or maps) can be depicted using diagrams with arrows drawn from each element of the domain to the corresponding element (or elements) of the range. If two arrows originate from any single element in the domain, then the mapping is not a function. Likewise, for a function, if each arrow is drawn to a unique value in the range (that is, there are no cases where more than one arrow is drawn to a given value in the range), then the relation is one-to-one.

Example: Determine the domain and range of this mapping.

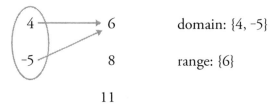

domain: {4, -5}

range: {6}

A function can be defined as a set of ordered pairs in which each element of the domain is paired with one and only one element of the range. The symbol $f(x)$ is read "f of x." A letter other than "f" can be used to represent a function. The letter "g" is commonly used as in $g(x)$.

Example: Given $f(x) = 4x^2 - 2x + 3$, find $f(-3)$.
(This question is asking for the range value that corresponds to the domain value of -3).

$$f(x) = 4x^2 - 2x + 3$$ 1. Replace x with -3.
$$f(-3) = 4(-3)^2 - 2(-3) + 3$$
$$f(-3) = 45$$ 2. Solve.

Example: Find f(3) and f(10), given f(x) = 7.

$f(x) = 7$ 1. There are no x values to substitute for.

$(3) = 7$ This is your answer.

$f(x) = 7$

$f(10) = 7$ 2. Same as above.

Notice that both answers are equal to the constant given.

SKILL **Represent relationships among variables using words, tables,**
24.4 **graphs, and rules**

See Skill 19.3

SKILL **Make use of algebraic functions to plot points, describe graphs,**
24.5 **determine slope, and extrapolate**

A first-degree equation has an equation of the form $ax + by = c$. To find the slope of a line, solve the equation for y. This gets the equation into slope-intercept form, $y = mx + b$. In this equation, m is the line's slope.

> Slope-intercept form is $y = mx + b$

The y intercept is the coordinate of the point where a line crosses the y-axis. To find the y intercept, substitute 0 for x and solve for y. This is the y intercept. In slope-intercept form, $y = mx + b$, b is the y intercept.

To find the x intercept, substitute 0 for y and solve for x. This is the x intercept. If the equation solves to $x = $ **any number**, then the graph is a vertical line, because it only has an x intercept. Its slope is undefined.

If the equation solves to $y = $ **any number**, then the graph is a horizontal line, because it only has a y intercept. Its slope is 0 (zero).

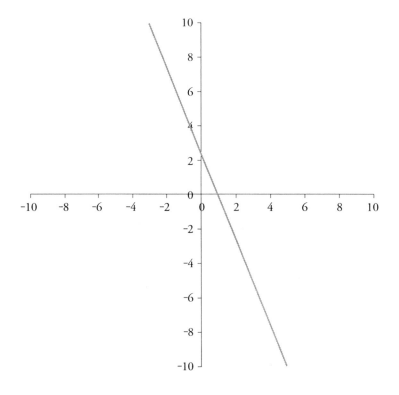

$$5x + 2y = 6$$
$$y = \frac{-5}{2x + 3}$$

The equation of a line from its graph can be found by finding its slope and its y intercept.

$$Y - y_a = m\ (X - x_a)$$

(x_a, y_a) can be (x_1, y_1) or (x_2, y_2) If m, the value of the slope, is distributed through the parentheses, the equation can be rewritten into other forms of the equation of a line.

Example: Find the equation of a line through (9, -6) and (-1, 2).

$$\text{slope} = \frac{y_2 - y_1}{x_2 - x_1} = \frac{2 - (\text{-}6)}{\text{-}1 - 9} = \frac{8}{210} = \frac{24}{5}$$

$$Y - y_a = m(X - x_a) \rightarrow Y - 2 = \frac{-4}{5(X - \text{-}1)} \rightarrow$$
$$Y - 2 = \frac{-4}{5(X + 1)} \rightarrow Y - 2 = -\frac{4}{5X} - \frac{4}{5} \qquad \text{This is the slope-intercept form.}$$
$$Y = \frac{-4}{5}X + \frac{6}{5}$$

Multiplying by 5 to eliminate fractions, it is:

$$5Y = -4X + 6 \rightarrow 4X + 5Y = 6 \qquad \text{Standard form.}$$

Example: Find the slope and intercepts of 3x + 2y = 14.

$$3x + 2y = 14$$
$$2y = -3x + 14$$
$$y = \frac{-3}{2}x + 7$$

The slope of the line is $\frac{-3}{2}$. The y-intercept of the line is 7. The x-intercept of the line is $\frac{14}{3}$.

The intercepts can also be found by substituting 0 in place of the other variables in the equation.

To find the y-intercept:
Let $x = 0$; $3(0) + 2y = 14$
$0 + 2y = 14$
$2y = 14$
$y = 7$
$(0, 7)$ is the y-intercept.

To find the x-intercept:
Let $y = 0$; $3x + 2(0) = 14$
$3x + 0 = 14$
$3x = 14$
$x = \frac{14}{3}$
$(\frac{14}{3}, 0)$ is the x-intercept.

Example: Sketch the graph of the line represented by 2x + 3y = 6.

Let $x = 0 \rightarrow 2(0) + 3y = 6$
$\rightarrow 3y = 6$
$\rightarrow y = 2$
$\rightarrow (0, 2)$ is the y-intercept

Let $y = 0 \rightarrow 2x + 3(0) = 6$
$\rightarrow 2x = 6$
$\rightarrow x = 3$
$\rightarrow (3, 0)$ is the x-intercept

Let $x = 1 \rightarrow 2(1) + 3y = 6$
$\rightarrow 2 + 3y = 6$
$\rightarrow 3y = 4$
$\rightarrow y = \frac{4}{3}$
$\rightarrow (1, \frac{4}{3})$ is the third point.

Plotting the three points on the coordinate system, we get the following:

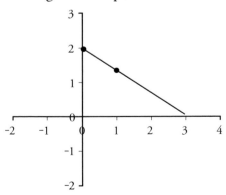

To graph an inequality, solve the inequality for y. This gets the inequality in slope intercept form ($y < mx + b$). The point $(0,b)$ is the y-intercept and m is the line's slope.

If the inequality solves to $x \geq$ **any number**, then the graph includes a vertical line.

If the inequality solves to $y \leq$ **any number,** then the graph includes a horizontal line.

When graphing a linear inequality, the line will be dotted if the inequality sign is $<$ or $>$. If the inequality sign is either $\geq$ or $\leq$, the line on the graph will be a solid line. Shade above the line when the inequality sign is $\geq$ or $>$. Shade below the line when the inequality sign is $\leq$ or $<$. For inequalities of the forms $x >$ number, $x \leq$ number, $x <$ number, or $x \geq$ number, draw a vertical line (solid or dotted). Shade to the right for $>$ or $\geq$. Shade to the left for $<$ or $\leq$.

Remember: Dividing or multiplying by a negative number will reverse the direction of the inequality sign.

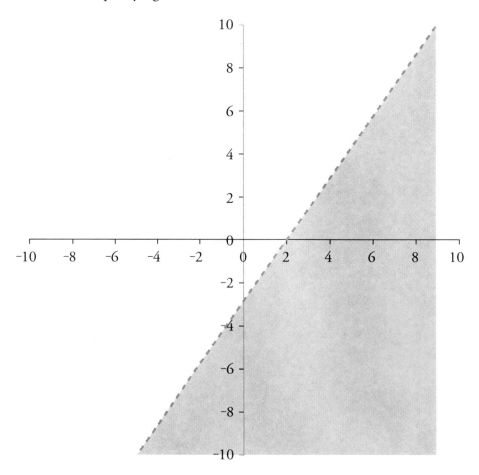

$3x - 2y \geq 6$
$y \leq \dfrac{3}{2x - 3}$

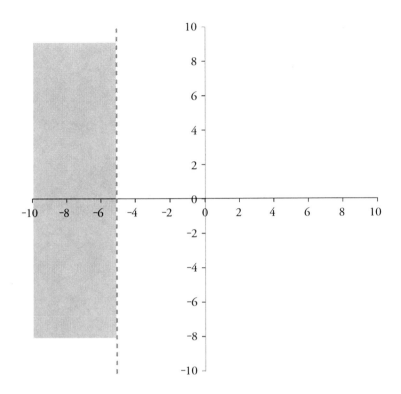

$3x + 12 < -3$
$x < -5$

Example: Solve by graphing.

    $x + y \leq 6$
    $x - 2y \leq 6$

Solving the inequalities for y, we find that they become:

    $y \leq -x + 6$ (y-intercept of 6 and slope = -1)
    $y \geq \frac{1}{2x - 3}$ (y-intercept of -3 and slope = $\frac{1}{2}$)

A graph with shading is shown below:

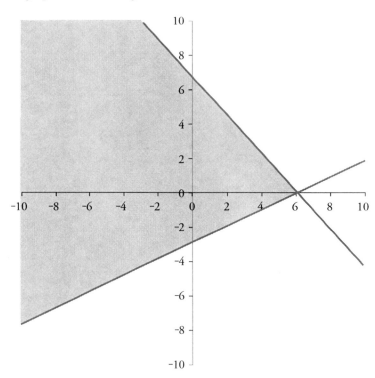

COMPETENCY 25

UNDERSTAND AND APPLY PRINCIPLES AND PROPERTIES OF GEOMETRY

SKILL Recognize the geometric properties of and relationships between
25.1 two- and three-dimensional figures

POLYGON: a simple, closed, two-dimensional figure composed of line segments

We name POLYGONS—simple, closed, two-dimensional figures composed of line segments—according to the number of sides they have.

A QUADRILATERAL is a polygon with four sides.

The sum of the measures of the angles of a quadrilateral is 360°.

A TRAPEZOID is a quadrilateral with exactly one pair of parallel sides.

In an ISOSCELES TRAPEZOID, the nonparallel sides are congruent.

A PARALLELOGRAM is a quadrilateral with two pairs of parallel sides.

In a parallelogram:

- The diagonals bisect each other
- Each diagonal divides the parallelogram into two congruent triangles
- Both pairs of opposite sides are congruent
- Both pairs of opposite angles are congruent
- Two adjacent angles are supplementary

A RECTANGLE is a parallelogram with a right angle.

A RHOMBUS is a parallelogram with all sides equal in length.

QUADRILATERAL: a polygon with four sides

TRAPEZOID: a quadrilateral with exactly *one* pair of parallel sides

ISOSCELES TRAPE-ZOID: a quadrilateral in which the nonparallel sides are congruent

PARALLELOGRAM: a quadrilateral with two pairs of parallel sides

RECTANGLE: a parallelogram with a right angle

RHOMBUS: a parallelogram with all sides equal in length

SQUARE: a rectangle with all sides equal in length

TRIANGLE: a polygon with three sides

ACUTE TRIANGLE: a triangle with three acute angles

ACUTE ANGLE: an angle that measures less than 90°

RIGHT TRIANGLE: a triangle with one *right* angle

RIGHT ANGLE: an angle that measures 90°

OBTUSE TRIANGLE: a triangle with one *obtuse* angle

OBTUSE ANGLE: an angle that measures between 90° and 180°

EQUILATERAL TRIANGLE: a triangle in which all sides are the same length

ISOSCELES TRIANGLE: a triangle in wich two sides are the same length

A SQUARE is a rectangle with all sides equal in length.

Example: True or false?

All squares are rhombuses	True
All parallelograms are rectangles	False—*some* parallelograms are rectangles
All rectangles are parallelograms	True
Some rhombuses are squares	True
Some rectangles are trapezoids	False—trapezoids have only *one* pair of parallel sides
All quadrilaterals are parallelograms	False—*some* quadrilaterals are parallelograms
Some squares are rectangles	False—*all* squares are rectangles
Some parallelograms are rhombuses	True

A TRIANGLE is a polygon with three sides. We can classify triangles by the types of their angles or the lengths of their sides.

An ACUTE TRIANGLE has three acute angles. An ACUTE ANGLE is an angle that measures less than 90°.

A RIGHT TRIANGLE has one right angle. A RIGHT ANGLE is an angle that measures 90°.

An OBTUSE TRIANGLE has one obtuse angle. An OBTUSE ANGLE measures between 90° and 180°.

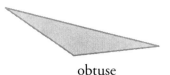

acute   right   obtuse

All three sides of an EQUILATERAL TRIANGLE are the same length.

Two sides of an ISOSCELES TRIANGLE are the same length.

None of the sides of a SCALENE TRIANGLE are the same length.

equilateral   isosceles   scalene

> **SCALENE TRIANGLE:** a triangle in which no sides are the same length

Example: Can a triangle have two right angles?

No. A right angle measures 90°; therefore, the sum of two right angles would be 180°, and there could not be a third angle.

Example: Can a triangle have two obtuse angles?

No. Since an obtuse angle measures more than 90°, the sum of two obtuse angles would be greater than 180°.

Three-dimensional figures

A CYLINDER is a space figure that has two parallel, congruent circular bases.

> **CYLINDER:** a space figure that has two parallel, congruent circular bases

A SPHERE is a space figure having all its points the same distance from the center.

> **SPHERE:** a space figure having all its points the same distance from the center

A CONE is a space figure having a circular base and a single vertex.

> **CONE:** a space figure having a circular base and a single vertex

A PYRAMID is a space figure with a square base and four triangle-shaped sides.

> **PYRAMID:** a space figure with a square base and four triangle-shaped sides

A TETRAHEDRON is a four-sided space triangle. Each face is a triangle.

> **TETRAHEDRON:** a four-sided space triangle; each face is a triangle

PRISM: a space figure with two congruent, parallel bases that are polygons

A **PRISM** is a space figure with two congruent, parallel bases that are polygons.

Congruent figures have the same size and shape. If one is placed above the other, they will fit exactly. Congruent lines have the same length. Congruent angles have equal measures.

The symbol for congruence is ≅.

The symbol for congruence is ≅.

Polygons (pentagons) *ABCDE* and *VWXYZ* are congruent. They are exactly the same size and shape.

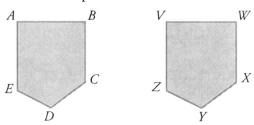

$$ABCDE \cong VWXYZ$$

Corresponding parts are the congruent angles and congruent sides. They are:

Corresponding Angles	Corresponding Sides
∠A ↔ ∠V	AB ↔ VW
∠B ↔ ∠W	BC ↔ WX
∠C ↔ ∠X	CD ↔ XY
∠D ↔ ∠Y	DE ↔ YZ
∠E ↔ ∠Z	AE ↔ VZ

Similarity

Two figures that have the same shape are similar. Polygons are similar if and only if corresponding angles are congruent and corresponding sides are in proportion. Corresponding parts of similar polygons are proportional.

Example: Given two similar quadrilaterals, find the lengths of sides x, y, and z.

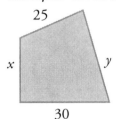
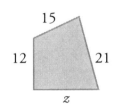

Since corresponding sides are proportional, the scale is:

$$\frac{12}{x} = \frac{3}{5} \qquad\qquad \frac{21}{y} = \frac{3}{5} \qquad\qquad \frac{z}{30} = \frac{3}{5}$$
$$3x = 60 \qquad\qquad 3y = 105 \qquad\qquad 5z = 90$$
$$x = 20 \qquad\qquad y = 35 \qquad\qquad z = 18$$

Example: Tommy draws and cuts out two triangles for a school project. One of them has sides of 3, 6, and 9 inches. The other triangle has sides of 2, 4, and 6 inches. Is there a relationship between the two triangles?

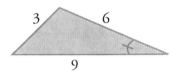
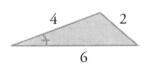

Take the proportion of the corresponding sides.

$$\frac{2}{3} \qquad\qquad \frac{4}{6} = \frac{2}{3} \qquad\qquad \frac{6}{9} = \frac{2}{3}$$

The smaller triangle is $\frac{2}{3}$ the size of the larger triangle.

The Pythagorean Theorem

Given any right triangle $\triangle ABC$, the square of the hypotenuse is equal to the sum of the squares of the other two sides.

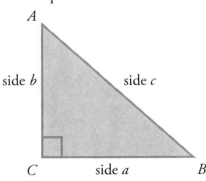

Hypotenuse (side opposite the 90° angle)

Given any right triangle $\triangle ABC$, the square of the hypotenuse is equal to the sum of the squares of the other two sides.

The Pythagorean Theorem states that $c^2 = a^2 + b^2$.

Example: Find the area and perimeter of a rectangle if its length is 12 inches and its diagonal is 15 inches.

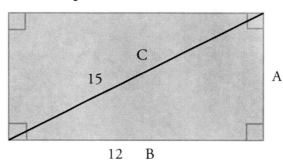

1. Draw and label sketch.
2. Since the height is still needed, use Pythagorean formula to find missing leg of the triangle.

$A^2 + B^2 = C^2$
$A^2 + 12^2 = 15^2$
$A^2 = 15^2 - 12^2$
$A^2 = 81$
$A = 9$

Now use this information to find the area and perimeter.

A = LW	P = 2(L + W)	1. Write formula.
A = (12)(9)	P = 2(12 + 9)	2. Substitute.
A = 108 in²	P = 42 inches	3. Solve.

Example: Two old cars leave a road intersection at the same time. One car traveled due north at 55 mph while the other car traveled due east. After 3 hours, the cars were 180 miles apart. Find the speed of the second car.

Using a right triangle to represent the problem, we get the figure below:

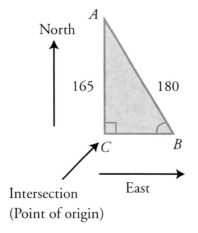

Traveling at 55 mph for 3 hours, the northbound car has driven (55)(3) = 165 miles. This is the side *AC*. The cars are 180 miles apart. This is side *AB*.

Since $\triangle ABC$ is a right triangle, then, by the Pythagorean Theorem, we get:

$(AB)^2 = (BC)^2 + (AC)^2$

$(BC)^2 = 180^2 + 165^2$
$(BC)^2 = 32400 + 27225$
$(BC)^2 = 5175$

Take the square root of both sides to get:

$\sqrt{(BC)^2} = \sqrt{5175} \approx 71.935$ miles

Since the east bound car has traveled 71.935 miles in 3 hours, then the average speed is:

$\frac{71.935}{3} \approx 23.97$ mph

SKILL 25.3 Identify and measure component parts of geometric figures (e.g., angles, lines, segments)

A point, a line, and a plane are actually undefined terms because we cannot give a satisfactory definition using simple terms. However, their properties and characteristics give a clear understanding of what they are.

A **POINT** indicates place or position. It has no length, width or thickness.

● point A

A

> **POINT:** indicates place or position

A **LINE** is considered a set of points. Lines may be straight or curved, but the term line commonly denotes a straight line. Lines extend indefinitely.

line *AB*

A   *B*

> **LINE:** is considered a set of points

A **PLANE** is a set of points composing a flat surface. A plane also has no boundaries.

plane *A*

A

> **PLANE:** a set of points composing a flat surface

A **LINE SEGMENT** has two endpoints.

segment *AB*

A   *B*

> **LINE SEGMENT:** has two endpoints

RAY: has exactly one endpoint and extends indefinitely in one direction

A RAY has exactly one endpoint and extends indefinitely in one direction.

ray *AB*

ANGLE: is formed by the intersection of two rays

An ANGLE is formed by the intersection of two rays.

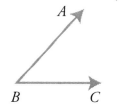

angle *ABC*

Angles are measured in degrees. $1° = \frac{1}{360}$ of a circle.

A right angle measures 90°.

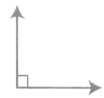

An acute angle measures more than 0° and less than 90°.

An obtuse angle measures more than 90° and less than 180°.

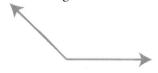

A straight angle measures 180°.

A REFLEXIVE ANGLE measures more than 180° and less than 360°.

REFLEXIVE ANGLE: measures more than 180° and less than 360°

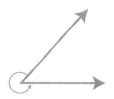

An infinite number of lines can be drawn through any point.

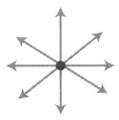

Exactly one line can be drawn through two points.

INTERSECTING LINES share a common point and INTERSECTING PLANES share a common set of points or line.

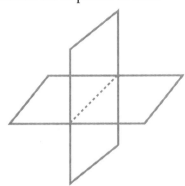

> **INTERSECTING LINES:** share a common point

> **INTERSECTING PLANES:** share a common set of points or line

SKEW LINES do not intersect and do not lie on the same plane.

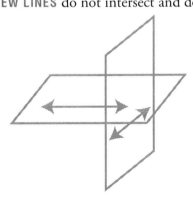

> **SKEW LINES:** do not intersect and do not lie on the same plane

PERPENDICULAR LINES or planes form a 90° angle to each other. Perpendicular lines have slopes that are negative reciprocals.

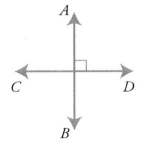

Line *AB* is perpendicular to line *CD*.

$AB \perp CD$

> **PERPENDICULAR LINES:** form a 90° angle to each other

PARALLEL LINES: or parallel planes do not intersect

PARALLEL LINES or planes do not intersect. Two parallel lines will have the same slope and are equidistant everywhere.

Line *AB* is parallel to line *CD*.

$AB \parallel CD$

SKILL 25.4 **Apply knowledge of symmetry and transformations** *(i.e., translation, glide, rotation, reflection)* **of geometric figures**

There are four basic transformational symmetries that can be used: *translation, rotation, reflection,* and *glide reflection*. The transformation of an object is called its image. If the original object was labeled with letters, such as *ABCD*, the image can be labeled with the same letters followed by a prime symbol: *A′B′C′D′*.

TRANSLATION: a transformation that "slides" an object a fixed distance in a given direction

A TRANSLATION is a transformation that "slides" an object a fixed distance in a given direction. The original object and its translation have the same shape and size, and they face in the same direction.

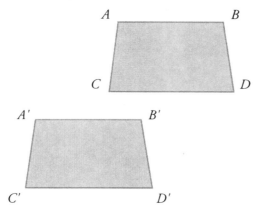

An example of a translation in architecture is stadium seating. The seats are the same size and the same shape and they face in the same direction.

ROTATION: a transformation that turns a figure about a fixed point called the center of rotation

A ROTATION is a transformation that turns a figure about a fixed point called the center of rotation. An object and its rotation are the same shape and size, but the figures may be turned in different directions. Rotations can occur in either a clockwise or a counterclockwise direction.

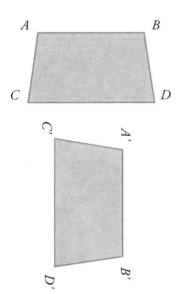

Rotations can be seen in wallpaper and art; sections of a Ferris wheel are an example of rotation.

An object and its REFLECTION have the same shape and size, but the figures face in opposite directions.

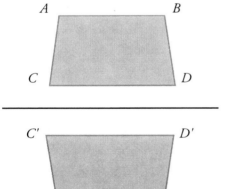

> **REFLECTION:** when figures have the same shape and size but face in opposite directions

The line (where a mirror may be placed) is called the LINE OF REFLECTION. The distance from a point to the line of reflection is the same as the distance from the point's image to the line of reflection.

> **LINE OF REFLECTION:** the line where a mirror may be placed; the distance from a point to this line is the same as the distance from the point's image to this line

GLIDE REFLECTION: a combination of a reflection and a translation

A GLIDE REFLECTION is a combination of a reflection and a translation.

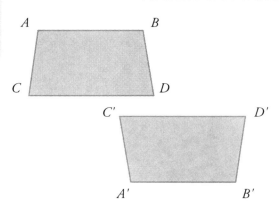

TANGENT: when objects make contact at a single point or along a line without crossing

Objects that are TANGENT make contact at a single point or along a line without crossing. Understanding tangency is critical in the construction industry, where architects and engineers must figure out how various elements fit together. An example is building a stair railing. The engineer must determine the points of tangency between the banisters, which might even be curved, and the posts supporting the banisters.

SYMMETRY: equal on both sides

Many types of flooring found in homes are examples of SYMMETRY: Persian carpets, tiling, patterned broadloom, etc. The human body is an example of symmetry, even though that symmetry is not perfect. If you split the torso down the middle, on each half you will find one ear, one eye, one nostril, one shoulder, one arm, one leg, and so on, in approximately the same places.

SKILL 25.5 **Make use of geometric models and properties of figures to solve problems**

We refer to three-dimensional figures in geometry as solids. A solid is the union of all points on a simple closed surface and all points in its interior. A polyhedron is a simple closed surface formed from planar polygonal regions. Each polygonal region is called a face of the polyhedron. The vertices and edges of the polygonal regions are called the vertices and edges of the polyhedron.

We can form a cube from three congruent squares. However, if we tried to put four squares around a single vertex, their interior angle measures would add up to 360° (i.e., four edge-to-edge squares with a common vertex lie in a common plane and therefore cannot form a corner figure of a regular polyhedron).

There are five ways to form corner figures with congruent regular polygons:

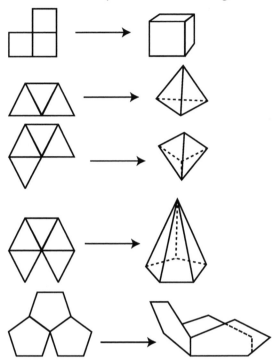

We can represent any two-dimensional geometric figure in the Cartesian or rectangular coordinate system. The Cartesian or rectangular coordinate system is formed by two perpendicular axes (coordinate axes): the X-axis and the Y-axis. If we know the dimensions of a two-dimensional, or planar, figure, we can use this coordinate system to visualize the shape of the figure.

COMPETENCY 26

UNDERSTAND CONCEPTS AND APPLICATIONS OF PROBABILITY

SKILL 26.1 Recognize real-world applications of probabilities and their consequences

> **SAMPLE SPACE:** a list of all possible outcomes of an experiment

In probability, a **SAMPLE SPACE** is a list of all possible outcomes of an experiment. For example, the sample space of tossing two coins is the set {HH, HT, TT, TH};

the sample space of rolling a six-sided die is the set {1, 2, 3, 4, 5, 6}; and the sample space of measuring the height of students in a class is the set of all real numbers {R}. PROBABILITY measures the chance of an event occurring. The probability of an event that *must* occur, a certain event, is **1**. When no outcome is favorable, the probability of an impossible event is **0**.

> **PROBABILITY:** the chance of an event occurring

$$P(\text{event}) = \frac{\text{number of favorable outcomes}}{\text{number of possible outcomes}}$$

Example: Given one die with faces numbered 1–6, the probability of tossing an even number on one throw of the die is $\frac{3}{6}$ or $\frac{1}{2}$, because there are three favorable outcomes (even faces) and six possible outcomes (faces).

Example: If we roll a fair die:

   A.   Find the probability of rolling an even number.
   B.   Find the probability of rolling a number less than 3.

   A.   The sample space is
       S ={1, 2, 3, 4, 5, 6}, and the event representing even numbers is
       E ={2, 4, 6}.
       Hence, the probability of rolling an even number is

$$p(\text{E}) = \frac{n(\text{E})}{n(\text{S})} = \frac{3}{6} = \frac{1}{2} \text{ or } 0.5$$

   B.   We represent the event of rolling a number less than 3 by
       A = {1, 2}
       Hence, the probability of rolling a number less than 3 is

$$p(\text{A}) = \frac{n(\text{A})}{n(\text{S})} = \frac{2}{6} = \frac{1}{3} \text{ or } 0.33$$

Example: A class has thirty students. Out of the thirty students, twenty-four are males. Assuming all the students have the same chance of being selected, find the probability of selecting a female. (Only one person is selected.)

The number of females in the class is

       30 − 24 = 6

       Hence, the probability of selecting a female is

$$p(\text{female}) = \frac{6}{30} = \frac{1}{5} \text{ or } 0.2$$

SKILL 26.2   **Recognize expressions of probabilities as fractions, ratios, and decimals**

See Skill 22.4

SKILL 26.3 Determine theoretical probabilities and make predications based on them

The absolute probability of some events cannot be determined. For instance, one cannot assume the probability of winning a tennis match is $\frac{1}{2}$ because, in general, winning and losing are not equally likely. In such cases, past results of similar events can be used to help predict future outcomes. The relative frequency of an event is the number of times an event has occurred divided by the number of attempts.

$$\text{Relative frequency} = \frac{\text{number of successful trials}}{\text{total number of trials}}$$

For example, if a weighted coin flipped 50 times lands on heads 40 times and tails 10 times, the relative frequency of heads is $\frac{40}{50} = \frac{4}{5}$. Thus, one can predict that if the coin is flipped 100 times, it will land on heads 80 times.

Example: Two tennis players, John and David, have played each other 20 times. John has won 15 of the previous matches and David has won 5.

    A. Estimate the probability that David will win the next match.

    B. Estimate the probability that John will win the next 3 matches.

    A. David has won 5 out of 20 matches. Thus, the relative frequency of David winning is $\frac{5}{20}$ or $\frac{1}{4}$. We can estimate that the probability of David winning the next match is $\frac{1}{4}$.

    B. John has won 15 out of 20 matches. The relative frequency of John winning is $\frac{15}{20}$ or $\frac{3}{4}$. We can estimate that the probability of John winning a future match is $\frac{3}{4}$. Thus, the probability that John will win the next three matches is $\frac{3}{4} \times \frac{3}{4} \times \frac{3}{4} = \frac{27}{64}$.

SKILL 26.4 Determine probabilities of dependent and independent events

If A and B are INDEPENDENT EVENTS, then the outcome of event A does not affect the outcome of event B, and vice versa. We use the multiplication rule to find joint probability.

$$p(\text{A and B}) = p(\text{A}) \times p(\text{B})$$

> **INDEPENDENT EVENTS:** when the outcome of event A does not affect the outcome of event B, and vice versa

Example: The probability that a patient is allergic to aspirin is .30. If the probability of a patient having a window in his room is .40, find the probability that the patient is allergic to aspirin and has a window in his room.

Defining the events:

A = the patient is allergic to aspirin

B = the patient has a window in his or her room

Events A and B are independent; hence

$p(A \text{ and } B) = p(A) \times p(B)$

$= (.30)(.40)$

$= .12 \text{ or } 12\%$

Example: Given a jar containing 10 marbles—3 red, 5 black, and 2 white— what is the probability of drawing a red marble and then a white marble if the marble is returned to the jar after choosing?

$\frac{3}{10} \times \frac{2}{10} = \frac{6}{100} = \frac{3}{50}$ or .06 or 6%

Dependent Events

> **DEPENDENT EVENTS:** when the outcome of event A affects the outcome of event B

When the outcome of the first event affects the outcome of the second event, the events are DEPENDENT EVENTS. Any two events that are not independent are dependent. This is also known as conditional probability.

Probability of (A and B) = $p(A) \times p(B \text{ given } A)$

Example: Two cards are drawn from a deck of 52 cards without replacement; that is, the first card is not returned to the deck before the second card is drawn. What is the probability of drawing a diamond?

A = drawing a diamond first

B = drawing a diamond second

$p(A) =$ drawing a diamond first

$p(B) =$ drawing a diamond second

$p(A) = \frac{13}{52} = \frac{1}{4}$ $p(B) = \frac{12}{52} = \frac{4}{17}$

$p(A \text{ and } B) = \frac{1}{4} \times \frac{4}{17} = \frac{1}{34}$

Example: A class of ten students consists of six males and four females. If two students are selected to represent the class, find the probability that:

A. The first is a male and the second is a female

B. The first is a female and the second is a male

C. Both are females

D. Both are males

Define the events:

F = a female is selected to represent the class

M = a male is selected to represent the class

$\frac{F}{M}$ = a female is selected after a male has been selected

$\frac{M}{F}$ = a male is selected after a female has been selected

A. Since F and M are dependent events, it follows that

$$p(M \text{ and } F) = p(M) \times p(\tfrac{F}{M})$$
$$= \tfrac{6}{10} \times \tfrac{4}{9} = \tfrac{3}{5} \times \tfrac{4}{9} = \tfrac{12}{45}$$

$p(\tfrac{F}{M}) = \tfrac{4}{9}$ instead of $\tfrac{4}{10}$ because the selection of a male first changed the sample space from ten to nine students.

B. $p(F \text{ and } M) = p(F) \times p(\tfrac{M}{F})$
$$= \tfrac{4}{10} \times \tfrac{6}{9} = \tfrac{2}{5} \times \tfrac{2}{3} = \tfrac{4}{15}$$

C. $p(F \text{ and } F) = p(F) \times p(\tfrac{F}{F})$
$$= \tfrac{4}{10} \times \tfrac{3}{9} = \tfrac{2}{5} \times \tfrac{1}{3} = \tfrac{2}{15}$$

D. $p(\text{both are males}) = p(M \text{ and } M)$
$$= \tfrac{6}{10} \times \tfrac{5}{9} = \tfrac{30}{90} = \tfrac{1}{3}$$

Using Tables

Example: The results of a survey of 47 students are summarized in the table below.

	BLACK HAIR	BLONDE HAIR	RED HAIR	TOTAL
Male	10	8	6	24
Female	6	12	5	23
Total	16	20	11	47

Use the table to answer questions A through C.

A. If one student is selected at random, find the probability of selecting a male student.

$$\frac{\text{Number of male students}}{\text{Number of students}} = \frac{24}{47}$$

B. If one student is selected at random, find the probability of selecting a female with red hair.

$$\frac{\text{Number of females with red hair}}{\text{Number of students}} = \frac{5}{47}$$

c. If one student is selected at random, find the probability of selecting a student who does not have red hair.

$$\frac{\text{Number of students with red hair}}{\text{Number of students}} = \frac{11}{47}$$

$$1 - \frac{11}{47} = \frac{36}{47}$$

SKILL 26.5 **Make use of tools** *(e.g., spinners, dice)* **to estimate probabilities**

Manipulatives and other tools are useful in introducing all mathematical concepts, but they are particularly critical for introducing the idea of probability because this requires a completely different way of thinking.

Manipulatives and other tools are useful in introducing all mathematical concepts, but they are particularly critical for introducing the idea of probability because this requires a completely different way of thinking. Most mathematical activities and calculations that children undertake in school produce exact results. Probability, on the other hand, involves *uncertainty*. No matter how much one may know about a particular sample space, *there is no way to predict the exact outcome of any one event.* One also cannot predict the exact proportion of different outcomes in a series of events. For instance, even though the probability of getting heads when a coin is flipped is half, there is no guarantee that if one flips ten coins that five of them will be heads. This idea is difficult to explain theoretically and is best demonstrated using tools such as coins, dice, and spinners. Children can observe for themselves that the same experiment (e.g., flipping ten coins) repeated several times produces slightly different results each time.

They can also try increasing the number of trials (say, 10, 20, 50, or 100 coin flips) and note how the experimental probability gets closer to the theoretical probability as the number of trials increases.

The use of tools is also extremely beneficial in exploring compound and conditional probabilities in different situations.

The use of tools is also extremely beneficial in exploring compound and conditional probabilities in different situations. Even young children can theoretically estimate, with a little practice, the probability of grabbing, unseen, a blue marble given the number of blue and red marbles in a bag. Compound probability, however, is much more difficult to visualize mentally. What is the probability of a match if two people spin two identical multicolored spinners, or what is the probability of getting a particular sum of numbers when two or more dice are rolled? Students can explore the answers to questions like this through experiment. This will make it much easier for them to understand the mathematical ideas of compound and conditional probability when they are introduced later.

Tools can provide a good introduction to the terminology of probability as well. Students learn through firsthand experience the meaning of terms such as dependent and independent events, mutually exclusive events, permutations, combinations, and so on. In addition to the tools mentioned above others can be used, including playing cards, raisin boxes (with varying numbers of raisins inside), dart boards, and software simulations.

COMPETENCY 27
UNDERSTAND CONCEPTS AND APPLICATIONS OF STATISTICS

SKILL 27.1 **Apply knowledge of methods for organizing data in a variety of formats** (e.g., frequency distributions, charts, tables, stem and leaf plots, bar graphs, histograms, line graphs, circle graphs)

To make a bar graph or a pictograph, we determine the scale for the graph. Then we determine the length of each bar on the graph or determine the number of pictures needed to represent each item of information. We need to be sure to include an explanation of the scale in the legend.

Example: A class had the following grades: 4 As, 9 Bs, 8 Cs, 1 D, 3 Fs. Graph these on a pictograph and a bar graph.

Grade	Number of Students
A	☺☺☺☺
B	☺☺☺☺☺☺☺☺☺
C	☺☺☺☺☺☺☺☺
D	☺
F	☺☺☺

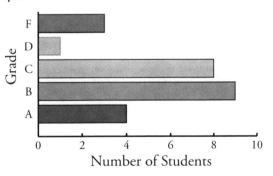

To make a line graph, we determine appropriate scales for both the vertical and horizontal axes (based on the information we are graphing). Describe what each axis represents and mark the scale periodically on each axis. Graph the individual points of the graph and connect the points on the graph from left to right.

Pictographs can be misleading, especially if drawn to represent 3-dimensional objects. If two or more dimensions are changed in reflecting ratio, the overall visual effect can be misinterpreted. Bar and line graphs can be misleading if the scales are changed. For example, using relatively small scale increments for large numbers will make the comparison differences seem much greater than if larger-scale increments are used. Circle graphs, or pie charts, are excellent for comparing relative amounts; however, they cannot be used to represent absolute amounts and, if interpreted as such, they are misleading.

Example: Graph the following information using a line graph.

THE NUMBER OF NATIONAL MERIT FINALISTS PER SCHOOL YEAR						
YEAR	**90–91**	**91–92**	**92–93**	**93–94**	**94–95**	**95–96**
Central	3	5	1	4	6	8
Wilson	4	2	3	2	3	2

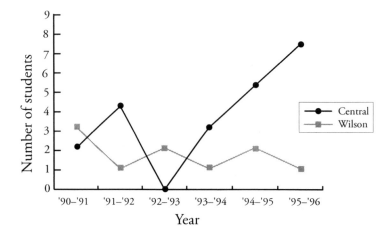

To make a circle graph, we total all the information that is to be included on the graph. We then determine the central angle to be used for each sector of the graph using the following formula:

$$\frac{\text{information}}{\text{total information}} \times 360° = \text{degrees in central} \sphericalangle$$

We lay out the central angles to these sizes, label each section, and include its percent.

Example: Graph the following information on a circle graph.

MONTHLY EXPENSES					
Rent	**Food**	**Utilities**	**Clothes**	**Church**	**Misc.**
$400	$150	$75	$75	$100	$200

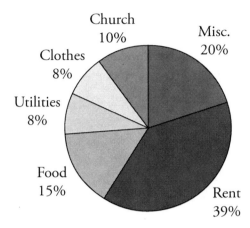

Scatter plots compare two characteristics of the same group of things or people and usually consist of a large body of data. They show how much one variable affects another. The relationship between the two variables is their **COR-RELATION**. The closer the data points come to forming a straight line when plotted, the closer the correlation.

> **CORRELATION:** the relationship between the two variables

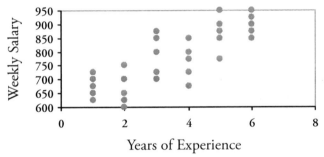

Stem-and-leaf plots are visually similar to line plots. The **stems** are the digits in the greatest place value of the data values, and the **leaves** are the digits in the next greatest place value. Stem-and-leaf plots are best suited for small sets of data and are especially useful for comparing two sets of data. The following is an example using test scores:

4	9
5	4 9
6	1 2 3 4 6 7 8 8
7	0 3 4 6 6 6 7 7 7 7 8 8 8 8
8	3 5 5 7 8
9	0 0 3 4 5
10	0 0

<table>
<tr><td>

FREQUENCY: the number of times any particular data value occurs

FREQUENCY OF THE INTERVAL: the number of data values in any interval

</td><td>

We use histograms to summarize information from large sets of data that we can naturally group into intervals. The vertical axis indicates FREQUENCY (the number of times any particular data value occurs), and the horizontal axis indicates data values or ranges of data values. The number of data values in any interval is the FREQUENCY OF THE INTERVAL.

</td></tr>
</table>

SKILL 27.2   Interpret statistical data expressed in various formats

PERCENTILES: divide a set of data into 100 equal parts

PERCENTILES divide data into 100 equal parts. A person whose score falls in the 65th percentile has outperformed 65 percent of all those who took the test. This does not mean that the score was 65 out of 100, nor does it mean that 65 percent of the questions were answered correctly. It means that the person's grade was higher than 65 percent of all the other grades.

STANINES: divide the bell curve into nine sections

STANINES, or "standard nines," scores combine the understandability of percentages with the properties of the normal probability curve. Stanines divide the bell curve into nine sections, the largest of which stretches from the 40th to the 60th percentile and is the "Fifth Stanine" (the average, taking into account error possibilities).

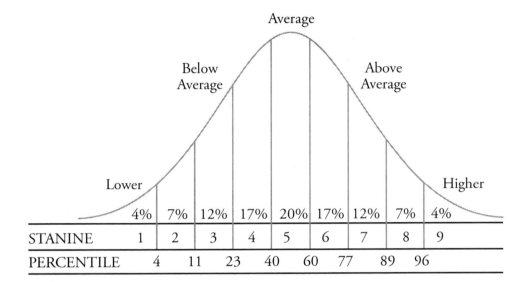

	4%	7%	12%	17%	20%	17%	12%	7%	4%
STANINE	1	2	3	4	5	6	7	8	9
PERCENTILE	4	11	23	40	60	77	89	96	

QUARTILES divide the data into four parts. First, find the median of the data set (Q2), then find the median of the upper (Q3) and lower (Q1) halves of the data set. If there is an odd number of values in the data set, include the median value in both halves when finding quartile values. For example, given the data set {1, 4, 9, 16, 25, 36, 49, 64, 81}, first find the median value, which is 25. This is the second quartile (Q2). Since there is an odd number of values in the data set (9), we include the median in both halves.

> **QUARTILES:** divide the data into four parts

To find the quartile values, we must find the medians of {1, 4, 9, 16, 25} and {25, 36, 49, 64, 81}. Since each of these subsets has an odd number of elements (5), we use the middle value. Thus, the first quartile value is 9 and the third quartile value is 49. If the data set has an even number of elements, average the middle two values. The quartile values are always either one of the data points or exactly halfway between two data points.

Example: Given the following set of data, find the percentile of the score 104.
70, 72, 82, 83, 84, 87, 100, 104, 108, 109, 110, 115
 Find the percentage of scores below 104.
 $\frac{7}{12}$ of the scores are less than 104. This is 58.333%; therefore, the score of 104 is in the 58th percentile.

Example: Find the first, second and third quartile for the data listed.
6, 7, 8, 9, 10, 12, 13, 14, 15, 16, 18, 23, 24, 25, 27, 29, 30, 33, 34, 37
 Quartile 1: The first quartile is the median of the lower half of the data set, which is 11.
 Quartile 2: The median of the data set is the second quartile, which is 17.
 Quartile 3: The third quartile is the median of the upper half of the data set, which is 28.

SKILL Identify assumptions, trends, and patterns in data
27.3

> **TREND LINE:** line on a line graph that shows the correlation between two sets of data

A **TREND LINE** on a line graph shows the correlation between two sets of data. A trend may show positive correlation (both sets of data get bigger together), negative correlation (one set of data gets bigger while the other gets smaller), or no correlation.

> **INFERENCE:** a statement that is derived from reasoning

An **INFERENCE** is a statement that is derived from reasoning. When reading a graph, inferences help us interpret the data that is presented. From this information, a conclusion and even predictions about what the data actually mean are possible.

Example: Katherine and Tom were both doing poorly in math class. Their teacher had a conference with each of them in November. The following graph shows their math test scores during the school year.

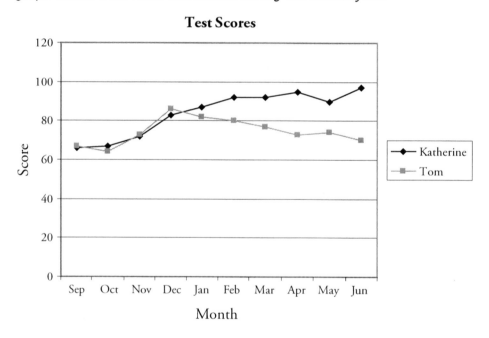

What kind of trend does this graph show?

> This graph shows that there is a positive trend in Katherine's test scores and a negative trend in Tom's test scores.

What inferences can you make from this graph?

> We can infer that Katherine's test scores rose steadily after November. Tom's test scores spiked in December but then began to fall again and became negatively trended.

What conclusion can you draw based upon this graph?

We can conclude that Katherine took her teacher's meeting seriously and began to study in order to do better on the exams. It seems as though Tom tried harder for a while, but his test scores eventually slipped back down to the level at which he began.

CORRELATION is a measure of association between two variables. It varies from -1 to 1, with 0 being a random relationship, 1 being a perfect positive linear relationship, and -1 being a perfect negative linear relationship.

The CORRELATION COEFFICIENT (r) is used to describe the strength of the association between the variables, as well as the direction of the association.

Example:

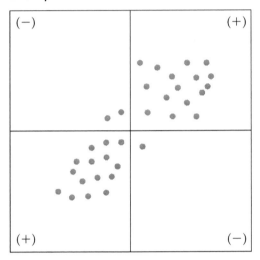

Horizontal and vertical lines are drawn through the POINT OF AVERAGES, which is the point on the respective averages of the x and y values. Doing this divides the scatter plot into four quadrants. If a point is in the lower left quadrant, the product of two negatives is positive; in the upper right quadrant, the product of two positives is positive. The positive quadrants are depicted with the positive sign (+). In the two remaining quadrants (upper left and lower right), the product of a negative and a positive is negative. The negative quadrants are depicted with the negative sign (−). If r is positive, then there are more points in the two positive quadrants; if is negative, then there are more points in the two negative quadrants.

REGRESSION is a form of statistical analysis used to predict a dependent variable (y) from values of an independent variable (x). A regression equation is derived from a known set of data.

The simplest regression analysis models the relationship between two variables using the equation $y = a + bx$, where y is the dependent variable and x is the

CORRELATION: a measure of association between two variables

CORRELATION COEFFICIENT: used to describe the strength of the association between the variables, as well as the direction of the association

POINT OF AVERAGES: the point on the respective averages of the *x* and *y* values

REGRESSION: a form of statistical analysis used to predict a dependent variable *(y)* from values of an independent variable *(x)*

independent variable. This simple equation denotes a linear relationship between x and y. This form would be appropriate if, when you plotted a graph of x and y, you saw the points roughly form along a straight line.

Example:

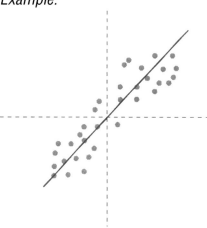

The line can then be used to make predictions.

If all of the data points fell on the line, there would be a perfect correlation ($r = 1.0$) between the x and y data points. These cases represent the best scenarios for prediction. A positive or negative value represents how y varies with x. When r is positive, y increases as x increases. When r is negative, y decreases as x increases.

A linear regression equation is of the form $y = a + bx$.

Example: A teacher wanted to determine how a practice test influenced a student's performance on the actual test. The practice test grade and the subsequent actual test grade for each student are given in the table below:

Practice Test (X)	94	95	92	87	82	80	75	65	50	20
Actual Test (Y)	98	94	95	89	85	78	73	67	45	40

We determine the equation for the linear regression line to be $y = 14.650 + 0.834x$.

A new student comes into the class and scores 78 on the practice test. Based on the equation obtained above, what score would the teacher predict this student would get on the actual test?

$y = 14.650 + 0.834(78)$
$y = 14.650 + 65.052$
$y = 80$
$\quad = 79.7$

It is predicted that the student will get an 80.

SKILL 27.4 Recognize limitations of data and models and their use in drawing conclusions

Both averages and graphs can be misleading if the data are not presented appropriately. The three types of averages used in statistics are mean, median, and mode. If a data set contains one very high or very low value, the mean will not be representative; for example, the teacher's height should not be included in the mean height of a class of elementary school students. If the data are clustered around two numbers with a large gap between them, the median will not be representative; for example, expressing the median height in a family of two parents and two small children would have little meaning. Modes are best used with categorical data. A mode of the sale of men's shoe sizes would be helpful to a store for reordering stock of men's shoes. However, finding the mode of men's and women's shoe sizes combined would not be a good indicator of the stock that needed to be reordered.

Pictographs can also be misleading, especially if they are drawn to represent three-dimensional objects. If two or more dimensions are changed in reflecting a ratio, the overall visual effect can be misinterpreted. Bar and line graphs can be misleading if the scales are changed; for example, using relatively small scale increments for large numbers will make the comparison differences seem much greater than if larger scale increments are used. Circle graphs, or pie charts, are excellent for comparing relative amounts. However, they cannot be used to represent absolute amounts, and if interpreted as such, they are misleading.

SKILL 27.5 Describe data using standard measures *(e.g., mean, median, mode, range, variability)*

The arithmetic MEAN (or average) of a set of numbers is the sum of the numbers divided by the number of items in the set.

Example: Find the mean. Round to the nearest tenth.
24.6, 57.3, 44.1, 39.8, 64.5
The sum is 230.3 ÷ 5 = 46.06, rounded to 46.1.

The MEDIAN of a set of numbers is the middle number when the numbers are arranged in order. To calculate the median, we must arrange the terms in order. If there is an even number of terms, the median is the mean of the two middle terms.

> **MEAN:** the sum of a set of numbers divided by the number of items in the set; also called the average

> **MEDIAN:** the middle number when a set of numbers is arranged in order

Example: Find the median.

12, 14, 27, 3, 13, 7, 17, 12, 22, 6, 16

    Rearrange the terms from least to greatest.

    3, 6, 7, 12, 12, 13, 14, 16, 17, 22, 27

    Since there are eleven numbers, the middle would be the sixth number, or 13.

> **MODE:** the number that occurs with the greatest frequency in a set of numbers

The **MODE** of a set of numbers is the number that occurs with the greatest frequency. A set can have no mode if each term appears exactly one time. Similarly, there can also be more than one mode.

Example: Find the mode.

26, 15, 37, **26**, 35, **26**, 15

    15 appears twice, but 26 appears three times. Therefore, the mode is 26.

> **RANGE:** the difference between the highest and lowest data value in a set of numbers

The **RANGE** of a set of numbers is the difference between the highest and lowest data value in the set.

Sum of the squares: this is the sum of the squares of the differences between each item and the mean.

$$Sx^2 = (X - \overline{X})^2$$

Variance: the sum of the squares quantity divided by the number of items in the set. The lowercase Greek letter sigma squared (σ^2) represents variance.

$$\frac{Sx^2}{N} = \sigma^2$$

> *The Greek letter sigma squared (σ^2) represents variance.*

The larger the value of the variance, the larger the spread.

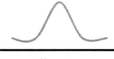

    small variation   larger variation

Standard deviation: the square root of the variance. The lowercase Greek letter sigma (σ) is used to represent standard deviation.

$$\sigma = \sqrt{\sigma^2}$$

> *The Greek letter sigma (σ) is used to represent standard deviation.*

Most statistical calculators have standard deviation keys and should be used to calculate statistical functions. It is important to become familiar with the calculator and the locations of the necessary keys.

Example: Given the ungrouped data below, calculate the mean, range, standard deviation, and variance.

15	22	28	25	34	38
18	25	30	33	19	23

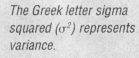

Mean $(\overline{X})$ = 25.8333333
Range: $38 - 15 = 23$
Standard deviation (σ) = 6.6936952
Variance (σ^2) = 44.805556

Different situations require different information. For example, examine the circumstances under which each of the following three scenarios use the numbers provided.

1. Over a 7-day period, the store owner collected data on the ice cream flavors sold. He found the mean number of scoops sold was 174 per day. The most frequently sold flavor was vanilla. This information was useful in determining how much ice cream to order overall, as well as the amounts of each flavor.

   In the case of the ice cream store, the median and range had little business value for the owner.

2. Consider the set of test scores from a math class: 0, 16, 19, 65, 65, 65, 68, 69, 70, 72, 73, 73, 75, 78, 80, 85, 88, and 92. The mean is 64.06 and the median is 71. Because there are only three scores less than the mean in the set, the median (71) is a more descriptive score.

3. Retail storeowners might be most concerned with the most common dress size so that they can order more of that size than of any other.

COMPETENCY 28
UNDERSTAND THE NATURE AND HISTORIES OF MATHEMATICS

SKILL 28.1 Recognize the histories and importance of mathematical ideas and the contribution of various cultures and individuals to mathematical knowledge

Mathematics goes back before recorded history. Prehistoric cave paintings with geometrical figures and slash counting have been dated prior to 20,000 BCE in Africa and France. The major early uses of mathematics were for astronomy, architecture, trading and taxation.

The early history of mathematics is found in Mesopotamia (Sumeria and Assyria), Egypt, Greece and Rome. Noted mathematicians from these times include Euclid, Pythagoras, Apollonius, Ptolemy, and Archimedes.

Islamic culture from the sixth through twelfth centuries CE drew from cultures ranging from Africa and Spain to India and China. This mix of cultures and ideas brought about developments in many areas, including the concept of algebra, our current numbering system, and major developments in algebra with concepts such as zero. India was the source of many of these developments. Notable scholars of this era include Omar Khayyam and Muhammad al-Khwarizmi.

Counting boards have been found in archeological digs in Babylonia and Greece. These include the Chinese abacus, the current form of which dates from approximately 1200 CE. Prior to the development of the zero, a counting board or abacus was the common method used for all types of calculations.

Abelard and Fibonacci brought Islamic texts to Europe in the 12th century CE. By the 17th century, major new works appeared from Galileo and Copernicus (astronomy), Newton and Leibnez (calculus), and Napier and Briggs (logarithms). Other significant mathematicians of this era include René Descartes, Carl Gauss, Pierre de Fermat, Leonhard Euler and Blaise Pascal.

The growth of mathematics since 1800 has been enormous and has affected nearly every area of life. Some names significant in the history of mathematics since 1800 and the work they are most known for are:

- Joseph-Louis Lagrange (theory of functions and of mechanics)
- Pierre-Simon LaPlace (celestial mechanics, probability theory)
- Joseph Fourier (number theory)
- Lobachevsky and Bolyai (non-Euclidean geometry)
- Charles Babbage (calculating machines, origin of the computer)
- Lady Ada Lovelace (first known program)
- Florence Nightingale (nursing, statistics of populations)
- Bernard Russel (logic)
- James Maxwell (differential calculus and analysis)
- John von Neumann (economics, quantum mechanics and game theory)
- Alan Turing (theoretical foundations of computer science)
- Albert Einstein (theory of relativity)
- Gustav Roch (topology)

A **SIMPLE STATEMENT** represents an idea that can be described as either true or false, but not both. A small letter of the alphabet represents a simple statement.

Example: "Today is Monday."
This is a simple statement because we can determine that this statement is either true or false. We can write p = "Today is Monday."

Example: "John, please be quiet."
We do not consider this a simple statement in our study of logic because we cannot assign a truth value to it.

Simple statements joined by connectives (*and, or, not, if…then,* and *if and only if*) result in **COMPOUND STATEMENTS**. Note that we can also form compound statements using *but, however,* or *nevertheless*. We can assign a truth value to a compound statement.

We frequently write conditional statements in *if-then* form. The *if* clause of the conditional statement is known as the **HYPOTHESIS**, and the *then* clause is called the **CONCLUSION**. In a proof, the hypothesis is the information that is assumed to be true, while the conclusion is what is to be proven true. We consider a conditional statement to be of the form "**if p, then q,**" where p is the hypothesis and q is the conclusion.

$p \rightarrow q$ is read "If p, then q."
$\sim$ (statement) is read "It is not true that (statement)."

QUANTIFIERS are words that describe a quantity under discussion. These include words such as *all, none* (or *no*), and *some*.

NEGATION of a statement: If a statement is true, then its negation must be false (and vice versa).

| A SUMMARY OF NEGATION RULES ||
STATEMENT	NEGATION
q	<u>not</u> *q*
<u>not</u> *q*	*q*

Continued on next page

SIMPLE STATEMENT: represents an idea that can be described as either true or false, but not both

COMPOUND STATE-MENTS: two simple statements joined by a connective *(and, or, not, if…then, if and only if, etc.)*

HYPOTHESIS: the *if* clause of an if-then statement

CONCLUSION: the *then* clause of an if-then statement

QUANTIFIERS: words that describe a quantity under discussion

NEGATION: in the case of a statement that is true, its negation must be false (and vice versa)

STATEMENT	NEGATION
π and s	(not π) or (not s)
π or s	(not π) and (not s)
if p, then q	(p) and (not q)

Example: Select the statement that is the negation of "Some winter nights are not cold."

    A. All winter nights are not cold.

    B. Some winter nights are cold.

    C. All winter nights are cold.

    D. None of the winter nights is cold.

The negation of *some are* is *none is*. Therefore, the negation statement is "None of the winter nights is cold." The answer is D.

Example. Select the statement that is the negation of "If it rains, then the beach party will not be held."

    A. If it does not rain, then the beach party will be held.

    B. If the beach party is held, then it will not rain.

    C. It does not rain, and the beach party will be held.

    D. It rains, and the beach party will be held.

The negation of "If p, then q" is "p and (not q)." The negation of the given statement is "It rains, and the beach party will be held." Select D.

Example: Select the negation of the statement "If they are elected, then all politicians go back on election promises."

    A. If they are elected, then many politicians go back on election promises.

    B. They are elected, and some politicians go back on election promises.

    C. If they are not elected, some politicians do not go back on election promises.

    D. None of the above statements is the negation of the given statement.

Identify the key words of "if...then" and "all...go back." The negation of the given statement is "They are elected, and none of the politicians goes back on election promises." So select response D, since statements A, B, and C are not the correct negations.

Example: Select the statement that is the negation of "The sun is shining brightly and I feel great."

    A. If the sun is not shining brightly, I do not feel great.

    B. The sun is not shining brightly, and I do not feel great.

    C. The sun is not shining brightly or I do not feel great.

    D. The sun is shining brightly, and I do not feel great.

The negation of "r and s" is "(not r) or (not s)." Therefore, the negation of the given statement is "The sun is not shining brightly or I do not feel great." We select response C.

We can diagram conditional statements using a **VENN DIAGRAM**. We can draw a diagram with one circle inside another circle. The inner circle represents the hypothesis. The outer circle represents the conclusion. If we take the hypothesis to be true, then we are located inside the inner circle. If we are located in the inner circle, then we are also inside the outer circle, so we have proved the conclusion true.

> **VENN DIAGRAM:** a diagram that illustrates conditional statements

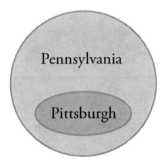

Example: If an angle has a measure of 90 degrees, then it is a right angle.
In this statement, "an angle has a measure of 90 degrees," is the hypothesis. In this statement, "it is a right angle" is the conclusion.

Example: If you are in Pittsburgh, then you are in Pennsylvania.
In this statement, "you are in Pittsburgh" is the hypothesis.
In this statement, "you are in Pennsylvania" is the conclusion.

DEDUCTIVE REASONING is the process of arriving at a conclusion based on other statements that are known to be true.

A symbolic argument consists of a set of premises and a conclusion in the format of if [premise 1 and premise 2], then [conclusion].

> **DEDUCTIVE REASONING:** the process of arriving at a conclusion based on other statements that are known to be true

VALID: an argument is valid when the conclusion follows necessarily from the premises

INVALID: an argument is invalid when the conclusion does not follow from the premises

An argument is VALID when the conclusion follows necessarily from the premises. An argument is INVALID or a fallacy when the conclusion does not follow from the premises.

FOUR STANDARD FORMS OF VALID ARGUMENTS		
Law of Detachment	If p, then q p Therefore, q	(premise 1) (premise 2)
Law of Contraposition	If p, then q not q Therefore, not p	
Law of Syllogism	If p, then q If q, then r Therefore, if p, then r	
Disjunctive Syllogism	p or q not p Therefore, q	

Example: Can we reach a conclusion from these two statements?

A. All swimmers are athletes.
    All athletes are scholars.

In "if-then" form, these would be:
If you are a swimmer, then you are an athlete.
If you are an athlete, then you are a scholar.

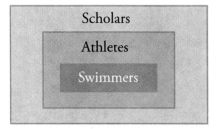

Clearly, if you are a swimmer, then you are also an athlete. This includes you in the group of scholars.

B. All swimmers are athletes.
All wrestlers are athletes.

In "if-then" form, these would be:
If you are a swimmer, then you are an athlete.
If you are a wrestler, then you are an athlete.

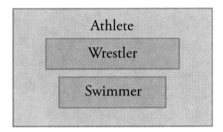

Clearly, if you are a swimmer or a wrestler, then you are also an athlete.
This does not allow you to come to any other conclusions.
A swimmer may or may not also be a wrestler. Therefore, no conclusion is possible.

Example: Determine whether statement A, B, C, or D can be deduced from the following:

(i) If John drives the big truck, then the shipment will be delivered.
(ii) The shipment will not be delivered.

A. John does not drive the big truck.

B. John drives the big truck.

C. The shipment will not be delivered.

D. None of the above conclusions is valid.
Let p: John drives the big truck.
q: The shipment is delivered.
Statement (i) gives p → q. Statement (ii) gives ∼ q (not q). This is the Law of Contraposition.
Therefore, the logical conclusion is ∼p (not p) or "John does not drive the big truck." The answer is response A.

Example: Determine which conclusion can be logically deduced by the following information:

(i) Peter is a jet pilot or Peter is a navigator.

(ii) Peter is not a jet pilot.

A. Peter is not a navigator.

B. Peter is a navigator.

C. Peter is neither a jet pilot nor a navigator.

D. None of the above is true.

Let p: Peter is a jet pilot.

q: Peter is a navigator.

So we have $p \lor q$ (p or q) from statement (i)

$\sim p$ (not p) from statement (ii)

The answer is response B.

Example: What conclusion, if any, can be reached? Assume each statement is true, regardless of any personal beliefs.

1. If the Red Sox win the World Series, I will die.
   I died.

2. If an angle's measure is between 0° and 90°, then the angle is acute.
   Angle B is not acute.

3. Students who do well in geometry will succeed in college.
   Annie is doing extremely well in geometry.

4. Left-handed people are witty and charming.
   You are left-handed.

Question #1	The Red Sox won the World Series.
Question #2	Angle B is not between 0 and 90 degrees.
Question #3	Annie will do well in college.
Question #4	You are witty and charming.

SKILL 28.3 Identify the roles and importance of mathematics in everyday life and in various occupations

Artists, musicians, scientists, social scientists, and people in business use mathematical modeling to solve problems in their disciplines. These disciplines rely on the tools and symbols of mathematics to model natural events and manipulate data.

Mathematics is a key aspect of visual art. Artists use the geometric properties of shapes, ratios, and proportions to create paintings and sculptures. For example, mathematics is essential to the concept of perspective. Artists must determine the appropriate lengths and heights of objects to realistically portray three-dimensional distance in two dimensions.

Mathematics is also an important part of music. Many musical terms have mathematical connections. For example, the musical octave contains twelve notes and spans a factor of two in frequency. In other words, the frequency (the speed of vibration that determines tone and sound quality) doubles from the first note in an octave to the last. Thus, starting from any note, we can determine the frequency of any other note with the following formula:

$$\text{Freq} = note \times 2^{N/12}$$

In this equation, N is the number of notes from the starting point, and *note* is the frequency of the starting note. Mathematical understanding of frequency plays an important role in tuning musical instruments.

In addition to the visual and auditory arts, mathematics is an integral part of most scientific disciplines. Physical scientists use vectors, functions, derivatives, and integrals to describe and model the movement of objects. Biologists and ecologists use mathematics to model ecosystems and study DNA. Chemists use mathematics to study the interaction of molecules and to determine the proper amounts and proportions of reactants in chemical reactions. Indeed, the uses of mathematics in science are almost endless.

Many social science disciplines use mathematics to model and solve problems as well. Economists, for example, use functions, graphs, and matrices to model the activities of producers, consumers, and firms. Political scientists use mathematics to model the behavior and opinions of the electorate. Finally, sociologists use mathematical functions to model the behavior of humans and human populations.

Finally, mathematical problem solving and modeling is essential to business planning and execution. For example, businesses rely on mathematical projections to plan business strategy. Additionally, stock market analysis and accounting rely on mathematical concepts.

DOMAIN VI
SCIENCE

Available for purchase at www.XAMonline.com:

eFlashcards: a digital representation of a card represented with words, numbers or symbols or any combination of each and briefly displayed as part of a learning drill. eFlashcards takes away the burden of carrying around traditional cards that could easily be disarranged, dropped, or soiled. Available at www.XAMonline.com/flashcards

More Sample Tests: more ways to assess how much you know and how much further you need to study. Ultimately, makes you more prepared and attain mastery in the skills and techniques of passing the test the FIRST TIME! Available at www.XAMonline.com/sampletests

PERSONALIZED STUDY PLAN

KNOWN MATERIAL/ SKIP IT

PAGE	COMPETENCY AND SKILL	
325	**29: Understand concepts and principles of physical science**	☐
	29.1: Recognize the structure and properties of matter	☐
	29.2: Identify chemical and physical changes	☐
	29.3: Identify fundamental forces and the motions resulting from them	☐
	29.4: Recognize concepts of conservation and transfer of energy, and analyze the interaction of energy and matter	☐
	29.5: Recognize basic principles of electricity and magnetism	☐
	29.6: Identify the characteristics of light and sound	☐
336	**30: Understand concepts and principles of life science**	☐
	30.1: Recognize the characteristics, structure, and functions of organisms	☐
	30.2: Analyze the life cycles of common organisms	☐
	30.3: Analyze the transmission of traits in living things	☐
	30.4: Recognize the interdependence of organisms in their natural environment	☐
	30.5: Analyze the effects of species, including humans, on an ecosystem	☐
	30.6: Recognize the diversity of organisms and the adaptations that help organisms survive	☐
347	**31: Understand concepts and principles of earth and space science**	☐
	31.1: Recognize the structure of Earth's lithosphere, hydrosphere, and atmosphere	☐
	31.2: Identify the properties of Earth's materials, and the availability and use of those materials	☐
	31.3: Analyze changes occurring within Earth's lithosphere, hydrosphere, and atmosphere	☐
	31.4: Analyze the relationships among the Earth, Sun, Moon, and solar system	☐
	31.5: Recognize changes that have occurred in Earth's history	☐

PERSONALIZED STUDY PLAN

COMPETENCY 29
UNDERSTAND CONCEPTS AND PRINCIPLES OF PHYSICAL SCIENCE

SKILL **Recognize the structure and properties of matter** *(e.g., boiling and*
29.1 *melting points, solubility, density)*

Matter, Mass, and Weight

Everything in our world is made up of MATTER, whether it is a rock, a building,
an animal, or a person. Matter is defined by its characteristics: it takes up space
and it has mass.

MASS is a measure of the amount of matter in an object. Two objects of equal
mass will balance each other on a simple balance scale no matter where the scale is
located. For instance, two rocks with the same amount of mass that are in balance
on Earth will also be in balance on the Moon. They will feel heavier on Earth than
on the Moon because of the gravitational pull of the Earth. So, although the two
rocks have the same mass, they will have different weights.

WEIGHT is the measure of the Earth's pull of gravity on an object. It can also be
defined as the pull of gravity between other bodies. The units of weight measurement commonly used are the pound (English measure) and the kilogram (metric
measure).

In addition to mass, matter also has the property of volume. VOLUME is the
amount of cubic space that an object occupies. Volume and mass together give
a more exact description of the object. Two objects may have the same volume,
but different mass, or the same mass but different volumes. For instance, consider
two cubes that are each one cubic centimeter, one made from plastic, one from
lead. They have the same volume, but the lead cube has more mass. The measure
that we use to describe the cubes takes into consideration both the mass and the
volume. DENSITY is the mass of a substance contained per unit of volume. If the
density of an object is less than the density of a liquid, the object will float in the
liquid. If the object is denser than the liquid, then the object will sink.

Density is stated in grams per cubic centimeter (g/cm^3) where the gram is the
standard unit of mass. To find an object's density, you must measure its mass and
its volume, and then divide the mass by the volume ($D = m/V$).

MATTER: anything that takes up space and has mass

MASS: a measure of the amount of matter in an object

WEIGHT: the measure of the Earth's pull of gravity on an object

VOLUME: amount of cubic space that an object occupies

DENSITY: the mass of a substance contained per unit of volume

To discover an object's density, first use a balance to find its mass. Then calculate its volume. If the object is a regular shape, you can find the volume by multiplying the length, width, and height together. However, if it is an irregular shape, you can find the volume by seeing how much water it displaces. Measure the water in a container before and after the object is submerged. The difference will be the volume of the object.

SPECIFIC GRAVITY is the ratio of the density of a substance to the density of water. For instance, the specific density of one liter of turpentine is calculated by comparing its mass (0.81 kg) to the mass of one liter of water (1 kg):

$$\frac{\text{mass of 1 L alcohol}}{\text{mass of 1 L water}} = \frac{0.81 \text{ kg}}{1.00 \text{ kg}} = 0.81$$

SOLUBILITY is defined as the amount of substance (referred to as solute) that will dissolve into another substance, called the solvent. The amount that will dissolve can vary according to various conditions, most notably temperature. The process is called solvation.

The freezing point of water is set at 0°C and the boiling point is 100°C. The interval between the two is divided into 100 equal parts called degrees Celsius.

MELTING POINT refers to the temperature at which a solid becomes a liquid. BOILING POINT refers to the temperature at which a liquid becomes a gas. Melting takes place when there is sufficient energy available to break the intermolecular forces that hold molecules together as a solid. Boiling occurs when there is enough energy available to break the intermolecular forces holding molecules together as a liquid.

HARDNESS describes how difficult it is to scratch or indent a substance. The hardest natural substance is diamond.

SPECIFIC GRAVITY: the ratio of the density of a substance to the density of water

SOLUBILITY: the amount of substance (referred to as solute) that will dissolve into another substance, called the solvent

MELTING POINT: the temperature at which a solid becomes a liquid

BOILING POINT: the temperature at which a liquid becomes a gas

HARDNESS: how difficult it is to scratch or indent a substance; the hardest natural substance is diamond

SKILL 29.2 Identify chemical and physical changes

Matter constantly changes. A physical change does not create a new substance. Atoms are not rearranged into different compounds. The material has the same chemical composition as it had before the change. Changes of state, as described in the previous section, are physical changes. Frozen water or gaseous water is still H_2O. Taking a piece of paper and tearing it up is a physical change. You simply have smaller pieces of paper.

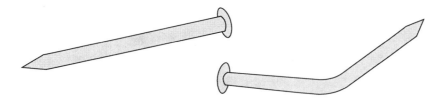

Compare these two nails. They are still iron nails, made of iron atoms. The difference is that one is bent while the other is straight. This is a physical change.

A chemical change is a chemical reaction. It converts one substance into another because atoms are rearranged to form a different compound. Paper undergoes a chemical change when you burn it. You no longer have paper. A chemical change to a pure substance alters its properties.

An iron nail rusts to form a rusty nail. The rusty nail, however, is not made up of the same iron atoms. It is now composed of iron (III) oxide molecules that form when the iron atoms combine with oxygen molecules during oxidation (rusting).

SKILL 29.3 Identify fundamental forces and the motions resulting from them

DYNAMICS is the study of the relationship between motion and the forces affecting motion. Force causes motion. Surfaces that touch each other have certain resistance to motion. This resistance is friction.

Mass and weight are not the same quantities. An object's mass gives it a reluctance to change its current state of motion. It is also the measure of an object's resistance to acceleration. The force that the earth's gravity exerts on an object with a specific mass is called the object's weight on earth. Weight is a force that is measured in Newtons. Weight (W) = mass times acceleration due to gravity ($W = mg$). To illustrate the difference between mass and weight, picture two rocks of equal mass on a balance scale. If the scale is balanced in one place, it will be balanced everywhere, regardless of the gravitational field. However, the weight of the stones would vary on a spring scale, depending upon the gravitational field. In other words, the stones would be balanced both on earth and on the moon. However, the weight of the stones would be greater on earth than on the moon.

DYNAMICS: the study of the relationship between motion and the forces affecting motion

Newton's Laws of Motion

Newton's first law of motion is also called the law of inertia. It states that an object at rest will remain at rest, and an object in motion will remain in motion at a constant velocity unless acted upon by an external force.

Newton's second law of motion states that if a net force acts on an object, it will cause the acceleration of the object. The relationship between force and motion is force equals mass times acceleration (F = ma).

Newton's third law of motion states that for every action there is an equal and opposite reaction. Therefore, if an object exerts a force on another object, that second object exerts an equal and opposite force on the first.

Other fundamental forces of motion

- Push and pull: Pushing a lawn mover or pulling a bowstring applies muscular force when the muscles expand and contract. Elastic force is when any object returns to its original shape (for example, when a bow is released).

- Rubbing: Friction opposes the motion of one surface past another. Friction is common when slowing down a car or sledding down a hill.

- Pull of gravity: The pull of gravity is a force of attraction between two objects. Gravity questions can be raised not only on earth but also between planets and even black holes.

- Forces on objects at rest: The formula F = m/a is shorthand for force equals mass over acceleration. An object will not move unless the force is strong enough to move the mass. Also, there can be opposing forces holding the object in place. For instance, a boat may want to be forced by the currents to drift away but an equal and opposite force is a rope holding it to a dock.

- Forces on a moving object: Inertia is the tendency of any object to oppose a change in motion. An object at rest tends to stay at rest. An object that is moving tends to keep moving.

- Inertia and circular motion: Centripetal force is provided by the high banking of the curved road, for example, and by friction between the wheels and the road. This inward force that keeps an object moving in a circle is called centripetal force.

SKILL 29.4 Recognize concepts of conservation and transfer of energy, and analyze the interaction of energy and matter

The law of conservation of energy states that energy is neither created nor destroyed. Thus, energy changes take place when energy transactions occur in nature. The following are the major forms energy can take.

- **Thermal energy:** The total internal energy of objects created by the vibration and movement of atoms and molecules. Heat is the transfer of thermal energy.

- **Acoustical energy,** or **sound energy:** The movement of energy through an object in waves. Energy that forces an object to vibrate creates sound.

- **Radiant energy:** The energy of electromagnetic waves. Light, visible and otherwise, is an example of radiant energy.

- **Electrical energy:** The movement of electrical charges in an electromagnetic field. Examples of electrical energy are electricity and lightning.

- **Chemical energy:** The energy stored in the chemical bonds of molecules. For example, the energy derived from gasoline is chemical energy.

- **Mechanical energy:** The potential and kinetic energy of a mechanical system. Rolling balls, car engines, and body parts in motion exemplify mechanical energy.

- **Nuclear energy:** The energy present in the nucleus of atoms. Division, combination, or collision of nuclei release nuclear energy.

Because the total energy in the universe is constant, energy continually transitions between forms. For example, an engine burns gasoline, converting the chemical energy of the gasoline into mechanical energy; a plant converts the radiant energy of the sun into the chemical energy found in glucose; or a battery converts chemical energy into electrical energy.

Interacting objects in the universe constantly exchange and transform energy. Total energy remains the same, but the form of the energy readily changes. Energy often changes from kinetic (motion) to potential (stored) or potential to kinetic. In reality, available energy, energy that is easily utilized, is rarely conserved in energy transformations. Heat energy is an example of relatively "useless" energy often generated during energy transformations. Exothermic reactions release heat and endothermic reactions require heat energy to proceed. For example, the human body is notoriously inefficient in converting chemical energy from food into mechanical energy. The digestion of food is exothermic and produces substantial heat energy.

The three laws of thermodynamics are as follows:

1. The total amount of energy in the universe is constant; energy cannot be created or destroyed, but can merely change form.

   Equation: $\Delta E = Q + W$

   Change in energy = (Heat energy entering or leaving) + (work done)

2. In energy transformations, entropy (disorder) increases and useful energy is lost (as heat).

   Equation: $\Delta S = \Delta Q/T$

   Change in entropy = (Heat transfer) / (Temperature)

3. As the temperature of a system approaches absolute zero, entropy (disorder) approaches a constant.

Sample Problems:

1. A car engine burns gasoline to power the car. An amount of gasoline containing 2000J of stored chemical energy produces 1500J of mechanical energy to power the engine. How much heat energy does the engine release?

   Solution:
$\Delta E = Q + W$	The first law of thermodynamics.
$2000J = Q + 1500J$	Apply the first law.
Q (work) = 500J	

2. 18200J of heat leaks out of a hot oven. The temperature of the room is 25°C (298K). What is the increase in entropy resulting from this heat transfer?

   Solution:
$\Delta S = \Delta Q/T$	The second law of thermodynamics.
$\Delta S = 18200J / 298K$	Apply the second law.
= 61.1 J/K	Solve.

SKILL 29.5 Recognize basic principles of electricity and magnetism

ELECTROSTATICS: the study of stationary electric charges

ELECTROSTATICS is the study of stationary electric charges. A plastic rod that is rubbed with fur or a glass rod that is rubbed with silk will become electrically charged and will attract small pieces of paper. The charge on the plastic rod rubbed with fur is negative and the charge on glass rod rubbed with silk is positive.

Electrically charged objects share these characteristics:

1. Like charges repel one another.

2. Opposite charges attract each other.

3. Charge is conserved. A neutral object has no net change. If the plastic rod and fur are initially neutral, when the rod becomes charged by the fur a negative charge is transferred from the fur to the rod. The net negative charge on the rod is equal to the net positive charge on the fur.

4. Materials through which electric charges can easily flow are called conductors. Metals that are good conductors include silicon and boron. On the other hand, an insulator is a material through which electric charges do not move easily, if at all. Examples of insulators are non-metal elements of the periodic table. A simple device used to indicate the existence of a positive or negative charge is called an electroscope. An electroscope is made up of a conducting knob and attached to it are very lightweight conducting leaves usually made of foil (gold or aluminum). When a charged object touches the knob, the leaves push away from each other because like charges repel. It is not possible to tell whether the charge is positive or negative.

An ELECTRIC CIRCUIT is a path along which electrons flow. A simple circuit can be created with a dry cell, wire, a bell, or a light bulb. When all are connected, the electrons flow from the negative terminal, through the wire to the device, and back to the positive terminal of the dry cell. If there are no breaks in the circuit, the device will work. The circuit is closed. Any break in the flow will create an open circuit and cause the device to shut off.

A SERIES CIRCUIT is one where the electrons have only one path along which they can move. When one load in a series circuit goes out, the circuit is open. An example of this is a string of Christmas tree lights that is missing a bulb. None of the bulbs will work.

A PARALLEL CIRCUIT is one where the electrons have more than one path along which to move. If a load goes out in a parallel circuit, the other load will still work because the electrons can still find a way to continue moving along the path.

When an electron goes through a load, it does work and therefore loses some of its energy. The measure of how much energy is lost is called the POTENTIAL DIFFERENCE. The potential difference between two points is the work needed to move a charge from one point to another.

> **ELECTRIC CIRCUIT:** a path along which electrons flow

> **SERIES CIRCUIT:** one where the electrons have only one path along which they can move

> **PARALLEL CIRCUIT:** one where the electrons have more than one path along which to move

> **POTENTIAL DIFFERENCE:** measure of how much energy is lost

VOLTAGE: the measure of potential difference

Potential difference is measured in a unit called the volt. VOLTAGE is potential difference. The higher the voltage, the more energy the electrons have. This energy is measured by a device called a voltmeter. To use a voltmeter, place it in a circuit parallel with the load you are measuring.

CURRENT: the number of electrons per second that flow past a point in a circuit

CURRENT is the number of electrons per second that flow past a point in a circuit. Current is measured with a device called an ammeter. To use an ammeter, put it in series with the load you are measuring.

RESISTANCE: the ability of a material to oppose the flow of electrons through it

As electrons flow through a wire, they lose potential energy. Some is changed into heat energy because of resistance. RESISTANCE is the ability of a material to oppose the flow of electrons through it. All substances have some resistance, even good conductors such as copper. This resistance is measured in units called OHMS. A thin wire will have more resistance than a thick one because it will have less room for electrons to travel. In a thicker wire, there are more possible paths for the electrons to flow. Resistance also depends upon the length of the wire. The longer the wire, the more resistance it will have.

OHMS: unit of measure of resistance

Potential difference, resistance, and current form a relationship know as *Ohm's Law*. Current (I) is measured in amperes and is equal to potential difference (V) divided by resistance (R).

$$I = V/R$$

If you have a wire with resistance of 5 ohms and a potential difference of 75 volts, you can calculate the current by

$$I = 75 \text{ volts}/5 \text{ ohms}$$
$$I = 15 \text{ amperes}$$

A current of 10 or more amperes will cause a wire to get hot. 22 amperes is about the maximum for a house circuit. Anything above 25 amperes can start a fire.

MAGNETIC FIELD: the space around a magnet where its force will affect objects

Magnets have a north pole and a south pole. Like poles repel and opposing poles attract. A MAGNETIC FIELD is the space around a magnet where its force will affect objects. The closer you are to a magnet, the stronger the force. As you move away, the force becomes weaker.

Some materials act as magnets and some do not. This is because magnetism is a result of electrons in motion. The most important motion in this case is the spinning of the individual electrons. Electrons spin in pairs in opposite directions in most atoms. Each spinning electron has the magnetic field that it creates canceled out by the electron that is spinning in the opposite direction.

MAGNETIC DOMAIN: small areas in the iron where atomic magnetic fields line up in the same direction

In an atom of iron, there are four unpaired electrons. The magnetic fields of these are not canceled out. Their fields add up to make a tiny magnet. There fields exert forces on each other setting up small areas in the iron called MAGNETIC DOMAINS where atomic magnetic fields line up in the same direction.

A magnet can be made out of a coil of wire by connecting the ends of the coil to a battery. When the current goes through the wire, the wire acts in the same way that a magnet does, and it is called an electromagnet. The poles of the electromagnet will depend upon which way the electric current runs. An electromagnet can be made more powerful in three ways:

1. Make more coils

2. Put an iron core (nail) inside the coils

3. Use more battery power

Telegraphs use electromagnets to work. When a telegraph key is pushed, current flows through a circuit, turning on an electromagnet that attracts an iron bar. The iron bar hits a sounding board, which responds with a click. Release the key and the electromagnet turns off. Messages can be sent around the world in this way.

Scrap metal can be removed from waste materials by the use of a large electromagnet that is suspended from a crane. When the electromagnet is turned on, the metal in the pile of waste will be attracted to it. All other materials will stay on the ground.

Air conditioners, vacuum cleaners, and washing machines use electric motors. An electric motor uses an electromagnet to change electric energy into mechanical energy.

SKILL 29.6 Identify the characteristics of light and sound

Shadows illustrate one of the basic properties of light. Light travels in a straight line. If you put your hand between a light source and a wall, you will interrupt the light and produce a shadow.

When light hits a surface, it is reflected. The angle of the incoming light (angle of incidence) is the same as the angle of the reflected light (angle of reflection). It is this reflected light that allows you to see objects. You see the objects when the reflected light reaches your eyes.

Different surfaces reflect light differently. Rough surfaces scatter light in many different directions. A smooth surface reflects the light in one direction. If it is smooth and shiny (like a mirror) you see your image in the surface.

REFRACTION: the bending of light when it enters a different medium

DIFFRACTED: light that bends around the edges of an object

When light enters a different medium, it bends. This bending, or change of speed, is called REFRACTION.

Light can be DIFFRACTED, or bent, around the edges of an object. Diffraction occurs when light goes through a narrow slit. As light passes through it, the light bends slightly around the edges of the slit. You can demonstrate this by pressing your thumb and forefinger together, making a very thin slit between them. Hold them about 8 cm from your eye and look at a distant source of light. The pattern you observe is caused by the diffraction of light.

The electromagnetic spectrum is measured in frequency (f) in hertz and wavelength (λ) in meters. The frequency times the wavelength of every electromagnetic wave equals the speed of light (3.0×10^9 meters/second).

Roughly, the range of wavelengths of the electromagnetic spectrum is:

	f	λ
Radio Waves	$10^5 - 10^{-1}$ hertz	$10^3 - 10^9$ meters
Microwaves	$10^{-1} - 10^{-3}$ hertz	$10^9 - 10^{11}$ meters
Infrared Radiation	$10^{-3} - 10^{-6}$ hertz	$10^{11.2} - 10^{14.3}$ meters
Visible Light	$10^{-6.2} - 10^{-6.9}$ hertz	$10^{14.3} - 10^{15}$ meters
Ultraviolet Radiation	$10^{-7} - 10^{-9}$ hertz	$10^{15} - 10^{17.2}$ meters
X-Rays	$10^{-9} - 10^{-11}$ hertz	$10^{17.2} - 10^{19}$ meters
Gamma Rays	$10^{-11} - 10^{-15}$ hertz	$10^{19} - 10^{23.25}$ meters

Radio waves are used for transmitting data. Common examples are television, cell phones, and wireless computer networks. Microwaves are used to heat food and deliver Wi-Fi service. Infrared waves are utilized in night vision goggles.

We are all familiar with visible light because the human eye is most sensitive to this wavelength range. UV light causes sunburns and would be even more harmful if most of it were not captured in the Earth's ozone layer. X-rays aid us in the medical field and gamma rays are useful in the field of astronomy.

Sound waves are produced by a vibrating body. The vibrating object moves forward and compresses the air in front of it, then reverses direction so that the pressure on the air is lessened and expansion of the air molecules occurs. One compression and expansion creates one longitudinal wave. Sound can be transmitted through any gas, liquid, or solid. However, it cannot be transmitted through a vacuum, because there are no particles present to vibrate and bump into their adjacent particles to transmit the wave.

The vibrating air molecules move back and forth parallel to the direction of the motion of the wave as they pass the energy from adjacent air molecules (closer to the source) to air molecules farther away from the source.

The pitch of a sound depends on the frequency that the ear receives. High-pitched sound waves have high frequencies. High notes are produced by an object that is vibrating at a greater number of times per second than one that produces a low note.

The intensity of a sound is the amount of energy that crosses a unit of area in a given unit of time. The loudness of the sound is subjective and depends upon the effect on the human ear. Two tones of the same intensity but different pitches may appear to have different loudness. The intensity level of sound is measured in decibels. Normal conversation is about 60 decibels. A power saw is about 110 decibels.

The amplitude of a sound wave determines its loudness. Loud sound waves have large amplitudes. The larger the sound wave, the more energy is needed to create the wave.

An oscilloscope is useful in studying waves because it gives a picture of the wave that shows the crest and trough of the wave. INTERFERENCE is the interaction of two or more waves that meet. If the waves interfere constructively, the crest of each one meets the crests of the others. They combine into a crest with greater amplitude. As a result, you hear a louder sound. If the waves interfere destructively, then the crest of one meets the trough of another. They produce a wave with lower amplitude that produces a softer sound.

INTERFERENCE: the interaction of two or more waves that meet

If you have two tuning forks that produce different pitches, then one will produce sounds of a slightly higher frequency. When you strike the two forks simultaneously, you may hear beats. BEATS are a series of loud and soft sounds. This is because when the waves meet, the crests combine at some points and produce loud sounds. At other points, they nearly cancel each other out and produce soft sounds.

BEATS: a series of loud and soft sounds

When a piano tuner tunes a piano, he only uses one tuning fork, even though there are many strings on the piano. He adjusts to first string to be the same as that of the tuning fork. Then he listens to the beats that occur when both the tuned and untuned strings are struck. He adjusts the untuned string until he can hear the correct number of beats per second. This process of striking the untuned and tuned strings together and timing the beats is repeated until all the piano strings are tuned.

NOISE: sounds that do not happen with regularity

DOPPLER EFFECT: change in experienced frequency due to relative motion of the source of the sound

Pleasant sounds have a regular wave pattern that is repeated over and over. Sounds that do not happen with regularity are unpleasant and are called NOISE.

Change in experienced frequency due to relative motion of the source of the sound is called the DOPPLER EFFECT. When a siren approaches, the pitch is high. When it passes, the pitch drops. As a moving sound source approaches a listener, the sound waves are closer together, causing an increase in frequency in the sound that is heard. As the source passes the listener, the waves spread out and the sound experienced by the listener is lower.

COMPETENCY 30
UNDERSTAND CONCEPTS AND PRINCIPLES OF LIFE SCIENCE

SKILL 30.1 Recognize the characteristics, structure, and functions of organisms

The Five Kingdoms of Living Organisms
Living organisms are divided into five major kingdoms:

- Monera
- Protista
- Fungi
- Plantae
- Animalia

Kingdom Monera
This kingdom includes bacteria and blue-green algae; these are prokaryotic, unicellular organisms with no true nucleus.

Bacteria are classified according to their morphology (shape). Bacilli are rod shaped, cocci are round, and spirillia are spiral shaped. The gram stain is a staining procedure used to identify bacteria. Gram-positive bacteria pick up the stain and turn purple. Gram-negative bacteria do not pick up the stain and are pink in color.

Methods of locomotion

Flagellates have a flagellum; ciliates have cilia; and ameboids move through use of pseudopodia.

Methods of reproduction

These organisms reproduce by binary fission, which is simply dividing in half and is asexual. All new organisms are exact clones of the parent. Sexual modes of reproduction provide more diversity. Bacteria can reproduce sexually through conjugation, where genetic material is exchanged.

Methods of obtaining nutrition

Photosynthetic organisms, or producers, convert sunlight to chemical energy, while consumers, or heterotrophs, eat other living things. Saprophytes are consumers that live off dead or decaying material.

Kingdom Protista

This kingdom includes eukaryotic, unicellular organisms; some are photosynthetic, and some are consumers. Microbiologists use methods of locomotion, reproduction, and how the organism obtains its food to classify protista.

Kingdom Fungi

Organisms in this kingdom are eukaryotic, multicellular, absorptive consumers, and contain a chitin cell wall.

Kingdom Plantae

This kingdom contains nonvascular plants and vascular plants.

Nonvascular plants

Small in size, these plants do not require vascular tissue (xylem and phloem) because individual cells are close to their environment. The nonvascular plants have no true leaves, stems, or roots.

- Division Bryophyta: Mosses and liverworts; these plants have a dominant gametophyte generation. They possess rhizoids, which are root-like structures. Moisture in their environment is required for reproduction and absorption.

Vascular plants

The development of vascular tissue enables these plants to grow in size. Xylem and phloem allow for the transport of water and minerals up to the top of the plant, as well as for the transport of food manufactured in the leaves to the bottom of the plant. All vascular plants have a dominant sporophyte generation.

- **Division Lycophyta:** Club mosses; these plants reproduce with spores and require water for reproduction.
- **Division Sphenophyta:** Horsetails; these plants also reproduce with spores. These plants have small, needle-like leaves and rhizoids. They require moisture for reproduction.
- **Division Pterophyta:** Ferns; they reproduce with spores and flagellated sperm. These plants have a true stem and need moisture for reproduction.
- **Gymnosperms:** The word means "naked seed." These were the first plants to evolve with seeds, which made them less dependent on water for reproduction. Their seeds can travel by wind; pollen from the male is also easily carried by the wind. Gymnosperms have cones that protect the seeds.
- **Division Cycadophyta:** Cycads; these plants look like palms with cones.
- **Divison Ghetophyta:** Desert dwellers.
- **Division Coniferophyta:** Pines; these plants have needles and cones.
- **Divison Ginkgophyta:** The ginkgo is the only member of this division.

Angiosperms (division Anthophyta)

The largest group in the plant kingdom. Plants in this kingdom are the flowering plants that produce true seeds for reproduction.

Kingdom Animalia

Annelida

This phylum includes the segmented worms. The Annelida have specialized tissue. The circulatory system is more advanced in these worms; it is a closed system with blood vessels. The nephridia are their excretory organs. They are hermaphroditic, and each worm fertilizes the other upon mating. They support themselves with a hydrostatic skeleton and have circular and longitudinal muscles for movement.

Mollusca

This phylum includes clams, octopi, and soft-bodied animals. These animals have a muscular foot for movement. They breathe through gills, and most are able to make a shell for protection from predators. They have an open circulatory system, with sinuses bathing the body regions.

Arthropoda

This phylum includes insects, crustaceans, and spiders; this is the largest group of the animal kingdom. Phylum Arthropoda accounts for about 85 percent of all the animal species. Animals in this phylum possess an exoskeleton made of chitin. They must molt to grow. Insects, for example, go through four stages of development. They begin as an egg, hatch into a larva, form a pupa, then emerge as an adult. Arthropods breathe through gills, trachea, or book lungs. Movement varies, with members being able to swim, fly, and crawl. There is a division of labor among the appendages (legs, antennae, etc.). This is an extremely successful phylum, with members occupying diverse habitats.

Echinodermata

This phylum includes sea urchins and starfish; these animals have spiny skin. Their habitat is marine. They have tube feet for locomotion and feeding.

Chordata

This phylum includes all animals with a notocord or a backbone. The classes in this phylum include Agnatha (jawless fish), Chondrichthyes (cartilage fish), Osteichthyes (bony fish), Amphibia (frogs and toads; gills that are replaced by lungs during development), Reptilia (snakes, lizards; the first to lay eggs with a protective covering), Aves (birds; warm-blooded with wings of a particular shape and composition designed for flight), and Mammalia (warm-blooded animals with body hair that bear their young alive and possess mammary glands for milk production).

The three-domain system of classification, introduced by Carl Woese in 1990, emphasizes the separation of the two types of prokaryotes. The following is a comparison of the cellular characteristics of members of the three domains of living organisms: Eukarya, Bacteria, and Archaea.

Domain Eukarya

The Eukarya domain includes all members of the protist, fungi, plant, and animal kingdoms. Eukaryotic cells possess a membrane-bound nucleus and other membranous organelles (e.g., mitochondria, Golgi, ribosomes). The chromosomes of Eukarya are linear and usually complexed with histones (protein spools). The cell membranes of eukaryotes consist of glycerol-ester lipids and sterols. The ribosomes of eukaryotes are 80 Svedburg (S) units in size. Finally, the cell walls of those eukaryotes that have them (i.e., plants, algae, fungi) are polysaccharide in nature.

Domain Bacteria

Prokaryotic members of the Kingdom Monera not classified as Archaea are members of the Bacteria domain. Bacteria lack a defined nucleus and other membranous organelles. The ribosomes of bacteria measure 70 S units in size.

The chromosome of Bacteria is usually a single, circular molecule that is not complexed with histones. The cell membranes of Bacteria lack sterols and consist of glycerol-ester lipids. Finally, most Bacteria possess a cell wall made of peptidoglycan.

Domain Archaea

Members of the Archaea domain are prokaryotic and similar to bacteria in most aspects of cell structure and metabolism. However, transcription and translation in Archaea are similar to the processes of eukaryotes, not bacteria. In addition, the cell membranes of Archaea consist of glycerol-ether lipids, in contrast to the glycerol-ester lipids of eukaryotic and bacterial membranes. Finally, the cell walls of Archaea are not made of peptidoglycan, but consist of other polysaccharides, protein, and glycoprotein.

SKILL 30.2 Analyze the life cycles of common organisms (e.g., butterfly, frog)

Bacteria are commonly used in laboratories for research. Bacteria reproduce by binary fission. This asexual process simply divides the bacterium in half. All new organisms are exact clones of the parent. The obvious advantage of asexual reproduction is that it does not require a partner. This is a huge advantage for organisms that do not move around. Not having to move around to reproduce also allows organisms to conserve energy. Asexual reproduction also tends to be faster. As asexual reproduction produces only exact copies of the parent organism, it does not allow for genetic variation, which means that mutations, or weaker qualities, will always be passed on.

Butterflies go through four different stages of life, but they only look like butterflies in the final stage. Many other animals also change as they grow. In the first stage, the adult butterfly lays an egg. In the second stage, the egg hatches into a caterpillar or larva. Next, the caterpillar forms the chrysalis or pupa. Finally, the chrysalis matures and the adult butterfly emerges.

Frogs also have multiple stages in their life cycle. Initially, and adult frog lays its eggs in the water (all amphibians require water for reproduction). In the second stage, tadpoles hatch from the eggs. The tadpoles swim in the water and use gills for breathing. Tadpoles have a tail that is used for locomotion, but they will grow legs as well. When it is between two and four months old, the tadpole is known as a froglet. You can recognize a froglet because the rim around its tail, which appeared more fish-like, has disappeared, its tail is shorter, and its four legs have grown to the extent that its rear legs are bent underneath it to allow for a spring-like jump. The final stage of a frog's life is spent as an adult. Its tail has been entirely reabsorbed, it has a chubby frog-like appearance instead of the tadpole's fish appearance, and as a mature frog it can lay eggs.

SKILL 30.3 Analyze the transmission of traits in living things

Gregor Mendel is recognized as the father of genetics. His work in the late 1800s is the basis of our knowledge of genetics. Although unaware of the presence of DNA or genes, Mendel realized there were factors (now known as genes) that were transferred from parents to their offspring. Mendel worked with pea plants; he fertilized the plants himself, keeping track of subsequent generations. His findings led to the Mendelian laws of genetics. Mendel found that two "factors" governed each trait, one from each parent. Traits or characteristics came in several forms, known as alleles. For example, the trait of flower color had white alleles and purple alleles.

> *Gregor Mendel is recognized as the father of genetics. His work in the late 1800s is the basis of our knowledge of genetics.*

Mendel established three laws:

- Law of dominance: In a pair of alleles, one trait may cover up the allele of the other trait. Example: Brown eyes are dominant (over blue eyes).

- Law of segregation: Only one of the two possible alleles from each parent is passed on to the offspring. (During meiosis, the haploid number ensures that half the sex cells get one allele and half get the other.)

- Law of independent assortment: Alleles sort independently of each other. (Many combinations are possible, depending on which sperm ends up with which egg. Compare this to the many combinations of hands possible when dealing a deck of cards.)

Punnet squares are used to show the possible ways that genes combine and indicate the probability of the occurrence of a certain genotype or phenotype. One parent's genes are put at the top of the box and the other parent's at the side of the box. Genes combine on the square just like numbers that are added in addition tables. Following is an example of a monohybrid cross, which is a cross using only one trait—in this case, a trait labeled *g*.

Punnet Square

	G	g
G	GG	Gg
g	Gg	gg

In a dihybrid cross, sixteen gene combinations are possible, because each cross has two traits.

Some definitions to know:

- Dominant: The stronger of two traits. If a dominant gene is present, it will be expressed. It is shown by a capital letter.

- Recessive: The weaker of two traits. In order for the recessive gene to be expressed, there must be two recessive genes present. It is shown by a lower case letter.

- Homozygous (purebred): Having two of the same genes present; an organism may be homozygous dominant with two dominant genes or homozygous recessive with two recessive genes.

- Heterozygous (hybrid): Having one dominant gene and one recessive gene. Due to the law of dominance, the dominant gene will be expressed.

- Genotype: The genes the organism has. Genes are represented with letters. AA, Bb, and tt are examples of genotypes.

- Phenotype: How the trait is expressed in an organism. Blue eyes, brown hair, and red flowers are examples of phenotypes.

- Incomplete dominance: Neither gene masks the other; a new phenotype is formed. For example, red flowers and white flowers may have equal strength. A heterozygote (Rr) would have pink flowers. If a problem occurs with a third phenotype, incomplete dominance occurs.

- Codominance: Genes may form new phenotypes. The ABO blood grouping is an example of codominance. A and B are of equal strength and O is recessive. Therefore, Type A blood may have the genotypes of AA or AO, Type B blood may have the genotypes of BB or BO, Type AB blood has the genotype A and B, and Type O blood has two recessive O genes.

- Linkage: Genes that are found on the same chromosome usually appear together unless crossing over has occurred in meiosis (e.g., blue eyes and blonde hair commonly occur together).

- **Lethal alleles:** These are usually recessive due to the early death of the offspring. If a 2:1 ratio of alleles is found in offspring, a lethal gene combination may be the reason. Some examples of lethal alleles include sickle cell anemia, Tay-Sachs disease, and cystic fibrosis. In most cases, the coding for an important protein is affected.

- **Inborn errors of metabolism:** These occur when the protein affected is an enzyme. Examples include PKU (phenylketonuria) and albinism.

- **Polygenic characters:** Many alleles code for a phenotype. There may be as many as twenty genes that code for skin color. This is why there is such a variety of skin tones. Another example is height. A couple of medium height may have very tall offspring.

- **Sex-linked traits:** The Y chromosome found only in males (XY) carries very little genetic information, whereas the X chromosome found in females (XX) carries very important information. Since men have no second X chromosome to cover up a recessive gene, the recessive trait is expressed more often in men. Women need the recessive gene on both X chromosomes to show the trait. Examples of sex-linked traits include hemophilia and color blindness.

- **Sex-influenced traits:** Traits are influenced by the sex hormones. Male pattern baldness is an example of a sex-influenced trait. Testosterone influences the expression of the gene. Many men lose their hair due to this trait.

SKILL 30.4 Recognize the interdependence of organisms in their natural environment

An environment is composed of all of the biotic and abiotic factors in a particular area. These biotic and abiotic factors are interdependent and make for a healthy environment. Changing any one of the biotic or abiotic factors can have disastrous effects.

An environment is composed of all of the biotic and abiotic factors in a particular area.

Ecosystems are vulnerable to effects from changes in the climate, human activity, introduction of nonnative species, and changes in population size. Changes in climate can alter the ability of certain organisms to grow. For example, during drought conditions, plants that are less succulent are unable to maintain water regulation and perish. Organisms that previously fed on that particular plant must find a new food source, or they too will perish. When one organism/colony dies, its space is made available for another. For example, after a brush fire, low-lying shrubs are the first to die off. Taller, well-established trees with tough bark are most likely to survive a forest fire. In addition, once the ground cools, new plats will emerge; some identical to the previous, but some new plants may be introduced because there is now a large, open surface area for new species to take root. It is in situations like these that ecosystems are especially vulnerable to the introduction of nonnative species.

> Invasive species are problematic because they reproduce rapidly, spread over large areas, and have few or no natural controls, such as diseases or predators, to keep them in check.

The introduction of a nonnative species can effectively wipe out an existing, or indigenous, species. For example, Zebra mussels and three different species of rat have all arrived in America as stowaways on ships. Zebra mussels are now established in all the Great Lakes, most of the large, navigable rivers of the eastern United States, and in many other lakes in the Great Lakes region. The presence of mussels in the Great Lakes and Hudson River has reduced the biomass of phytoplankton significantly since their accidental introduction in 1980. These nonnative muscles are consuming the phytoplankton on which native species previously fed, and the non-native species are reproducing faster than the native species. Therefore, not only are native mussels affected, but the local food web is affected by a decrease in its nourishment.

As populations increase in size they naturally consume more resources and excrete more waste. These paradoxical behaviors are a drain on an ecosystem. Sometimes an ecosystem can recover from these changes, but sometimes the damage is too severe. This has never been truer than with the human species. Humans are continuously searching for new places to form communities. This encroachment on the environment leads to the destruction of wildlife communities. Conservationists focus on endangered species, but the primary focus should be on protecting the entire biome. If a biome becomes extinct, the wildlife dies or invades another biome. Preservations established by the government aim at protecting small parts of biomes.

While beneficial in the conservation of a few areas, the majority of the environment is still unprotected.

SKILL 30.5 Analyze the effects of species, including humans, on an ecosystem

The basic stability of ecosystems depends on the interaction and contributions of a wide variety of species. For example, all living organisms require nitrogen to live. Only a select few species of microorganisms can convert atmospheric nitrogen into a form that is usable by most other organisms (nitrogen fixation). Thus, humans and all other organisms depend on the existence of the nitrogen-fixing microbes. In addition, the cycling of carbon, oxygen, and water depends on the contributions of many different types of plants, animals, and microorganisms. Finally, the existence and functioning of a diverse range of species creates healthy, stable ecosystems. Stable ecosystems are more adaptable and less susceptible to extreme events like floods and droughts.

Humans have a tremendous impact on the world's natural resources. The world's natural water supplies are affected by human use. Waterways are major sources of recreation and freight transportation. Oil and wastes from boats and cargo ships pollute the aquatic environment. The aquatic plant and animal life is affected by this contamination.

Plant resources also make up a large part of the world's natural resources. Plant resources are renewable and can be regrown and restocked. Plant resources can be used by humans to make clothing, buildings, and medicines, and can also be directly consumed. Forestry is the study and management of growing forests. Deforestation for urban development has resulted in the extinction or relocation of several species of plants and animals. Animals are forced to leave their forest homes or perish amongst the destruction. The number of plant and animal species that have become extinct due to deforestation is unknown. Scientists have only identified a fraction of the species on Earth. It is known that if the destruction of natural resources continues, there may be no plants or animals successfully reproducing in the wild.

SKILL 30.6 Recognize the diversity of organisms and the adaptations that help organisms survive

Biological diversity is the extraordinary variety of living things and ecological communities interacting with each other throughout the world. Maintaining biological diversity is important for many reasons. First, we derive many products used by humans from living organisms in nature. Second, the stability and habitability of the environment depends on the varied contributions of many different organisms. Finally, the cultural traditions of human populations depend on the diversity of the natural world.

Many pharmacological products important to human health have their origins in nature. For example, scientists first harvested aspirin, a derivative of salicylic acid, from the bark of willow trees. In addition, nature is also the source of many medicines including antibiotics, anti-malarial drugs, and cancer fighting compounds. However, scientists have yet to study the potential medicinal properties of many plant species, including the majority of rainforest plants. Thus, losing such plants to extinction may result in the loss of promising treatments for human diseases.

Aside from its scientific value, biological diversity greatly affects human culture and cultural diversity. Human life and culture is tied to natural resources. For example, the availability of certain types of fish defines the culture of many coastal human populations. The disappearance of fish populations because of environmental disruptions changes the entire way of life of a group of people. The loss of cultural diversity, like the loss of biological diversity, diminishes the very fabric of the world population.

Variations occur naturally within a population. Some of these variations will aid an individual, others will harm, and still others will have no effect on one's survival. Those individuals with positive variations will survive best, and produce offspring that are more adapted to the environment. The colorations of plants and animals serve as camouflage or as warning in their environments. Cryptic coloration is that color or pattern that serves to conceal. For example, moths with light-colored wings are nearly invisible on birch trees (their chosen home), but are obvious to all birds, and therefore eaten, when they land on a dark tree trunk. Only green grasshoppers are seen in areas where there is abundant lush grass, but only tan and brown ones are seen in dry prairie areas. Those that do not match their environment do not survive to reproduce. Most animals (including many birds and insects) are darker on their backs than underneath. This tends to conceal them because most light comes from above and is absorbed by the darkness of their upper bodies.

According to the theory of cryptic coloration by natural selection animals have a hereditary variation in color and pattern. Some variations are more likely to deceive predators than others. Typically, predators will find and kill more of the less well-protected variants. This will leave a population in a given location that is better concealed and better protected.

On the other hand, many insects have unpleasant tastes, bristles, or stings that make them disagreeable as food. These do not help the insects if the predator does not know about them prior to killing and tasting that insect, so many also have colorations that serve to warn the predator.

COMPETENCY 31

UNDERSTAND CONCEPTS AND PRINCIPLES OF EARTH AND SPACE SCIENCE

Lithosphere

PLATES are rigid blocks of the Earth's crust and upper mantle. These rigid solid blocks make up the lithosphere. The Earth's lithosphere is broken into nine large sections and several small ones. These moving slabs are called plates. The major plates are named after the continents they are "transporting." The plates float on and move with a layer of hot, plastic-like rock in the upper mantle. Geologists believe that the heat currents circulating within the mantle cause this plastic zone of rock to slowly flow, carrying along the overlying crustal plates.

Movement of these crustal plates creates areas where the plates diverge as well as areas where the plates converge. A major area of divergence is located in the Mid-Atlantic. Currents of hot mantle rock rise and separate at this point of divergence, creating new oceanic crust at the rate of two to ten centimeters per year. Convergence is when the oceanic crust collides with either another oceanic plate or a continental plate. The oceanic crust sinks, forming an enormous trench and generating volcanic activity. Convergence also includes continent-to-continent plate collisions. When two plates slide past one another, a transform fault is created.

These movements produce many major features of the Earth's surface, such as mountain ranges, volcanoes, and earthquake zones. Most of these features are located at plate boundaries, where the plates interact by spreading apart, pressing together, or sliding past each other. These movements are very slow, averaging only a few centimeters a year.

Hydrosphere

Water that falls to Earth in the form of rain and snow is called PRECIPITATION. Precipitation is part of a continuous process in which water at the Earth's surface evaporates, condenses into clouds, and returns to Earth. This process is termed

PLATES: rigid blocks of the Earth's crust and upper mantle

PRECIPITATION: water that falls to Earth in the form of rain and snow; precipitation is part of a continuous process in which water at the Earth's surface evaporates, condenses into clouds, and returns to Earth

the water cycle. The water located below the surface of the Earth is called groundwater.

The impacts of altitude upon climatic conditions are primarily related to temperature and precipitation. As altitude increases, climatic conditions become increasingly drier and colder. Solar radiation becomes more severe as altitude increases while the effects of convection forces are minimized. Climatic changes as a function of latitude follow a similar pattern (as a reference, latitude moves either north or south from the equator). The climate becomes colder and drier as the distance from the equator increases. Proximity to land or water masses produces climatic conditions based upon the available moisture. Dry and arid climates prevail where moisture is scarce; lush tropical climates prevail where moisture is abundant. Climate, as described above, depends upon the specific combination of conditions making up an area's environment. Man impacts all environments by producing pollutants in earth, air, and water. It follows then, that man is a major player in world climatic conditions.

Atmosphere

Dry air has three basic components: dry gas, water vapor, and solid particles (dust from soil, etc.).

The most abundant dry gases in the atmosphere are:

(N_2) Nitrogen 78.09 %   (AR) Argon 0.93 %
(O_2) Oxygen 20.95 %   (CO_2) Carbon Dioxide 0.03 %

The atmosphere is divided into four main layers based on temperature:

- Troposphere: This layer is the closest to the Earth's surface. All weather phenomena occur here because it is the layer with the most water vapor and dust. Air temperature decreases with increasing altitude. The average thickness of the troposphere is seven miles (eleven kilometers).

- Stratosphere: This layer contains very little water. Clouds within this layer are extremely rare. The ozone layer is located in the upper portions of the stratosphere. Air temperature is fairly constant but does increase somewhat with height due to the absorption of solar energy and ultraviolet rays from the ozone layer.

- Mesosphere: Air temperature again decreases with height in this layer. This is the coldest layer, with temperatures in the range of -1000°C at the top.

- Thermosphere: This layer extends upward into space. Oxygen molecules in this layer absorb energy from the Sun, causing temperatures to increase with height. The lower part of the thermosphere is called the ionosphere.

Here, charged particles (ions) and free electrons can be found. When gases in the ionosphere are excited by solar radiation, the gases give off light and glow in the sky. These glowing lights are called the aurora borealis in the Northern Hemisphere and aurora australis in the Southern Hemisphere. The upper portion of the thermosphere is called the exosphere. Gas molecules are very far apart in this layer. Layers of exosphere are also known as the Van Allen belts and are held together by the Earth's magnetic field.

SKILL 31.2 Identify the properties of Earth's materials, and the availability and use of those materials

Humans have a tremendous impact on the world's natural resources. Plant and animal life is affected by the pollution that humans introduce to the water supply, and to obtain drinking water, contaminants such as parasites, pollutants and bacteria are removed from raw water through a purification process involving various screening, conditioning and chlorination steps. Most uses of water resources, such as drinking and crop irrigation, require fresh water. Only 2.5% of water on Earth is fresh water, and more than two thirds of this fresh water is frozen in glaciers and polar ice caps. Consequently, in many parts of the world, water use greatly exceeds supply. This problem is expected to increase in the future.

Plant resources also make up a large part of the world's natural resources. The forestry industry provides the wood that is essential for use as construction timber or paper. Cotton is a common plant found on farms of the Southern United States. Cotton is used to produce fabric for clothing, sheets, furniture, etc. Another example of a plant resource that is not directly consumed is straw, which is harvested for use in plant growth and farm animal care. The list of plants grown to provide food for the people of the world is extensive. Major crops include corn, potatoes, wheat, sugar, barley, peas, beans, beets, flax, lentils, sunflowers, soybeans, canola, and rice. These crops may have alternate uses as well. For example, corn is used to manufacture cornstarch, ethanol fuel, high fructose corn syrup, ink, biodegradable plastics, chemicals used in cosmetics and pharmaceuticals, adhesives, and paper products.

Other resources used by humans are known as "non-renewable" resources. Such resources, including fossil fuels, cannot be remade and do not naturally reform at a rate that could sustain human use. Non-renewable resources are therefore depleted and not restored. Presently, non-renewable resources provide the main source of energy for humans. Common fossil fuels used by humans are coal, petroleum and natural gas, which all form from the remains of dead plants and animals through natural processes over millions of years. Because of their high carbon content, when burnt these substances generate high amounts of energy as well as carbon dioxide, which is released back into the atmosphere, increasing global warming. To create electricity, energy from the burning of fossil fuels is harnessed to power a rotary engine called a turbine. Implementation of the use of fossil fuels as an energy source allowed for large-scale industrial development.

Mineral resources are concentrations of naturally occurring inorganic elements and compounds located in the Earth's crust that are extracted through mining for human use. Minerals have a definite chemical composition and are stable over a range of temperatures and pressures. Construction and manufacturing rely heavily on metals and industrial mineral resources. These metals include iron, bronze, lead, zinc, nickel, copper, and tin. Other industrial minerals are divided into two categories: bulk rocks and ore minerals. Bulk rocks, including limestone, clay, shale and sandstone, are used as aggregate in construction, in ceramics, and in concrete. Common ore minerals include calcite, barite and gypsum. Energy from some minerals can be utilized to produce electricity fuel and industrial materials. Mineral resources are also used as fertilizers and pesticides.

SKILL 31.3 Analyze changes occurring within Earth's lithosphere, hydrosphere, and atmosphere and interactions among those systems

While the hydrosphere, lithosphere, and atmosphere can be described and considered separately, they are actually constantly interacting with one another. Energy and matter flows freely between these different spheres. For instance, in the water cycle, water beneath the Earth's surface and in rocks (in the lithosphere) is exchanged with vapor in the atmosphere and liquid water in lakes and the ocean (the hydrosphere). Similarly, significant events in one sphere almost always affect the other spheres. The recent increase in greenhouse gases is an example of this ripple effect. Additional greenhouse gases produced by human activities are released into the atmosphere, where they build up and cause widening holes in certain areas of the atmosphere and global warming. These increasing temperatures have had many effects on the hydrosphere: rising sea levels, increasing water temperature, and climate changes. These lead to even more changes in the lithosphere, such as glacier retreat and alterations in the patterns of water-rock interaction (run-off, erosion, etc.).

Earth is the third planet away from the Sun in our solar system. Earth's numerous types of motion and states of orientation greatly affect global conditions, such as seasons, tides, and lunar phases. The Earth orbits the Sun over a period of 365 days. During this orbit, the average distance between the Earth and Sun is 93 million miles. The shape of the Earth's orbit around the Sun deviates from the shape of a circle only slightly. This deviation, known as the Earth's eccentricity, has a very small affect on the Earth's climate. The Earth is closest to the Sun at perihelion, occurring around January 2 of each year, and is farthest from the Sun at aphelion, occurring around July 2. Because the Earth is closest to the sun in January, the northern winter is slightly warmer than the southern winter.

Seasons

The rotation axis of the Earth is not perpendicular to the orbital (ecliptic) plane. The axis of the Earth is tilted 23.45 degrees from the perpendicular; the tilt of this axis is known as the obliquity of the ecliptic, and is responsible for the four seasons of the year by influencing the intensity of solar rays received by the Northern and Southern hemispheres.

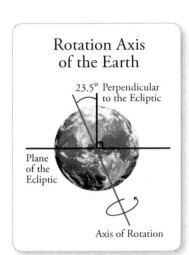

Rotation Axis of the Earth

23.5° Perpendicular to the Ecliptic

Plane of the Ecliptic

Axis of Rotation

The four seasons—spring, summer, fall, and winter—are extended periods of characteristic average temperature, rainfall, storm frequency, and vegetation growth or dormancy. The effect of the Earth's tilt on climate is best demonstrated at the solstices, the two days of the year when the Sun is farthest from the Earth's equatorial plane. At the summer solstice (June), the Earth's tilt on its axis causes the Northern Hemisphere to lean toward the Sun, while the Southern Hemisphere leans away. Consequently, the Northern Hemisphere receives more intense rays from the Sun and experiences summer during this time, while the Southern Hemisphere experiences winter. At the winter solstice (December), it is the Southern Hemisphere that leans toward the Sun and thus experiences summer. Spring and fall are produced by varying degrees of leaning toward or away from the Sun.

Tides

The orientation of and gravitational interaction between the Earth and the moon are responsible for the ocean tides that occur on Earth. The term tide refers to the cyclic rise and fall of large bodies of water. Gravitational attraction is defined as the force of attraction between all bodies in the universe. At the location on Earth closest to the moon, the gravitational attraction of the moon draws seawater toward the moon in the form of a tidal bulge. On the opposite side of the Earth, another tidal bulge forms in the direction away from the moon because at this point, the moon's gravitational pull is the weakest.

SPRING TIDES are the especially strong tides that occur when the Earth, Sun, and moon are in line, allowing both the Sun and the moon to exert gravitational force on the Earth, thereby increasing tidal bulge height. These tides occur during the full moon and the new moon. NEAP TIDES are especially weak tides occurring when the gravitational forces of the moon and the Sun are perpendicular to one another. These tides occur during quarter moons.

Phases of the Moon

The Earth's orientation in relation to the solar system is also responsible for our perception of the phases of the moon. While the Earth orbits the Sun over a period of 365 days, the moon orbits the Earth every twenty-seven days. As the moon circles the Earth, its shape in the night sky appears to change. The changes in the appearance of the moon from the Earth are known as LUNAR PHASES.

These phases vary cyclically according to the relative positions of the moon, the Earth, and the Sun. At all times, half of the moon is facing the Sun; thus, it is illuminated by reflecting the Sun's light. As the moon orbits the Earth and the Earth orbits the Sun, the half of the moon that faces the Sun changes. However, the moon is in synchronous rotation around the Earth, meaning that nearly the same side of the moon faces the Earth at all times. This side is referred to as the near side of the moon. Lunar phases occur as the Earth and moon orbit the Sun and the fractional illumination of the moon's near side changes.

When the Sun and moon are on opposite sides of the Earth, observers on Earth perceive a full moon, meaning that the moon appears circular because the entire illuminated half of the moon is visible. As the moon orbits the Earth, the moon "wanes" as the amount of the illuminated half of the moon that is visible from Earth decreases. A gibbous moon is between a full moon and a half moon, or between a half moon and a full moon. When the Sun and the moon are on the same side of Earth, the illuminated half of the moon is facing away from Earth, and the moon appears invisible. This lunar phase is known as the new moon. The time between full moons is approximately 29.53 days.

SPRING TIDES: occurring during the full and new moon, the especially strong tides that occur when the Earth, Sun, and moon are in line, allowing both the Sun and the moon to exert gravitational force on the Earth, thereby increasing tidal bulge height

NEAP TIDES: occurring during quarter moons, especially weak tides during which the gravitational forces of the moon and the Sun are perpendicular to one another

LUNAR PHASES: the changes in the appearance of the moon from the Earth

PHASES OF THE MOON		
New Moon	●	The moon is invisible or the first signs of a crescent appear
Waxing Crescent	◑	The right crescent of the moon is visible
First Quarter	◐	The right quarter of the moon is visible
Waxing Gibbous	◐	Only the left crescent is not illuminated
Full Moon	○	The entire illuminated half of the moon is visible
Waning Gibbous	◑	Only the right crescent of the moon is not illuminated
Last Quarter	◑	The left quarter of the moon is illuminated
Waning Crescent	◐	Only the left crescent of the moon is illuminated

Viewing the moon from the Southern Hemisphere causes these phases to occur in the opposite order.

Eclipses

Eclipses are defined as the passing of one object into the shadow of another object. A LUNAR ECLIPSE occurs when the moon travels through the shadow of the earth. A SOLAR ECLIPSE occurs when the moon positions itself between the Sun and Earth.

LUNAR ECLIPSE: occurs when the moon travels through the shadow of the earth

SOLAR ECLIPSE: occurs when the moon positions itself between the Sun and Earth

Recognize changes that have occurred in Earth's history
(e.g., glaciation, mass extinction, plate tectonics)

Earth's Plates

PLATE TECTONICS: a theory that explains not only the movement of the continents but also the changes in the Earth's crust caused by internal forces

Data obtained from many sources led scientists to develop the theory of PLATE TECTONICS. This theory is the most current model that explains not only the movement of the continents but also the changes in the Earth's crust caused by internal forces.

Boundaries form between spreading plates where the crust is forced apart in a process called rifting. Rifting generally occurs at mid-ocean ridges. Rifting can also take place within a continent, splitting the continent into smaller landmasses that drift away from each other, forming an ocean basin between them. The Red Sea is a product of rifting. As the seafloor spreading takes place, new material is added to the inner edges of the separating plates. In this way the plates grow larger, and the ocean basin widens. This is the process that broke up the supercontinent Pangaea and created the Atlantic Ocean.

Boundaries between plates that are colliding are zones of intense crustal activity. When a plate of ocean crust collides with a plate of continental crust, the more dense oceanic plate slides under the lighter continental plate and plunges into the mantle. This process is called subduction, and the site where it takes place is called a subduction zone. A subduction zone is usually seen on the sea floor as a deep depression called a trench.

The crustal movement identified by plates sliding sideways past each other produces a plate boundary characterized by major faults that are capable of unleashing powerful earthquakes. The San Andreas fault forms such a boundary between the Pacific plate and the North American plate.

A mountain is terrain that has been raised high above the surrounding landscape by volcanic action or some form of tectonic plate collisions. The plate collisions could be intercontinental or ocean floor collisions with a continental crust (subduction). The physical composition of mountains includes igneous, metamorphic, or sedimentary rocks; some may have rock layers that are tilted or distorted by plate collision forces.

A continental glacier covered a large part of North America during the most recent ice age. Evidence of this glacial coverage remains as abrasive grooves, large boulders from northern environments dropped in southerly locations, glacial troughs created by the rounding out of steep valleys by glacial scouring, and the remains of glacial sources called cirques that were created by frost wedging the rock at the bottom of the glacier. Remains of plants and animals found in warm climates have been discovered in moraines and outwash plains help to support the theory of periods of warmth during the past ice ages.

The Ice Age began about 2 to 3 million years ago. This age saw the advancement and retreat of glacial ice over millions of years. Theories relating to the origin of glacial activity include Plate Tectonics, which demonstrates that some continental masses, now in temperate climates, were at one time blanketed by ice and snow. Another theory involves changes in the earth's orbit around the sun, changes in the angle of the earth's axis, and the wobbling of the earth's axis. Support for the validity of this last theory has come from deep ocean research that indicates a correlation between climatic sensitive micro-organisms and the changes in the earth's orbital status.

About 12,000 years ago, a vast sheet of ice covered a large part of the northern United States. This huge, frozen mass had moved southward from the northern regions of Canada as several large bodies of slow-moving ice, or glaciers. A time period in which glaciers advance over a large portion of a continent is called an ICE AGE. A glacier is a large mass of ice that moves or flows over the land in response to gravity. Glaciers form among high mountains and in other cold regions.

> **ICE AGE:** a time period in which glaciers advance over a large portion of a continent

There are two main types of glaciers: valley glaciers and continental glaciers.

Erosion by valley glaciers is evidenced by U-shaped erosion. They produce sharp peaked mountains such as the Matterhorn in Switzerland. Continental glaciers often ride over mountains in their paths leaving smoothed, rounded mountains and ridges.

The history of the earth is partitioned into four major eras, which are further divided into major periods. The latter periods are refined into groupings called epochs.

Earth's history extends over more than four billion years and is reckoned in terms of a scale. Paleontologists who study the history of the Earth have divided this huge period of time into four large time units called eons. Eons are divided into smaller units of time called eras. An era refers to a time interval in which particular plants and animals were dominant, or present in great abundance. The end of an era is most often characterized by a general uplifting of the crust, the extinction of the dominant plants or animals, and the appearance of new life-forms.

See also Skill 31.1

COMPETENCY 32
UNDERSTAND CONCEPTS AND PRINCIPLES OF SCIENTIFIC INQUIRY AND INVESTIGATION

SKILL 32.1 Demonstrate knowledge of methods used for making observations and for formulating and expressing scientific questions or hypotheses to be investigated based on the observations

---

The Scientific Method

The scientific method is the basic process behind science. It involves several steps beginning with hypothesis formulation and working through to the conclusion.

> The scientific method is the basic process behind science

Posing a Question	Although many discoveries happen by chance, the standard thought process of a scientist begins with forming a question to research. The more limited the question, the easier it is to set up an experiment to answer it.
Form a Hypothesis	Once the question is formulated, take an educated guess about the answer to the problem or question. This "best guess" is your hypothesis.
Doing the Experiment	To make an experiment fair, data from an experiment must have a VARIABLE such as temperature or mass. A good experiment will try to manipulate as few variables as possible so as to see which variable is responsible for the result. This requires a second example called CONTROL.
Observe and Record the Data	Reporting the data should state specifics of how the measurements were calculated. A graduated cylinder needs to be read with proper procedures. As beginning students, technique must be part of the instructional process so as to give validity to the data.
Drawing a Conclusion	After recording data, compare your data with that of other groups. A conclusion is the judgment derived from the data results.
Graphing Data	Graphing utilizes numbers to demonstrate patterns. The patterns offer a visual representation, making it easier to draw conclusions.

> **VARIABLE:** any condition that can be changed

> **CONTROL:** an extra setup in which all the conditions are the same except for the variable being tested

Apply Knowledge of Designing and Performing Investigations

Normally, knowledge is integrated in the form of a lab report. A report has many sections. It should include a specific title and tell exactly what is being studied. The ABSTRACT is a summary of the report written at the beginning of the paper. The PURPOSE should always be defined and will state the problem. The purpose should include the HYPOTHESIS (educated guess) of what is expected from the outcome of the experiment. The entire experiment should relate to this problem.

It is important to describe exactly what was done to prove or disprove a hypothesis. A control is necessary to prove that the results occurred from the changed conditions and would not have happened normally. Only one variable should be manipulated at a time. OBSERVATIONS and RESULTS of the experiment should be recorded, including all results. Drawings, graphs, and illustrations should be included to support the results. Observations are objective, whereas analysis and interpretation is subjective. A CONCLUSION should explain why the results of the experiment either proved or disproved the hypothesis.

A SCIENTIFIC THEORY is an explanation of a set of related observations based on a proven hypothesis. A scientific law usually lasts longer than a scientific theory and has more experimental data to support it.

ABSTRACT: a summary of the report written at the beginning of the paper

PURPOSE: defines and states the problem

HYPOTHESIS: an educated guess of what is the expected outcome

OBSERVATIONS AND RESULTS: the recorded outcomes of the experiment

CONCLUSION: explains why the results proved or disproved the hypothesis

SCIENTIFIC THEORY: an explanation of a set of related observations based on a proven hypothesis

---

SKILL 32.2 Identify methods for conducting scientific investigations to address and explain questions or hypotheses

---

SCIENTIFIC INQUIRY is an understanding of science through questioning, experimentation and drawing conclusions.

The basic skills involved in this important process are:

1. Observing

2. Identifying problem

3. Gathering information/research

4. Hypothesizing

5. Experimental design, which includes identifying control, constants, independent and dependent variables

6. Conducting experiment and repeating the experiment for validity

7. Interpreting, analyzing, and evaluating data

8. Drawing conclusions

9. Communicating conclusions

SCIENTIFIC INQUIRY: an understanding of science through questioning, experimentation and drawing conclusions

What are the uses of scientific inquiry?

- Finding solutions for world problems

- Encouraging a problem solving approach to thinking, learning and understanding

- Applying math and language skills

- Confirming by experimentation that which is already known to the scientific community

- Offering explanations, conclusions, and critical evaluations

- Encouraging the use of modern technology for research, experiments, analysis, and to communicate data

- Staying up to date with recent advances in science

Scientific inquiry is a very powerful and highly interesting tool to teach and learn. Armed with knowledge of the subject matter, students can effectively conduct investigations. They need to learn to think critically and logically to connect evidence with explanations. This includes deciding what evidence should be used and accounting for unusual data. Based upon data collected during experimentation, basic statistical analysis and measures of probability can be used to make predictions and develop interpretations.

Students should be able to review the data, summarize, and form a logical argument about cause-and-effect relationships. It is important to differentiate between causes and effects and determine when causality is uncertain.

When developing proposed explanations, the students should be able to express their level of confidence in the proposed explanations and point out possible sources of uncertainty and error. When formulating explanations, it is important to distinguish between error and unanticipated results. Possible sources of error include assumptions of models and measuring techniques or devices.

With confidence in the proposed explanations, the students need to identify what would be required to reject the proposed explanations. Based upon their experience, they should develop new questions to promote further inquiry.

Different types of questions and hypotheses require different approaches to conducting scientific investigations. Some investigations involve making models; some involve discovery of new phenomena and objects; some involve observing and describing objects, organisms, or events; some involve experiments; some involve collecting specimens; and some involve seeking more information.

Different scientific domains use different methods, core theories, and standards.

Scientific investigations sometimes result in new ideas and phenomena to study, generate new procedures or methods for an investigation, or develop new technologies to improve data collection. All of these results can lead to new investigations.

SKILL 32.3 Identify strategies for collecting, organizing, analyzing, and displaying scientific data

The type of graphic representation used to display observations depends on the data that is collected. Line graphs are used to compare different sets of related data or to predict data that has not yet be measured. An example of a line graph would be comparing the rate of activity of different enzymes at varying temperatures. A bar graph or histogram is used to compare different items and make comparisons based on this data. An example of a bar graph would be comparing the ages of children in a classroom. A pie chart is useful when organizing data as part of a whole. A good use for a pie chart would be displaying the percent of time students spend on various after school activities.

As noted before, the independent variable is controlled by the experimenter. This variable is placed on the *x*-axis (horizontal axis). The dependent variable is influenced by the independent variable and is placed on the *y*-axis (vertical axis). It is important to choose the appropriate units for labeling the axes. It is best to take the largest value to be plotted and divide it by the number of blocks, and then rounding to the nearest whole number.

Careful research and statistically significant figures will be your best allies should you need to defend your work. For this reason, make sure to use controls, work in a systematic fashion, keep clear records, and have reproducible results.

See also skills 27.1, 32.1, and 32.2

SKILL 32.4 Demonstrate knowledge of systems of measurement used in science

Science uses the metric system because it is accepted worldwide and allows easier comparison among experiments done by scientists around the world. Learn the following basic units and prefixes:

meter	measure of length
liter	measure of volume
gram	measure of mass

deca-(meter, liter, gram)	=	10X the base unit	**deci**	=	1/10 the base unit
hecto-(meter, liter, gram)	=	100X the base unit	**centi**	=	1/100 the base unit
kilo-(meter, liter, gram)	=	1000X the base unit	**milli**	=	1/1000 the base unit

The common instrument used for measuring volume is the graduated cylinder. The unit of measurement is usually in milliliters (mL). It is important for accurate measure to read the liquid in the cylinder at the bottom of the meniscus, the curved surface of the liquid.

The common instrument used is measuring mass is the triple beam balance. The triple beam balance is measured in as low as tenths of a gram and can be estimated to the hundredths of a gram.

Rulers or meter sticks are the most commonly used instruments for measuring length. Measurements in science should always be measured in metric units. Be sure when measuring length that the metric units are used.

SKILL 32.5 Identify strategies for summarizing and analyzing scientific information, including possible sources of error, and suggesting reasonable and accurate interpretations and implications

Biologists use a variety of tools and technologies to perform tests, collect and display data, and analyze relationships. Examples of commonly used tools include computer-linked probes, spreadsheets, and graphing calculators.

Biologists use computer-linked probes to measure various environmental factors including temperature, dissolved oxygen, pH, ionic concentration, and pressure. The advantage of computer-linked probes, as compared to more traditional observational tools, is that the probes automatically gather data and present it in an accessible format. This property of computer-linked probes eliminates the need for constant human observation and manipulation.

Biologists use spreadsheets to organize, analyze, and display data. For example, conservation ecologists use spreadsheets to model population growth and development, apply sampling techniques, and create statistical distributions to analyze relationships. Spreadsheet use simplifies data collection and manipulation and allows the presentation of data in a logical and understandable format.

Graphing calculators are another technology with many applications to biology. For example, biologists use algebraic functions to analyze growth, development and other natural processes. Graphing calculators can manipulate algebraic data and create graphs for analysis and observation. In addition, biologists use the matrix function of graphing calculators to model problems in genetics. The use of graphing calculators simplifies the creation of graphical displays including histograms, scatter plots, and line graphs. Biologists can also transfer data and displays to computers for further analysis. Finally, biologists connect computer-linked probes, used to collect data, to graphing calculators to ease the collection, transmission, and analysis of data.

Error

All experimental uncertainty is due to either random errors or systematic errors.

RANDOM ERRORS are statistical fluctuations in the measured data due to the precision limitations of the measurement device. Random errors usually result from the experimenter's inability to take the same measurement in exactly the same way to get identical results.

SYSTEMATIC ERRORS, by contrast, are reproducible inaccuracies that are consistently in the same direction. Systematic errors are often due to a problem that persists throughout the entire experiment.

Systematic and random errors refer to problems associated with making measurements. Mistakes made in the calculations or in reading the instrument are not considered in error analysis.

> **RANDOM ERRORS:** statistical fluctuations in the measured data due to the precision limitations of the measurement device

> **SYSTEMATIC ERRORS:** reproducible inaccuracies that are consistently in the same direction

COMPETENCY 33
UNDERSTAND THE RELATIONSHIPS AMONG SCIENCE, TECHNOLOGY, AND SOCIETY

SKILL **Analyze the effects of science and technology on society**
33.1

Scientific and technological breakthroughs greatly influence other fields of study and the job market. All academic disciplines utilize computer and information technology to simplify research and information sharing. Advances in science and technology influence the types of available jobs and the desired work skills. Machines and computers now perform many jobs previously done by people, and computer and technological literacy is now a requirement for many jobs and careers. Because of science and technology's great influence on all areas of the economy and the continuing scientific and technological breakthroughs, careers can be far less stable than in past eras.

Local, state, national, and global governments and organizations must increasingly consider policy issues related to science and technology. For example, local and state governments must analyze the impact of proposed development and growth on the environment. Governments and communities must balance the demands of an expanding human population with the local ecology to ensure sustainable growth.

In addition, advances in science and technology create challenges and ethical dilemmas that national governments and global organizations must attempt to solve. Genetic research and manipulation, antibiotic resistance, stem cell research, and cloning are but a few of the issues facing national governments and global organizations.

In all cases, policy makers must analyze all sides of an issue and attempt to find a solution that protects society while limiting scientific inquiry as little as possible.

SKILL **Analyze the influence of society on science and technology**
33.2

The influence of social and cultural factors on science can be profound. Some early societies had trouble accepting science, especially when the science exposed some cultural beliefs as myths. This created a dilemma concerning whether or not to accept the proven facts provided by scientific investigations or to cling to cultural norms. This struggle went on for centuries. It took a long time for societies to accept scientific facts and to leave some cultural beliefs behind or modify them.

It can be extremely difficult for some societies to come to terms with technological advances. Even today, some cultures are not using modern technology, but, at the same time, they are using technology in principle—using simple machines for farming rather than using complex machines like tractors.

Other cultures have so readily adapted to technology that lives are intertwined with it—intertwined so much that we utilize the computer, television, microwave, dishwasher, washing machine, cell phone, etc. on a daily basis. It is surprising to realize that human society began with no technology and now are surrounded with it.

The religious beliefs and institutions of a culture can greatly influence scientific research and technological innovation. Political factors have affected scientific advancement as well, especially in cultures that partially support scientific research with public money. Warfare has traditionally been a strong driver of technological advancement as cultures strive to outpace their neighbors with better weapons and defenses. Technologies developed for military purposes often find their way into the mainstream. Significant advances in flight technology, for example, were made during the two World Wars.

Socially, many cultures have come to value innovation and welcome new products and improvements to older products. This desire to always be advancing and obtaining the latest, newest technology creates economic incentive for innovation.

SKILL 33.3 Identify the advantages and risks of scientific and technological changes

With any rapid change, there are always good and bad things associated with it. At the same time, we need technology in our lives, and we should make use of these developments and reap the benefits for the good of humanity.

Environment

The environment is constantly and rapidly undergoing tremendous changes.

The positive effects of technology on the environment include the ability to predict hurricanes; measuring changes in radioactivity present in our environment;

predicting the levels of carbon monoxide, carbon dioxide, and other harmful gases; and understanding phenomena like the green house effect, ozone layer, and UV radiation, to name a few.

The negative aspects of the effect of technology on our environment are numerous. The first and foremost is pollution of various kinds—water, air, and noise. Others include the greenhouse effect, the indiscriminate use of fertilizers and pesticides, the use of various additives to our food, deforestation, and the unprecedented exploitation of nonrenewable resources.

Human Biology

The strides science and technology have made have lasting effects on human biology. A few examples are organ transplants, in-vitro fertilization, cloning, new drugs, new understanding of various diseases, reconstructive surgery, use of computers in operations, lasers in medicine, and forensic science. As always, there are pros and cons to these changes.

The positive aspects are that people with organ transplants have renewed hope. Their life spans are increased, and their quality of life has improved with the use of technology such as pacemakers. Couples who experienced infertility can often have babies. Corrective and cosmetic surgeries are giving new confidence to patients. Glasses to correct vision problems are being replaced by laser surgery in some cases.

The negative aspects are some medical blunders, the indiscriminate use of corrective and cosmetic surgery, and the overuse of, and dependence on, often unnecessarily complex medical tests and procedures.

Society and Culture

The use of technology has changed our lifestyles, our behavior, our ethical and moral thinking, and our economy, and our career opportunities.

The computer has contributed a lot to these changes. Normal household chores are being done by machines, giving relief through a cost-effective and timesaving means for upkeep of kitchen and home.

The positive aspects are that technology is uniting us to a certain extent (e.g., it is possible to communicate with a person of any culture even when we are not seeing them face to face). It makes business and personal communication much easier over long distances. E-mail has made communication between remote cultures and individuals possible, fostering greater understanding among cultures.

Modern methods of travel are changing the way we think about relationships, possibilities, and career opportunities. We can now visit places previously inaccessible and experience other cultures first-hand.

The negative aspects include increased dependency on technology. In addition, electronic communication often replaces real, face-to-face human interactions.

On the whole, we can safely conclude that science and technology are part of our lives, and we must exercise caution when we are adapting to new ideas and new thinking.

SKILL 33.4   Identify career opportunities in the fields of science and technology

Science is an interesting, innovative, and thoroughly enjoyable subject. Science careers can be challenging and stimulating. The possibilities for scientific careers are endless.

Why Do People Choose Careers in Science?

This is a very important question. The reasons are manifold.

1. A passion for science

2. A desire to experiment and gain knowledge and contribute to society's betterment

3. An inquiring mind

4. Wanting to work in a team, and many more.

There are a number of opportunities in science:

1. Biological sciences
2. Physical sciences
3. Earth science
4. Space science
5. Forensic science
6. Medical science
7. Agricultural science

Let's take each category and examine the opportunities available.

- Biological sciences: The study of living organisms and their life cycles, medicinal properties, and the like
  - Botanist
  - Microbiologist

- Physical science: The study of matter and energy
  - Analytical chemist
  - Biochemist
  - Chemist
  - Physicist

- Earth science: The study of the Earth, its changes over the years, and natural disasters such as earthquakes and hurricanes
  - Geologist
  - Meteorologist
  - Oceanographer
  - Seismologist
  - Volcanologist

- Space science: The study of space, the universe, and planets
  - Astrophysicist
  - Space scientist

- Forensic science: The solving of crimes using various techniques
  - Forensic pathologist

- Medical science: Science with practical applications in the care and cure of diseases
  - Biomedical scientist
  - Clinical scientist

- Agricultural science: The use of science to grow and improve upon crops
  - Agriculturist
  - Agricultural service industry worker
  - Agronomist
  - Veterinary science worker

There are many career opportunities available, but it is up to each student to choose the right career. The students need to be made aware of the connection between today's learning and their future lives. It is especially important to impress upon them how science is everywhere, and its truly useful applications. When this is made clear to them, they may seriously consider science as a career.

COMPETENCY 34
UNDERSTAND THE NATURE AND HISTORY OF SCIENCE

SKILL 34.1 Recognize the history of important scientific ideas and the contributions of various cultures and individuals to scientific knowledge

The history of biology traces mans' understanding of the living world from the earliest recorded history to modern times. Though the concept of biology as a field of science arose only in the 19th century, the origin of biological sciences can be traced back to ancient Greeks (Galen and Aristotle).

During the Renaissance and the Age of Discovery, renewed interest in the rapidly increasing number of known organisms generated lot of interest in biology.

Andreas Vesalius (1514–1564), a Belgian anatomist and physician, performed dissections of the human body and the descriptions of his findings helped to correct the misconceptions of the time. The books Vesalius wrote on anatomy were the most accurate and comprehensive anatomical texts to date.

Anton van Leeuwenhoek is known as the father of microscopy. In the 1650s, Leeuwenhoek began making tiny lenses that gave magnifications up to 300 times. He was the first to see and describe bacteria, yeast plants, and the microscopic life found in water. Over the years, light microscopes have advanced to produce greater clarity and magnification. The scanning electron microscope (SEM) was developed in the 1950s. Instead of light, a beam of electrons passes through the specimen. Scanning electron microscopes have a resolution about one thousand times greater than light microscopes. The disadvantage of the SEM is that the chemical and physical methods used to prepare the sample result in the death of the specimen.

Robert Hooke (1635–1703) was a renowned inventor, a natural philosopher, astronomer, experimenter and a cell biologist. He deserves more recognition than he has reeceived. He is remembered mainly for Hooke's laws an equation describing elasticity that is still used today. He was the type of scientist that was then called a "virtuoso," able to contribute findings of major importance in any field of science. Hooke published *Micrographia* in 1665. Hooke devised the compound microscope and illumination system, one of the best such microscopes of his time, and used it in his demonstrations at the Royal Society's meetings. With it he observed organisms as diverse as insects, sponges, bryozoans, foraminifera, and bird feathers. *Micrographia* is an accurate and detailed record of his observations, illustrated with magnificent drawings.

Carl Von Linnaeus (1707–1778), a Swedish botanist, physician and zoologist, is well known for his contributions in ecology and taxonomy. Linnaeus is famous for his binomial system of nomenclature in which each living organism has two names, a genus and a species name. He is considered as the father of modern ecology and taxonomy.

In the late 1800s, Pasteur discovered the role of microorganisms as the cause of disease, and invented pasteurization and the rabies vaccine. Koch took this observations one step further by formulating that specific diseases are caused by specific pathogens. Koch's postulates are still used as guidelines in the field of microbiology: the same pathogen must be found in every diseased person, the pathogen must be isolated and grown in culture, the disease from the culture is induced in experimental animals, and the same pathogen must be isolated from the experimental animal.

Mattias Schleiden, a German botanist, is famous for his cell theory. He observed plant cells microscopically and concluded that the cell is the common structural unit of plants. He proposed the cell theory along with Schwann, a zoologist, who observed cells in animals.

In the 18th century, many fields of science like botany, zoology and geology began to evolve as scientific disciplines in the modern sense.

In the 20th century, the rediscovery of Mendel's work led to the rapid development of genetics by Thomas Hunt Morgan and his students.

DNA structure was another key event in biological study. In the 1950s, James Watson and Francis Crick discovered that the structure of a DNA molecule is a double helix. This structure made it possible to explain DNA's ability to replicate and to control the synthesis of proteins.

Francois Jacob and Jacques Monod contributed greatly to the field of lysogeny and bacterial reproduction and both of them won Nobel Prize for their contributions.

Following the cracking of the genetic code, biology has been largely split between organismal biology—consisting of ecology, ethology, systematics, paleontology—and evolutionary biology, developmental biology, and other disciplines that deal with whole organisms or group of organisms; and the disciplines related to molecular biology, including cell biology, biophysics, biochemistry, neuroscience, immunology, and many other similar subjects.

The use of animals in biological research has expedited many scientific discoveries. Animal research has allowed scientists to learn more about animal biological systems, including the circulatory and reproductive systems. One significant use of animals is for the testing of drugs, vaccines, and other products (such as perfumes and shampoos) before use or consumption by humans. Along with the pros of animal research, the cons are also very significant. The debate about the ethical treatment of animals has been ongoing since the introduction of animals in research. Many people believe the use of animals in research is cruel and unnecessary. Animal use is federally and locally regulated. The purpose of the Institutional Animal Care and Use Committee (IACUC) is to oversee and evaluate all aspects of an institution's animal care and use program.

SKILL 34.2 Recognize unifying concepts of science *(e.g., systems, equilibrium)*

Biological science is closely connected to technology and the other sciences and greatly impacts society and everyday life. Scientific discoveries often lead to technological advances and, conversely, technology is often necessary for scientific investigation and advances in technology often expand the reach of scientific discoveries. In addition, biology and the other scientific disciplines share several concepts and processes that help unify the study of science. Finally, because biology is the science of living systems, it directly impacts society and everyday life.

Unifying Concepts and Processes Among the Sciences

The following are the concepts and processes generally recognized as common to all scientific disciplines:

- Systems, order, and organization
- Evidence, models, and explanation
- Constancy, change, and measurement
- Evolution and equilibrium
- Form and function

Systems, Order, and Organization

Because the natural world is so complex, the study of science involves the organization of items into smaller groups based on interaction or interdependence. These groups are called systems. Examples of organization are the periodic table of elements and the five-kingdom classification scheme for living organisms. Examples of systems are the solar system, cardiovascular system, Newton's laws of force and motion, and the laws of conservation.

Order refers to the behavior and measurability of organisms and events in nature. The arrangement of planets in the solar system and the life cycle of bacterial cells are examples of order.

Evidence, Models, and Explanations

Scientists use evidence and models to form explanations of natural events. Models are miniaturized representations of a larger event or system. Evidence is anything that furnishes proof.

Constancy, Change, and Measurement

CONSTANCY AND CHANGE describe the observable properties of natural organisms and events. Scientists use different systems of measurement to observe change and constancy; for example, the freezing and melting points of given substances and the speed of sound. Growth, decay, and erosion are all examples of natural change.

CONSTANCY AND CHANGE: the observable properties of natural organisms and events

Evolution and Equilibrium

EVOLUTION is the process of change over a long period of time. While biological evolution is the most common example, one can also classify technological advancement, changes in the universe, and changes in the environment as evolution.

EVOLUTION: the process of change over a long period of time

EQUILIBRIUM is the state of balance between opposing forces of change. Homeostasis and ecological balance are examples of equilibrium.

EQUILIBRIUM: the state of balance between opposing forces of change

Form and Function

FORM AND FUNCTION are properties of organisms and systems that are closely related. The function of an object usually dictates its form and the form of an object usually facilitates its function. For example, the form of the heart (e.g., muscle, valves) allows it to perform its function of circulating blood through the body.

FORM AND FUNCTION: properties of organisms and systems that are closely related

SKILL **Identify inherent values of science** (e.g., using logical arguments, avoiding
34.3 researcher bias, acknowledging paradigm shifts)

See also Skills 32.1, 32.2, 34.2, and 34.4

Scientific research serves two purposes:

1. To investigate and acquire knowledge that is theoretical

2. To do research of practical value

Science is in a unique position to be able to serve humanity. Scientific research comes from inquiry. An inquiring mind is always trying to find answers. The two most important questions—why and how—are the starting points. A person who is inquisitive asks questions and wants to find out answers.

Scientific research uses the scientific method to methodically answer questions. Those who research follow the scientific method, which consists of a series of steps designed to solve a problem or find answer to a problem.

The aim of the scientific method is to eliminate bias or prejudice from the scientist researcher. As human beings, we are inherently biased, and this method helps to eliminate that. If all the steps of the scientific method are followed as outlined, there is the maximum elimination of bias.

SKILL **Recognize the process and importance of peer review of scientific**
34.4 **findings**

Science Is Empirical, Verifiable, and Logical

Observations, however general they may seem, lead scientists to create a viable question and an educated guess (hypothesis) about what to expect from an experiment. While scientists often have laboratories set up to study a specific thing, it is likely that along the way they will find an unexpected result. It is always important to be open-minded and to look at all of the information. An open-minded approach to science provides room for more questioning, and, hence, more learning. A central concept in science is that all evidence is empirical. This means that all evidence must be is observed by the five senses. The phenomenon must be both observable and measurable, with reproducible results.

The question stage of scientific inquiry involves repetition. By repeating the experiment you discover whether or not you have reproducibility. If results are reproducible, the hypothesis is valid. If the results are not reproducible, one has more questions to ask. It is also important to recognize that one experiment is often a stepping-stone for another. It is possible that data will be retested (by the same scientist or by another), and that a different conclusion might be found. In this way, scientific competition acts as a system of checks and balances.

Evaluating Scientific Claims

Because people often attempt to use scientific evidence in support of political or personal agendas, the ability to evaluate the credibility of scientific claims is a necessary skill. In evaluating scientific claims made in the media, public debates, and advertising, one should follow several guidelines.

1. Scientific, peer-reviewed journals are the most accepted source of information on scientific experiments and studies. One should carefully scrutinize any claim that does not reference peer-reviewed literature.

2. The media and those with an agenda to advance (advertisers, debaters, etc.) often overemphasize the certainty and importance of experimental results. One should question any scientific claim that sounds fantastical or overly certain.

3. Knowledge of experimental design and the scientific method is important in evaluating the credibility of studies. For example, one should look for the inclusion of control groups and the presence of data to support the given conclusions.

DOMAIN VII
HEALTH AND PHYSICAL EDUCATION

Available for purchase at www.XAMonline.com:

eFlashcards: a digital representation of a card represented with words, numbers or symbols or any combination of each and briefly displayed as part of a learning drill. eFlashcards takes away the burden of carrying around traditional cards that could easily be disarranged, dropped, or soiled. Available at www.XAMonline.com/flashcards

More Sample Tests: more ways to assess how much you know and how much further you need to study. Ultimately, makes you more prepared and attain mastery in the skills and techniques of passing the test the FIRST TIME! Available at www. XAMonline.com/sampletests

PERSONALIZED STUDY PLAN

KNOWN MATERIAL/ SKIP IT

PAGE	COMPETENCY AND SKILL	
375	**35: Understand basic principles and practices related to personal and community health and safety**	☐
	35.1: Recognize basic processes of human growth, development, and body systems	☐
	35.2: Identify strategies for maintaining personal mental and physical health	☐
	35.3: Recognize the role culture plays in mental and physical well-being	☐
	35.4: Recognize common health issues of children	☐
	35.5: Recognize the influence of various factors on personal and community health and safety	☐
	35.6: Recognize the importance of positive interventions on personal and community health and safety	☐
393	**36: Understand basic principles and practices related to lifetime physical fitness**	☐
	36.1: Identify components of fitness	☐
	36.2: Identify activities that promote lifetime physical fitness	☐
	36.3: Recognize ways to prevent or lower the risk of injury and disease	☐
	36.4: Recognize the influence of media on health choices, body image, and self-confidence	☐
	36.5: Recognize consequences of substance use and abuse	☐
	36.6: Identify strategies for promoting students' ability to use skills that contribute to good health	☐
399	**37: Understand basic principles and practices of physical education**	☐
	37.1: Identify basic locomotor patterns	☐
	37.2: Recognize principles of training, conditioning, and practicing for specific physical activities	☐
	37.3: Identify safety practices associated with physical activities	☐
	37.4: Recognize appropriate rules and strategies for physical activities, cooperative and competitive games, and sports	☐
	37.5: Demonstrate knowledge of physical activities, games, and sports	☐
	37.6: Recognize cross-cultural origins of physical activities, games, and sports	☐

COMPETENCY 35
UNDERSTAND BASIC PRINCIPLES AND PRACTICES RELATED TO PERSONAL AND COMMUNITY HEALTH AND SAFETY

SKILL 35.1 **Recognize basic processes of human growth, development, and body systems**

Physical Development

Small children (ages 3-5) have a propensity for engaging in periods of intense physical activity, punctuated by a need for a lot of rest. Children at this stage lack fine motor skills and cannot focus on small objects for very long. Their bones are still developing. At this age, girls tend to be better coordinated, and boys tend to be stronger.

The lag in fine motor skills continues during the early elementary school years (ages 6-8).

Pre-adolescent children (ages 9-11) become stronger, leaner, and taller. Their motor skills improve, and they are able to sit still and focus for longer periods. Growth during this period is constant. This is also the time when gender physical predispositions will begin to manifest. Pre-adolescents are at risk of obesity without proper nutrition and adequate activity.

Young adolescents (ages 12-14) experience drastic physical growth (girls earlier than boys), and are often preoccupied with their physical appearance.

As children proceed to the later stages of adolescence (ages 15-17), girls will reach their full height, while boys will continue to grow.

Cognitive Development

Language development is the most important aspect of cognitive development in small children (ages 3-5).

Early elementary school children (ages 6-8) have a very literal understanding of rules and verbal instructions and must develop strong listening skills.

Pre-adolescent children (ages 9-11) display increased logical thought. Differences in cognitive styles develop at this age (e.g., field dependant or independent preferences). In early adolescence (ages 12-14), boys tend to score higher on mechanical/spatial reasoning tasks, and girls on spelling, language, and clerical tasks. Boys are better with mental imagery, and girls can better access and retrieve information from memory. Self-efficacy (the ability to self-evaluate) becomes very important at this stage.

In later adolescence (ages 15-17), children are capable of formal thought.

Body Systems

Major systems of the human body consist of organs working together to perform important physiological tasks. In this section, we will discuss several major body systems including the musculoskeletal system, the cardiovascular system, the respiratory/excretory system, the nervous system, the endocrine system, the reproductive system, and the immune system. In addition, we will discuss how these systems adapt to physical activity, produce movement, and contribute to fitness.

Structures, Locations, and Functions of the Three Types of Muscular Tissue

The main function of the muscular system is movement. There are three types of muscle tissue: skeletal, cardiac, and smooth.

Skeletal muscle is voluntary. These muscles are attached to bones and are responsible for their movement. Skeletal muscle consists of long fibers and is striated due to the repeating patterns of the myofilaments (made of the proteins actin and myosin) that make up the fibers.

Cardiac muscle is found in the heart. Cardiac muscle is striated like skeletal muscle, but differs in that the plasma membrane of the cardiac muscle causes the muscle to beat even when away from the heart. The action potentials of cardiac and skeletal muscles also differ.

Smooth muscle is involuntary. It is found in organs and enables functions such as digestion and respiration. Unlike skeletal and cardiac muscle, smooth muscle is not striated. Smooth muscle has less myosin and does not generate as much tension as skeletal muscle.

Mechanism of Skeletal Muscle Contraction

A nerve impulse strikes a muscle fiber. This causes calcium ions to flood the sarcomere. Calcium ions allow ATP to expend energy. The myosin fibers creep along the actin, causing the muscle to contract. Once the nerve impulse has passed, calcium is pumped out and the contraction ends.

Movement of Body Joints

The axial skeleton consists of the bones of the skull and vertebrae. The appendicular skeleton consists of the bones of the legs, arms, and shoulder girdle. Bone is a connective tissue. Parts of the bone include compact bone that gives strength, spongy bone that contains red marrow to make blood cells and yellow marrow in the center of long bones to store fat cells, and the periosteum that is the protective covering on the outside of the bone.

A joint is a place where two bones meet. Joints enable movement. Ligaments attach bone to bone, and tendons attach bone to muscle. Joints allow great flexibility in movement.

THREE TYPES OF JOINTS	
Ball and socket	Allows for rotational movement. An example is the joint between the shoulder and the humerus. Ball and socket joints allow humans to move their arms and legs in many different ways.
Hinge	Movement is restricted to a single plane. An example is the joint between the humerus and the ulna.
Pivot	Allows for the rotation of the forearm at the elbow and the hands at the wrist.

Human Nervous and Endocrine Systems

The central nervous system (CNS) consists of the brain and spinal cord. The CNS is responsible for the body's response to environmental stimuli. The spinal cord is located inside the spine. It sends out motor commands for movement in response to stimuli. The brain is where responses to more complex stimuli occur. The meninges are the connective tissues that protect the CNS. The CNS contains fluid-filled spaces called ventricles. These ventricles are filled with cerebrospinal fluid, which is formed in the brain. This fluid cushions the brain and circulates nutrients, white blood cells, and hormones. The CNS's response to stimuli is a reflex. A reflex is an unconscious, automatic response.

The peripheral nervous system (PNS) consists of the nerves that connect the CNS to the rest of the body. The sensory division of the PNS brings information to the CNS from sensory receptors and the motor division of the PNS sends signals from the CNS to effector cells. The motor division consists of the somatic nervous system and the autonomic nervous system. The body consciously controls the somatic nervous system in response to external stimuli. The hypothalamus in the brain unconsciously controls the autonomic nervous system to regulate the internal environment. This system is responsible for the movement of smooth muscles, cardiac muscles, and the muscles of other organ systems.

HORMONES: proteins that circulate in the bloodstream and stimulate actions when they interact with target tissue

The function of the endocrine system is to manufacture proteins called hormones. HORMONES circulate in the bloodstream and stimulate actions when they interact with target tissue. There are two classes of hormones. Steroid hormones come from cholesterol and include the sex hormones. Amino acids are the source of peptide hormones. Hormones are specific and fit receptors on the target tissue cell surface. The receptor activates an enzyme that converts ATP to cyclic AMP. Cyclic AMP (cAMP) is a second messenger from the cell membrane to the nucleus. The genes found in the nucleus turn on or off to cause a specific response.

Endocrine cells, which make up endocrine glands, secrete hormones.

MAJOR ENDOCRINE GLANDS AND THEIR HORMONES	
Hypothalamus	Located in the lower brain; signals the pituitary gland.
Pituitary gland	Located at the base of the hypothalamus; releases growth hormones and antidiuretic hormone (retention of water in kidneys).
Thyroid gland	Located on the trachea; lowers blood calcium levels (calcitonin) and maintains metabolic processes (thyroxine).
Gonads	Located in the testes of the male and the ovaries of the female; testes release androgens to support sperm formation and ovaries release estrogens to stimulate uterine lining growth and progesterone to promote uterine lining growth.
Pancreas	Secretes insulin to lower blood glucose levels and glucagon to raise blood glucose levels.

Role of Nerve Impulses and Neurons

NEURON: basic unit of the nervous system, consisting of an axon, a dendrite, and the cell body

The NEURON is the basic unit of the nervous system. It consists of the axon, which carries impulses away from the cell body to the tip of the neuron; the dendrite, which carries impulses toward the cell body; and the cell body, which contains the nucleus. Synapses are spaces between neurons. Chemicals called neurotransmitters are found close to the synapse. The myelin sheath, composed of Schwann cells, covers the neurons and provides insulation.

Nerve action depends on depolarization and an imbalance of electrical charges across the neuron. A polarized nerve has a positive charge outside the neuron. A depolarized nerve has a negative charge outside the neuron. Neurotransmitters turn off the sodium pump, which results in depolarization of the membrane. This wave of depolarization (as it moves from neuron to neuron) carries an electrical impulse. This is actually a wave of opening and closing gates that allows for the flow of ions across the synapse. Nerves have an action potential. There is a threshold of the level of chemicals that must be met or exceeded in order for muscles to respond. This is the "all or nothing" response.

Structure and Function of the Skin

The skin consists of two distinct layers, the epidermis and the dermis. The epidermis is the thinner outer layer and the dermis is the thicker inner layer. Layers of tightly packed epithelial cells make up the epidermis. The tight packaging of the epithelial cells supports the skin's function as a protective barrier against infection.

The top layer of the epidermis consists of dead skin cells and contains keratin, a waterproofing protein. The dermis layer consists of connective tissue. It contains blood vessels, hair follicles, sweat glands, and sebaceous glands. The body releases an oily secretion called sebum, produced by the sebaceous gland, to the outer epidermis through the hair follicles. Sebum maintains the pH of the skin between 3 and 5, which inhibits most microorganism growth.

The skin also plays a role in thermoregulation. Increased body temperature causes skin blood vessels to dilate, causing heat to radiate from the skin's surface. Increased temperature also activates sweat glands, increasing evaporative cooling. Decreased body temperature causes skin blood vessels to constrict. This diverts blood from the skin to deeper tissues and reduces heat loss from the surface of the skin.

Human Respiratory and Excretory Systems

Surface area, volume, and function of the respiratory and excretory systems

The lungs are the respiratory surface of the human respiratory system. A dense net of capillaries contained just beneath the epithelium form the respiratory surface. The surface area of the epithelium is about 100m² in humans. Based on the surface area, the volume of air inhaled and exhaled is the tidal volume. This is normally about 500mL in adults. Vital capacity is the maximum volume the lungs can inhale and exhale. This is usually around 3400mL.

The kidneys are the primary organ in the excretory system. Each of the two kidneys in humans is about 10cm long. Despite their small size, they receive about 20 percent of the blood pumped with each heartbeat. The function of the excretory system is to rid the body of nitrogenous wastes in the form of urea.

The respiratory system allows the gas exchange of oxygen and carbon dioxide waste. The respiratory system delivers oxygen to the bloodstream and picks up carbon dioxide for release from the body. Air enters the mouth and nose, where it is warmed, moistened, and filtered of dust and particles. Cilia in the trachea trap and expel unwanted material in mucus. The trachea splits into two bronchial tubes and the bronchial tubes divide into smaller and smaller bronchioles in the lungs. The internal surface of the lung is composed of alveoli, which are thin-walled air sacs. These allow for a large surface area for gas exchange. Capillaries line the alveoli. Oxygen diffuses into the bloodstream and carbon dioxide diffuses out of the capillaries and is exhaled from the lungs due to partial pressure. Hemoglobin, a protein containing iron, carries the oxygenated blood to the heart and all parts of the body.

The thoracic cavity holds the lungs. The diaphragm muscle below the lungs makes inhalation possible. As the volume of the thoracic cavity increases, the diaphragm muscle flattens out and inhalation occurs. When the diaphragm relaxes, exhalation occurs.

Human Circulatory and Immune Systems

Structure, function, and regulation of the heart

The function of the closed circulatory system (cardiovascular system) is to carry oxygenated blood and nutrients to all cells of the body and return carbon dioxide waste to the lungs for expulsion. The heart, blood vessels, and blood make up the cardiovascular system. This diagram shows the structure of the heart:

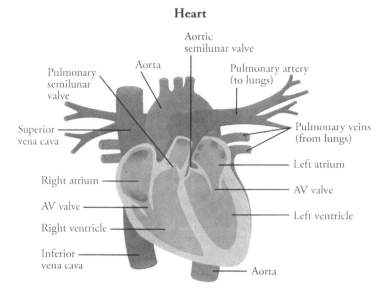

Heart

The atria are the chambers that receive blood returning to the heart and the ventricles are the chambers that pump blood out of the heart. There are four valves, two atrioventricular (AV) valves and two semilunar valves. The AV valves are located between each atrium and ventricle. The contraction of the ventricles closes the AV valves to keep blood from flowing back into the atria. The semilunar valves are located where the aorta leaves the left ventricle and where the pulmonary artery leaves the right ventricle. Ventricular contraction opens the semilunar valves, pumping blood out into the arteries, and ventricular relaxation closes the valves.

The cardiac output is the volume of blood that the left ventricle pumps per minute. This output depends on the heart rate and stroke volume. The heart rate is the number of times the heart beats per minute and the stroke volume is the amount of blood pumped by the left ventricle each time it contracts. Humans have an average cardiac output of about 5.25 L/min. Heavy exercise can increase cardiac output up to five times. Epinephrine and increased body temperature also increase heart rate and, thus, the cardiac output.

Cardiac muscle can contract without any signal from the nervous system. The sinoatrial node is the pacemaker of the heart. It is located on the wall of the right atrium and generates electrical impulses that make the cardiac muscle cells contract in unison. The atrioventricular node briefly delays the electrical impulse to ensure the atria is empty before the ventricles contract.

Structure, function, and regulation of the immune system

The immune system is responsible for defending the body against foreign invaders.

TWO OF THE BODY'S DEFENSE MECHANISMS	
Nonspecific	This immune mechanism has two lines of defense. The first is the physical barriers of the body. These include the skin and mucous membranes. The skin prevents the penetration of bacteria and viruses as long as there are no abrasions on the skin. Mucous membranes form a protective barrier around the digestive, respiratory, and genitourinary tracts. In addition, the pH of the skin and mucous membranes inhibit the growth of many microbes. Mucous secretions (tears and saliva) wash away many microbes and contain lysozyme that kills microbes. The second line of defense includes white blood cells and the inflammatory response. Phagocytosis is the ingestion of foreign particles. Neutrophils make up about seventy percent of all white blood cells. Monocytes mature to become macrophages, which are the largest phagocytic cells. Eosinophils are also phagocytic. Natural killer cells destroy the body's own infected cells instead of the invading the microbe directly. Another second line of defense is the inflammatory response. The blood supply to the injured area increases, causing redness and heat. Swelling also typically occurs with inflammation. Basophils and mast cells release histamine in response to cell injury. This triggers the inflammatory response.

Continued on next page

Specific	This immune mechanism recognizes specific foreign material and responds by destroying the invader. These mechanisms are specific and diverse. They are able to recognize individual pathogens. An antigen is any foreign particle that elicits an immune response. The body manufactures antibodies that recognize and latch onto antigens, hopefully destroying them. They also discriminate between foreign material and self material. Memory of the invaders provides immunity upon further exposure.

IMMUNITY: the body's ability to recognize and destroy an antigen

IMMUNITY is the body's ability to recognize and destroy an antigen before it causes harm. Active immunity develops after recovery from an infectious disease (e.g., chicken pox) or after a vaccination (e.g., mumps, measles, and rubella). Passive immunity may be passed from one individual to another and is not permanent. A good example of passive immunity is the immunities passed from mother to nursing child. A baby's immune system is not well developed and the passive immunity a baby receives through nursing keeps the baby healthier.

TWO PHYSICAL RESPONSES TO AN ANTIGEN	
Humoral Response	Free antigens activate this response and B cells (lymphocytes from bone marrow) give rise to plasma cells that secrete antibodies and memory cells that will recognize future exposures to the same antigen. The antibodies defend against extracellular pathogens by binding to the antigens and making them an easy target for phagocytes to engulf and destroy. Antibodies are in a class of proteins called immunoglobulins. The five major classes of immunoglobulins (Ig) involved in the humoral response are: IgM, IgG, IgA, IgD, and IgE.
Cell Mediated Response	Infected cells activate T-cells (lymphocytes from the thymus). These activated T-cells defend against pathogens in the cells or cancer cells by binding to the infected cells and destroying them along with the antigen. T-cell receptors on the T helper cells recognize antigens bound to the body's own cells. T helper cells release IL-2, which stimulates other lymphocytes (cytotoxic T-cells and B cells). Cytotoxic T-cells kill infected host cells by recognizing specific antigens.

Vaccines are antigens given in very small amounts. They stimulate both humoral and cell mediated responses. After vaccination, memory cells recognize future exposure to the antigen so the body can produce antibodies much more quickly.

Human Digestive System

Roles of basic nutrients found in foods

The function of the digestive system is to break food down into nutrients, absorb them into the blood stream, and deliver them to all cells of the body for use in cellular respiration.

Essential nutrients are those nutrients that the body needs but cannot make. There are four groups of essential nutrients: essential amino acids, essential fatty acids, vitamins, and minerals.

There are about eight essential amino acids that humans need. A lack of these amino acids results in protein deficiency. There are only a few essential fatty acids.

Vitamins are organic molecules essential for a nutritionally adequate diet. Scientists have identified thirteen vitamins essential to humans. There are two groups of vitamins: water-soluble (including the vitamin B complex and vitamin C) and water insoluble (vitamins A, D and K). Vitamin deficiencies can cause severe problems.

Unlike vitamins, minerals are inorganic molecules. Calcium is important in bone construction and maintenance. Iron is important in cellular respiration and is a major component of hemoglobin.

Carbohydrates, fats, and proteins are fuel for the generation of ATP. Water is necessary to keep the body hydrated.

Essential Amino Acids	Essential Vitamins
Arginine	Vitamin A
Histidine	Vitamin B complex (8 vitamins)
Isoleucine	Vitamin C
Leucine	Vitamin D
Lysine	Vitamin E
Methionine	Vitamin K
Phenylalanine	
Threonine	
Tryptophan	
Valine	

Mechanical and chemical digestion

The teeth and saliva begin digestion by breaking food down into smaller pieces and lubricating it to allow swallowing. The lips, cheeks, and tongue form a bolus or ball of food. The process of peristalsis (wave-like contractions) carries the food down the pharynx where it enters the stomach through the sphincter, which closes to keep food from going back up. In the stomach, pepsinogen and hydrochloric acid form pepsin, the enzyme that hydrolyzes proteins. This chemical action breaks the food down further and churns into a semifluid mass called acid chyme. The pyloric sphincter muscle opens to allow the food to enter the small intestine. Most nutrient absorption occurs in the small intestine. Its large surface area, resulting from its length and protrusions called villi and microvilli, allows for a great absorptive surface into the bloodstream. Neutralization of the chyme after arrival from the acidic stomach allows the local enzymes to function. Accessory organs function in the production of necessary enzymes and bile. The pancreas makes many enzymes to break down food in the small intestine. The liver makes bile, which breaks down and emulsifies fatty acids. Any food left after the trip through the small intestine enters the large intestine. The large intestine functions to reabsorb water and produce vitamin K. The feces, or remaining waste, pass out through the anus.

Human Reproductive System

Hormone control and development and function of male and female reproductive systems

Hormones regulate sexual maturation in humans. Humans cannot reproduce until puberty, about the age of 8-14 depending on the individual. The hypothalamus begins secreting hormones that help mature the reproductive system and develop the secondary sex characteristics. Reproductive maturity in girls occurs with their first menstruation and occurs in boys with the first ejaculation of viable sperm.

Hormones also regulate reproduction. In males, the primary sex hormones are the androgens, testosterone being the most important. The testes produce androgens that dictate the primary and secondary sex characteristics of the male. Female hormone patterns are cyclic and complex. Most women have a reproductive cycle length of about 28 days. The menstrual cycle is specific to the changes in the uterus. The ovarian cycle results in ovulation and occurs in parallel with the menstrual cycle. Hormones regulate these cycles. Five hormones participate in this regulation, most notably estrogen and progesterone. Estrogen and progesterone play an important role in the development and maintenance of the endometrium. Estrogens also dictate the secondary sex characteristics of females.

Gametogenesis, fertilization, and birth control

GAMETOGENESIS is the production of the sperm and egg cells.

Spermatogenesis begins at puberty in the male. One spermatogonia, the diploid precursor of sperm, produces four sperm. The sperm mature in the seminiferous tubules located in the testes. Oogenesis, the production of egg cells (ova), is usually complete by the birth of a female. Females do not release egg cells until menstruation begins at puberty. Meiosis forms one ovum with all the cytoplasm and three polar bodies that the body reabsorbs. The ovaries store the ova and release one each month from puberty to menopause.

> **GAMETOGENESIS:** the production of the sperm and egg cells

Seminiferous tubules in the testes house sperm, where they mature. The epididymis, located on top of the testes, contains mature sperm. After ejaculation, the sperm travel up the vas deferens where they mix with semen made in the prostate and seminal vesicles and travel out the urethra.

Ovulation releases the egg into the fallopian tubes where cilia move the egg along the length of the tubes. Fertilization of the egg by the sperm normally occurs in the fallopian tube. If pregnancy does not occur, the egg passes through the uterus and is expelled through the vagina during menstruation. Levels of progesterone and estrogen stimulate menstruation. Implantation of a fertilized egg regulates the levels, stopping menstruation.

There are many methods of contraception (birth control) that affect different stages of fertilization. Chemical contraception (birth control pills) prevents ovulation by synthetic estrogen and progesterone. Several barrier methods of contraception are available. Male and female condoms block semen from contacting the egg. Sterilization is another method of birth control. Tubal ligation in women prevents eggs from entering the uterus. A vasectomy in men involves the cutting of the vas deferens, which prevents the sperm from entering the urethra. The most effective method of contraception is abstinence.

SKILL 35.2 Identify strategies for maintaining personal mental and physical health (e.g., hygiene, sleep, exercise, nutrition)

Lifestyle choices and personal behaviors greatly affect personal mental and physical health. Strategies for maintaining mental and physical health include regular exercise, proper nutrition, adequate sleep, and attention to personal hygiene.

Nutrition and exercise are closely related concepts important to student health. An important responsibility of physical education instructors is to teach students about proper nutrition and exercise and how they relate to each other. The two key components of a healthy lifestyle are consumption of a balanced diet and regular physical activity. Nutrition can affect physical performance. Proper nutrition produces high energy levels and allows for peak performance. Inadequate or improper nutrition can impair physical performance and lead to short-term and long-term health problems (e.g., depressed immune system and heart disease, respectively). Regular exercise improves overall health. Benefits of regular exercise include a stronger immune system, stronger muscles, bones, and joints, reduced risk of premature death, reduced risk of heart disease, improved psychological well-being, and weight management.

Sleep gives the body a break from the normal tasks of daily living. During sleep the body performs many important cleansing and restoration tasks. The immune and excretory systems clear waste and repair cellular damage that accumulates in the body each day. Similarly, the body requires adequate rest and sleep to build and repair muscles. Without adequate rest, even the most strenuous exercise program will not produce muscular development. Finally, lack of rest and sleep leaves the body vulnerable to infection and disease.

Personal hygiene is routine grooming and cleaning practices. Personal hygiene is important for health, general wellness, and pleasurable social interaction. A basic personal hygiene program should include regular washing of the body and hair, more frequent washing of the hands and face, brushing the teeth twice a day, applying deodorant daily, and cleaning the clothes and place of residence.

SKILL 35.3 Recognize the role culture plays in mental and physical well-being

Cultural norms have a significant and sometimes overlooked influence on decisions relating to health behaviors. Students may not feel motivated to participate in certain physical activities, sometimes because the activities are not associated with the student's sense of identity or because the student's culture discourages these activities. For example, students from cultures with strict dress codes may not be comfortable with swimming activities. On the same note, students (especially older children) may be uncomfortable with physical activities in inter-gender situations. Educators must keep such cultural considerations in mind when planning physical education curricula and educating students about physical activity.

Cultural beliefs can also have a strong influence on health behaviors and the use of health services. They may cause individuals to avoid treatments of certain types or to avoid health services altogether, and they may cause individuals to be very uncomfortable admitting to certain types of problems and seeking treatment.

Two major areas in which cultural beliefs can have a strong impact on health behaviors and the use of health services are health issues related to sexuality and mental health.

Sexual matters are taboo in many cultures, and parents may not be willing to accept the fact that their child has a certain sexual health condition, or that their child might have performed the actions that can lead to the development of the condition (i.e., parents may be unwilling to accept the fact that their child is sexually active). This can make it very difficult to help a student receive necessary treatment.

Many cultures view mental health issues as deficiencies or defects, and mental health intervention as an admission of "craziness." These views can make it very difficult for students with mental health conditions to receive treatment. This is especially so in the case of conditions like clinical depression, which makes it difficult for the individual to help themselves. In these cases, helping the student will hinge on educating the parents about the real nature of mental health conditions.

> **SKILL 35.4**
> **Recognize common health issues of children, the signs and symptoms of health problems** (e.g., allergies, asthma, conjunctivitis, pediculosis), **and how they can be prevented or treated**

Common health issues among children include allergies, asthma, conjunctivitis (pink eye), and pediculosis (lice). Physical educators should be able to recognize the signs and symptoms of these conditions, and should know how to treat and prevent them.

Allergies

Allergies result when the body identifies a generally innocuous substance (e.g., peanuts) as toxic, and responds the same way it would to a toxic element introduced into the body. Excessive activation of mast cells and basophils results in a systematic inflammatory response. This can result in symptoms ranging from a runny nose to life-threatening anaphylactic shock and death.

Many allergic reactions selectively affect particular organs or parts of the body. For example, the nasal passages and airways might swell up, eyes might become itchy and red, ears might feel stuffed and painful, and skin might develop rashes. Occasionally, headaches also accompany allergic reactions.

There is limited mainstream medical treatment for allergies. The most important factor in rehabilitation is the removal of sources of allergens from the home and school environment. Once the individual has experienced an allergic reaction, however, the student may require medical attention to keep him in stable condition.

Asthma

Asthma is a chronic disease of the respiratory system in which the airways will occasionally constrict, become inflamed, and become lined with excessive amounts of mucus. This happens in response to one or more triggers, which can include allergens, cold air, exercise or exertion, and emotional stress. In children, the most common triggers tend to be viral illnesses like the common cold. The narrowing of the airways causes symptoms such as wheezing, shortness of breath, chest tightness, and coughing.

The most effective treatment for asthma is identifying triggers (which can include, for example, pets or aspirin), and limiting or eliminating exposure to them. Smoking adversely affects asthmatics in several ways, and asthmatics should neither smoke nor expose themselves to second-hand smoke. For students who experience asthma attacks induced by exercise, higher levels of ventilation and cold, dry air will tend to exacerbate attacks. For these reasons, such students should avoid activities such as skiing and outdoor running, in which they will breathe large amounts of cold, dry air. Activities such as swimming in an indoor, heated pool are a better option. There are various medical treatments available for asthmatics. Consult a physician for details specific to the case in question.

Conjunctivitis (pink eye)

Conjunctivitis is an inflammation of the outermost layer of the eye and the inner surface of the eyelid that is usually due to an allergic reaction or an infection. Other possible causes include overuse of contact lenses, foreign bodies in the eyes, vitamin deficiency, and dryness of the eye. Symptoms include redness, irritation, and watering of the eyes, with a variable level of itchiness depending on the cause of conjunctivitis.

Treatment is usually a routine of antibiotics prescribed by a physician, though this may vary depending on the cause of the infection. Soothing drops and cold compresses can provide relief. Conjunctivitis is highly contagious and it is important to isolate infected students. Since conjunctivitis spreads by touch (infected students rub their eyes, touch their hands to other students, who then rub their own eyes), it is important to maintain good hygiene through frequent hand washings.

Pediculosis (lice)

Pediculosis is an infestation of lice (parasitic insects) on the bodies of humans. The condition is commonly known as head lice, body lice, or pubic lice (depending on where the lice happen to congregate). The most common form of pediculosis among children is head lice, which spread through direct head-to-head contact with an infested person. Body lice spread through direct contact with the skin, clothing, or other personal items of a person already carrying lice. Pubic lice generally spread by intimate contact with an infested person. Lice do not have wings, and cannot jump from one individual to another. Human lice are different from dog lice, and the two species are not interchangeable (so you can't get lice from your dog, or vice versa).

The most common symptom of lice infestation is itching. Excessive scratching of the infested area can cause sores, which may become infected. Treatment of lice infestation usually includes medicated shampoos or cream rinses. We can also use fine combs to remove lice and eggs from the hair. Laundering clothes at high temperatures can eliminate body lice. Treatment should focus on the hair, body, or clothes, not on the home environment.

It is important to remember, though, that despite having a solid base of knowledge from which to draw, physical education professionals are not qualified to provide students or parents with medical advice of any kind. If there is concern that a student may have a significant health risk, instructors should refer them to a certified physician.

SKILL 35.5 Recognize the influence of various factors on personal and community health and safety

Family Health

The primary factors that affect family health include environmental conditions such as pollution and proximity to industrial areas, smoking and drinking habits of family members, economic conditions that affect nutrition, and general levels of education among family members about healthy living habits.

The relative levels of pollution in the family's area can significantly contribute to family health. For example, proximity to industrial areas, which may be releasing carcinogenic emissions, can be dangerous. Similarly, a smoking habit within the home environment is highly detrimental, as it will negatively affect the respiratory and circulatory systems of all members of the household. A drinking habit can also pose a risk both to the individual and to those in proximity to him or her.

Economic conditions can affect family health because lower economic means can lead to neglect of some nutritional factors (which are critical to healthy living and proper physical and cognitive development). Similarly, families with two working parents may not have as much time to spend with children to prepare food and monitor their eating habits. Education levels among family members about healthy living habits are also significant. Even with all of the required financial means, parents or caregivers may not have the requisite knowledge to direct them to habits for healthy living.

Public Health

Factors that influence public health include availability of health care in the community, pollution levels, community resources to promote and facilitate healthy living habits, and awareness of healthy living habits among adults in the community.

Availability of health care in the community that is both accessible and affordable has a critical influence on public health. When health care is not readily available to the community, relatively minor problems will tend to go untreated, and may develop into bigger problems.

Pollution levels in the community can affect public health by exposing the community as a whole to toxic and carcinogenic chemicals that negatively affect systems, including (but not limited to) the circulatory and respiratory systems.

Community resources are an important influence on public health. When financing is available to support health education and programs that encourage the development of healthy living habits, the health of the community will benefit. Conversely, if the community does not dedicate resources to this cause, the health of the community will suffer. Related to this is the issue of awareness of healthy living habits among adults in the community. A strong personal commitment among responsible community members sets an important example for others to follow.

Health Care

There are a variety of health care providers, agencies, and organizations involved in the maintenance of student health. On site, the school nurse assists ill or injured students, maintains health records, and performs health screenings. School nurses also assist students who have long-term illnesses such as diabetes, asthma, epilepsy, or heart conditions. Most schools maintain relationships with other outside health care agencies in order to offer more extensive health care services to students. These community partnerships offer students services such as vaccinations, physical examinations and screenings, eye care, treatment of minor injuries and ailments, dental treatment, and psychological therapy. These community partnerships may include relationships with the following types of health care professionals: physicians, psychiatrists, optometrists, dentists, nurses, audiologists, occupational therapists, physical therapists, dieticians, respiratory therapists, and speech pathologists.

Physicians are health care professionals licensed to practice medicine. A physician may choose to specialize in a specific area of medicine or to work in primary care. A psychiatrist is a physician who specializes in the care of psychological disorders.

Optometrists are health care practitioners who conduct eye examinations and prescribe corrective lenses. Dentists are health care professionals who provide care of the teeth. They may either work in general practice or specialize in areas such as orthodontics (correction of abnormalities of the teeth). Nurses are allied health care professionals who provide medical care under the supervision of a medical doctor. Audiologists conduct screenings to detect hearing problems. An occupational therapist helps people with disabilities learn skills needed for activities of daily living. They also help people who have sustained injuries regain their fine motor skills. Physical therapists are allied health care professionals who help people with disabilities and injuries regain their gross motor skills. Dieticians provide counseling regarding nutrition and perform meal planning. Respiratory therapists specialize in identification and treatment of breathing disorders. Speech pathologists help people with speech problems.

There are also various agencies and organizations involved in maintaining the well-being of students. The state and local health departments provide a wide range of services such as services for children with disabilities, chronic disease control, communicable disease control, mental health programs, consumer safety, and health education. The state department of human services investigates reports of child abuse or neglect. The police department prevents crime and captures offenders. Police also work with schools to provide violence and substance abuse prevention programs. Firefighters extinguish fires, check for fire hazards, install smoke detectors, check fire alarms, and give presentations on fire safety. The National Health Information Center is a federal agency that provides references for trustworthy health information.

SKILL 35.6 **Recognize the importance of positive interventions** (e.g., community involvement, nonviolent conflict resolution) **on personal and community health and safety**

Proactive intervention and education can protect personal and community health and safety. Important topics in intervention include conflict resolution and violence prevention.

Conflict Resolution

Interpersonal conflict is a major source of stress and worry. Teaching students to successfully manage conflict will help them reduce stress levels throughout their lives, thereby limiting the adverse health effects of stress. The following is a list of conflict resolution principles and techniques.

1. Think before reacting: In a conflict situation, it is important to resist the temptation to react immediately. You should step back, consider the situation, and plan an appropriate response. In addition, do not react to petty situations with anger.

2. Listen: Be sure to listen carefully to the opposing party. Try to understand the other person's point of view.

3. Find common ground: Try to find some common ground as soon as possible. Early compromise can help ease the tension.

4. Accept responsibility: In every conflict there is plenty of blame to go around. Admitting when you are wrong shows you are committed to resolving the conflict.

5. Attack the problem, not the person: Personal attacks are never beneficial and usually lead to greater conflict and hard feelings.

6. Focus on the future: Instead of trying to assign blame for past events, focus on what to do differently to avoid future conflict.

Violence Prevention

Violence is a concern of educators. Assault, rape, suicide, gang violence, and weapons in school are major issues confronting educators in today's schools. Violence is no longer an issue confined to secondary schools in large urban areas. Violence involving younger students at the elementary level and in rural areas is also on the rise. Additionally, more adolescents are regularly witnessing violence in their communities. Clearly, violence poses a serious threat to students' personal safety; however, violence also creates another challenge for schools. The fear of possible violence negatively affects students' growth, development, and ability to learn. In order to promote learning and healthy growth and development, schools must be violence-free. In order to accomplish this, schools must enact policies and procedures that promote an environment free from crime, drugs, and weapons. For some schools, this may include locker searches, full-time school security officers, and metal detectors. Some school systems may choose to utilize separate alternative schools for students proven to be violent or abusive.

In addition to experiencing violence at school, students may also be involved in various harmful relationships in their homes or communities. Harmful relationships may include abuse, violence, and co-dependence. Students can use self-protection strategies to decrease the risk of becoming a victim of violence in their school, home, and community. Students should learn to trust their feelings about people and situations. If their instincts indicate that a person or situation is potentially dangerous, they should trust their feeling and remove themselves from the situation. They should always be attentive and aware of the actions of the people near them. They should avoid situations that increase the chance that something harmful will happen. Lastly, adult mentors can play a vital role in helping young people to stay safe. Educators are in a unique position to mentor young people and to act as a resource to help students avoid violence.

COMPETENCY 36
UNDERSTAND BASIC PRINCIPLES AND PRACTICES RELATED TO LIFETIME PHYSICAL FITNESS

SKILL 36.1 **Identify components of fitness** (e.g., cardiovascular endurance, flexibility, coordination)

The components of fitness are body composition, cardiovascular fitness, muscular strength, muscular endurance, and flexibility.

Body composition describes the physical make-up of the body. The two components of body composition are fat tissue and lean tissue (i.e., muscle, bone, etc.). We can measure body mass by circumference and skinfold measurements. A more practical method of measuring body composition is the Body Mass Index (BMI). We use the BMI to assess body weight relative to height. BMI equals weight in kilograms divided by height in meters, squared (kg/m2). Although this method does not distinguish between fat mass and muscle mass, a BMI of 25 or higher increases many health risks such as high blood pressure, high cholesterol, type 2 diabetes, heart attack and stroke. Normal values fall between 18.5 and 24.9.

Cardiovascular fitness relates to the ability to perform moderate to high intensity exercise for a prolonged period. Peak levels of cardiovascular fitness usually occur around age 20-25 and decrease by approximately 10% each decade thereafter (one percent per year). Low levels of fitness increase the risk of premature death from cardiovascular disease. High levels of fitness reduce the risk of premature death from many causes and provide many health benefits. Men often have higher levels of cardiovascular fitness than women do. Everyone should engage in cardiovascular exercise three to five days per week, for 20-60 minutes, at an intensity of

55-90% of maximum heart rate (220 – age). The mode of exercise should engage large muscle groups in a continuous, rhythmic motion. In addition, everyone should choose a mode they enjoy to increase adherence to an exercise routine.

Muscular fitness relates to how much force a muscle group can generate (strength) and how effectively the muscle group can sustain that force over a period of time (endurance). Gains in strength, muscle mass, and endurance require different training methods. Lifting heavy weights 4 to 8 repetitions per exercise encourages strength development. Lifting moderate weights 8 to 12 repetitions per exercise leads to an increase in muscle size (hypertrophy). Lifting light weights 12 to 15 repetitions per exercise develops muscular endurance. A minimum weight training regimen consists of one set of eight to twelve repetitions using ten of the primary muscle groups (four lower body, six upper body) on two non-consecutive days of the week. Generally, men show greater muscular fitness levels than women, but with age, the margin becomes smaller. Peak levels of muscular fitness occur in the second decade of life.

Flexibility is the ability of a joint to move through its range of motion (ROM). Measurements of flexibility are joint specific, so it is difficult to gauge overall flexibility by just one test. Like cardiovascular and muscular fitness, flexibility decreases with age. Minimal requirements to improve flexibility include stretching each major joint to tightness, holding for 15-30 seconds, repeating each stretch 2 to 4 times per session, and engaging in flexibility training 2 to 4 days per week.

Improvement in each of these categories leads to a decreased risk of injury and disease and allows performance of normal, everyday activities with greater ease. Strategies for enhancing adherence to these fitness programs include appropriately maintaining facilities and equipment, emphasizing short-term goals, minimizing injuries, encouraging group participation, emphasizing variety and enjoyment, and recruiting support and motivation from family and friends.

SKILL 36.2 Identify activities that promote lifetime physical fitness

Several activities can promote lifetime physical fitness. All of these activities are based on the concept of providing individuals with the knowledge of both why fitness is important and how they can pleasantly integrate fitness into their lifestyles. This includes exposing students to a range of physical activities, emphasizing health and fitness education (theory as well as practice), and organizing events that target both the entire family (students with their parents) and that target parents only.

Exposing students to a wide range of physical fitness activities in school is the first step towards empowering them to choose a fitness activity that they enjoy and want to integrate into their lifestyles. A small range of activities is more likely to leave some students without a fitness activity that they enjoy.

Health and fitness education in school that provides a solid understanding of the importance of fitness education (i.e., classes that don't only get students moving, but explain to them why that movement is valuable) is very important if students are to make conscious choices to engage in physical activity later in life. Even if they are familiar with activities that they enjoy, they still need motivation to integrate them into their lifestyles.

Also beneficial is the organization of activities that target the entire family (i.e., students with their parents, and possibly siblings and other relatives). This can happen in the form of a school-sponsored "family fun day," where families learn about enjoyable physical education activities that they can participate in together and receive background information on the importance of integrating physical fitness into their lifestyles. Taking this concept a step further, instructors and schools can organize parent nights with the express purpose of teaching adults why physical fitness activities are important.

Integrating Physical Activity into Daily Life

One of the most important tasks for physical education instructors is to introduce students to strategies to incorporate physical activity into everyday situations. For example, instructors can recommend that students walk or ride a bike to school, rather than drive or ride the bus. In addition, there are a number of everyday activities that promote fitness including yard work, sports and games, walking, and climbing stairs. Beyond these everyday activities, physical education instructors must also be able to design physical fitness programs to meet the needs of students.

SKILL 36.3 **Recognize ways to prevent or lower the risk of injury and disease**

Basic healthy behaviors reduce the risk of injuries, illness, disease, and other health problems.

Safety precautions that can help decrease the risk of injury include using rubber mats in bathtubs and showers, using safety gates to block young children from stairs, wearing appropriate safety equipment during physical activity, and promptly removing ice and snow from steps and sidewalks.

Positive health behaviors can help decrease the risk of illness and disease. Good nutrition and regular exercise can help prevent everyday illnesses such as colds and flu, and chronic diseases such as heart disease and cancer. Exercise and a healthy diet help maintain a healthy body composition, reduce cholesterol levels, strengthen the heart, lungs, and musculoskeletal system, and strengthen the body's immune system.

SKILL 36.4 **Recognize the influence of media on health choices, body image, and self-confidence**

> Media-based expectations influence the development of self-concept and body image and individual health choices by setting media-based role models as the benchmarks against which students will measure their traits.

Media-based expectations influence the development of self-concept and body image and individual health choices by setting media-based role models as the benchmarks against which students will measure their traits. Self-concept is a set of statements describing the child's own cognitive, physical, emotional, and social self-assessment. These statements will usually tend to be fairly objective ("good at baseball" or "has red hair"); media-based expectations can change the statements to be measurements against role models ("athletic like this actor" or "thin like that model").

Current trends in media advertising and marketing practices related to fitness, recreational, and sports products and programs will typically display happy and fit individuals participating in the activity or making use of the advertised product. This trend has positive and negative ramifications for the work of physical educators.

On the positive side, the media advertising and marketing trend paints physical activity in a very positive light (as it should). The exposure that students have to the media today makes this a helpful reinforcement of the messages that physical education professionals work to promote in the classroom and school gymnasium. On the negative side, these trends ignore the reality that the current national level of fitness is poor, and obesity and heart disease are on the rise.

SKILL 36.5 **Recognize consequences of substance use and abuse**

Substance abuse can lead to adverse behaviors and increased risk of injury and disease. Any substance affecting the normal functions of the body, illegal or not, is potentially dangerous and students and athletes should avoid them completely.

- Anabolic steroids: The alleged benefit is an increase in muscle mass and strength. However, these substances are illegal and produce harmful side effects. Premature closure of growth plates in bones can occur if a teenager abuses steroids, limiting adult height. Other effects include bloody cysts in the liver, increased risk of cardiovascular disease, increased blood pressure, and dysfunction of the reproductive system.

- Alcohol: This is a legal substance for adults but is very commonly abused. Moderate to excessive consumption can lead to an increased risk of cardiovascular disease, nutritional deficiencies, and dehydration. Alcohol also causes negative effects on various aspects of performance such as reaction time, coordination, accuracy, balance, and strength.

- Nicotine: This is another legal but often abused substance that can increase the risk of cardiovascular disease, pulmonary disease, and cancers of the mouth. Nicotine consumption through smoking severely hinders athletic performance by compromising lung function. Smoking especially affects performance in endurance activities.

- Marijuana: This is the most commonly abused illegal substance. Adverse effects include a loss of focus and motivation, decreased coordination, and lack of concentration.

- Cocaine: This is another illegal and somewhat commonly abused substance. Effects include increased alertness and excitability. This drug can give the user a sense of overconfidence and invincibility, leading to a false sense of one's ability to perform certain activities. A high heart rate is associated with the use of cocaine, leading to an increased risk of heart attack, stroke, potentially deadly arrhythmias, and seizures.

Substance Abuse—Treatment and Alternatives

Alternatives to substance use and abuse include regular participation in stress-relieving activities like meditation, exercise, and therapy, all of which can have a relaxing effect (a healthy habit is, for example, to train oneself to substitute exercise for a substance abuse problem). More importantly, the acquisition of longer-term coping strategies (for example, self-empowerment via the practice of problem-solving techniques) is key to maintaining a commitment to alternatives to substance use and abuse.

Aspects of substance abuse treatment that we must consider include the processes of physical and psychological withdrawal from the addictive substance, acquisition of coping strategies and replacement techniques to fill the void left by the addictive substance, limiting access to the addictive substance, and acquiring self-control strategies.

Withdrawal from an addictive substance has both psychological and physical symptoms. The psychological symptoms include depression, anxiety, and strong cravings for the substance. Physical withdrawal symptoms occur when the body, adapted to a steady intake of the addictive substance, adapts to accommodate for the no-longer available substance. Depending on the substance, medical intervention may be necessary.

Coping strategies and replacement techniques, as discussed earlier, center around providing the individual with an effective alternative to the addictive substance as a solution to the situations that they feel necessitate the substance.

Limiting access to the addictive substance (opportunities for use) is important, because the symptoms of withdrawal and the experiences associated with the substance can provide a strong impetus to return to using it. Finally, recovering addicts should learn strategies of self-control and self-discipline to help them stay off the addictive substance.

SKILL 36.6 Identify strategies for promoting students' ability to use skills that contribute to good health (e.g., problem solving, decision making, locating and evaluating information about health services)

The key to improving the ability of consumers to evaluate physical education programs is increased education about the subject matter. That is, a public that understands some of the mechanisms of physical education and the value and benefits of physical activity is better equipped to evaluate different types of programs and strategies. Educators can lead seminars for parents supplementary to the school's physical education curriculum for the children. In this way, parents can learn to appraise and evaluate the contributions of various programs and activities that may be available to their children (and to themselves).

Educators can use interactive technology to teach parents and their children about the benefits of physical activity. In addition, the Internet is a valuable and easily accessible source of information about physical education. Of course, educators should also encourage parents to approach the school's physical education professionals with questions that they have about the fitness activities they are considering and in which their children participate.

Positive health choices and behavior must be supported by proper education, which includes fitness and health education. Obviously, without an understanding of the various choices available and the ramifications of each choice, it is difficult to make a wise decision regarding personal and family health choices and behavior. This education should include an introduction to research skills, so that the individual has the ability to find pertinent information when new situations arise that call for them to make health decisions. Good venues for these personal research habits include the Internet, local libraries, and fitness and health-care professionals in the community.

Positive health choices and behavior also require a layer of economic support, because healthy lifestyle choices are often more expensive than the less healthy alternative. It is also important for the environment to be conducive to positive choices and behaviors. For example, the availability of resources (both educational and practical) and facilities (medical and fitness) in proximity to the individual can positively impact the decision-making process.

COMPETENCY 37
UNDERSTAND BASIC PRINCIPLES AND PRACTICES OF PHYSICAL EDUCATION

> ### SKILL 37.1 Identify basic locomotor patterns *(e.g., run, gallop, slide, horizontal jump, hop, leap, skip, starting and stopping)*

Locomotor skills move an individual from one point to another. Examples of locomotor skills are:

1. Crawling: A form of locomotion where the person moves in a prone position with the body resting on or close to the ground or on the hands and knees

2. Creeping: A slightly more advanced form of locomotion in which the person moves on the hands and knees

3. Walking: With one foot contacting the surface at all times, walking shifts one's weight from one foot to the other while legs swing alternately in front of the body

4. Running: An extension of walking that has a phase where the body is propelled with no base of support (speed is faster, stride is longer, and arms add power)

5. Jumping: Projectile movements that momentarily suspend the body in midair

6. Vaulting: Coordinated movements that allow one to spring over an obstacle

7. Leaping: Similar to running, but with greater height, flight, and distance

8. Hopping: Using the same foot to take off from a surface and land

9. Galloping: Forward or backward advanced elongation of walking combined and coordinated with a leap

10. Sliding: Sideward stepping pattern that is uneven, long, or short

11. Body Rolling: Moving across a surface by rocking back and forth, by turning over and over, or by shaping the body into a revolving mass

12. Climbing: Ascending or descending using the hands and feet with the upper body exerting the most control

Nonlocomotor skills are stability skills that require little or no movement of one's base of support and do not result in change of position. Examples of nonlocomotor skills are:

1. Bending: Movement around a joint where two body parts meet

2. Dodging: Sharp change of direction from original line of movement such as away from a person or object

3. Stretching: Extending/hyper-extending joints to make body parts as straight or as long as possible

4. Twisting: Rotating body/body parts around an axis with a stationary base

5. Turning: Circular movements through space releasing the base of support

6. Swinging: Circular/pendular movements of the body/body parts below an axis

7. Swaying: Same as swinging but movement is above an axis

8. Pushing: Applying force against an object or person to move it away from one's body or to move one's body away from the object or person

9. Pulling: Executing force to cause objects/people to move toward one's body

SKILL 37.2 Recognize principles of training, conditioning, and practicing for specific physical activities *(e.g., swimming, running)*

Basic Training Principles

The Overload Principle is exercising at an above normal level to improve physical or physiological capacity (a higher than normal workload).

The Specificity Principle is overloading a particular fitness component. In order to improve a component of fitness, you must isolate and work on a single component. Metabolic and physiological adaptations depend on the type of overload; hence, specific exercise produces specific adaptations, creating specific training effects.

The Progression Principle states that once the body adapts to the original load or stress, no further improvement of a component of fitness will occur without the addition of an additional load.

There is also a Reversibility-of-Training Principle in which all gains in fitness are lost when a training program is discontinued.

Modifications of Overload

We can modify overload by varying frequency, intensity, and time. Frequency is the number of times we implement a training program in a given period (e.g., three days per week). Intensity is the amount of effort put forth or the amount of stress placed on the body. Time is the duration of each training session.

PRINCIPLES OF OVERLOAD, PROGRESSION, AND SPECIFICITY APPLIED TO IMPROVEMENT OF HEALTH-RELATED COMPONENTS OF FITNESS		
OVERLOADING	**PROGRESSION**	**SPECIFICITY**
Cardio-Respiratory Fitness		
• **Frequency** = minimum of 3 days/week • **Intensity** = exercising in target heart-rate zone • **Time** = minimum of 15 minutes	• Begin at a frequency of 3 days/week and work up to no more than 6 days/week • Begin at an intensity near THR threshold and work up to 80% of THR • Begin at 15 minutes and work up to 60 minutes	• To develop cardiovascular fitness, you must perform aerobic (with oxygen) activities for at least fifteen minutes without developing an oxygen debt. Aerobic activities include, but are not limited to, brisk walking, jogging, bicycling, and swimming.

Continued on next page

OVERLOADING	PROGRESSION	SPECIFICITY
Muscle Strength		
• **Frequency** = every other day • **Intensity** = 60% to 90% of assessed muscle strength • **Time** = 3 sets of 3 to 8 reps (high resistance with a low number of repetitions)	• Begin 3 days/week and work up to every other day • Begin near 60% of determined muscle strength and work up to no more than 90% of muscle strength • Begin with 1 set of 3 reps and work up to 3 sets of 8 reps	• To increase muscle strength for a specific part of the body, you must target that part of the body.
Muscle Endurance		
• **Frequency** = every other day • **Intensity** = 30% to 60% of assessed muscle strength • **Time** = 3 sets of 12 to 20 reps (low resistance with a high number of repetitions)	• Begin 3 days/week and work up to every other day • Begin at 20% to 30% of muscle strength and work up to no more than 60% of muscle strength • Begin with 1 set of 12 reps and work up to 3 sets of 20 reps	• Same as muscle strength.
Flexibility		
• **Frequency** = 3 to 7 days/week • **Intensity** = stretch muscle beyond its normal length • **Time** = 3 sets of 3 reps holding stretch 15 to 60 seconds	• Begin 3 days/week and work up to every day • Begin stretching with slow movement as far as possible without pain, holding at the end of the range of motion (ROM), and work up to stretching no more than 10% beyond the normal ROM • Begin with 1 set of 1 rep, holding stretches 15 seconds, and work up to 3 sets of 3 reps, holding stretches for 60 seconds	• ROM is joint specific.

Continued on next page

OVERLOADING	PROGRESSION	SPECIFICITY
Body Composition		
• **Frequency** = daily aerobic exercise • **Intensity** = low • **Time** = approximately one hour	• Begin daily • Begin a low aerobic intensity and work up to a longer duration (see cardio-respiratory progression) • Begin low-intensity aerobic exercise for 30 minutes and work up to 60 minutes	• Increase aerobic exercise and decrease caloric intake.

Cardiovascular Activities

Walking is a good generic cardiorespiratory activity for promoting basic fitness. Instructors can incorporate it into a variety of class settings (not only physical education instructors—for example, a biology class might include a field trip to a natural setting that would involve a great deal of walking). Walking is appropriate for all age groups, but can only serve as noteworthy exercise for students who lead a fairly sedentary lifestyle (athletic students who train regularly or participate in some sport will not benefit greatly from walking).

Jogging or Running is a classic cardiorespiratory activity in which instructors can adjust the difficulty level by modifying the running speed or the incline of the track. It is important to stress proper footwear and gradual increase of intensity to prevent overuse injuries (e.g., stress fractures or shin splints).

Bicycling is another good cardiorespiratory activity that is appropriate for most age groups. Obviously, knowing how to ride a bicycle is a prerequisite, and it is important to follow safety procedures (e.g., ensuring that students wear helmets). An additional benefit of bicycle riding is that it places less strain on the knee joints than walking or running.

Swimming is an excellent cardiorespiratory activity that has the added benefit of working more of the body's muscles more evenly than most other exercises, without excessive resistance to any one part of the body that could result in an overuse injury. To use swimming as an educational cardiorespiratory activity, there must be qualified lifeguards present, and all students must have passed basic tests of swimming ability.

There are many alternatives for cardiorespiratory activities, like inline skating and cross-country skiing. More importantly, instructors should modify the above exercises to match the developmental needs of the students—for example, younger students should receive most of their exercise in the form of games. An instructor could incorporate running in the form of a game of tag, soccer, or a relay race.

SKILL **Identify safety practices associated with physical activities**
37.3

Instructors and participants should make safety and injury prevention the top priority in exercise activities. There are a number of potential risks associated with physical activity, and instructors must be familiar with all the risks to prevent an emergency situation.

Equipment

Exercise equipment in poor condition has the potential for malfunction. Instructors should perform weekly checks to ensure that all equipment is in proper working order. If it is not, the instructor or maintenance staff must repair the equipment before students use it. Placement of exercise equipment is also important. There should be adequate space between machines and benches to ensure a safe environment.

Technique

Instructors should stress proper exercise technique at all times, especially with beginners, to prevent development of bad habits. Whether it's weightlifting, running, or stretching, participants should not force any body part beyond the normal range of motion. Pain is a good indicator of overextension. Living by the phrase "No pain, no gain" is potentially dangerous. Participants should use slow and controlled movements. In addition, participants must engage in a proper warm-up and cool-down before and after exercise. When lifting weights, lifters should always have a partner. A spotter can help correct the lifter's technique and help lift the weight to safety if the lifter is unable to do so. A partner can also offer encouragement and motivation. Flexibility is an often overlooked, yet important, part of exercise that can play a key role in injury prevention. Participants should perform stretching exercises after each workout session.

Environment

Environmental conditions can be very dangerous and potentially life threatening. Be cautious when exercising in extremely hot, cold, or humid conditions. High humidity can slow the body's release of heat, increasing the chances of heat-related illnesses. Hydration in hot environments is very important. Drink two cups of water two hours before exercise and hydrate regularly during exercise at the same rate that sweat is lost. In exercise lasting for a long period, it is possible to drink too much water, resulting in a condition known as hyponutremia, or low sodium content in the body. Water cannot replace the sodium and other electrolytes lost through sweat. Drinking sports drinks can solve this problem. Cold environments can also be a problem when exercising. The human body works more efficiently at its normal temperature. Wear many layers of clothing to prevent cold-related illnesses such as frostbite and hypothermia. In populations suffering from asthma, wearing a cloth over the mouth during exercise increases the moisture of the air breathed in and can help prevent an attack.

Emergency Action Plans

The first step in establishing a safe physical education environment is creating an Emergency Action Plan (EAP). The formation of a well-planned EAP can make a significant difference in the outcome of an injury situation.

Components of an emergency action plan

To ensure the safety of students during physical activity, an EAP should be easily comprehensible yet detailed enough to facilitate prompt, thorough action.

Communication

Instructors should communicate rules and expectations clearly to students. This information should include pre-participation guidelines, emergency procedures, and proper game etiquette. Instructors should collect emergency information sheets from students at the start of each school year. First-aid kits, facility maps, and incident report forms should also be readily available. Open communication between students and teachers is essential. Creating a positive environment within the classroom allows students to feel comfortable enough to approach an adult or teacher if she feels she has sustained a potential injury.

Teacher education

At the start of each school year, every student should undergo a pre-participation physical examination. This allows a teacher to recognize the "high-risk" students before activity commences. The teacher should also take note of any student that requires any form of medication or special care. When teachers are aware of their students' conditions, the learning environment is a lot safer.

Facilities and equipment

It is the responsibility of the teacher and school district to provide a safe environment, playing area, and equipment for students. Instructors and maintenance staff should regularly inspect school facilities to confirm that the equipment and location is adequate and safe for student use.

First aid equipment

It is essential to have a properly stocked first aid kit in an easily reachable location. Instructors may need to include asthma inhalers and special care items to meet the specific needs of certain students. Instructors should clearly mark these special care items to avoid a potentially harmful mix-up.

Implementing the emergency plan

> *The main thing to keep in mind when implementing an EAP is to remain calm.*

The main thing to keep in mind when implementing an EAP is to remain calm. Maintaining a sufficient level of control and activating appropriate medical assistance will facilitate the process and will leave less room for error.

Strategies for Injury Prevention

- Participant screenings: Evaluate injury history, anticipate and prevent potential injuries, watch for hidden injuries and reoccurrence of an injury, and maintain communication.

- Standards and discipline: Ensure that athletes obey rules of sportsmanship, supervision, and biomechanics.

- Education and knowledge: Stay current in knowledge of first aid, sports medicine, sport technique, and injury prevention through clinics, workshops, and communication with staff and trainers.

- Conditioning: Programs should be yearlong and participants should have access to conditioning facilities in and out of season to produce more fit and knowledgeable athletes that are less prone to injury.

- Equipment: Perform regular inspections; ensure proper fit and proper use.

- Facilities: Maintain standards and use safe equipment.

- Field care: Establish emergency procedures for serious injury.

- Rehabilitation: Use objective measures such as power output on an isokinetic dynamometer.

Prevention of Common Athletic Injuries

- **Foot:** Start with good footwear, foot exercises.

- **Ankle:** Use high top shoes and tape support; strengthen plantar (calf), dorsiflexor (shin), and ankle eversion (ankle outward).

- **Shin splints:** Strengthen ankle dorsiflexors.

- **Achilles tendon:** Stretch dorsiflexion and strengthen plantar flexion (heel raises).

- **Knee:** Increase strength and flexibility of calf and thigh muscles.

- **Back:** Use proper body mechanics.

- **Tennis elbow:** Lateral epicondylitis caused by bent elbow, hitting late, not stepping into the ball, heavy rackets, and rackets with strings that are too tight.

- **Head and neck injuries:** Avoid dangerous techniques (i.e., grabbing facemask) and carefully supervise dangerous activities like the trampoline.

Equipment Selection

School officials and instructors should base equipment selection on quality and safety; goals of physical education and athletics; participants' interests, age, sex, skills, and limitations; and trends in athletic equipment and uniforms. Knowledgeable personnel should select equipment, keeping in mind continuous service and replacement considerations (i.e., what's best in the year of selection may not be best the following year). One final consideration is the possibility of reconditioning versus the purchase new equipment.

Injury Follow-up and Reporting

Responding to accidents and injuries is an important responsibility of physical educators. After an injury occurs, instructors must follow up with parents and school personnel. Instructors must also complete an accident report.

Instructors should contact an injured student's parents or guardians as soon as possible after the injury. Such contact makes the parents aware of the injury and allows them to make necessary arrangements.

Instructors must also complete an accident report. Accident reports describe and explain the circumstances surrounding the accident and the nature of the injury. Such reports are important for recordkeeping, future evaluations, and protection against lawsuits.

Finally, the physical education instructor should notify the school administration of any accidents or injuries. In addition, if the injured student requires immediate first aid, the instructor should notify the school nurse.

> ### SKILL 37.4 Recognize appropriate rules and strategies for physical activities, cooperative and competitive games, and sports

Individual and Dual Sport Strategies

Archery strategies for correcting errors in aiming and releasing

- Shifting position

- Relaxing both the arms and shoulders at the moment of release

- Reaching point of aim before releasing string

- Pointing aim to the right or left of direct line between the archer and the target's center

- Aiming with the left eye

- Sighting with both eyes

- Using the proper arrow

Bowling for spares strategies

- Identifying the key pin and determining where to hit it to pick up remaining pins

- Using the three basic alignments: center position for center pins, left position for left pins, and right position for right pins

- Rolling the spare ball in the same manner as rolled for the first ball of frame

- Concentrating harder for the spare ball because of the reduced opportunity for pin action and margin of error

Badminton strategies

Strategies for Return of Service

- Returning serves with shots that are straight ahead

- Returning service so that opponent must move out of his/her starting position

- Returning long serves with an overhead clear or drop shot to near corner

- Returning short serves with underhand clear or a net drop to near corner

Strategies for serving

- Serving long to the backcourt near centerline

- Serving short when opponent is standing too deep in his/her receiving court to return the serve, or using a short serve to eliminate a smash return if opponent has a powerful smash from the backcourt

Handball or racquetball strategies

- Identifying opponent's strengths and weaknesses

- Making opponent use less dominant hand or backhand shots if they are weaker

- Frequently alternating fastballs and lobs to change the pace (changing the pace is particularly effective for serving)

- Maintaining position near middle of court (the well) that is close enough to play low balls and corner shots

- Placing shots that keep opponent's position at a disadvantage to return cross-court and angle shots

- Using high lob shots that go overhead but do not hit the back wall with enough force to rebound to drive an opponent out of position when he/she persistently plays close to the front wall

Tennis strategies

- Using a high, lob shot for defense giving the player more time to get back into position

- Identifying opponent's weaknesses, attacking them, and recognizing and protecting one's own weaknesses

- Outrunning and out-thinking an opponent

- Using change of pace, lobs, spins, approaching the net, and deception at the correct time

- Hitting cross-court (from corner to corner of the court) for maximum safety and opportunity to regain position

Team Sport Strategies

Basketball strategies

Use a zone defense

- To prevent drive-ins for easy lay-up shots
- When playing area is small
- When team is in foul trouble
- To keep an excellent rebounder near opponents' basket
- When opponents' outside shooting is weak
- When opponents have an advantage in height
- When opponents have an exceptional offensive player, or when the best defenders cannot handle one-on-one defense

Offensive strategies against zone defense

- Using quick, sharp passing to penetrate zone forcing opposing player out of assigned position
- Overloading and mismatching

Offensive strategies for one-on-one defense

- Using the "pick-and-roll" and the "give-and-go" to screen defensive players to open up offensive players for shot attempts
- Teams may use freelancing (spontaneous one-one-one offense), but more commonly they use "sets" of plays

Soccer strategies

- Heading: Using the head to pass, shoot, or clear the ball
- Tackling: Objective is to take possession of the ball from an opponent; successful play requires knowledgeable utilization of space

Volleyball strategies

- Using forearm passes (bumps, digs, or passes) to play balls below the waist, to play balls that are driven hard, to pass the serve, and to contact balls that are distant from a player

Rules of Individual and Dual Sports

Archery

- Arrows that bounce off the target or go through the target count as 7 points
- Arrows landing on lines between two rings receive the higher score of the two rings
- Arrows hitting the petticoat receive no score

Badminton

- Intentionally balking opponent or making preliminary feints results in a fault (side in = loss of serve; side out = point awarded to side in)
- When a shuttlecock falls on a line, it is in play (i.e., a fair play)
- If the striking team hits shuttlecock before it crosses net it is a fault
- Touching the net when the shuttlecock is in play is a fault
- The same player hitting the shuttlecock twice is a fault
- The shuttlecock going through the net is a fault

Bowling

- No score for a pin knocked down by a pinsetter (human or mechanical)
- There is no score for the pins when any part of the foot, hand, or arm extends or crosses over the foul line (even after ball leaves the hand) or if any part of the body contacts division boards, walls, or uprights that are beyond the foul line
- There is no count for pins displaced or knocked down by a ball leaving the lane before it reaches the pins
- There is no count when balls rebound from the rear cushion

Racquetball/handball

- A server stepping outside service area when serving is a fault
- The server is out (relinquishes serve) if he/she steps outside of serving zone twice in succession while serving
- Server is out if he/she fails to hit the ball rebounding off the floor during the serve

- The opponent must have a chance to take a position or the referee must call for play before the server can serve the ball

- The server reserves the ball if the receiver is not behind the short line at the time of the serve

- A served ball that hits the front line and does not land back of the short line is "short"; therefore, it is a fault. The ball is also short when it hits the front wall and two sidewalls before it lands on the floor back of the short line

- A serve is a fault when the ball touches the ceiling from rebounding off the front wall

- A fault occurs when any part of the foot steps over the outer edges of the service or the short line while serving

- A hinder (dead ball) is called when a returned ball hits an opponent on its way to the front wall—even if the ball continues to the front wall

- A hinder is any intentional or unintentional interference with an opponent's opportunity to return the ball

Tennis

A player loses a point when:

- The ball bounces twice on the player's side of the net

- The player returns the ball to any place outside the designated areas

- The player stops or touches the ball in the air before it lands out-of-bounds

- The player intentionally strikes the ball twice with the racket

- The ball strikes any part of a player or racket after the initial attempt to hit the ball

- A player reaches over the net to hit the ball

- A player throws the racket at the ball

- The ball strikes any permanent fixture that is out-of-bounds (other than the net)

- a ball touching the net and landing inside the boundary lines is in play (except on the serve, where a ball contacting the net results in a "let"—replay of the point)

- A player fails, on two consecutive attempts, to serve the ball into the designated area (i.e., double fault)

Rules of Team Sports

Basketball

- A player touching the floor on or outside the boundary line is out-of-bounds
- The ball is out of bounds if it touches anything (a player, the floor, an object, or any person) that is on or outside the boundary line
- An offensive player remaining in the three-second zone of the free-throw lane for more than three seconds is a violation
- A ball firmly held by two opposing players results in a jump ball
- A throw-in is awarded to the opposing team of the last player who touches a ball that goes out-of-bounds

Soccer

The following are direct free-kick offenses:

- Hand or arm contact with the ball
- Using hands to hold an opponent
- Pushing an opponent
- Striking/kicking/tripping or attempting to strike/kick/trip an opponent
- Goalie using the ball to strike an opponent
- Jumping at or charging an opponent
- Kneeing an opponent
- Any contact fouls

The following are indirect free-kick offenses

- Same player playing the ball twice at the kickoff, on a throw-in, on a goal kick, on a free kick, or on a corner kick
- The goalie delaying the game by holding the ball or carrying the ball more than four steps
- Failure to notify the referee of substitutions/re-substitutions and that player then handling the ball in the penalty area
- Any person who is not a player entering playing field without a referee's permission

- Unsportsmanlike actions or words in reference to a referee's decision

- Dangerously lowering the head or raising the foot too high to make a play

- A player resuming play after being ordered off the field

- Offsides: an offensive player must have two defenders between him and the goal when a teammate passes the ball to him or else he is offsides

- Attempting to kick the ball when the goalkeeper has possession or interference with the goalkeeper to hinder him from releasing the ball

- Illegal charging

- Leaving the playing field without referee's permission while the ball is in play

Softball

- Each team plays nine players in the field (sometimes 10 for slow pitch)

- Field positions are one pitcher, one catcher, four infielders, and three outfielders (four outfielders in ten player formats)

- The four bases are 60 feet apart

- Any ball hit outside of the first or third base line is a foul ball (i.e., runners cannot advance and the pitch counts as a strike against the batter)

- If a batter receives three strikes (i.e., failed attempts at hitting the ball) in a single at bat the player strikes out.

- The pitcher must start with both feet on the pitcher's rubber and can only take one step forward when delivering the underhand pitch

- A base runner is out if:

  – The opposition tags him with the ball before he reaches a base

  – The ball reaches first base before he does

  – The player runs outside of the base path to avoid a tag

  – A batted ball strikes him in fair territory

- A team must maintain the same batting order throughout the game

- Runners cannot lead off and base stealing is illegal

- Runners may overrun first base, but can be tagged out if they overrun any other base

Volleyball

The following infractions by the receiving team result in a point awarded to the serving side and an infraction by serving team results in side-out:

- Illegal serves or serving out of turn

- Illegal returns or catching or holding the ball

- Dribbling, or a player touching the ball twice in succession

- Contact with the net (two opposing players making contact with the net at the same time results in a replay of the point)

- Touching the ball after it has been played three times without passing over the net

- A player's foot completely touching the floor over the centerline

- Reaching under the net and touching a player or the ball while the ball is in play

- Players changing positions prior to the serve

Sample Officiating Situations

Basketball situation: Actions of the spectators interfere with the progression of the game.

Ruling: An official may call a foul on the team whose supporters are interfering with the game.

Basketball situation: A1 is attempting a field goal and B1 fouls him. A1 continues with the field goal attempt and, before releasing the ball, crashes into B2 who has a legal position on the floor. A1 successfully completes the field goal.

Ruling: The ball was immediately dead when A1 fouled B2; therefore, the field goal does not count. However, since B1 fouled A1 while attempting the field goal, A1 receives two free throws.

Basketball situation: The official in the frontcourt runs into a pass thrown from the backcourt by A1 and the ball goes out-of-bounds.

Ruling: B receives a throw-in. The official is part of the court.

> **Note:**
> Because rules change yearly, acquiring new rulebooks every year is necessary for proper officiating.

Basketball Situation: A1 catches the ball in mid-air and lands with the right foot first and then the left foot. A1 pivots on the left foot.

Ruling: A violation has occurred because A1 can only pivot on the foot that first lands on the floor, which was the right foot.

Soccer situation: The ball is alive when a substitute enters the playing field.

Ruling: A non-player foul. Referee can either penalize at location of the next dead ball or at the place of entry (usually when the team offended is at an advantage).

Soccer situation: B1 charges A1's goalie in A1's penalty area.

Ruling: Team A receives a direct free kick at the spot of foul. A flagrant charge awards team A a penalty-kick at the other end of the field, and B1 is red-carded.

Soccer situation: The goalie is out of position when a back on team B heads the ball out and falls into the net. A2 gets the ball, passes it to A1, and has only the goalie to beat.

Ruling: A1 is not offside because the B back left the field during legal play.

Volleyball situation: Team A's second volley hits an obstruction directly over the net, returns to A's playing area, and team A plays it again.

Ruling: Fair play and the next play is team A's third play.

Volleyball situation: The serving team has three front line players standing close together in front of the server at the spiking line.

Ruling: Illegal alignment is called for intentional screening.

Volleyball situation: RB and CB on the receiving team are overlapping at the time of the serve, and the serve lands out-of-bounds.

Ruling: Serving team receives a point because of receiving team's illegal alignment.

Volleyball situation: LB on team B saves a spiked ball and it deflects off his/her shoulder.

Ruling: A legal hit.

SKILL 37.5 **Demonstrate knowledge of physical activities, games, and sports for individuals at various activity levels**

There are physical activities, games, and sports available to individuals of all activity levels. Physical education instructors must be familiar with fitness activities, competitive games, cooperative games, individual and dual sports, and team sports.

Activities for Various Objectives, Situations, and Developmental Levels

The following is a list of physical activities that may reduce specific health risks, improve overall health, and develop skill-related components of physical activity. Some of these activities, such as walking and calisthenics, are more suitable to students at beginning developmental levels, while others, such as circuit training and rowing, are best suited for students at more advanced levels of development.

PHYSICAL ACTIVITY	HEALTH-RELATED COMPONENTS OF FITNESS	SKILL-RELATED COMPONENTS OF FITNESS
Aerobic Dance	cardio-respiratory, body composition	agility, coordination
Bicycling	cardio-respiratory, muscle	balance
Calisthenics	cardio-respiratory, muscle strength, muscle endurance, flexibility, body composition	agility
Circuit Training	cardio-respiratory, muscle strength, muscle endurance, body composition	power
Cross Country Skiing	cardio-respiratory, muscle strength, muscle endurance, body composition	agility, coordination, power
Jogging/Running	cardio-respiratory, body composition	
Jumping Rope	cardio-respiratory, body composition	agility, coordination, reaction time, speed
Rowing	cardio-respiratory, muscle strength, muscle endurance, body composition	agility, coordination, power
Skating	cardio-respiratory, body composition	agility, balance, coordination, speed
Swimming/Water Exercises	cardio-respiratory, muscle strength, muscle endurance, flexibility, body composition	agility, coordination
Brisk Walking	cardio-respiratory, body composition	

In general, teachers may need to modify instructional methods to accommodate students with disabilities participating in physical education class. The physical educator should ensure that students with disabilities understand the purpose of the lesson before the activity begins. The teacher should design lesson plans that include alternate activities in the event that the originally planned activity does not work well for the students with disabilities. Teachers should not place students with disabilities in activities where they have no chance of success. Thus, teachers should avoid elimination games. The physical educator should praise even minor displays of progress and achievement. The teacher should work with the students with disabilities to set achievable goals, because goal attainment is a wonderful motivator.

Individual/Dual Sport Activities Appropriate for Various Developmental Levels and Purposes

Team sports form a major part of the physical education curriculum. Designed mainly for promoting physical fitness among students, children, and adults, such sport activities include concepts and strategies, which help students to develop healthy physical, motor, emotional, social, and psychological skills.

These activities have defined steps that help gradually increase the physical development of the students. Apart from this, physical activities associated with team sports also keep diseases and other body ailments at bay. Physical activity inherent in sports can help remedy and prevent potential body ailments such as obesity, weakness, and heart disease.

Physical activities usually involve the utilization of motor skills in harmony with physical, emotional, psychological, psychomotor, and mental skills. Sports activities are a combination of movements and rules that often lead to healthy physical development in a child. In turn, the child is likely to become stronger and fitter, making various other tasks in life easier. These types of activities lead to other qualities such as sportsmanship, mutual respect, and cooperation. Children also develop intellectually during the course of play and motor skills development. For example, rock climbing and other adventure activities require forethought and planning. Participation in such activities promotes the development of critical thinking, problem solving, and decision making skills.

Further, regard for others and learning to work cooperatively with peers are necessary skills for success in team sports. In addition, participation in sports provides experience in dealing with interpersonal conflict (e.g., between teammates or competitors) and helps develop leadership skills. Children also develop respect for rules, acquire motor skills, and gain the ability to enjoy physical activity early in life, or as soon as they engage in organized or free play.

Cooperative and Competitive Games

Cooperative games are a class of games that promote teamwork and social interaction. The emphasis is on activity, fitness, skill development, and cooperation, rather than competition. There are many cooperative games available to the physical education instructor that help develop various coordination skills and teamwork. Examples of cooperative games include throwing and catching, freeze tag, and parachute.

Competitive games are a class of games that emphasize points and winning. Physical education instructors should integrate competitive games into the curriculum to generate student interest and teach concepts of fair play and sportsmanship. Competitive games are most suitable for students that are more mature and possess more developed skills. All traditional sporting events are competitive games.

Individual and Dual Sports and Activities—Overview

Archery

Skills that students study in archery classes include proper care of their equipment, properly stringing the bow, drawing, and shooting with accuracy (including compensating for distance, angle, and wind).

Safety practices in archery include respectful handling of the equipment (which is potentially dangerous) and ensuring that students only draw bows when pointed at a (non-living) target. Finally, instructors should keep students away from the path between firing students and their targets at all times.

Proper equipment for archery classes includes a bow and arrows, which can vary greatly in technical complexity and cost, and a target.

Badminton

Students in a badminton class will have to master the strokes as basic skills and should learn at least some of them by name (e.g., types of serves, net shot, net kills, drive, push, lift). Students should also know which strokes are appropriate from which areas of the court.

Bocce ball

Bocce requires a flat, level playing surface (packed dirt, gravel or grass are ideal). The instructor divides students into two teams of one, two, or four players each. Each team gets four balls, divided equally among the players. A player from the starting team stands behind the foul line (10 feet from the throwing end of the court) and throws the small ball ("pallina") toward the opposite end of the playing surface. The player then throws one of the larger balls ("boccia"), trying to get it as close to the pallina as possible without touching it. Players from the opposing team take turns throwing their balls until one of the balls stops closer to the pallina than the starting player's ball. If they fail to do so, the starting team tries to outdo its first attempt. Teams continue to take turns in this manner until they have thrown all the balls. The team with closest ball gets a point. This game emphasizes throwing skills (coordination and gross and fine motor skills).

Bowling

Skills that students will learn in bowling classes include learning to select a ball of comfortable weight and appropriate for the shot they need to make, properly controlling the ball so it hits the pins they are aiming for, and learning the dynamics of pin interaction to plan the proper angle of entry for the ball.

Safety practices in bowling include wearing proper footwear, handling the balls cautiously, and preventing horseplay (to avoid situations where a heavy bowling ball may drop inopportunely and cause injury).

Equipment needed for a bowling class includes proper footwear, a bowling ball, pins, and a lane.

Cross-country running

Much like track and field, cross-country running will teach the students proper running form, the ability to pace their energy expenditure relative to the length of the course, and the ability to adapt their running technique to the terrain.

Cross-country running strategy focuses on adapting energy expenditure relative to the length of the course and psychological training to minimize responsiveness to physical exhaustion. Runners should familiarize themselves with a course before running it.

Safety practices, for all running sports, focus on proper attention to warm-ups and cool-downs and remaining attentive to the course, which may be quite rugged. Because cross-country running often takes place in fairly remote, natural settings, it is important to coordinate the availability of first aid.

Equipment required for cross-country running includes proper footwear and water to prevent dehydration on longer runs.

Frisbee golf

Skills that students will acquire in a Frisbee golf class include methods of throwing the Frisbee (primarily forehand, side arm, and backhand throws). Students will also gain an intuitive sense of the physics governing the movement of the Frisbee (e.g., stability and speed range).

Frisbee golf strategy focuses on gauging distances and the amount of force and angle of throw required to land the disc in the target.

Frisbee golf safety practices involve ensuring that students don't wander in areas where a disc is in play, because this may result in injury. Instructors should also instruct students to remain alert and not throw the disc if they perceive there is a possibility that they might hit an individual.

Equipment needed for Frisbee golf includes a proper disc (though you can substitute a regular Frisbee for school purposes), target nets, and a playing area large enough to accommodate the game without excessive risk of the Frisbee flying irretrievably out of bounds.

Golf

The most fundamental skills for students to learn when studying golf include the correct way to execute a golf swing with proper posture and how to correctly judge distance for shot selection. Further, students should learn specific shots and their names (e.g., tee shot, fairway shot, bunker shot, putt).

Strategy in golf centers on properly gauging distances and required force to control the ball to the best extent possible.

Safety practices in golf, especially with students, involve ensuring that the course is clear and that there are no students nearby when players are swinging. Instructors should also remind students that golf clubs are not toys, and that misuse can result in injury.

Equipment necessary for a golf class includes a proper set of clubs and golf balls (a golf course or open area for hitting balls is also necessary).

Handball

Skills that students will learn in a handball class include catching and accurately throwing the ball, taking steps while bouncing it (similar to basketball's dribble), and quick analysis of the playing situation to determine the best target for a pass.

Strategy in handball centers on staying one step ahead of the opposing team. Keep them guessing and have multiple contingencies for given situations, so that game play doesn't become predictable (and easier to counter). Specific tactics can include types of shots that are harder for the opponent to hit, and shots that will put the ball out of play (when it is advantageous to do so).

Pickleball

Skills that students will learn in pickleball classes include manipulation of the ball with the racket and the variety of strokes.

Pickleball strategy is similar to tennis. Students should learn to vary their strokes to keep their opponents guessing, with the goal of reaching the frontcourt in a net volley position first. This places the students in the best position to win the point.

Table tennis (ping pong)

Skills that students will study when learning table tennis include the variety of grips (e.g., penhold, shakehand, V-grip), and the various types of offensive and defensive strokes. Students will also learn to gauge the force needed to manipulate the ball properly.

Strategies for success in table tennis involve manipulating and minimizing the opponent's ability to return a shot. This includes learning to hit to the opponent's weak side, putting a spin on the ball to make its movement less predictable, and setting the opponent up to receive a shot that he cannot return.

Tennis

Skills that students will learn when studying tennis include the proper grips of the racket and stroke techniques, which they should know by name (e.g., flat serve, topspin serve, twist serve, forehand, backhand, volley, overhead).

Shuffleboard

Depending on whether students are playing deck shuffleboard or table shuffleboard, they will learn to manipulate the discs, either with or without sticks.

Strategy requires students to properly gauge and apply the force needed to propel the disc accurately to a particular spot on the playing area.

Safety practices in shuffleboard include properly instructing and monitoring students to avoid horseplay, which may result in injury caused by the playing equipment.

Equipment needed for a shuffleboard class includes a disc with which to play, the equipment to manipulate the disc (this will vary depending on whether the shuffleboard game is played on a deck or on a table), and the appropriate playing area.

Track and field

In track and field practice, students will acquire proper running form, the ability to pace their energy expenditure relative to the length of the track, and the ability to manipulate objects in field events.

Track and field strategy focuses on learning to pace energy expenditure relative to the length of the track and analyzing the psychological interaction with other racers and competitors.

Safety practices in track and field include adhering to proper warm up and cool down procedures to prevent injury and handling field equipment (e.g., discus, javelin, shot) with care.

Equipment that is important to track events is minimal, with the most important requirement being appropriate footwear. Field events require specialized equipment. For example, throwing events require a discus, shot, or javelin. Jumping events require a landing area and height or length measuring device.

Combative Activities—Overview

Basic knowledge of wrestling includes knowledge of basic techniques (familiarity with pins, reversals, and positioning transitions), drills for practicing technique (e.g., students can drill shooting and sprawling, drill reversals from pinned positions, etc.), and terminology (naming the techniques, e.g., shoot, sprawl, half nelson, full nelson, etc.).

Basic knowledge of self-defense includes familiarity with basic striking techniques (punches and kicks), blocks and evasions, knowledge of major vital points on the body (eyes, nose, ears, jaw, throat, solar plexus, groin, knees, instep), knowledge of basic escape techniques (from chokes, grabs and bear-hugs) and some situational training (to prevent "freezing" in a real-life encounter). Martial arts (e.g., judo, karate) are common forms of self-defense that physical education instructors can teach to students.

Fencing practice will teach students proficiency in proper fencing form, techniques (for example, parries and strikes), and an awareness of open target areas on their opponents. Students will also acquire efficient movement skills.

Fencing strategy focuses on minimizing the number and size of vulnerable target areas on the body, while maneuvering (with the feet, body, and foil) to maximize the vulnerability of opponent's target areas in order to score a point.

Safety practices include proper attention to full protective gear, proper form, and careful monitoring of students in practice. Instructors should remind students frequently that they should not take frustrations out on training partners.

Equipment required for fencing practice includes the full gamut of protective gear (suit and helmet), appropriate footwear, and, of course, the fencing foil or saber. Higher technology suits that record points are also available, but are not required.

In-class focus should be placed on strategies for conflict recognition (based on developing an understanding of threat factors, like individuals in a hostile frame of mind), avoidance (physically avoiding potentially dangerous situations), and diffusion (overview of the psychology of confrontations, evaluation of the motivations behind a hostile encounter, understanding of the way body language and eye contact can impact the situation).

Team Passing Sports—Overview

Basketball

The fundamental skills of basketball include passing, dribbling, and shooting. As students' skills improve, they may begin to specialize in playing a specific position (point guard, shooting guard, small forward, power forward or center).

Touch/flag football

Skills that students will practice include running and passing. Tackling is not used in touch or flag football situations. As students improve, they may begin to specialize in playing specific positions (e.g., quarterbacks or receivers). They may also become more involved in the study and implementation of strategy.

The main goal of offensive strategy in football is to move closer to the opposing team's end zone, to the point where the ball is close enough to score either a touchdown or a field goal. The aim of defensive strategies is to prevent this same movement towards the end zone by the opposition. Both offensive and defensive strategies make important use of concepts of time management and the possibility of "running out the clock." Formations are central to football strategy, both on offense and on defense, and students should become familiar with simple formations for both.

Lacrosse

Lacrosse players must master the skills of catching and throwing the ball with their sticks and cradling (the motion that allows players to run with the ball in their stick).

Lacrosse strategy has many parallels to other team sports like basketball, soccer, and field hockey. In all of these sports, the team of players has to maneuver to outflank and outsmart their opponents in order to score a goal.

Soccer

Soccer players must master the skills of running, accurate kicking, manipulation of the ball, and footwork that allows them to maneuver when in motion.

The key to soccer strategy is to get the ball to the right person's feet—the one who has the most time and space and is in the most advantageous position to score or make a goal-scoring pass. Broadly, offensive strategy will spread the team out, to allow for coverage of more of the field. Defensive strategy will have the team compress to a compact unit that is able to cover the goal effectively.

Team handball

Skills that students will learn in a handball class will include catching and accurately throwing the ball, taking steps while bouncing the ball (similar to basketball's dribble), and quick analysis of the playing situation to ascertain the best target for a pass.

Strategy in handball centers around staying one step ahead of the opposing team, keeping them guessing, and having multiple contingencies for given situations so that game play doesn't become predictable (and easier to counter). Specific tactics can include types of shots that are harder for the opponent to hit and shots that will put the ball out of play (when it is advantageous to do so).

Ultimate Frisbee

Skills that students must acquire to play ultimate Frisbee proficiently include catching the Frisbee, accurately throwing the Frisbee, and running. Instructors should also emphasize strategic thinking, because there is limited time to select a destination and execute a throw.

The goal of offensive strategy in ultimate Frisbee is to create open lanes in the field that are free of defenders. Common offensive strategies include the "vertical stack" and "horizontal stack" (similar to a spread offense in football). Defensive strategy aims to gain control of the Frisbee and deflect passes made by the opposing team. A basic defensive principle is the "force," which calls for the defense to cut off the handler's access to half of the field, thereby forcing the offensive player to throw the Frisbee to the other side of the field.

Team Striking/Fielding Sports—Overview

Baseball

Skills that students studying baseball will acquire include accurate throwing and catching and the correct way to swing and hit with a baseball bat.

Defensive strategy in baseball focuses on the pitcher, who is responsible for trying to strike out the team that is at bat. Offensive strategy in baseball centers on batting and attempting to turn batters into runners.

Safety practices in baseball include maintaining discipline among the students, because horseplay and lack of attentiveness can lead to injury (e.g., a ball could hit a student who isn't paying attention). In addition, instructors should remind students that the baseball bat is not a toy, and they should handle it with care and not swing it near other students.

Equipment required for baseball practice includes baseball bats, baseballs, baseball gloves (though for some educational situations, the gloves are not necessary), base markers of some kind, and protective padding for the catcher.

Cricket

Skills that students in cricket class will acquire include accurate throwing and catching, swinging the bat correctly, and the proper form for the execution of an effective pitch.

Unlike baseball and softball, where pitching controls the game, batting controls the game in cricket. Since the batter can hit in any direction around him, he will focus on weak spots in the opposing team's field deployment, and the defensive strategy of the opposing team will focus on minimizing weak spots for the batter to exploit.

Safety practices in cricket are similar to those in baseball and softball: enforcing discipline and maximizing attentiveness to prevent the chance of injury, and reminding students that they should not swing the bat when other students are in the vicinity.

Equipment required for cricket practice includes cricket bats, cricket balls, appropriate protective gear, and base markers.

Field hockey

Skills that students of field hockey will acquire include running, tactical thinking on the field, and the ability to manipulate the ball with the stick (including running with the ball and different types of shots).

Offensive strategy in field hockey focuses on maneuvering the ball between team members to prevent the opposing team from intercepting and to get close enough to the opposing team's net to score a goal. Defensive strategy will strive to create solid coverage of the advancing team to enable interception of the ball.

Safety practices include emphasizing mindfulness on the part of the students to prevent accidents, and reinforcing the safety regulations of the game concerning legal use of the hockey stick.

Equipment needed for the practice of field hockey with students includes an appropriate ball, sticks for the students, and appropriate protective gear.

Softball

Skills students in softball classes will acquire include accurate throwing and catching and the correct way to swing and hit with a softball bat.

Softball is similar in strategy to baseball. Defensive strategy focuses on the pitcher, who is responsible for trying to strike out the team that is at bat. Offensive strategy centers on batting and attempting to turn batters into runners.

Safety practices in softball are also similar to baseball. Enforcing discipline and maintaining student attentiveness to prevent the chance of injury is of utmost importance. Instructors must also emphasize that students should not swing the bat when other students are in the area.

Equipment required for softball practice includes a softball bat and softball, fielding gloves, appropriate protective gear, and base markers of some sort.

SKILL **Recognize cross-cultural origins of physical activities, games, and**
37.6 **sports**

Throughout history, many cultures have contributed to the development of physical activities, games, and sports.

Contributions of Early Societies to Physical Activity, Games, and Sports

Historically, sports and games often had a practical, educational aim, like playing house. In addition, games such as gladiatorial games had political aims. Economic games included fishing and hunting. Families played board games. There were ceremonial reasons for games found in dances. Finally, ball games provided an opportunity for socialization.

Early society

The common activities performed in early societies included war-like games, chariot racing, boating and fishing, equestrian, hunting, music and dancing, boxing and wrestling, bow and arrow activities, dice, and knucklebones.

Egyptian

The common activities performed in Egypt were acrobatics, gymnastics, tug of war, hoop and kick games, ball and stick games, juggling, knife-throwing games of chance, board games, and guessing games (e.g., how many fingers are concealed).

Bronze Age

The activities performed during the Bronze Age (3000 to 1000 BCE) were bullfights, dancing, boxing, hunting, archery, running, and board games.

Greek Age

The Greeks are best known for the Olympic Games, but their other contributions were the pentathlon, which included the jump, the discus, and the javelin. The Pankration was a combination of boxing and wrestling. The Greeks also played on seesaws, enjoyed swinging, hand guessing games, blind man's bluff, dice games (losers had to carry their partner's pick-a-back), and hoop and board games. There also were funeral games described in *The Iliad*.

Romans

The Romans kept slaves and were advocates of "blood sports." Their philosophy was to die well. Roman baths were popular, as were ball games, stuffed feathers, pila trigonalis, follis, and balloon or bladder ball. The Capitoline games were held in 86 CE. These union guild athletes were paid for their activities, which included artificial fly-fishing. The games that were popular during this period were top spinning, odds and evens, riding a long stick, knucklebones, and hide and seek.

Chinese

The Chinese contributed the following: jujitsu, fighting cocks, dog racing, and football. In Korea, Japan, and China, children played with toys and lanterns. Common activities included building snowmen, playing with dolls, making/playing with shadows, flying kites, and fighting kites. Children enjoyed ropewalker toys, windmills, turnip lanterns, ring puzzles, and playing horse. Noblemen engaged in hopping, jumping, leapfrog, jump rope, seesaw, and drawing.

Major Events in the History of Physical Education and the Historical Relationship of Physical Education to Health and Fitness

Egypt: Sport dancing among the nobility, physical skills among the masses, and physical training for wars

Spartan and Greeks: Emphasized severe physical training and NOT competitive sport

Athenians: Believed in the harmonious development of the body, mind and spirit

Romans: The Romans established the worth of physical education.

During the dark ages, children learned fitness and horsemanship. The Romans combined the physical and mental aspects of exercise in their daily routines. The squires learned how to become knights by boxing and fencing. Swimming was also popular.

During the Renaissance, people developed the body for health reasons.

1349-1428: Physical education was necessary for a person's total education and also a means of recreation.

1546: Martin Luther saw physical education as a substitute for vice and evil.

Sweden: Ling, in 1839, strove to make physical education a science.

Colonial period: Religions denounced play. Pleasures were either banned or frowned upon.

The National period began in 1823. Games and sports were available as after school activities. There was an introduction of gymnastics and calisthenics.

Civil War (1860): Gymnastics and non-military use of physical education. Physical Education became organized. It became part of the school curriculum and held a respectable status among other subjects. YMCAs were founded. Gulick was the Director of physical education at NYC, and Dudley Allen Sargent was teaching physical education at Harvard.

Great Depression of the 1930s and the birth of the physical fitness movement: Bowling was the number one activity. Dance, gymnastics and sports were popular. The Heisman Trophy was awarded in 1935. After WWII, outdoor pools were common for the average American.

SAMPLE TEST

The test that follows is a short, 30-question diagnostic test.

 Visit *www.XAMonline.com* for the full ORELA Multiple Subjects 001, 002, 003 sample test, which includes full rationales for the correct answer choices.

SAMPLE TEST

(Rigorous)

1. **All of the following are common types of narratives EXCEPT:**

    A. Legends

    B. Short stories

    C. Poems

    D. Memoirs

(Easy)

2. **All of the following are examples of transitional phrases EXCEPT:**

    A. The

    B. However

    C. Furthermore

    D. Although

(Average)

3. **Which of the following is NOT a characteristic of a fable?**

    A. Animals that feel and talk like humans

    B. Happy solutions to human dilemmas

    C. Teaches a moral or standard for behavior

    D. Illustrates specific peoples or groups without directly naming them

(Rigorous)

4. **Effective reading and comprehension requires:**

    A. Encoding

    B. Decoding

    C. Both A and B

    D. Neither A nor B

(Average)

5. **A sixth-grade science teacher has given her class a paper to read on the relationship between food and weight gain. The writing contains signal words such as "because," "consequently," "this is how," and "due to." This paper has which text structure?**

    A. Cause and effect

    B. Compare and contrast

    C. Description

    D. Sequencing

(Rigorous)

6. **All of the following are correctly capitalized EXCEPT:**

    A. Queen Elizabeth

    B. Congressman McKay

    C. commander Alger

    D. the president of the United States

(Easy)

7. **A student has written a paper with the following characteristics: written in first person; characters, setting, and plot; some dialogue; and events organized in chronological sequence with some flashbacks. In what genre has the student written?**

    A. Expository writing

    B. Narrative writing

    C. Persuasive writing

    D. Technical writing

(Average)

8. When students present information orally, they should keep the following in mind:

    A. Volume

    B. Pace

    C. Body language

    D. All of the above

(Rigorous)

9. **Which of the following is an irrational number?**

    A. .36262626262…

    B. 4

    C. 8.2

    D. -5

(Easy)

10. **4,087,361**

    What number represents the ten-thousands place?

    A. 4

    B. 6

    C. 0

    D. 8

(Rigorous)

11. Two kids are selling lemonade on the side of the road and want to raise at least $320. If the materials needed (lemons, pitcher, table, etc.) to run a lemonade stand costs $15, how many glasses of lemonade will they need to sell if each glass costs $6?

    A. 210 glasses

    B. 61 glasses

    C. 74 glasses

    D. 53 glasses

(Average)

12. If a right triangle has a hypotenuse of 10 cm and one leg of 6 cm, what is the measure of the other leg?

    A. 7 cm

    B. 5 cm

    C. 8 cm

    D. 9 cm

(Easy)

13. 3 km is equivalent to:

    A. 300 cm

    B. 300 m

    C. 3000 cm

    D. 3000 m

(Average)

14. All of the following are examples of obtuse angles EXCEPT:

    A. 110 degrees

    B. 90 degrees

    C. 135 degrees

    D. 91 degrees

(Average)

15. Given the formula *d* = *rt* (where *d* = distance, *r* = rate, and *t* = time), calculate the time required for a vehicle to travel 585 miles at a rate of 65 miles per hour.

    A. 8.5 hours

    B. 6.5 hours

    C. 9.5 hours

    D. 9 hours

(Rigorous)

16. Permutation is:

    A. The number of possible arrangements, without repetition, where order of selection is not important

    B. The number of possible arrangements, with repetition, where order of selection is not important

    C. The number of possible arrangements of items, without repetition, where order of selection is important

    D. The number of possible arrangements of items, with repetition, where order of selection is important

(Easy)

17. All of the following are oceans EXCEPT:

    A. Pacific

    B. Atlantic

    C. Mediterranean

    D. Indian

(Rigorous)

18. Which civilization invented the wheel?

    A. Egyptians

    B. Romans

    C. Assyrians

    D. Sumerians

(Rigorous)

19. What was the long-term importance of the Mayflower Compact?

    A. It established the foundation of all later agreements with the Native peoples

    B. It established freedom of religion in the original English colonies

    C. It ended the war in Europe between Spain, France, and England

    D. It established a model of small, town-based government that was adopted throughout the New England colonies

(Easy)

20. The belief that the United States should control all of North America was called:

    A. Westward expansion

    B. Pan Americanism

    C. Manifest Destiny

    D. Nationalism

(Average)

21. The Westward expansion occurred for a number of reasons; however, the most important reason was:

    A. Colonization

    B. Slavery

    C. Independence

    D. Economics

(Easy)

22. The economic collapse of the United States in 1929 is known as the:

    A. Cold War

    B. New Deal

    C. Unhappy times

    D. Great Depression

(Easy)

23. Activities that enhance team socialization include all of the following EXCEPT:

    A. Basketball

    B. Soccer

    C. Golf

    D. Volleyball

(Rigorous)

24. Cultural diffusion is:

    A. The process that individuals and societies go through in changing their behavior and organization to cope with social, economic, and environmental pressures

    B. The complete disappearance of a culture

    C. The exchange or adoption of cultural features when two cultures come into regular direct contact

    D. The movement of cultural ideas or materials between populations independent of the movement of those populations

(Rigorous)

25. Which of the following is the best definition for *meteorite*?

    A. A meteorite is a mineral composed of mica and feldspar

    B. A meteorite is material from outer space that has struck the Earth's surface

    C. A meteorite is an element that has properties of both metals and nonmetals

    D. A meteorite is a very small unit of length measurement

(Rigorous)

26. Identify the correct sequence of organization of living things from lower to higher order:

    A. Cell, Organelle, Organ, Tissue, System, Organism

    B. Cell, Tissue, Organ, Organelle, System, Organism

    C. Organelle, Cell, Tissue, Organ, System, Organism

    D. Organelle, Tissue, Cell, Organ, System, Organism

(Average)

27. The following are examples of chemical reactions EXCEPT:

    A. Melting ice into water

    B. Dissolving a seltzer tablet in water

    C. Using a fire-cracker

    D. Burning a piece of plastic

(Average)

28. **All of the following professions are classified under "Earth sciences" EXCEPT:**

    A. Geologist

    B. Meteorologist

    C. Seismologist

    D. Biochemist

(Average)

29. **The Bill of Rights consists of which Amendments?**

    A. Amendments 1-5

    B. Amendments 1-10

    C. Amendments 1 and 2

    D. Amendments 1-22

(Average)

30. **Social skills and values developed by activity include all of the following EXCEPT:**

    A. Winning at all costs

    B. Making judgments in groups

    C. Communicating and cooperating

    D. Respecting rules and property

Answer Key

ANSWER KEY					
1. C	6. C	11. B	16. C	21. D	26. C
2. A	7. B	12. C	17. C	22. D	27. A
3. D	8. D	13. D	18. D	23. C	28. D
4. C	9. A	14. B	19. D	24. D	29. B
5. A	10. D	15. D	20. C	25. B	30. A

ORELA? Praxis? We've got you covered!

XAMonline has study guides for both the ORELA and the Praxis Series. Aligned with current standards, these guides offer a comprehensive review of the core test content and include practice test questions to help you prepare for the actual exam. If you need certification success the first time, you need an XAMonline guide!

Featured Title:

ORELA Protecting Student and Civil Rights in the Educational Environment Examination

From understanding federal and state laws that protect individual civil rights to the implications of student diversity for teaching and learning, this comprehensive guide covers all the core competencies within the two subareas of legal foundations and equity in the school environment. Once you've mastered the content, test your knowledge with 60 sample questions.

XAMonline also has study guides for the entire Praxis series:

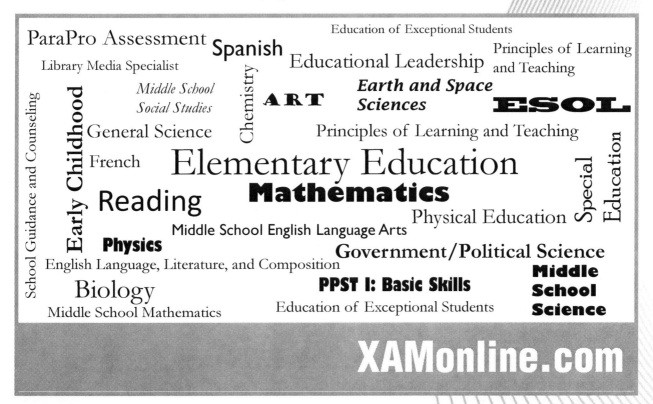

ParaPro Assessment
Education of Exceptional Students
Spanish
Educational Leadership
Principles of Learning and Teaching
Library Media Specialist
School Guidance and Counseling
Middle School Social Studies
Chemistry
ART
Earth and Space Sciences
ESOL
Early Childhood
General Science
Principles of Learning and Teaching
Special Education
French
Elementary Education
Reading
Mathematics
Physical Education
Middle School English Language Arts
Physics
Government/Political Science
English Language, Literature, and Composition
PPST I: Basic Skills
Middle School Science
Biology
Education of Exceptional Students
Middle School Mathematics

XAMonline.com

Find XAM on

XAMonline.com

Teaching in another state? XAMonline carries 14 other state-specific series including the WEST, CBEST and CSET. Also check out our 30+ Praxis titles!

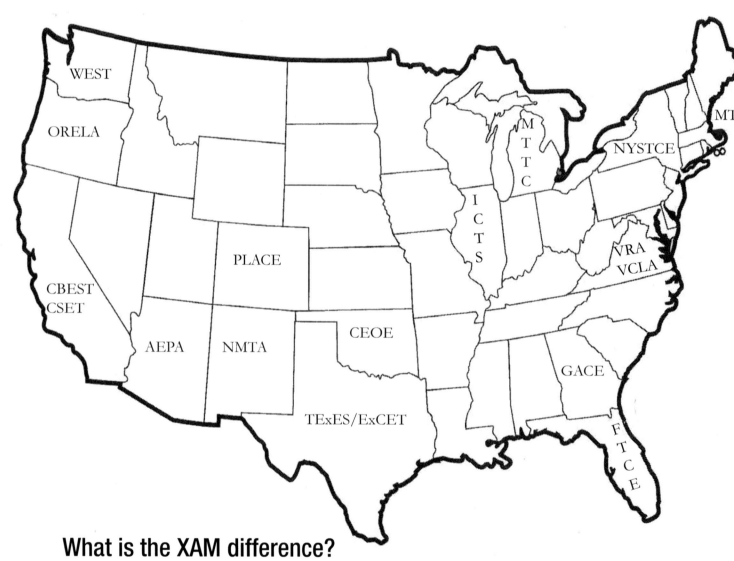

WEST

ORELA

CBEST
CSET

AEPA

NMTA

PLACE

CEOE

TExES/ExCET

M T T C

I C T S

NYSTCE

MT

VRA
VCLA

GACE

F T C E

What is the XAM difference?

- State-aligned, current and comprehensive content
- Reviews all required competencies and skills
- Practice test questions aligned to actual test in both number and rigor level
- Questions include full answer rationale and skill reference for easy, efficient study
- Additional resources available online: diagnostic tests, flashcards, timed and scored practice tests and study/test tips

Breinigsville, PA USA
16 December 2010
251586BV00005B/1-64/P

9 781607 870159